FORM AND BEING

**STUDIES IN PHILOSOPHY
AND THE HISTORY OF PHILOSOPHY**

General Editor: Jude P. Dougherty

Studies in Philosophy
and the History of Philosophy   Volume 45

Form and Being

Studies in Thomistic Metaphysics

Lawrence Dewan, O.P.

THE CATHOLIC UNIVERSITY OF AMERICA PRESS
Washington, D.C.

The paper used in this publication meets the minimum requirements of the
American National Standards for Information Science—Permanence of Paper
for Printed Library Materials, ANSI z39.48-1984.
∞

LIBRARY OF CONGRESS CATALOGING-IN-PUBLICATION DATA
Dewan, Lawrence, 1932–
    Form and being : studies in Thomistic metaphysics / Lawrence Dewan.
       p. cm. — (Studies in philosophy and the history of philosophy ; v. 45)
    Includes bibliographical references and index.
ISBN-13: 978-0-8132-1461-0 (cloth : alk. paper)
ISBN-13: 978-0-8132-2759-7 (pbk.)
    1. Thomas, Aquinas, Saint, 1225?–1274.   I. Title.   II. Series.
    B21.S78 vol. 45
    [B765.T54]
    100 s—dc22
    [189'.4]   2005033359

Contents

Acknowledgments

The following chapters are reprinted with permission of the original publishers.

Chapter 1, "What Is Metaphysics?" appeared in *Études Maritainiennes/ Maritain Studies* 9 (1993), 145–60; chapter 2, "What Does It Mean to Study Being 'as Being'?" in *International Journal of Philosophy* [Taipei] (July 2004), 63–86; chapter 3, "St. Thomas and the Ground of Metaphysics," in *Philosophical Knowledge*, edited by John B. Brough, Daniel O. Dahlstrom, and Henry B. Veatch, *Proceedings of the American Catholic Philosophical Association*, vol. 54 (Washington, 1980), 144–54; chapter 4, "St. Thomas, Physics, and the Principle of Metaphysics," in *The Thomist* 61 (1997), 549–66; chapter 5, "St. Thomas and the Principle of Causality," in *Jacques Maritain: philosophe dans la cite* [*A Philosopher in the World*] (1985), 53–71, and chapter 10, "St Thomas, Form, and Incorruptibility," in *Être et Savoir* (1989), 77–90, both edited by Jean-Louis Allard and reprinted by permission of the University of Ottawa Press.

Chapter 7, "The Importance of Substance" (1997), and chapter 12, "Nature as a Metaphysical Object" (2001), were originally published on the website of the Jacques Maritain Center at the University of Notre Dame. Chapter 8, "St. Thomas, Metaphysics, and Formal Causality," appeared in *Laval théologique et philosophique* 36 (1980): 285–316; chapter 9, "St. Thomas, Metaphysical Procedure, and the Formal Cause," in *The New Scholasticism* 63 (1989): 173–82; chapter 11, "St. Thomas and the Distinction between Form and *Esse* in Caused Things," in *Gregorianum* 60 (1999): 353–70; and chapter 13, "The Individual as a Mode of Being according to Thomas Aquinas," in *The Thomist* 63 (1997): 403–24.

Introduction

The present collection of papers, the earliest of which originally appeared in 1980, has been selected from more than a hundred published over the years. If there is a dominant theme in these thirteen, it is the centrality of form in metaphysics. I hope to publish subsequently collections on the doctrine of the act of being, and on natural theology. The general outlook in these papers is fairly uniform, and so I am placing them in a somewhat systematic, rather than chronological, order: from the general to the particular, and from principles to conclusion.

I begin with a paper providing a kind of caveat. It focuses on the objectivity and certainty, yet the difficulty for the human mind, proper to metaphysics. While every human being possesses the seed of metaphysics, not all possess the soil in which it can grow. The very first article of the first question of Thomas Aquinas's *Summa theologiae* speaks of how rare real metaphysical knowledge of divine things is, and how necessary it is that we have the benefit of revelation as regards the very conclusions of this natural knowledge.

The second paper is a general statement of the metaphysical task, an overall conception of the science, presented in some detail. As will be seen, I insist not only on the need to begin with sensible, material things, but also on the need to establish the existence of a higher mode of being, absolutely imperishable substance. The field of the science is hierarchical, including the contingent and the necessary. It is such a field that constitutes the spiritual trampoline or launching pad, leading to the consideration of something still higher, the highest cause, the first principle.

The third and fourth papers have much in common. That on "the seed of metaphysics" was an eye-opener for me. The subject, of course, is an inevitable one for the metaphysician, bearing as it does on the knowledge which one must possess at the outset, in order for metaphysics to be possible. The teaching of Thomas Aquinas is clear, that our first intellectual knowledge bears upon what is expressed by the words "a being" or "that which is" [Latin: *ens*], but the analysis of this situation is something else. The paper's title, as originally published, used the term "ground" rather than "seed"; this was in conformity with Cornelio Fabro's paper (which I criticize), but I have since often wished I had used the more Thomistic word "seed." Hence, the change here. My research for this led to my close reading of the *ST* 1-2 on the formation of our intellectual knowledge as a self-perfecting process.

I use this doctrine again in the paper opposing the so-called "River Forest School" of Thomists; while I argue against them on the basis of Thomas's *Commentaries* on Aristotle (the River Forest contention being that one there finds Thomas's philosophy best expressed), the *ST* 1-2 teaching on self-development and the nature of its seed really seem to go to the heart of the matter. I might add that what I am saying does not appear to me to square with the view of those, such as Jacques Maritain, who distinguish between "first known" being and the "being" which is the subject of metaphysics.

The fifth paper still has us very much at the level of our original knowledge. Against the background of the Humean skepticism which forms so important a part of the modern philosophical tradition, a right conception of our intellectual awareness of causal connection is most salutary.

I have placed an analogy paper next. On the one hand, we are still in the zone of beginnings, since, of course, Thomas teaches us that the very first of all predicates, "a being," is an analogical term.[1] Furthermore, this feature of our metaphysical knowledge is the basis for the reduction of the discussion to substance as primary, the issue we will look at next. The analogy paper stresses the dominant role of the metaphysical mind regarding the principles of all sciences, metaphysics itself included.

"Substance" names what presents us most of all with the aspect of being, yet it is terribly neglected. I attempt to recall myself (and, if need be, the reader) from obliviousness to this reality. Thomas's teaching on the substantial form—and in particular the soul, as present as a whole in every part of the body—I see as the best means of taking us in this regard beyond mere imagination to intellectual appreciation. With the help of Charles De Koninck, I also seek to exhibit some of the difficulty to be found in this domain.

The paper on "metaphysics and formal causality" undertakes a reading of Thomas's own reading of the central books of Aristotle's *Metaphysics*, or, at least, of Books 7 and 8. Thomas teaches that metaphysics demonstrates primarily by the formal cause. Can we observe him actually finding that to be the case in very basic metaphysical discussion? This turns out to be a lesson on the centrality of substantial form for the study of metaphysics. There is likewise the great lesson (in opposition to Plato) that the essence of material things includes matter.

---

1. *ST* 1.13.5.*ad* 1.

The next three papers make clear that form, as cause, is a principle of the act of being [*esse*]. One cannot dissociate the notion of causality from the notion of the act of being. A thing has a cause inasmuch as it has a cause of its *esse*.[2] While form's role as principle of being was already in evidence in the previous paper, I look more closely at this in these three papers.

The first criticizes Joseph Owens's view that the act of being is an accidental associate [*per accidens*] of the created thing, and so also accidental relative to the thing's form. I bring out the teaching of Thomas, that, far from that being the case, it is even more intimate to the form than what are called "properties."

In the second, we see that the indissociability of form and act of being is the key premise for Thomas's demonstration of the incorruptibility, the immortality, of the human soul. Thomas seems to have taken a little time to see this line of thinking, but once he does it becomes standard in his treatments.

The third comes to what has sometimes been called "the fundamental truth of Christian philosophy,"[3] the distinction between the essence or form and the act of being. My contention is that a healthy conception of form should tend to confuse it with the act of being; this is precisely because of the kinship between the two, i.e. the intimate relationship I have been stressing in the preceding papers. It is only by appreciating the implications of efficient causal hierarchy that the necessity to conclude to a real distinction between form and *esse* in caused things is rightly seen.

The paper on nature as a metaphysical object presents essence and form as principle of operation. In its latter half I show how Thomas exhibits the human soul, the human substantial form, as source of operative power and of operation, i.e. he exhibits it as a *nature*.

The last paper moves away from the focus on form, and has to do with another ineluctable target of metaphysical attention, the *subsisting* thing as such. (Following St. Thomas, I consider that there are three such targets: the subsisting thing, the essence or form, and the act of being.)[4] Fr. Owens, whose opinion is endorsed by others, has presented as the teaching of St. Thomas the doctrine of the act of being as a global principle of individuation. I focus very precisely on "individual" as signifying the measure or mode of being proper to substance as such, and show that it

2. *Expositio libri Posteriorum* 2.7 (Leonine ed., lines 34–35; Spiazzi, 471).
3. Cf. Norbert del Prado, *De veritate Fundamentali Philosophiae Christianae,* Fribourg, 1911: Consoc. Sancti Pauli.
4. *SCG* 4.11 (ed. Pera, 3472–3473) is a passage from St. Thomas which shows the ineluctable variety of intelligible roles of the various items in the metaphysical analysis; it is quoted in chapter 2, at n. 34.

is found diversely but analogously realized in material things, in separate forms, and in God, who is the subsisting act of being.

My philosophical education began mainly at St. Michael's College in the University of Toronto, and at the associated Toronto Graduate Philosophy Department and the Pontifical Institute of Mediaeval Studies. This campus, in the years I was there as a student and fledgling teacher (1949–59), was a remarkable place of learning. One of the first things I remember doing on arriving there, at age seventeen, was to obtain a copy of Fr. Armand Maurer's translation of the *De ente et essentia.* As undergraduates we were taught to take the text of St. Thomas very seriously, and there was also a strong interest in Jacques Maritain. In the university's graduate philosophy program we were able to partake of the philosophy offerings of the Pontifical Institute; there, the interest was, of course, in the lines of thinking of Etienne Gilson and Joseph Owens.

Accordingly, I was interested from the start in the doctrine of the act of being, and went on to do my doctoral work, at Professor Gilson's suggestion, on Johannes Capreolus's presentation of Thomas's doctrine of *esse.* I am very much of the view that my teachers were entirely correct to feature Thomas's doctrine of *esse,* the act of being. However, over the years it has occurred to me to take positions somewhat different from theirs. The reader will find in some papers criticism of the views of Fr. Owens and Professor Gilson. In general, I am much more inclined than they were to stress the continuity of thought between Aristotle and Thomas, even as to the doctrine of the act of being.[5] I have, too, tried to bring out the need for a fuller appreciation of the role of essence or form than I think I found in my teachers.[6]

Nevertheless, my gratitude is complete as regards their communication of high seriousness in the pursuit of truth. This is also true as regards the many teachers I have subsequently had at longer range, especially Charles De Koninck.

Lastly, I would like to add some words from an earlier paper. I almost always give papers presenting what I take to be the doctrine of St. Thomas. Usually they get placed in the "history of philosophy" category. Generally my aim is philosophical, and, with Thomas, I insist that ". . . the study of philosophy is not in order to know what it is people have thought,

5. I have a paper currently posted on the website of the Maritain Center, University of Notre Dame, among the papers of the Summer Thomistic Institute for the year 2000: "Aristotle as a Source of St. Thomas's Doctrine of *esse.*"

6. I might mention my professor and friend Marshall McLuhan, so human a presence in those student days. In his inimitable aphoristic (and enigmatic) style he once, years later, encouraged me: "Larry, be the first to discover formal causality!" It was already a little late for that, but I hope these papers on form and being do help.

but what is the truth about reality."[7] However, agreeing as I do with my teacher Etienne Gilson that "great philosophers are very scarce,"[8] and that the soundest approach in philosophical education is to live a sort of apprenticeship with a great philosopher, I have lived an apprenticeship with Thomas Aquinas. That at this relatively late date in my life I am still presenting his views, as well as I can, simply means that I am still an apprentice.[9]

These papers have been published for different particular occasions and inevitably involve some repetition. Still, that repetition itself will help indicate that certain points are fundamental.

7. ". . . *studium philosophiae non est ad hoc quod sciatur quid homines senserint sed qualiter se habeat veritas rerum.*": Thomas Aquinas, *In libros Aristotelis De caelo et mundo expositio,* 1.22 (ed. R. Spiazzi, Rome/Turin, 1952: Marietti, 228 [8]).

8. Etienne Gilson, *History of Philosophy and Philosophical Education,* Milwaukee, 1948: Marquette University Press, p. 21.

9. Cf. "Truth and Happiness," *American Catholic Philosophical Quarterly* 67 (1993) [Annual Supplement: ACPA Proceedings], pp. 1–21, at pp. 1–2.

Abbreviations

For the following works of St. Thomas Aquinas:

CM	*Commentary on Aristotle's Metaphysics*
CP	*Commentary on Aristotle's Physics*
DP	*Quaestiones disputatae de potentia Dei*
Sent.	*Commentary on the Sentences of Peter Lombard*
SCG	*Summa contra gentiles*
ST	*Summa theologiae*
DV	*Quaestiones disputatae de veritate*

For Aristotle:

EN	*Nicomachean Ethics*
Metaph.	*Metaphysics*
Phys.	*Physics*

FORM AND BEING

Chapter 1

WHAT IS METAPHYSICS?

INTRODUCTION

If the question is the straight "what is metaphysics?" one, then I would reply that it is the "science of being as being." In order to explain this, I would refer first of all to Plato. In the *Theaetetus*,[1] distinguishing knowledge from sense perception, Plato presents the soul as comparing things from the viewpoint of being. In the *Timaeus*[2] he presents the three ways of existing of the Ideas, the Receptacle, and the Phenomena. And there is the entire enterprise of philosophical education in the *Republic*, to turn the whole soul toward an interest in being.[3] And I think of the demand in the account of the perpetual war about being, in the *Sophist*,[4] that being must somehow include both the changeless and the changing.

Secondly, I would refer to Aristotle, from whom comes the formula: science which treats of that which is inasmuch as it is that which is [*to on he on*].[5] And I think of the doctrine of being as divided by the categories, and being as divided by act and potency.[6]

---

1. Plato, *Theaetetus* 184b–186e.
2. Plato, *Timaeus* (52d): ". . . *einai tria triche* . . ."
3. Plato, *Republic* 7 (518c–e). On degree or measure or mode of being, see especially *Republic* 9 (585b–586b).
4. Plato, *Sophist* 249d.
5. Aristotle, *Metaph.* 4.1 (1003a21).
6. Aristotle, *Metaph.* 5.7 (1017a22–b9). Thinking about the project of presenting metaphysics as *objective,* I was led to consider the word "theory." The reason is that what I mean by "objectivity" in this context is what is expressed in Aristotle's classification of the sciences by the Greek term: *"theoretikos"* (cf. e.g. *Metaph.* 11.7 [1064a10–18], and 2.1 [993b19–31]). Do I wish to use the word "theory," as in such expressions as the "theory of being as divided by act and potency"? It seems to me unsuitable. The reason is that, in modern English usage, it means an *interpretation* of the *data.* In this way, it opens the door to *other* theories concerning the same data. Such a conception suggests that certain items or a certain zone constitute in a somewhat evident way the "data," whereas what else is on the scene is not "data." Now, just what pertains to "the data" may be the crucial question. Some have spoken of *"sense data."* Bergson spoke of the "immediate data of *consciousness.*" I would like to consider the "immediate data of *intelligence.*" Accordingly, I prefer to speak of the metaphysical *"doctrine"* (rather than *"theory"*) of "being as divided by act and potency."

I think of Avicenna, too, and his description of the task of the metaphysician as determining the modes of being.[7] I think of how this task is
taken up and presented by Thomas Aquinas, in a work such as *De ente et
essentia* (modeled, in important respects, on Aristotle's *De anima*), presenting the grades of *essentia* and its associate, *esse*. Metaphysics considers
modes or grades or intensities of being.[8]

Of particular importance, as we can see in Thomas Aquinas, is the extent to which the task of the metaphysician consists in large part in distinguishing what have more the nature of principles of metaphysical knowledge (our "original lights," the "seeds of wisdom"),[9] and showing how
other truths necessarily follow from them. It seems to me that our minds
stand in constant danger of taking for self-evident things which are not
self-evident. This results in confusion and disagreement about supposedly "most basic" things. In fact, the entire domain of metaphysics is such
that even when we hit upon the truth, it seems that we are doing so by
"intuition," and that the truths seen are self-evident. The contribution of
the metaphysician is often simply to isolate the real starting point, and to
show how the truth does indeed follow.[10]

METAPHYSICS MOST DIFFICULT

Wishing, as I do, to stress the objectivity of metaphysics, I am conscious of the danger that I be misunderstood as finding metaphysical
judgments "easy," as though everyone should easily agree with me. I recognize the need to explore the nature of the *individual* metaphysician's
hold or grasp of his subject. In this regard, I think of certain remarks of
Aristotle, not to mention Plato, about the difficulties of metaphysics. Aristotle tells us that "these things, the most universal, are on the whole the
hardest for men to know; for they are farthest from the senses."[11] Again,
in the same place,[12] having argued that wisdom is non-utilitarian but rather
sought for its own intrinsic worth, it is seen as perhaps not a suitable pur-

7. Avicenna, *Avicenna Latinus. Liber de philosophia prima sive scientia divina* I–IV (ed. S.
Van Riet), Louvain/Leiden, 1977: Peeters/Brill, tr. 1, cap. 2 (pp. 10–11), where the expression *"modus essendi"* and the like are much in evidence.
8. See below, chapter 2.
9. See below, chapter 3.
10. Thomas Aquinas, *SCG* 3.38 (ed. Pera et al., 2161); also 1.10 (59) and 1.11 (66).
See also Thomas's *In Boethii De trin.* 6.1, third set of responses, *ad* 1 (ed. Decker, p. 212,
lines 26–30; in the Maurer transl., 4th ed., p. 73). From this line of thinking, we see why
someone like Thomas or Aristotle or Plato credits others with having "hit upon the truth"
or having spoken "as if forced by truth itself," even though they do not agree with the procedure used by that other thinker.
11. *Metaph.* 1.2 (982a23–25, Oxford tr.).
12. *Metaph.* 1.2 (982b25–32).

suit for human beings, whose nature is servile, i.e. must in large part be absorbed in the pursuit of the useful. Aristotle rejects this view, but he goes on to admit that one of the reasons wisdom should be regarded as "most divine" is that "God alone can have it, or God above all others."[13]

In the *Nicomachean Ethics,* in the discussion of human happiness, the life of contemplation of truth is proposed as the most appropriate candidate to qualify as human happiness. An objection is raised, precisely on the grounds that "such a life would be too high for man; for it is not insofar as he is man that he will live so, but insofar as something divine is present in him."[14] To this, it is countered that we "must, so far as we can, make ourselves immortal, and strain every nerve to live in accordance with the best thing in us."[15] But Aristotle does not leave the matter there. He goes on:

. . . This would seem, too, to be each man himself, since it is the authoritative and better part of him. It would be strange, then, if he were to choose not the life of his self but that of something else . . . for man, the life according to reason is best and pleasantest, since reason more than anything else *is* man.[16]

That is, in this argument, human nature itself is seen as something akin to divine nature. Still, and this is my constant point, the activity in question is viewed as requiring extraordinary effort. It is not presented as easy.

Similar testimony could be elicited from Plato or Thomas Aquinas. Since my own philosophical apprenticeship is with Thomas Aquinas, I will at least note how rare he finds the presence of truly mature metaphysical acumen.[17] Thus, he certainly accuses Averroes of having failed to take up the properly metaphysical outlook in discussing the grades of causality.[18] Still, he views metaphysics as most certain and most in touch with reality.

On the one hand, we should be able to say that, e.g., the priority of act

13. *Metaph.* 1.2 (983a9–10, Oxford tr.).
14. *EN* 10.7 (1177b25–27, Oxford tr.).
15. *EN* 10.7 (1177b35).
16. *EN* 10.7 (1178a2–8, Oxford tr.; italics theirs).
17. In fact, this is the point of the very first article of the *Summa theologiae,* insofar as it includes within the appropriate content of meta-philosophical divine revelation even those truths which the human mind can discover naturally about God. As is well known, his presentation there has its background in earlier observation by Moses Maimonides.
In this regard, viz. the accessibility or inaccessibility of metaphysical truth, an interesting item is Étienne Gilson's early study (first published in 1921), "L'innéisme cartésien et la théologie," in *Etudes sur le rôle de la pensée médiévale dans la formation du système cartésien* (4th ed.), Paris, 1975: Vrin, pp. 9–50; he points out a historical diversity of positions, some seeing the knowledge of God as readily available, others seeing it as most difficult of access.
18. See Thomas, *CP* 8.2 (ed. Maggiòlo, 974 [4]–975 [5]).

over potency is a most certain truth, and, on the other hand, that nevertheless many have stumbled in connection with it.[19] Indeed, we have in
the *Metaphysics*, right at the outset so to speak (book 4), Aristotle facing
the fact that very responsible philosophers have gone wrong concerning the most certain of all principles, and have done so because of real
scientific concerns.[20] When one says that metaphysics is "objective," it
should at the same time be made clear that one has not forgotten the
real world of metaphysical controversy.

METAPHYSICS MOST CERTAIN

In his *Commentary on the Metaphysics* (henceforth, "*CM*") 4.6, Thomas
comments on Aristotle, *Metaph.* 4.3 (1005b8 and ff.). Aristotle, relating
certitude of knowledge in particular fields with knowledge of the most
certain principles for that field, presents the metaphysician as knowing the most certain principles of all, those bearing on beings as beings.
Thomas notes that this was one of the points established concerning the
wise man in the *proemium* of the entire work, i.e. that he was the one with
most certain knowledge of the causes.[21] Thomas's commentary on this
latter text is of great importance.[22] Aristotle has made the point that the
more certain science is the one which includes *fewer* things in its consideration: thus, arithmetic is more certain than geometry. Thomas carries
this further by then presenting metaphysics as most certain. He says:

... particular sciences are posterior, according to nature, to universal sciences,
because their subjects add to the subjects of the universal sciences: as it is clear
that *movable being*, which natural philosophy is about, adds to *being, unqualifiedly*,
which metaphysics is about, and to *quantal being*, which mathematics is about.
Thus, the science which is about being and the maximally universal things is
most certain ...

19. Cf. Aristotle, *Metaph.* 12.6 (1071b22–1072a7); Thomas, *CM* 12.6 (2500–2507).
20. Aristotle, *Metaph.* 4.5 (1009a22). For the seriousness and source of the difficulty,
see 1009b33–1010a3:

And it is in this direction that the consequences are most difficult. For if those who
have seen most of such truth as is possible for us (and these are those who seek and
love it most)–if these have such opinions and express these views about the truth, is
it not natural that beginners in philosophy should lose heart? For to seek the truth
would be to follow flying game.–But the reason why these thinkers held this opinion is
that while they were inquiring into the truth of that which is, they thought "that which
is" was identical with the sensible world [*ta aistheta*] . . . [Oxford tr.]

Aristotle is confident that these thinkers themselves would be easily persuaded by his
clarifications, which are *not difficult* to grasp: 4.6 (1011a14).
21. See *Metaph.* 1.2 (982a12–13, and 25–28).
22. *CM* 1.2 (47).

If we go back now to *CM* 4.6, we see that the most certain principle regarding the being of things is introduced as having three conditions: one cannot err concerning it (thus it belongs to it to be most known of all);[23] it is not dependent on any other thing, as is the case with conditional knowledge: it is known just by virtue of itself; and thirdly, it is not acquired by demonstration or some similar process, but comes *naturally* to the possessor; one simply has to know the terms of the principle, through sense, memory, experience, and the light of the agent intellect.[24]

Thomas goes on to consider the principle, viz. *that it is impossible for the same thing to be and not to be at once and in the same respect etc.* He follows Aristotle's argument that, indeed, one cannot *think* otherwise, since to do so would require the co-existence of contrary opinions in the one mind. One simply cannot be in error about this, and it is thus naturally the principle and the axiom of all axioms. As presupposed by all demonstrations, it is not a conditional principle, and as naturally first, it is naturally possessed by the possessor, not acquired through demonstration.

It is what Thomas then adds which is most important, i.e. a presentation of *"a being"* or *"that which is"* [*ens*] as that which is first known by the *first* operation of the mind, called "the understanding of indivisibles," so that this principle, viz. the aforementioned axiom of axioms, based on knowledge of *ens*, is first in the order of the *second* operation of the mind, called "composing and dividing." I say that this is most important, for it corresponds somewhat to what he says at the end of 4.5 regarding the metaphysician's work of treating of the first principles, viz. that he does so, not by demonstrating, but by "treating the notions of the terms, such as what a whole is and what a part is, and so on" [*rationes terminorum tradendo, ut quid totum et quid pars et sic de aliis*].[25] Thus, ultimately, one sees the task as a focusing on what we get at with our talk and thought about *beings and their being.*

TURNING OUR REFLECTIONS TOWARD BEING

I had at first thought that, my interest being in metaphysics as objective, or as contemplation of truth, it might be as well to take the differ-

---

23. Cf. Etienne Gilson, *Being and Some Philosophers,* Toronto, 1952 (2nd ed.; 1st ed. 1949): Pontifical Institute of Mediaeval Studies (p. ix):

> The present book is not an attempt to show what comes first in reality, for all philosophers know it inasmuch as they are, not philosophers, but men. Our only problem will be to know how it is that what men so infallibly know *qua* men, they so often overlook *qua* philosophers.

24. *CM* 4.6 (597–599).
25. *CM* 4.5 (595).

ence between Plato and Aristotle as a problem, since such differing of great minds might suggest that the difference itself has a basis, not in the domain of cognition, but in something more like choice or fundamental inclination. However, I have since decided that such a case is itself too particular, and that it would be more appropriate to consider a more primary task.[26]

What I was looking for was a difference closer to metaphysical generalities, and where we can more immediately see ourselves in the course of fundamental contemplation. And so I ask help from both Plato and Aristotle, and I ask where they undertake to usher us into consideration of things from the viewpoint of being.

Plato's recommendation in the *Republic*[27] as to what awakens the mind to reflect on being is *single* sensible things which give rise to *multiple considerations*. The example is the group of three fingers with the one in the middle smaller than one of its associates and larger than the other. This one finger is then grasped as both "big" and "small," and we are led to ask, as these are two and yet the thing is one, *what* the big and the small *are*.[28] The point is that the *two* in *one* has excited the mind to ask questions about *being*. The capacity to view things from the viewpoint of being is present, and requires only the appropriate techniques of stimulation.[29]

Other passages in Plato come to mind. There is the text in the *Sophist* in which the Eleatic Stranger attempts to lead those who hold that "only bodies have being" to the fundamental truth one might say they have hit upon but are badly expressing, namely that being is the power to be an origin of action on something else or a receiver of action.[30] One cannot help thinking, too, of the use Plato makes of representations (reflections

---

26. Cf. *CM* 3.9 (443): the question: whether there is something separate from sensible things, which is their principle. Thomas paraphrases Aristotle as follows:

... that it is *the most difficult of all the problems of this science*. Which is shown from this, that *the most eminent philosophers judged diversely about it*. For the Platonists held that the universals are separate, with the other philosophers holding the contrary.–Thirdly, he says about it, that it is most necessary to consider, because *on it depends the entire knowledge of substances, sensible as well as immaterial*. [my italics]

27. Plato, *Republic* 7 (523c–525a).
28. More precisely, what we are seeing is *relations* caused by *quantity*, i.e. if the fingers are A, B, and C, with A the smallest and C the biggest, then, in B, we see both "bigger than A" and "smaller than C"; and we could, of course, be even more thoroughly descriptive.
29. Plato, *Republic* 7 (518b–519b).
30. Plato, *Sophist* (246d–247e, especially 247d–e). Plato here is proposing a doctrine very close to, if not identical with, Aristotle's division of being by act and potency (here, it is more a case of active potency and passive potency). Aristotle criticized the Platonic Forms as not *productive*: cf. e.g. *Metaph.* 1.9 (991a8–11, also a19–23, and 991b3–9; 992a24–26). Since Plato here seems to be making the same point, one wonders why Aristotle criticized him in just that way.

in water, etc.) as contrasted with the represented sensible things themselves, as a trampoline or launching pad for the mind to turn its attention to higher modes or measures of being.[31]

However, the passage which I wish to recall particularly today is the moment in the *Phaedo* when Socrates undertakes to discuss the causes of coming to be and ceasing to be and being. He expresses his dissatisfaction with the methods of the physicists, and with their conception of causal explanation. He approves of Anaxagoras's consideration of mind as a cause, but sees this as requiring a vision of the good of each thing. He himself undertakes to approach beings from the viewpoint of the notion [*logos*] as contrasted with beings in the concrete [*ergon*].[32]

In recounting his decision to become a "dropout" from the school of the physicists,[33] Socrates presents their typical questions:

Do heat and cold, by a sort of fermentation, bring about the organization of animals, as some people say? Is it the blood, or air, or fire by which we think? Or is it none of these, and does the brain furnish the sensations of hearing and sight and smell, and do memory and opinion arise from these, and does knowledge come from memory and opinion in a state of rest?[34]

What Socrates complains of is not that the physicists give a role to this or that factor, but that they regard it as truly causal and as explanatory in an ultimate and satisfying way. He compares their explanations of natural phenomena to someone attempting to say why he, Socrates, is there in prison, and speaking only of his body and its bones and sinews—or

---

Notice also that in this same context, Aristotle criticizes the Forms as having no relevance for *final causality*, i.e. the good. And he has just mentioned the part of the *Phaedo* where Plato speaks of the appropriateness of a doctrine of mind looking toward the good (though Plato also says he has not been able to proceed in this direction, and so has started with the Forms: *Phaedo* [99c]). Aristotle considers Plato's Forms as too purely along the lines of mathematicals, it would seem (See *Physics* 2.2 [193b35–194a6]). It looks as though, for Aristotle, there must be fusion of agency and form-as-intelligible-goal, a fusion found in mind, for an adequate doctrine of the supreme cause: for him, in mind the medical art (the *productive* cause) and health (the *final* cause) are one: see *Metaph.* 12.10 (1075b8–10). This goes counter to what many historians hold about Aristotle's supreme cause, viz. that it is purely a final and not an efficient cause. See my paper, "St. Thomas, Aristotle, and Creation," in *Dionysius* (annual of the classics department, Dalhousie University, Halifax, N.S.) 15 (1991), pp. 81–90.

31. Plato, *Republic* 6 (509e–510a).
32. Plato, *Phaedo* (100a).
33. Plato, *Phaedo* (96a).
34. Plato, *Phaedo* (96b) [tr. H. N. Fowler, Cambridge, Mass., 1960 (original 1914): Harvard University Press]. The question about the organization of animals from "fermentation" by "the hot and the cold" brings to mind the quest for the origin of life by bolts of lightning affecting a prebiotic mixture: cf. Michael J. Behe, *Darwin's Black Box: The Biochemical Challenge to Evolution,* New York, 1996: The Free Press, pp. 166–170, reporting on the work of Stanley Miller and others.

someone saying that the causes of our talking were "voice" and "air" and "hearing." He himself cites as "cause" "the choice of what is best."[35]

In general, Socrates favors as cause mind contemplating the good, but he admits to having difficulty following out this pathway in the natural world. The cause he proposes is the *form*, e.g. beauty itself, and the causal influence is participation (on the side of the effect), presence or communication (on the side of the cause). The cause of something being *two* is *participation in duality.*[36]

This primacy of form as contrasted with what is perfected by the form corresponds to the Aristotelian primacy of form and act over matter and potency. Aristotle, it is true, accepts matter as a cause, but he clearly does not see "cause" as said of all types of cause as though they were *equally* causal.[37]

Aristotle criticizes Plato for not having the adequate doctrine of the moving cause, origin of events.[38] What is it that does any work, looking toward the Ideas?[39] In sum, without something along the lines of mind as agent, the forms will not be *final* causes. The good will not be considered as a cause in the way *proper* to its being a cause.[40] Even in the Anaxagorean view of mind (looking toward the good), mind will not be first, and something will be beyond it, viz. the good.[41] What will explain the *unity* of the good and the mind which "works, looking toward it"? Does the good just *happen* to be the sort of thing which appeals to that mind? Or is that mind *by nature* akin to the good? If it just happens to appeal, then "the universe" would be merely a series of episodes.[42] No, Aristotle's doctrine has a primary *unity* of mover and goal, one being which is both final cause and efficient cause of *all*. In that way, end, form, and agent all stand together in the perfecting of matter, and act is absolutely prior to potency.[43]

Still, it is not the difference between Plato and Aristotle that occupies me here, and I must say that, in view of the things Plato says, especially

35. Plato, *Phaedo* (99b).

36. Plato, *Phaedo* (101c).

37. See Aristotle, *Metaph.* 12.10 (1075a37), on the good as maximally a principle.

38. Notice that Aristotle, *Metaph.* 9.8 (1050b35–1051a2), regards the Ideas as mere potencies; thus there will be something more actual and prior in perfection to the Ideas: "science-itself" seems to name something still open to a diversity of actualizations, whereas operating mind is determinately of this or that. This objection, while rather particular to the cases of science itself and motion itself, seems nevertheless to be applicable to the doctrine of Ideas generally, including even the Good.

39. Aristotle, *Metaph.* 1.9 (991a22–23 and 991b3–5).

40. Aristotle, *Metaph.* 1.7 (988b11–16).

41. Aristotle, *Metaph.* 12.10 (1075b8–10).

42. This is an expression used by Aristotle at *Metaph.* 12.10 (1075b34–1076a4), in criticizing those who fail to give an adequate account of the unity of all being.

43. Cf. Aristotle, *Metaph.* 12.10 (1075b34–1076a4). I am very far from thinking that what I say here jumps right out from this text.

in the *Sophist*,[44] about the need for there to be intelligence and life in the highest being, I am not sure why Aristotle criticizes him in just the way he does. Was it simply that the *Phaedo* and the *Republic* were the widely read Plato, and the *Sophist* relatively recondite?

The reason I focused on Socrates' autobiography in the *Phaedo* was, rather, to highlight something common to Plato and Aristotle, namely the insistence on form and goodness, on the priority of act over potency, and on a certain line of criticism of the earlier physicists. These things seem to me the perennial fundamental lesson, and "gateway to metaphysics." When I read in the Science Reports in the *New York Times* what representative scientists think about the "Big Bang," I am more and more convinced of the need for metaphysical education.[45] They put me in mind of the theologians referred to by Aristotle, who, he tells us, "gen-

---

44. Plato, *Sophist* (248e).

45. Malcolm W. Browne, "Despite New Data, Mysteries of Creation Persist," *New York Times,* May 12, 1992, pp. C1 and C10. We are told:

> One of the major mysteries that have long vexed astrophysicists has to do with the origin of structure in the universe. Just after the Big Bang event in which most scientists believe the universe sprang into existence, the initial fireball is generally thought to have been smooth and homogeneous, lacking any structure. By contrast, the present-day universe is lumpy and has lots of structure. Its visible matter is clumped into galaxies, clusters of galaxies, and clusters of clusters. This structure, indeed, was essential for the origin and evolution of life.
>
> Once the free-wheeling atoms of matter in the early universe began to clump together, the formation of galaxies and clusters of galaxies could be readily explained in terms of the growing gravitational attraction of the snowballing clumps. But the central mystery remained: when and how did the very first clumping of matter, the genesis of universal structure, arise? (C1).

This particular report has to do with the finding of "slight irregularities in the universal background of microwave radiation surviving from the earliest time to which astronomers can look back, a mere 300,000 years after the Big Bang creation event." It quotes Dr. Steven Weinberg, "winner of the Nobel Prize in Physics and a leading cosmological theorist," as saying that if the long-sought evidence of early structure in the universe had not been eventually discovered, "there's no theory that would have survived." (C1) Still, we are eventually told:

> But the discovery leaves unresolved the more fundamental question of how structure originated. [C10]

And it goes on to indicate various theories and to tell something of the arguments among their advocates.

The "Letters" section of the following day's *Times* (May 13, 1992) devotes a quarter of a page to letters received in comment on the original *Times* reporting of the discovery (front page, April 24). One is from a professor of philosophy (Adolf Grunbaum, University of Pittsburgh) saying that they should not have spoken of "a beginning of time" in connection with the Bang, since "the concept of a finite but unbounded past is unfamiliar to common sense, but unproblematic in mathematical physics." Another is from a professor of mathematics (Irving E. Segal, Massachusetts Institute of Technology), telling us that Big Bang theory in its entirety is "seriously flawed by its incompatibility with redshift observations and by its deficiency of other predictions that are subject to model-independent direct observational confirmation, not to mention the considerable cost of its abandonment of global energy conservation as a fundamental physical principle."

erate all things from night" or "the natural philosophers who says that 'all things were together.'"[46] So also, to speak very generally, theoreticians of evolution who assign a truly ultimate role to chance in their explanations are speaking against their own awareness of the primacy of form: chance ultimately has to be a derivative of form.[47]

Commenting on Aristotle's remark that in a sense potency is prior to act, while in another sense act is prior to potency, Thomas Aquinas resumes the doctrine as follows:

> . . . act is prior to potency unqualifiedly; but in one and the same thing, which is developed from potency into act, potency is temporally prior to act, even though act is prior to potency as to its nature and perfection.[48]

Metaphysics is a constant development of the implications of this knowledge.

ADDENDUM ON THE BIG BANG

If I may add some remarks on Big Bang popular discussions, I would protest the Bang's being presented as an altogether first event, if this is conceived as something really integral to what I would call "observational" physical science.

Let us suppose the Big Bang can be scientifically established. What does it come to? That a cosmos once dense is now rare. This would indeed make an interesting point regarding the comportment of corporeal reality, but it would say nothing about the origin of the cosmos (unless, quite arbitrarily, one limits one's cosmoses to rare ones). Aristotle, in the fourth century B.C., pointed out that there could be no such thing as a "first event," looking at things from a strictly physical perspective. If things had to begin to become rare (a big bang), the question is: "why only then, why not earlier?" The answer has to be: "conditions were not yet right." What was it for "conditions to become right"? Something had to happen *first* (i.e. before the big bang). Thus, there is always an event presupposed by any posited "first event." The Big Bang, even if it is science, is only an interesting event.

46. Aristotle, *Metaph.* 12.6 (1071b26–28).
47. Aristotle, *Phys.* 2.6 (198a5–13):
> . . . Spontaneity and chance are causes of effects which, though they might result from intelligence or nature, have in fact been caused by something *incidentally.* Now since nothing which is incidental is prior to what is *per se,* it is clear that no incidental cause can be prior to a cause *per se.* Spontaneity and chance, therefore, are posterior to intelligence and nature. Hence, however true it may be that the heavens are due to spontaneity, it will still be true that intelligence and nature will be prior causes of this All and of many things in it besides. [Oxford tr.]

48. *CM* 12.6 (2506), concerning Aristotle at 12.6 (1072a3–4).

The question of *creation,* understood as the emanation of all being from a supreme being (whether the emanated reality be of finite duration going towards the past, or has always existed in complete, through and through, dependence on higher reality) has occupied the philosophical and religious mind for centuries, and is not part of the same discussion as a Big Bang. Still, physical scientists are also human beings, and human beings are (I am glad to say) interested in questions of absolute origin.

My purpose in referring to Aristotle was not so much to invoke an authority as to indicate that the argument has been in the public domain for quite a while. The argument, I believe, is too clear to require an authority. It is based on a principle needed for the existence of any experimental science, namely that an event occurs if and only if the appropriate conditions obtain.

Notice, however, that a first event is not impossible, viewing the physical world from a metaphysical point of view. A transcendent cause, acting voluntarily, can create either a physical world wherein there is no first event or else one in which there is a first event. Still, the metaphysical observer cannot say which of these two is the actual world.

A religious believer, basing himself on divine revelation, may say that the world has finite duration going toward the past, and so there is a first moment of time and a beginning of movement. As a Roman Catholic, I actually say that this is the truth about the world. However, I do not say it on the basis of metaphysics and, still less, on the basis of physical science.

A mathematical physicist may find it appropriate, in view of certain observed phenomena, to develop the hypothesis of an (otherwise unobservable) first event. (There is no real "before" in relation to a first event. In the thirteenth century, this was exactly the way Thomas Aquinas argued to show the intelligibility of a model of the universe having a first moment.) Still, even if there are observational reasons for so envisioning the history of the corporeal universe, how ultimately satisfactory could such a hypothesis be, even in its own order? Such hypotheses seem *provisional* by their very nature. The reason is that nothing would seem to qualify as an observationally determinable "all-encompassing" physical phenomenon. I dare say that the very envisaging of an "original situation" or "first event" obliges us to cross the frontier from mathematical physics to straight mathematics.

The tendency of the Big Bang to drift across the line from physics into mathematics can be seen in expressions used in accounts of it. Consider some of the things said by J. Richard Gott (with others) in the article "Will the Universe Expand Forever?," *Scientific American,* March 1976. He says: "... at some unique time in the past all the matter in the universe was compressed to an arbitrarily *great* density . . ." Then we read: ". . . crushed together at *infinite* density." Then, ". . . the initial state is one of . . . *high* density . . ." We alternate between the "high" or "great" (which sounds measurable) and the "infinite." So also, though we are told that "matter was compressed," we are also told that "space and time were created in that event *and so was all the matter in the universe*" (matter seems to have to *be*, in order to be infinitely dense, and *not to be*, in order to result from the bang). We are also told: "The point-universe was not an object isolated in space; it was the entire universe . . ." Thus, the universe was a "point." Quite aside from the fact that the universe seems to be present both at the origin of the creative event (hence, "point-universe") and at its achievement, the notion of a point taken all by itself is rather purely mathematical. Is the move from density to rarity, or from no dimensions to dimensionality?

Chapter 2

WHAT DOES IT MEAN TO STUDY BEING "AS BEING"?

INTRODUCTION[1]

What does it mean to study being "as being"? Anyone at all familiar with Aristotelian discussion of metaphysics has heard the expression: "the science (or study) of being as being."[2] Sometimes, in the mouths of oldsters recalling their student days, it symbolizes a certain gobbledy-gook or double talk. Sometimes, in the mouths of neophytes, it seems to encapsulate a mysterious enterprise whose promise is extraordinary.

The mere form of expression should not cause difficulty. To consider a doctor precisely as a doctor is obviously different from the infinity of possible incidental considerations of a doctor. Sentences expressing *per accidens* considerations are familiar, and their denial provides comedy. If I say "doctors do not make money," I am greeted (I hope) with laughter. Yet precisely *qua* doctor, the doctor does not make money; the doctor heals. It is as a human being with material needs that the doctor asks for recompense. Studying the medical art is one thing. Studying business practice is something else.

No, in the expression "studying being as being," the source of puzzlement, the source of obscurity, is the repeated word: "being." How much does it really say? "Dog" says something, and "cat" says something; but "being"? Since it is said of everything whatsoever, it has seemed to many not to say anything at all, a pseudo-word. Being, it might be thought, is like "the night in which all cows are black."

Of course, it can be insisted that to say something "is" signifies that one is not merely dealing with fantasies or dreams. Beings are what is

---

1. This paper was originally read at the philosophy conference "Thomas Aquinas and the Subject of Metaphysics–Findings and Issues," held at the Pontificia Università della Santa Croce, Rome, Feb. 27–28, 2003. I have not removed occasional references to that context.

2. Aristotle, *Metaph.* 4.1 (1003a21).

real. Still, that seems to be a rather homogeneous check mark to place after a thing's name. It hardly expresses anything intelligible about the thing.

In short, it is easy to convince oneself that "being" either means exactly the same thing, even when said of the most radically diverse items, or else that "being," since it is said of the most radically diverse items, has no one meaning at all.

Fortunately we are not alone. We have predecessors with whom we can still communicate. We have such people as Plato of Athens, Aristotle of Stagira, and Thomas Aquinas the Neapolitan. In fact, our conference is entitled "*Thomas Aquinas* and the Subject of Metaphysics—Findings and Issues." In a sense, then, it is a historical investigation. What did this thirteenth-century thinker understand concerning the subject of metaphysics? On the other hand, if we take to heart Thomas's own view of philosophy, we will not see ourselves as engaged in "mere history." With Thomas, we will insist that ". . . the study of philosophy is not in order to know what it is people have thought, but what is the truth about reality."[3] If we go back to Thomas in our study of philosophy, it is because, in the words of Étienne Gilson: "Great philosophers are very scarce."[4]

It is not necessary, then, to *discover*, as though for the first time, an answer to the question: What does it mean to study being "as being"? Aristotle, the originator of the formula, already provided an answer, and Thomas Aquinas took it upon himself to explain that answer. I propose to review their presentations, and, above all, to recall the way they undertook the study itself. Without some exploration of their practice, the answer might remain incomprehensible.

Aristotle's own presentation offers considerable difficulty, owing in part to the exploratory procedure in his *Metaphysics*, in part to the nature of those writings of Aristotle which have come down to us.[5] That is a reason to appreciate the commentary[6] provided by Thomas. We are better off the more penetrating the philosophical mind of the commentator.[7] Accordingly, I will generally rely on Thomas for the presentation of

---

3. Thomas Aquinas, *In Aristotelis libros De caelo et mundo expositio*, 1.22 (ed. R. Spiazzi, Rome/Turin, 1952: Marietti, 228 [8]):

> . . . studium philosophiae non est ad hoc quod sciatur quid homines senserint sed qualiter se habeat veritas rerum.

4. Étienne Gilson, *History of Philosophy and Philosophical Education*, Milwaukee, 1948: Marquette University Press, p. 21.

5. Cf. Joseph Owens, *History of Ancient Western Philosophy*, New York, 1959: Appleton-Century-Crofts, pp. 285–294.

6. By "the commentary" here, I do not mean simply the work of St. Thomas which undertakes the line-by-line commentary of Aristotle's *Metaphysics;* I mean the metaphysical doctrine expressed in all the works of Thomas.

7. Gilson held constantly to the view that one must be a philosopher to be adequate as a historian of philosophy, and one must be a historian of philosophy to be a philosopher.

Aristotle, though I am well aware of the distance which often separates Thomas from our contemporaries as regards Aristotle's meaning.

In the *Republic* of Plato, the task of philosophical education is precisely to turn the soul toward the consideration of being. "Being" in Plato obviously names a field of investigation which incorporates a variety of intensities: some things *"are"* more, some things *"are"* less.[8]

It is Aristotle who, in undertaking the most ambitious of human studies, the only study which can satisfy the radical human natural desire, the desire to know,[9] eventually presents it as "a science of being as being." He had already said he was seeking the highest causes. Pursuing this point, he noted that a cause must be the cause of some nature. Of what nature could the highest cause be cause, if not of the nature of being? In confirmation of this, he pointed to the ancient Greek cosmologists. *They* sought the highest causes, and, clearly, they were seeking the causes of being as being.[10]

Cf. "Wisdom and Time," published in French in *Lumière et Vie* 1 (1951), pp. 77–92, and in English translation by Anton C. Pegis in *A Gilson Reader,* ed. Anton C. Pegis, Garden City, N.Y., 1957: Doubleday Image Books, pp. 328–341:

> ... one can be a scientist without knowing the history of the sciences, whereas one cannot be a philosopher without knowing the history of philosophy. [337]

And E. Gilson, "Doctrinal History and its Interpretation," *Speculum* 24 (1949), pp. 483–492, at pp. 488–489:

> ... no man can write a single line of history of philosophy without handling his subject as a philosopher. Such is the main reason why doctrinal history is full of philosophical controversies about historical facts, which we mistake for historical controversies.

8. On degree or measure or mode of being, see especially Plato, *Republic* 9 (585b–586b). The project, viz. treating being as being, is a *distinctive* one. One thinks immediately of the project envisaged in Plato's *Republic* 7.4 (518c–d):

> ... [T]he present argument ... indicates that this power is in the soul of each, and that the instrument with which each learns–just as an eye is not able to turn toward the light from the dark without the whole body–must be turned around from that which *is coming into being* [*ek tou gignomenou*] together with the whole soul until it is able to endure looking at that which *is* [*to on*] and the brightest part of that which *is* [*tou ontos*]. And we affirm that this is the good, do we not? [Plato, *Republic* 7.4 (518c–d), tr. Allan Bloom, New York, 1968: Basic Books (italics Bloom's).]

In the *Theaetetus* (184b–186e), Plato, distinguishing knowledge [*episteme*] from sense perception, presents the soul as comparing things from the viewpoint of *being.* He speaks [185c] of "what is common to all things"; being [*ousia*], more than anything else, belongs to all things [186a]. In the *Timaeus* (52d): ". . . *einai tria triche* . . .": he presents *the three ways of being* of the Ideas, the Receptacle, and the Phenomena. And let us recall the demand in the account of the perpetual war about being in the *Sophist* (249d), that being must somehow include both the changeless and the changing.

9. Aristotle, *Metaph.* 1.1 (980a21).

10. Aristotle, *Metaph.* 4.1 (1003a21–32); St. Thomas, *CM* 4.1 (ed. Cathala, 529–533):

> [533]Then, when [Aristotle] says "But because . . . ," here he shows that this science which we have in our hands has *that-which-is* for its subject, with this sort of argument. Every principle is the essential principle and cause of some *nature*. But we are seeking the *first* principles of things and the *highest* causes, as was said in the first book: therefore, *they* are the essential cause of some *nature*. But of no other [nature] than that of

Aristotle's presentation of being as being as the field of the metaphysician is thus a doctrine of "being" as the name of a *nature*, a nature seen in its community as coinciding with the field of influence of the highest of all causes. This picture is several times presented by St. Thomas when considering God as creator. To take a well-known text, consider his explanation of God as cause of primary matter. Thomas reviews the history of philosophy of causal influence. The early philosophers thought that the substance of things was uncaused, and conceived of causes merely as sources of accidental form. Later, having analyzed generable and corruptible substance itself into form and matter, they understood such substance as caused, but conceived of matter as uncaused: thus, the causes they conceived were limited to originating particular kinds of things. Ultimately, such philosophers as Plato and Aristotle achieved an unqualifiedly universal outlook, considering being as being, and so they came to affirm the existence of unqualifiedly universal causality, causality of total substance, and so even of matter.[11]

To study being as being, then, means that one catch sight of being as a nature, i.e. something somehow common to things, in function of which they fall within the proper field of influence of the highest of all causes.[12] Thomas had already indicated this in the prologue he wrote for his *Commentary on the Metaphysics:*

The aforementioned separate substances are the universal and first causes *of being* [*universales et primae causae essendi*]. Now, it pertains to the same science to consider the proper causes of some genus and the genus itself: for example, the natural [scientist] considers the principles of natural body [*corporis naturalis*]. Hence, it is necessary that it pertain to the same science to consider the separate substances and *common being* [*ens commune*], which is the genus of which the aforementioned substances are the common and universal causes.

---

being [*entis*]. Which is clear from this fact, that *all the philosophers seeking the elements* [*of beings*] *inasmuch as they are beings* sought these sorts of principle, viz. the first and highest; therefore, in this science we are seeking the principles of that-which-is inasmuch as it is that-which-is; therefore, that-which-is is the subject of this science, because every science is seeking the proper causes of its subject.

In the above I have inserted the words "of beings" [*entium*] which appears to have been omitted by scribal error, since it is in Thomas's Aristotle text, and is needed for Thomas's argument. Socrates also, as presented by Plato in *Phaedo* 96a–b and 97b, 97e, saw the early physicists as seeking the causes of being.

11. Thomas, *ST* 1.44.2 (and 1); and cf. *CP* 8.2 (975 [5]).

12. Cf. *ST* 1.4.3, where Thomas, seeking to explain how all creatures are like God, speaks of the analogical community constituted by being:

. . . according to some sort of analogy, the way being itself [*ipsum esse*] is common to all. And in this way those things which are from God are assimilated to him inasmuch as they are beings [*entia*], as to the first and universal principle of all being [*totius esse*].

What I wish to underline is the treatment of being as a *single unified field,* called here a "genus." We know that Thomas must be using the word "genus" in a wide sense, since he always maintains that being is not a genus, properly speaking.[13] Still, it must name a *per se* unified field.[14]

THE UNITY OF THE FIELD

Aristotle saw the difficulty of seeing "being" as naming the objects in a unified field: we say "is" even of what is not: "Non-being *is* non-being."[15] Without reviewing in detail Aristotle's doctrine that "being" is said in many ways, but as reducible to substance, I would recall the systematization provided by Thomas Aquinas of this doctrine, since it shows us a pedagogy aimed at developing the vision of the unity of the field of metaphysics, the unity of being. After following carefully the text of Aristotle, Thomas presents four "modes" or "measures" or "intensities" or "degrees" of being, beginning with the weakest, the least, and moving toward the strongest. The four are (1) negations and privations, (2) generations and corruptions and movements, (3) inhering accidents, and (4) substances. We read:

One should know that the aforementioned modes of being [*modi essendi*] can be reduced to four. For one of them, which is *the weakest, "is"* only *in the mind,* namely *negation* and *privation;* we say they *"are"* in the mind, because the mind treats them as though they were some sort of beings, when it affirms or negates something in their regard. (The difference between negation and privation will be explained later.)

Another mode is *close to the first as regards weakness,* according to which *generation* and *corruption* and *movement* are called *"beings."* The reason [they are weak] is that they have, mixed in, something of negation and privation. Thus, it is said in [Aristotle's] *Physics,* book 3, that movement is *imperfect* actuality.

13. Cf. *CM* 3.8 (433), Thomas paraphrasing Aristotle at 3.3 (998b20), arguing that "one" and "being" cannot be genera. Cf. also *CM* 4.4 (583), where Thomas is commenting on Aristotle at 4.2 (1005a2). The Latin translation Thomas had there speaks of "being" and "one" as genera. Thomas says:

. . . not that they are truly genera, but they have a resemblance to genera, by reason of their commonness.

14. In *CM* 6.4 (1243–1244), Thomas, commenting on Aristotle at *Metaph.* 6.3 (1028a1–2) as to why both "being" in the sense of "the true" and "being" as that which "is" *per accidens* are to be set aside in the principal study, says:

And another reason is that both, viz. true being and being *per accidens,* are about some genus of being, not about being unqualifiedly *per se* which is in things [*ens simpliciter per se quod est in rebus*], and *they do not show any other* nature of being [*aliquam aliam naturam entis*] *existing outside per se* beings.

15. Aristotle, *Metaph.* 4.2 (1003b10).

Now, in third place those items are called ["beings"] that have no admixture of not-being, and yet *still have weak being*, because they *"are,"* not *by themselves*, but *in another*, the way *qualities, quantities,* and *properties of substances* "are."

But it is the fourth kind which is *the most perfect*, namely that which has being *in nature* [i.e. not merely in the mind], and without an admixture of privation [the way mere processes have], and has *solid* and *firm* being, as *existing by virtue of itself*, the way *substances* "are." And to this, as to what is first and principal, all the others are referred back. Thus, qualities and quantities are said to "be," inasmuch as they have "being-*in*" substances; movements and generations [are said to "be"] inasmuch as they *tend* toward substance, or to one of the others [i.e. quality or quantity]; and privations and negations [are said to "be"], inasmuch as they *remove* something pertaining to the other three modes.[16]

Privations, such as *blindness*, have "being" attributed to them by our minds so that they may be dealt with in discussion. Blindness is not some positive reality in nature, but rather, by such a word, we focus on the *absence* of something that *ought to be present:* i.e. absence of *sight* in *eyes*. Still, we say that blindness "is" in the eyes. In so speaking, we understand that we are not attributing to blindness an extra-mental *nature*. Such "beings," *"beings of reason,"* we treat as beings so as to be able to talk about them.[17]

Movement, while it is not *wholly* a mere being of reason, nevertheless cannot be thought of without introducing negation and so involving beings of reason. When we say a thing *"is in motion,"* we consider it both as *"not yet* arrived" and as *"no longer* where it was." The *absence* of the thing from its point of origin and from its point of arrival is essential for an intelligible conception of movement. Also, movement can "be" *only* in the movable thing. It has neither stability nor solidity.[18]

Thirdly, St. Thomas comes to the qualities and quantities and other properties (e.g. relations) which we find *in* things. They are stable and wholly in extra-mental reality, unlike movements. But they *inhere* in substances, and so lack the "solidity" which substances have. Their "being" is a mere "being *in*."

And lastly we come to substances (i.e. those items which we focus on by means of such words as "dog," "cat," "spider," "tree," "iron," "hydrogen," etc.) which fully *"are,"* inasmuch as they are (1) outside the mind, and are (2) stable, and (3) do not merely inhere.

Thomas here is considering "is" as the sign of an *actuality* which is attributed to what one is talking about, a *perfection* seen in the thing: much as one would see the sculptor's block of wood as perfected by the con-

16. Thomas Aquinas, *CM* 4.1 (ed. Cathala, 540–543).

17. "Negations" differ from privations merely because what is seen as absent is not something that *ought* to be present; e.g. absence of *sight* in *trees:* their "not having sight" is a mere negation, not a privation, not a "lack."

18. For a detailed presentation of this point, cf. *CP* 3.5 (ed. Maggiòlo, 324 [17]).

ferred shape. "Now, the wood *is like David*." "Is like David" is the actuality or perfection which has been conferred by the sculptor on the block of wood. And St. Thomas is saying that the "is" will be stronger or weaker, depending on its resemblance to or remoteness from *substantial actuality*. "To be" is used in the unqualified, we might say "uninhibited," "full blast," way when it is said with reference to the thing's very substantiality: to be is *to be a human being*, or *to be a horse*, or *to be a tree*. "To be able to play the piano" is a *quality* added to the human being, a secondary "being." The person who has it is said to "be qualified" in that respect. "To be six feet tall" (the "being" of *quantity*) is a secondary "to be," *presupposing*, as it does, the substantial being of the thing to which it is attributed. "To be getting there" (the being of movement) is even weaker. "To be broken" (the being of privation) (said, for example, of a bird's wing or of your arm) is more of a lament for the being you would like to see in your arm or in the wing (and which it *ought* to have), but which you can only envisage in your mind.

Thomas, again, has been encouraging us to consider the words "be" and "is" as found in propositions, i.e. in actual predication, as a *verb*. He is favoring this, for the moment, over considerations of the *noun:* "a being" (as in "John is *a being*" or "*a being* from outer space"). "Is" is *said of* a subject, and does not normally stand in the place of a subject (as "a being" might do). "Is" is said of a subject, and that subject is primarily *the subsisting thing* or *substance*. It is the substance which *is*, i.e. which *is a man* (substantial predicate), *is tall* (quantity predicate), *is dark complexioned* (quality predicate), *is en route to class* (predicate of movement to place), *is late* (time predicate), etc. St. Thomas is encouraging us to see the *subject* as affected by a *variety* of *"acts of being."* The acts are all related to, said of, the *one* subject. However, there is a *variety* among the acts, and that variety is expressed, not simply by the word "is," which is repeatedly being used, but by the word "is" along with the accompanying word: "is *a man*," "is *tall*," etc. These accompanying words express a *form* or *essence*, a factor in the domain of "programming," we might say. There is a proportion, a kinship, between the *form* (named by a word like "man" or "tree" or "tall") and the corresponding *act of being* (named by the word "is"),[19] but, as we eventually see, they are not to be *identified* with each other (except in the case of God).[20]

The doctrine of *the analogy of being*, i.e. that the word "being" is used in a variety of senses, one sense having a proportion to another (and one sense having primacy) is developed, not only as to "being" and "is," but as

19. Cf. especially *SCG* 4.14 (ed. Pera, 3508), on the hierarchy of stronger and weaker acts of accidental being.
20. On this, cf. below, chapter 11.

to the whole field of metaphysical items. Terms like "cause," "form," "perfection," etc. are all said with a variety of meanings, some primary, some secondary and derivative. And this is not merely a matter of "the way we *talk*"; rather, we talk the way we do, and think the way we do, because of the nature of being.

St. Thomas uses the term *"analogy"* to describe this situation and this use of words. He presents analogy as a middle position between pure *equivocity* (as with "pen" said of a writing instrument and an enclosure: same word, said of two different things, with two completely different meanings) and pure *univocity* ("animal" said of a dog and of a cat: same word, said of two different things, but with the same meaning). With analogy, one has the same word, said of different things, and with different meanings one deriving from another. There is reduction to one meaning and one nature.

Now, I have presented this doctrine as a bridge, taking us toward what happens in books 7 and 8 of Aristotle's *Metaphysics*. Pierre Aubenque has called *Metaphysics* 4.2 a *"crux commentatorum."*[21] He does not believe that one can take seriously Aristotle's word *"phusis,"* i.e. "nature," in 4.1.[22] He reads 4.2 (1004a5) as speaking of a dividing of "the sciences" in keeping with a dividing of the Aristotelian categories of being.[23] St. Thomas, on the other hand, has this paraphrase of the pertinent passage:

> [563] Here [Aristotle] shows that the parts of philosophy are distinguished in keeping with the parts of "a being" and "one." And he says that the parts of philosophy are as many as the parts of substance, about which principally "a being" and "one" are said, and concerning which is the principal consideration and aim of this science. And because the parts of substance are ordered to one another: for immaterial substance is naturally prior to sensible substance, therefore it is necessary that among the parts of philosophy there be some first. Nevertheless, that [part] which is *about sensible substance* is first in the order of teaching, because it is necessary to begin teaching from what are more known to us; and concerning that there is treatment in the seventh and eighth books of this work. However, that [part] which is *about immaterial substances* is prior in dignity and in the aim of this science; concerning which there is treatment in book twelve of this work. And nevertheless whatever are first must be continuous with the other parts, because *all the parts have for genus "one" and "a being."* Hence, in the consideration of "one" and "a being" the diverse parts of this science are united, even though they are about *diverse parts of substance:* in such a way that it is *one* science inasmuch as the aforementioned parts are following on this, i.e. *"one" and "a being,"* as *what are common to substance*. And in this respect the philosopher is like the mathematician. For mathematics has diverse parts, one principal, viz. arithmetic, and one

21. Cf. Pierre Aubenque, "Sens et structure de la *Métaphysique* aristotélicienne" (Séance du 23 mars 1963), *Bulletin de la Société française de Philosophie* 58 (1964), p. 13.

22. Ibid., pp. 10–11.

23. Ibid., p. 14.

secondary, viz. geometry, and others following upon these, such as optics, astronomy, and music.[24]

That is, Thomas interprets the division as into *parts of primary philosophy*, which has as subject, as just said, substance. Thus, Aristotle speaks, not of the categories of being, but of a division within the domain of substance itself.[25]

THE FIRST PART: ON SENSIBLE SUBSTANCE

Here we must recall the discussions in books 7 and 8 as the foundational metaphysical step for us. It is an investigation of *essence or formal cause* in generable and corruptible substance. This is in accord with the doctrine of metaphysics, insofar as it considers that which is [*"considerativa entis"*], as demonstrating especially by the formal cause. Thus Thomas tells us:

. . . [Aristotle] determines in Book 4 that this science considers *ens* inasmuch as it is *ens;* and so it belongs to it to consider the primary substances, and not to natural science: because above mobile substance there are other substances. But every substance either is *ens* through itself, if it is form alone, or else, if it is composed out of matter and form, it is *ens* through its own form; hence, inasmuch as this science undertakes to consider *ens*, it considers most of all the formal cause.[26]

Already at the beginning of book 7, Thomas sees the primary interest of Aristotle as bearing on substance in the sense of subject.[27] Then, in the subject, it is the substantial form which is to be the chief target of investigation.[28] He speaks of it as particular substantial form [*forma particularis*].[29] The studies have the aim of exhibiting it as of a nature to perfect matter. In this, Aristotle is refuting the doctrine of Plato, who dissociated the forms of the things we know from matter. Establishing the view of material substance as a "this in this," form in matter,[30] meant rejecting the doctrine that the universals encountered in our knowledge of things are themselves separate substances. In book 3 Aristotle had called this

24. Thomas, *CM* 4.2 (563), commenting on Aristotle, *Metaph.* 4.2 (1004a2–9).

25. Ultimately one would have to distinguish between the immaterial substances that Thomas includes here within the "genus" of being, and the absolutely first cause, which is not included within the subject of metaphysics.

26. Thomas, *CM* 3.4 (384). This text concerns specifically the causes used by the science in order to demonstrate. It explains that we cannot know the primary substances through formal causality because of our own limitations, though we can have knowledge of final causality and of a sort of "cause of motion" in this part. It completely rules out demonstration by the material cause in metaphysics. Cf. below, chapter 8, ca. n. 6.

27. *CM* 7.2 (1274), concerning Aristotle at 1028b37–29a1.

28. *CM* 7.2 (1296).

29. *CM* 7.2 (1276–1277).

30. *CM* 7.11 (1517), concerning Aristotle at 7.11 (1036b22–32).

the most difficult question facing philosophy. Thomas explained this remark by the fact that two such great philosophers as Plato and Aristotle could fail to agree on its correct solution. We read:

Concerning this problem [Aristotle] speaks thus: . . . *that it is the most difficult of all the problems of this science.* Which is shown from this, that *the most eminent philosophers judged diversely about it.* For the Platonists held that the universals are separate, with the other philosophers holding the contrary.—[And] . . . he says . . . that it is most necessary to consider, because *on it depends the entire knowledge of substances, sensible as well as immaterial.*[31]

Thomas reads these books as working out the doctrine that "a being through essence *has being*" [*ens per essentiam habet esse*],[32] and, more particularly, that "form gives being to matter" [*forma dat esse materiae*].[33] This brings to our attention the importance of the threefold "structure," what we might call "integral parts," of being as being: *ens, essentia, esse.* One text I keep quoting because it seems to me to be at odds with much that my teachers liked to think is in the *Summa contra gentiles,* and runs:

. . . those things which in creatures are divided are unqualifiedly one in God: thus, for example, in the creature essence and being [*esse*] are other; and in some [creatures] that which subsists in its own essence is also other than its essence or nature: for this man is neither his own humanity nor his being [*esse*]; but God is his essence and his being.

And though these in God are one in the truest way, nevertheless in God there is *whatever pertains to the intelligible role* [*ratio*] of the subsisting thing, or of the essence, or of the being [*esse*]; for it belongs to him not to be in another, inasmuch as he is subsisting; to be a what [*esse quid*], inasmuch as he is essence; and being in act [*esse in actu*], by reason of being itself [*ipsius esse*].[34]

We have all encountered people who try to eliminate essence from the highest cause. This, I submit, is fatal for metaphysics.

There is another point raised most explicitly in Thomas's discussion of books 7 and 8 which is of great philosophical importance. It is the question of the use of dialectic as preliminary, and then moving to the more properly philosophical doctrine. Thomas sees this in books 7 and 8. It is a question which doctrines, which arguments in Thomas's own work, he would see as more dialectical.[35]

---

31. *CM* 3.9 (443): my italics.
32. For this doctrine, cf. e.g. Thomas, *De ente et essentia,* c. 1 (Leonine ed., lines 50–52), the explanation of the word "essence":

Sed essentia dicitur secundum quod per eam et in ea ens habet esse.

33. For this doctrine, cf. e.g. Thomas, *De ente et essentia,* c. 4 (Leonine ed., line 46).
34. *SCG* 4.11 (ed. Pera, 3472–3473).
35. On dialectical argument in Thomas's metaphysical presentations, cf. Armand Maurer, C.S.B., "Dialectic in the *De ente et essentia* of St. Thomas Aquinas," in *Roma, magistra*

The crucial achievement of books 7 and 8 is the doctrine of a mode of substantial form whose immediate raison d'être is to be the perfection of a matter. This is a definitely different picture than the conception of sensible phenomena such as fire, as given in the *Timaeus* of Plato.[36] Aristotle has formulated a conception of sensible phenomena as substances, as beings.

AN APPROACH TO PART II: SEPARATE SUBSTANCE

What we wish to pursue here is the move to separate substance. My reason for doing so is that it seems to me clearest that we have a hierarchy of being as being when we have established a hierarchy of substance as substance. We can then consider reasoning to a cause of being as being, substance as substance.

In hierarchies of substance, Thomas regularly located the celestial bodies between generable and corruptible substance and immaterial substance; they were considered incorruptible.[37] Given that there is now no empirical object to which his theory of the celestial bodies could be applied, the importance of our knowledge of our own soul as an immaterial substance, possessed by nature of incorruptibility, is obvious. An incorruptible substance is an absolutely necessary being.[38] Establishing the existence of such a being provides our access to the other general mode of the nature of being, since that nature is properly divided into the contingent and the necessary.[39]

---

mundi. Itineraria culturae medievalis, Mélanges offerts au Père L. E. Boyle à l'occasion de son 75ᵉ anniversaire, ed. J. Hamesse, Louvain-la-Neuve, 1998: Fédération Internationale des Instituts d'Etudes Médiévales, pp. 573–583. Cf. also chapter 8, below.

36. In the *Timaeus,* 49d, the phenomenal element, e.g. fire, is not a "this," but a mere "such"; moreover, it is ontologically inferior to the receptacle, which is a "this" (49e); the receptacle has the role of mother: the phenomenal element is a mere offspring (50d).

37. Cf. *ST* 1.9.2; 1.66.2; 1.115.3; *SCG* 2.30 (ed. Pera, 1073 (a)); *DP* 5.8; etc.

38. Cf. *DP* 5.3.*ad* 12:

It is to be said that though, admittedly, incorruptible creatures depend on the will of God, who is able both to bestow being on them and not to do so, nevertheless they obtain from the divine will *absolute necessity of being* [*absolutam necessitatem essendi*], inasmuch as they are caused in such a nature in which there is no possibility relative to not being: for all created things *are,* precisely, in the *way* that God willed them to *be* [*talia enim sunt cuncta creata, qualia deus esse ea voluit*], as Hilary says in the book *On Synods.*

Cf. also *ST* 1.44.1.*ad* 2.

39. Cf. *SCG* 3.72 (2481):

It pertains to divine providence that *the grades of being which are possible be fulfilled,* as is clear from what has been said [in the preceding chapter on goodness]. But *being is divided by the contingent and the necessary, and it is a proper division of being* [*Ens autem dividitur per contingens et necessarium: et est per se divisio entis*]. If therefore divine providence excluded all contingency, not all the grades of beings would be preserved.

And cf. my paper, "Thomas Aquinas and Being as a Nature," *Acta Philosophica* 12 (2003), pp. 123–135.

What I wish to underline here is our dependence on the hylomorphic ontology developed in *Metaph.* 7–9. Up to now I have mentioned only 7 and 8, since it is there that the focus is directly on substance. Concerning book 9, on being as divided by act and potency, I will only note here that Thomas presents these considerations as wider, more all-embracing, than consideration merely of being as divided by the categories. This latter consideration, as such, he sees as bearing only on perfect being, whereas being as divided by act and potency includes even imperfect being.[40] When I speak of the "hylomorphic ontology," I mean the doctrine which presents the primary matter and the substantial form as potency and act in the category of substance, with form as principle of being.

I might note that, in focusing on this doctrine of being, I do not wish to have it thought something easily accessible. Aristotle on one occasion says that *both matter and form are difficult to know*, pertaining to the highest study, being difficult to view in isolation from each other. They are "at the very apex of speculative thought" [Philip Wicksteed tr.], *"altissimam habent speculationem"* in the translation commented upon by Thomas.[41] And in *De generatione et corruptione* Aristotle shows how difficult it is to conceive of unqualified coming to be, precisely because of the difficulty of conceiving of primary matter, that which is potentially a substantial actuality.[42] Only when it is realized that such matter never does and indeed cannot exist separately from form is there a satisfactory solution to what Aristotle describes as the "wondrous difficulty." Primary matter can exist only as part of the composite of form and matter.[43] Aristotle is thus very far from treating his primary items of analysis as ones which are familiar to all.[44] As regards his predecessors, one of his main points was their fail-

40. Cf. *CM* 5.9 (889).

41. Aristotle, *Phys.* 4.2 (209b18–21): ". . . *tén akrotatén ekei théan* . . ."; cf. Thomas, *CP* 4.3 (428 [7]); Wicksteed's translation is in the Loeb Classical Library edition, Cambridge, Mass., 1929: Harvard University Press.

42. Aristotle says:

. . . it is extraordinarily difficult [*thaumasten aporian*] to see how there can be "unqualified coming-to-be" (whether we suppose it to occur out of what potentially "is" [*ek dunamei ontos*], or in some other way), and we must recall this problem for further examination. [(317b18–20), Oxford tr.: Harold H. Joachim]

Thomas's paraphrase, *In De gen.* 1.6 (49 [8]), runs:

. . . because even after the preceding determination there still looms a *wondrous difficulty* [*mirabilis dubitatio*], one must once more attempt [to determine] how unqualified coming to be occurs [*sit*], whether out of being in potency or how it comes about in any other way.

43. Aristotle, *De gen. et corr.* 1.3 (317a32–318a27); cf. Thomas, *In De gen.* 1.6–7.

44. At the beginning of *De anima* [1.1 (402a1–12)] Aristotle speaks of the intrinsic worth of knowledge of the soul, but also of its great difficulty; the soul-body composition is, of course, that of the substantial form and primary matter of living things: cf. *De anima* 2.1 (412a6–b9).

ure to conceive of the causes properly, among which, of course, are the matter and the form.[45]

Along with other generable and corruptible substances, the human being is grasped as a composite of form and matter.[46] As a living substance, its substantial form is called a "soul," where the first, general definition of soul is "first grade of actuality in a body potentially having life," i.e. an organized body. "First grade of actuality" is form. "Body" is on the side of matter.[47] We recall how souls are graded by the operations of which they are principles. The question raised by Aristotle and answered by St. Thomas is whether there is any operation stemming from soul which is properly the operation of the soul alone, or are all the operations operations of the composite of soul and body.[48] Thomas's answer is that intellection cannot be an operation of the body. It must be an operation of the soul alone. This generates a conception of the mode of being of the intellective soul. It cannot be conceived, as other souls must be conceived, viz. as inhering rather than subsisting. It must be conceived as *subsisting*.[49]

This means that if it is to cease to be, it cannot be conceived as ceasing to be merely through association with something else. It must cease to be on its own account. That is, it cannot cease to be merely because the composite of soul and body, the human being, ceases to be. If it cease to be, it must cease to be as regards its own intrinsic resources.[50]

It is then seen that, as pure form[51] subsisting, the intellective soul *cannot* cease to be. Form is the proper principle of being. Form and being are indissoluble.[52] The intellective soul is a necessary being, a necessary substance.

I wished to recall rapidly this line of thinking before considering its foundations. The association of subsistent being with being a source of operation is certainly strongly affirmed by Aristotle. He himself introduces it in the *De anima* in relation to the question of a soul's separability from the composite.[53] It relates to his locating of actions, as such, in things taken in their singularity.[54] It relates, moreover, to his explana-

45. Aristotle, *Metaph.* 1.7 (988a34–b1); 1.8 (988b28–29); 1.10 (993a11–16).
46. Thomas, *ST* 1.75.4.
47. Aristotle, *De anima* 2.1 (412a3–b9); Thomas, *In De anima* 2.1 *(in toto).*
48. For the question, cf. Aristotle, *De anima* 1.1 (403a3–10).
49. Cf. Thomas, *In De anima* (Leonine ed.) 1.2 (lines 46–81); also, *ST* 1.75.2.
50. *ST* 1.75.6 (ed. Ottawa, 445a33–52).
51. Thomas makes the distinct point that the subsisting, incorporeal human soul is pure form at *ST* 1.75.5.
52. *ST* 1.75.6 (ed. Ottawa, 445a52–b9); cf. also 1.50.5.
53. Aristotle, *De anima* 1.1 (403a10–12).
54. Aristotle, *Metaph.* 1.1 (981a15–20).

tion of the use of a vocabulary stemming from discussions of motion and change in order to talk about actual existence.[55] That which has an action of its own has being as its own. And *having* being, *possessing* being as one's *own*, is what is meant by "subsisting."[56]

What about the other premises? Form as the principle of being is no surprise.[57] What we have to consider is the doctrine that intellection cannot be the operation of the composite of form and matter. Here we are led back to Aristotle's conception of cognition as form without matter, embraced by Thomas.[58] The text to which I would first refer is *ST* 1.14.1: does God possess knowledge? Thomas presents cognition as related to perfection, to that fullness of being which he calls "immateriality." We read:

> . . . things that know are distinguished from things that do not know in [precisely] this [respect], that things that do not know have nothing but their own form alone, whereas the thing that knows is of such a nature as to have the form also of another thing: for the specific likeness [*species*] of the thing known is in the knower. Hence, it is obvious that the nature of the non-knowing thing is confined and limited; whereas the nature of knowers has greater fullness and extension [*amplitudinem et extensionem*]. For this reason the Philosopher [Aristotle] says, in *De anima* 3 [431b21], that "the soul is in a way all things."
>
> Now, the *confinedness* of form stems from *matter*; and so we said earlier [1.7.1][59] that forms, according as they are more immaterial, attain more to a measure of infinity.

55. Aristotle, *Metaph.* 9.3 (1047a30–b2).
56. Thomas, *ST* 1.45.4; 1.90.2.
57. Thomas, *ST* 1.42.1.*ad* 1; 1.1–2.85.6. Cf. *CM* 7.17 (1678–1680).
58. Cf. e.g. *In De anima* 2.24 (Leonine ed., lines 13–59), concerning Aristotle, 424a17.
59. Because of the importance of this text, one entirely expressed in terms of the hylomorphic ontology, I include the body of the article in its entirety:

> . . . it is to be considered that something is called *"infinitum"* from the fact that it is *not finitum* ["finished"]. Now, matter is finished in a way by form, and also form is finished [in a way] by matter: matter by form, inasmuch as matter, before it receives form, is in potency to many forms; but when it receives one, it is rendered determinate [*terminatur*] by it; but form is finished by matter, inasmuch as the form, considered in itself, is common to many; but by the fact that it is received in matter, it is rendered determinately the form of *this* thing.
>
> Now, matter is perfected by the form by which it is finished; and so the "infinite," according as it is attributed to matter, has the character of the imperfect: for it is, so to speak, matter not having form.
>
> Form, however, is not perfected by matter, but rather its fullness is constricted by it: hence, the "infinite," inasmuch as it stands on the side of form not determined by matter, has the character of the perfect.
>
> Now, this precise item, *being* [*esse*], is that which is most *formal* of all, as is clear from earlier [discussions] [cf. 1.4.1.*ad* 3].
>
> Therefore, since the divine *esse* is *esse* not received in anything, but he himself is his own subsisting *esse*, as was shown earlier, it is evident that God himself is infinite and perfect.

Hence, it is clear that the *immateriality* of a thing is the factor which renders it cognitive; and according to the *grade* of its immateriality is the grade of its knowing.

Thus, in *De anima* 2 [424a32–b3], it is said that plants do not know, because of their materiality. Sense is cognitive, because it is receptive of forms [*specierum*] without matter;[60] and intellect is still more cognitive, because it is more separated from matter and "unmixed," as is said in *De anima* 3 [429a18].

Hence, since God is at the summit of immateriality, as is clear from things previously said [1.7.1], it follows that he is at the summit of knowing.[61]

What I wish to stress is the reliance on the hylomorphic ontology for the conception of knowledge and the nature of the knower as such. One begins with the non-knower as a matter-form composite, in which form is completely limited by the matter. The contrast between sense and intellect provides grounds for conceiving of greater or lesser freedom from the confining role of matter. Immateriality, freedom from matter, is the root of the ability to know.[62]

In presenting the knowledge proper to the intellective soul, Thomas insists that it involves reception of forms absolutely. We have reached a certain plateau in the immaterial mode of reception of form. The argument is presented in *ST* 1.75.5. It runs:

It is evident that everything which is *received in* something is received in it in function of the *mode* [or measure] *of the receiver.*

But it is thus that each thing is known, viz. according as its *form* is *in* the one who knows.

But the intellective soul knows a thing in its nature *absolutely*, for example the stone inasmuch as it is a stone, absolutely.

Therefore, the *form* of the stone, *absolutely*, according to its *proper formal* character, is in the intellective soul.

Therefore, the intellective soul *is* an *absolute* [or pure] *form*, not a thing composed of matter and form.

---

60. Animals, of course, are the beings which have sense knowledge; thus, Aristotle says in *Parts of Animals* 1.3 (643a25):

. . . no part of an animal is purely material or purely immaterial.

Aristotelian animals are very different from Cartesian animals.

61. *ST* 1.14.1.

62. Cf. *ST* 1.84.2 (513b37–514a3):

. . . it is necessary that material things known exist in the knowing being, not materially but immaterially. And the reason for this is that the act of knowing extends to those things which are outside the knowing being: for we know even those things which are outside us. Now, through *matter* the form of the thing is *confined* to something one. Hence, it is evident that the nature of knowing stands in opposition to the nature of materiality [. . . *ratio cognitionis ex opposito se habet ad rationem materialitatis* . . .].

For if the intellective soul were composed of matter and form, the forms of things would be received in it *as individual;* and thus it would know only *the singular,* just as occurs in the sensitive powers, which receive the forms of things in a corporeal organ: *for matter is the principle of individuation of forms.*

Therefore, the conclusion is that the intellective soul, and every intellectual substance knowing forms absolutely, is without the composition of form and matter.

As we see, the judgment about the soul itself is based on the sort of *reception* which the soul provides for the form of the thing known. Outside the soul, in its own proper being, the form is individuated by matter; and even when the senses know the thing, the form is received in the knower in a material organ, so that the knowledge is merely of the thing as individuated by the matter. In the intellect, on the other hand, the form is isolated from matter, i.e. is considered "all by itself" or "absolutely." This mode of reception of the form tells us about the soul's own nature, a nature which makes this mode of receiving forms possible. The soul itself cannot contain matter, for if it did, it would *individuate* the form in receiving it.[63] The soul itself must be pure form.[64]

Thus, we have arrived at the existence of *pure form subsisting.*

Thomas actually moves more slowly and gradually than this in the *ST* 1.75, first arguing for the incorporeal subsistence of the human intellective soul,[65] and then going on to the argument for its being pure form. My interest here is to stress the role of the hylomorphic ontology for the conception of knowledge and thus for the conception of the soul as source of such an operation.

63. Here I would say that the argument presupposes that we are speaking of our knowledge of material things, whose forms are properly the perfections of matter.

64. Cf. the following argument against Ibn Gebirol's universal hylomorphism, presented in *De substantiis separatis,* c. 7:

> Since receiving is proper to matter as such, if there is the same matter for spiritual and corporeal substances, then it is necessary that there be the same mode of reception in both. But the matter of corporeal things receives the form *particularly,* that is, not in function of the universal scope of the form [*non secundum communem rationem formae*]. Nor does corporeal matter have this [way of receiving] inasmuch as it is lying under dimensions or under corporeal form, because corporeal matter receives *individually* even the very corporeal form itself. Hence it becomes clear that this belongs to such matter stemming from [its] very nature as matter, which, because it is lowest, receives form in the weakest way: for receiving comes about in accordance with the capacity [*modum*] of the recipient. And in function of this it falls short of the complete reception of form, which is as to its own totality, receiving it [merely] particularly. But it is evident that all intellectual substance receives understood form in function of its totality; otherwise, it would not be able to understand it in its totality: for it is thus that the intellect understands a thing, viz. according as [the thing's] form exists in it. It remains, therefore, that matter, if there is any in spiritual substances, is not the same as the matter of corporeal things, but much higher and more sublime, as receiving form as regards its universal scope [*secundum eius totalitatem,* in function of the form's totality].

65. Cf. *ST* 1.75.2.

Once the human intellective soul is presented as pure form subsisting, it is then argued that it is incorruptible. As we have recalled, as subsisting, its ceasing to be must occur because of what belongs to it just in itself, not in function of its association with a body. This is a move in the argument for incorruptibility which corresponds to the moment in Plato's *Phaedo* when Simmias worries that the soul may be a harmony, and thus disappear with the destruction of the body in which it is. As a subsisting thing, not a mere harmony, its ceasing to be must be strictly its own. Socrates thus allows the comparison of the subsisting soul, at this stage of the discussion, to the tailor who makes successive coats (bodies) for himself. The next problem is thus that the tailor too is a thing which can wear out, and some day will make his last coat. The task then becomes: showing that the soul is simply not, in its own being, the sort of thing subject to wearing out (Socrates' argument to answer Cebes).[66]

Thomas, having the advantage of the Aristotelian hylomorphic ontology, can argue that the subsisting soul, as form without matter, cannot cease to be. St. Thomas's argument for the soul's immortality or incorruptibility is entirely dependent on the nature of *form* and form's relation to *the act of being*. We read:

... the human soul cannot be corrupted, unless it be itself directly corrupted. And this is altogether impossible, not only for it, but for any subsisting thing which is form alone [or "pure form"].

(1) For it is evident that that which belongs to something just by virtue of itself is inseparable from it.

(2) But *being* [*esse*] belongs to form, which is act, just by virtue of [form] itself: thus, matter just on this account acquires *being actually*, that it acquires *form;* while just by this does corruption occur [in matter], that *form* is separated from it.

(3) Hence, it is impossible that a subsisting form cease to be.[67]

Notice that this argument is based on the *inseparability* of *form* and *act of being* [*esse*]. And this relationship is grasped through our experience of the coming to be and ceasing to be of sensible, material things. This is to say that form is the *principle* of being. The *intrinsic* character of form is such that it brings *existence* with it wherever it goes.

Once this is seen, the rest of the argument is not difficult. The human intellective soul is not a composite of matter and form. It is a pure form, subsisting with its own act of being. Hence, it simply *does not have the ontological structure of what can cease to be*. There is no matter in it which might be separated from a form. Its ontological structure is that of a necessary being.

66. Cf. Plato, *Phaedo* 91c–107a; and see below, chapter 10 in its entirety.
67. *ST* 1.75.6 (445a50–b9). Cf. *ST* 1.50.5.

Suppose we have demonstrated the incorruptibility of the human soul. What then? I would say that we have a most suitable starting point for the Fourth Way, among Thomas's famous five ways of demonstrating the existence of a God. I say a starting point, though I am conscious of the fact that the proper starting points of this way might be considered (at least) threefold:

We find in things some more and something less good, true, noble, and the like.[68] We are asked to envisage hierarchy in the order of goodness, in the order of truth, and in the order of nobility. It is only through the link between being and truth that we are made to envisage what we are speaking of from the viewpoint most precisely of *being*. Yet, as I have elsewhere argued,[69] this presentation has its background in *Metaph.* 9.9–10, wherein Aristotle presents act as more noble than, better than, more intelligible than, truer than, potency. Thus, as it seems to me, the ultimate vision on which it rests is the vision of being itself, i.e. substance, as found according to act and potency, or more and less. And as Thomas tells us:

Act has *more* of the nature of being than potency has.[70]

That is, the division of being in function of act and potency is a division according to the more and the less. This seems most evidently[71] to be found in the division of substance into the necessary and the contingent (or corruptible).

Thus, we are led to the conclusion that there exists a maximal in the

---

68. *ST* 1.2.3.

69. Cf. "Number and Order of St. Thomas's Five Ways," *Downside Review* 92 (1974), pp. 1–18.

70. Cf. *De substantiis separatis*, c. 7:

Manifestum est autem quod cum ens per potentiam et actum dividatur, quod actus est potentia perfectior, et *magis habet de ratione essendi:* non enim simpliciter esse dicimus quod est in potentia, sed solum quod est actu. [It is evident that while *ens* is divided by potency and act, act is more perfect than potency, and has *more* of *the nature of being:* for we do not say "is," unqualifiedly, of that which is in potency, but only of that which is in act.]

71. Cf. *CM* 9.9, where Thomas interprets Aristotle's procedure in contrasting act and potency as found in incorruptible and corruptible substance, respectively, as "more evident"; Aristotle is arguing that act is prior to potency as to perfection:

Firstly, [Aristotle] shows the point, and does so using this argument: everlasting things are related to corruptible things as act to potency. [This is so] because everlasting things, precisely as such, are not in potency, whereas corruptible things, precisely as such, are in potency. But everlasting things are prior to corruptible things from the viewpoint of substance and perfection: this is evident. Therefore, act is prior to potency as to substance and perfection. [Aristotle] says that by this argument the point is shown "more properly" because act and potency are not taken in one same thing, but rather in diverse things. This makes the proof more evident.

order of being, something which is the cause of being for all beings. The vision of being according to more and less is properly the vision of being as the effect of creative causality. It is subsisting things as such which are the proper termini of the act of creation.[72]

THE COMPLETE PICTURE

With the complete picture of the nature of being, we are in a position to move to the existence and causality of the cause of the nature of being, which Thomas in the Fourth Way calls the "maximal being" [*maxime ens*]. I am particularly interested in underlining the problems for which Thomas uses this complete vision as a solution. Their importance implies the importance of the overall view of metaphysics as the study of being *as a nature*.

We should note first of all how universal providence is shown to be compatible with the existence of the contingent. In Thomas Aquinas's *Commentary on Aristotle's Metaphysics*, one finds a remarkable treatment of the implications of divine providence. It occurs in book 6, where Aristotle has just set aside from his theological philosophy[73] the study of being by coincidence [*to on . . . to kata sumbebékos*].[74] Does not this position of Aristotle's, in that it acknowledges the existence of mere haphazard, destroy the doctrine of providence? Does not "providence" suggest that everything happens of necessity? After all, divine providence cannot fail.

Thomas solves as follows:

[1219]But one must know that on the same cause depends the effect and all those [items] which are essential accidents [*per se accidentia;* "properties"] of that effect. For example, just as man is [caused] by nature, so also are all his essential accidents, such as capability of laughter, and susceptibility to mental discipline. But if some cause does not make man, unqualifiedly, but [makes] man *such*, it will not belong to it to constitute those things which are the essential accidents of man, but merely to take advantage of them. For example, the ruler [*politicus*] makes a man a good citizen [*civilem*]; still, he does not make him to be susceptible to discipline of the mind; rather, he makes use of that property of [man] in order to make of him a good citizen.

[1220]But, as has been said, *being inasmuch as it is being* [*ens inquantum ens est*] *has as cause God himself; hence, just as to the divine providence being itself* [*ipsum ens*] *is submitted, so also are all the accidents of being as being, among which are the necessary and*

---

72. Cf. *ST* 1.45.4. Concerning the fourth way and its relation to the discovery of the createdness of reality, cf. my paper, "St. Thomas, the Fourth Way, and Creation," *The Thomist* 59 (1995), pp. 371–378.

73. Cf. Aristotle, *Metaph.* 6.1 (1026a19).

74. Ibid. 6.2 (in its entirety).

the contingent. Therefore, to divine providence it pertains, not merely to make this being, but that it give to it contingence or necessity . . .[75]

And Thomas goes on to make the point that no other cause gives to its effects the modes of necessity and contingency; this is proper to the cause of being as being.

In his *Commentary on Aristotle's Perihermeneias,* he again raises the question of providence and necessity. Considering the difference of the divine will from human wills, he says:

. . . the divine will is to be understood as standing outside the order of beings [*ut extra ordinem entium existens*], as a cause pouring forth being in its entirety [*totum ens*] and all its differences. *Now, the possible and the necessary are differences of being* [*differentie entis*], and so it is from the divine will itself that necessity and contingency in things have their origin, and the distinction of both in virtue of the proximate causes: [thus] for the effects that he willed to be necessary he established necessary causes, and for the effects that he willed to be contingently he ordered causes acting contingently, i.e. able to fail; and according to the condition of these causes, the effects are called "necessary" or "contingent," even though all depend on the divine will as on *a first cause which transcends the order of necessity and contingency.* But this cannot be said of the human will, nor of any other cause, because every other cause already falls under the order of necessity or contingency, and so it is necessary that either the cause itself can fail, or that its effect is not contingent but necessary. But the divine will cannot fail, and nevertheless not all its effects are necessary, but some are contingent . . .[76]

Clearly, everything depends on considering being as a nature with its proper differences or proper accidents. The general point also applies to the existence of human free choice, which is a mode of contingent causation.[77]

The cause of the nature of being is also, and by the same token, cause of the nature of goodness: "the good" and "that which is" are convertible.[78] A most important application of the doctrine we are following concerns the problem of the existence of the *bad* in a created universe produced by an omnipotent cause who is the essence of goodness. Thus far I have noted only the role of God as *efficient* cause in the production of things, but of course the ultimate causal explanation is that in function of final causality, the causality proper to goodness as such. God produces things in view of his own goodness, that it be communicated to creatures

75. *CM* 6.3 (1218–1220).
76. Thomas, *Expositio libri Peryermenias* 1.14 (Leonine ed., t. 1*1, Rome/Paris, 1989: Commissio Leonina/Vrin, lines 438–461).
77. Cf. *SCG* 3.72 (2481), on providence and contingency in general; and *SCG* 3.73 (2488): the application to human choice.
78. Cf. *ST* 1.5.1–3; 1–2.18.1.

and represented through them.[79] It is the universe as apt to represent the divine goodness which is appealed to in explaining the existence of the bad. This aptitude requires a certain perfection of the universe. We read:

> . . . the perfection of the universe requires that there be inequality in things, *in order that all the grades of goodness be brought to completion.* Now, one grade of goodness is that something be good in such a way that it never can fail. But another grade of goodness is that something be good in such a way that it can fail. *These grades are also to be found in being itself* [*in ipso esse*]*:* for some things are, which cannot lose their being, such as incorporeal [beings]; but some are, which can lose being, such as corporeal [beings]. Therefore, just as *the perfection of the universe requires that there be not only incorruptible beings, but also corruptible beings,* so also the perfection of the universe requires that there be some which can fail as to goodness, and thus it follows that they do sometimes fail. But the note of the bad consists in this, i.e. that something fail as to goodness [*deficiat a bono*]. Hence, it is evident that the bad is to be found in things, just as corruption [is]; for corruption itself is an instance of the bad.[80]

It is the *nature* of being and goodness that requires that there be these grades in the universe.[81]

Before finishing, I would like to add one point concerning God as the

79. *ST* 1.47.1 (300b6–26); cf. also 1.44.4.*ad* 1.

80. *ST* 1.48.2 (305a34–b4). Notice that Thomas affirms the proposition that it belongs to the best agent to produce his total effect as something best [*optimum*]. Thus, God established the entire universe as best, in accordance with the mode of created being: 1.47.2.*ad* 1. And the bad does not pertain to the perfection of the universe, nor is it included within the order of the universe, save through association [*per accidens*], by reason of the associated good: 1.48.1.*ad* 5.

81. It should not be thought that this discussion is only about the so-called "physical" as contrasted with "moral" evil. Thus, in the *ad* 3, we get a rapid but complete picture. The objector held that God, as making what is best, would admit no evil to his effects. The reply is:

> . . . God and nature and any agent whatsoever makes what is better in the whole, but not what is better in each part, save as ordered to the whole, as has been said [1.47.2.*ad* 1]. But the whole which is the universe of creatures is better and more perfect if in it there are some things which can fail as to goodness, and which indeed do sometimes fail, given that God does not impede this. For [one reason, he does not impede since] "it belongs to providence, not to destroy but to preserve," as Dionysius says, in *On the Divine Names,* ch. 4: now, the very nature of things has this [feature], that those which can fail sometimes do fail. For [another reason], since as Augustine says in *Enchiridion,* "God is so powerful, that he can bring out good from the bad." Hence, many good things would be done away with if God did not permit any bad to be. For there would not be generated any fire if air did not suffer corruption; nor would the life of the lion be maintained if the deer were not killed; *nor would one praise vindicating justice and long-suffering patience if there were no injustice.* [my italics]

One sees the extent to which the doctrine of God as cause of being and its proper modes plays a role here, and how certain modes of the good can only exist as a response to the bad.

cause of being as being. The program, I note, already includes discussions of analogy and of whether God is included in the subject of metaphysics. Accordingly, I will say only this. We have seen a conception of the first cause as transcending all else, thus transcending being, in a remarkable way. The divine will is pouring forth being in its entirety [*totum ens*], and transcending the order of necessity and contingency. Yet the Fourth Way arrives at that cause as "maximally a being" [*maxime ens*]. This will certainly call for a discussion of analogy. I call attention to a fine passage in Thomas's *Commentary on the Divine Names of the pseudo-Dionysius:* The nature of the divine transcendence is variously expressed by Thomas in various places, but here is a passage which, I would say, illustrates the point I wish to make:

. . . he [Dionysius] shows how being [*esse*] stands with respect to God; and he says that being itself, taken as a universal [or formally: *ipsum esse commune*], is from the first *being* [*ex primo Ente*], which is God; and from this it follows that being, as a universal [*esse commune*], stands otherwise with respect to God than [to] other existents [*alia existentia*], in three ways. Firstly, . . . other existents depend on universal being [*ab esse communi*], but not God: rather, universal being depends on God . . . Secondly, . . . all existents are contained under being, as a universal, but not God: rather, universal being is contained under his power, for the divine power reaches farther [*plus extenditur*] than created reality [*ipsum esse creatum*] . . . Thirdly, . . . all other existents participate in being, but not God: rather, created being itself [*ipsum esse creatum*] is a certain participation vis-à-vis God and a likeness of him . . . God does not "have being," as though he were a participant in being . . .[82]

What I believe one must take seriously here is how much the universality of being, among other universals, is being featured, as a means of approaching the divine transcendence. In fact, as soon as the expression "created being" is introduced, we spontaneously tend to set up a *wider* universal which would "contain under it" both creator and creatures.[83] Against this, the whole point of the above text is that creation is the sort of origin of things that, to be properly understood, requires a therapy against just that sort of grossly deceptive convenience.

82. Thomas, *In librum beati Dionysii De divinis nominibus expositio,* ed. C. Pera, O.P., Rome/Turin, 1950: Marietti, 5.2 (660).

83. Thus, fighting such a move, in *ST* 1.13.5 Thomas explains the analogy which applies to names (e.g. "good") said of creatures as compared to names (e.g. "good") said of God; he rules out a model in which two items are compared to a third ("healthy" said of the medicine and of the urine, both relative to the health of the animal), and uses a *two*-member model ("healthy," said of the animal and of the medicine).

Chapter 3

ST. THOMAS AND THE SEED OF METAPHYSICS

An interpreter of St. Thomas's doctrines concerning knowledge, metaphysics, and being itself can hardly avoid discussing the knowledge of *ens*, which St. Thomas often declares to be the principle of all intellectual knowledge.[1] However, among the interpreters prominent in the last forty years, one can certainly find a considerable variety of opinion in this matter. In a paper published in English translation in 1966, Cornelio Fabro, while laudably insistent on the importance of the issue of the primacy of *ens*, proposes some views which seem to me particularly foreign to the thought of St. Thomas.[2] Speaking of "*how* the mind grasps such a notion [i.e. *ens*]" (423), he says:

In a famous youthful text, when he still thought of the origin of the first principles in a way slightly influenced by Augustinian illuminationism, he attributes

1. Cf. *Summa theologiae* 1–2.94.2 (Ottawa ed., 1225b8–10). Most subsequent references to the *Summa theologiae* (henceforth "*ST*") will be made in the body of the article, with, where helpful, the pagination of the Ottawa edition. I have elsewhere argued that the doctrine of the concept (and so also of *words*) pertains properly to *reflexive* cognition; cf. "St. Thomas, Ideas, and Immediate Knowledge," *Dialogue* 18 (1979), pp. 392–404; my interest here is in the original *apprehension* of things which ultimately gives rise to the concept of *ens*, and to the word "*ens*": cf. *ST* 1.16.4.*ad* 2:

> Intellectus . . . per prius apprehendit ipsum ens . . . [the intellect firstly apprehends the precise item: that which is . . .]

Notice that it is only subsequently, according to St. Thomas in this text and elsewhere, that the intellect apprehends ". . . *se intelligere ens* . . . [itself intellectually apprehending that which is]," i.e. reflects. I have left the word "*ens*" in Latin; the best English equivalents would be "a being" (taken concretely) or "that which is." I will use the Latin term "*ens*" throughout the paper, particularly because it is very important to distinguish it from *esse*, i.e. "being," as signifying in a way similar to a word like "running" (this is also called the "*actus essendi*," the act of being).

2. Fabro, C., "The Transcendentality of *Ens-Esse* and the Ground of Metaphysics," *International Philosophical Quarterly* 6 (1966), pp. 389–427, especially pp. 423–427. Further reference to this article will be made in the body of the paper, merely citing the page number.

the origin of the *notio entis* to the abstractive process of the agent intellect: "There pre-exist in us certain seeds of the sciences, namely the first conceptions of the intellect, *which immediately by the light of the agent intellect are known through species abstracted from sensible things, whether they be the complex ones such as the axioms, or the incomplex ones, such as the notions: ens, unum, and other such,* which the intellect immediately apprehends. From these universal principles all principles follow, as from certain seminal notions." (423–424)[3]

Fabro goes on to object that the notion cannot be the fruit of abstraction "in the ordinary sense" (424). The reason he gives is that *ens* includes in itself both the essence and the *actus essendi,* while "ordinary" abstraction abstracts only the essence. Thus he says:

Insofar as the *notio entis* properly includes *esse* as its distinguishing characteristic, it rivets and connects consciousness of necessity to reality in act, from which, for this reason, the mind cannot abstract. (425)

This position of Fabro's provides the occasion for the following observations.

A. THE SEEDS OF WISDOM

Can we set aside the cited passage from the *De veritate,* in which the agent intellect's abstraction from sensible things is made the origin of the knowledge of *ens,* as a view later explicitly rejected by St. Thomas, or even as something about which he ceased to speak? On the contrary, we find the very same doctrine carefully worked into *ST* 1–2. Thus, speaking of the fact that the intellectual *habitus* (something like a "knack") called "the understanding of principles" [*intellectus principiorum*] is partly but not entirely naturally pre-existent and inborn, St. Thomas says that while by the very nature of the intellectual soul, it belongs to man that immediately, once it is known what a whole is and what a part is, he knows that every whole is greater than its part, still what a whole is and what a part is he cannot know except through intelligible *species* received from the phantasms (*ST* 1–2.51.1: 978b24–31). Obviously, if St. Thomas meant to exclude *ens* from the number of objects known through intelligible *species* received from the phantasms he would have to say so, since such a doctrine would at least strongly suggest there was a completely inborn *habitus* after all.

Next, we should note the doctrine that the virtues, including the intellectual virtues (understanding, the sciences, and wisdom), are caused

3. Fabro gave the Latin of St. Thomas; the translation is my own, but the italics are Fabro's. The text is *De veritate* 11.1 (Leonine ed., lines 266–275).

in us by the acts we perform. It is explained that where an agent has in itself both active and passive principles, it can act on itself, and in so doing, render the passive principle more appropriately disposed to the influence of the active. The active principle, as such, is *not perfectible* by the agent's operation. In his examples of the development of intellectual virtues in these texts, St. Thomas constantly uses as active principle a *per se nota* proposition. And he says that all this supposes the greater nobility of the active principle: the understanding of principles is a more noble principle than the science of conclusions (*ST* 1–2.51.2: 979b41–51 and ibid. *ad* 2). Later on, when it is objected that the acts we perform cannot cause the virtues, because the acts performed prior to the presence in us of the virtues are less perfect than the virtue, St. Thomas says that the seeds [*semina*] naturally present in us prior to the existence of the virtues are more noble than the virtues themselves which are acquired through their power: thus, he repeats by way of example, the understanding of principles is more noble than the science of conclusions (*ST* 1–2.63.2. *ad* 3).

But the ultimate step in this doctrine is seen when the virtue of wisdom is presented as supreme among intellectual virtues. The objection is raised that the knowledge of principles is more noble than the knowledge of conclusions. Thus, since wisdom concludes from the indemonstrable principles, which pertain to the virtue of understanding [*intellectus*], clearly understanding is a more noble virtue than wisdom. St. Thomas replies that the truth and knowledge of the indemonstrable principles depend on the notions of the terms: when one knows what a whole is and what a part is, immediately one knows that every whole is greater than its part. Furthermore, to know the notions *ens, non ens,* whole, part, and the others that follow upon *ens,* out of which as out of terms the indemonstrable principles are constituted, *pertains to wisdom.* The reason is that wisdom considers as its object the highest cause, God, and *ens commune* is the proper effect of the highest cause. That is why wisdom not only uses the indemonstrable principles, concluding from them, but even judges concerning them, and disputes against those who deny them. And he concludes that wisdom is a greater virtue than understanding (*ST* 1–2.66.5.*ad* 4). Now, for this reply to be effective, it must mean that *ens,* precisely as known by priority to the indemonstrable principles, already has a *nobility* which is prior to the understanding of first principles [*intellectus*], i.e. already has in itself the status of *seed of wisdom,* is indeed the most perfect of all our intellectual acts considered as to their intrinsic perfection.[4] It is the *ens* whose knowledge is presupposed to the under-

4. Here I am speaking of absolute or intrinsic perfection, not of the perfection which can be obtained by adding notion to notion.

standing of principles which is the "proper effect of the highest cause." That is why it has the role of seed of wisdom, wisdom which eventually is developed into knowledge of the highest cause.

If this perfection, right from the start, of the knowledge of *ens* surprises, one should consider that it is *natural* and is thus the "movement" in the mind of the very "generator" of mind. I am here referring to the extended application St. Thomas makes of the idea that the mover for natural movements is the generator, applying it to the cases of spiritual operation. Thus, the natural movement of the will is an influence of the first cause, God (*ST* 1–2.9.6). So also, at *ST* 2–2.2.3, we read that in every inferior nature there is the movement of the nature superior to it, and that precisely it is the rational creature which has an immediate order to God. The sign of this immediate order is that creature's attaining to something universal: "the rational nature, inasmuch as it knows the universal notions *bonum* and *ens*, has an immediate order to the universal principle of being [*essendi*]." While, in this text, the superior movement primarily meant is the movement of faith, not the movement of natural intellect, nevertheless the grasp of the universal notion, *ens*, is the sign of the immediate relation to God.

Another notable text along these lines is *ST* 1–2.3.6 (732b29–39). There St. Thomas argues that something cannot be perfected by some other inferior thing, except inasmuch as the inferior has in it a participation in something superior. Thus, since the form of the stone or of any sensible thing is inferior to man, the form of the stone cannot perfect the human intellect inasmuch as it (the form of the stone) is a particular form [*talis forma*], but inasmuch as in it there is a participated likeness of something above the human intellect, namely the intelligible light or something like that.[5] Precisely, the form of the stone can have the role of an intelligible *species* only inasmuch as it is subsumed under the intelligible, *ens*, the likeness of the first cause. That this is the correct interpretation of the text is confirmed by the fact that it is in just this way that St. Thomas describes even angelic intellect. When an objector argues that the act of understanding and the act of being are identical in angels, because they both have the same cause, namely the very form or essence of the angel, St. Thomas replies that though the very essence of the angel is the entire principle [*ratio*] of the angel's being, it is not the entire principle of its understanding. The essence of the angel is compared to the understanding of the angel according to the intelligibility [*ratio*] of a more universal object, namely *verum* or *ens*. It is only as so taken that the essence of the angel is principle of understanding. That is, even the an-

5. Notice St. Thomas says "intelligible," not "intellectual," i.e. he is speaking about a perfection on the side of the object as an object.

gel's very own essence is properly principle of intellection only inasmuch as it participates in the likeness of a higher principle, through the *ratio entis* (*ST* 1.54.2.*ad* 2).

But let us not think that this knowledge of *ens* is completely innate (in the case of human intellect). It is the fruit of abstraction. On the side of the knower, as active, all that is innate is the agent intellect. Its initial act of abstraction is not an act of *knowing*, of understanding. Rather, for understanding, one must have the operations of both agent and possible intellect.[6] The abstractive power of the agent intellect is rather to be envisaged as a light to shine upon the imagination.[7] On the side of things known there are the intelligible *species* as representative of sensible and material things, in which things we *find* the likeness of the first principle. The intelligible *species* are reduced as to a first cause to a principle which is intelligible by its very own essence, i.e. to God, but they come forth from that principle through the mediation of the forms of sensible and material things, from which we gather science (*ST* 1.84.4.*ad* 1). The forms of sensible things, precisely as apt to generate science in us, are truly "something *divine* in things."[8]

Having said enough to counteract the suggestion that what Fabro quoted from the *De veritate* was something later abandoned by St. Thomas, let us now consider more closely the abstractive character of our knowledge of *ens*.

B. KNOWLEDGE OF 'ENS' ABSTRACTIVE

Here I wish to touch on two points. First, it seems to me that in recent decades abstraction has been subjected to undeserved abuse. I should like to stress that for St. Thomas it is definitely part of the vision of human perfection or nobility. Secondly, I wish to say something about the type of abstraction which St. Thomas attributes to our knowledge of *ens*.

As to the nobility of abstraction, I would refer primarily to *ST* 1.12.4 *in corp.* and *ad* 3. Speaking of our soul as a knower which has as its connatural object those things whose nature does not have *esse* except in "this individual matter," St. Thomas distinguishes two knowing powers, (1) the

---

6. Cf. *Quaestiones de anima* 4.*ad* 8.
7. Cf. *SCG* 2.78 (paras. 5–7).
8. Cf. *In De caelo* 3.2 (ed. Spiazzi/Leonine Manual, 552):

For though there is some science concerning things subject to generation and corruption, this is so only inasmuch as there is in them something ungenerated and incorruptible, according to participation in those natures which in themselves are ungenerated and incorruptible; for they are known according to their forms: now, form is something divine in things, inasmuch as it is some sort of participation in the first act [*quaedam participatio primi actus*].

sense, to which it is connatural to know things according as they are in individual matter, and (2) the intellect, to which it is connatural to know natures which indeed have *esse* only in individual matter; but to know them not according as they are in individual matter, but according as they are abstracted from it through the consideration of intellect. Thus, through intellect, we can know this mode of things (i.e. those that have *esse* only in individual matter) universally [*in universali*]: and this universal consideration, says St. Thomas, is *beyond* the power of sense [*supra facultatem sensus*]. Clearly, here, where St. Thomas is engaged in a discussion of modes of knowing, precisely with a view to answering the question: can any created intellect by its natural power see the divine essence, he is measuring knowing powers as regards their proximity to a vision of the object: being itself subsisting [*ipsum esse subsistens*]. And it is in this light that one should see his presentation of human intellect as having a capacity which surpasses the senses: to grasp even the things which can only have *esse* in individual matter, as abstracted from that matter, and so to grasp them universally, is a mode of knowing closer in nature to the knowing which grasps *ipsum esse subsistens*.

If this insistence on the sense of the argument in the *corpus* of the article seems forced, it will no longer seem so once we have looked at the reply to the third objection. There St. Thomas is arguing that created intellect, human and angelic, unlike sense, can be elevated by grace to the vision of an object beyond its connatural object. He says that a sign of this elevability of intellect, as contrasted with sense, is found in the fact that the sense of sight can in no way consider in abstraction that which it knows in the concrete. It can perceive a nature no other way than as "this." But our intellect can consider in the abstract what it knows in the concrete. Though it knows things having form in matter, nevertheless it resolves the composite into the two, and considers the form itself just by itself. And similarly the angelic intellect, though it is connatural for it to know *esse* as concretized in a particular nature, nevertheless can isolate *esse* itself by the power of its intellect, when it knows that it itself is not identical with its *esse*. And these powers of created intellect, viz. that it is natural for it to apprehend concrete form and concrete *esse* in abstraction, by means of some sort of power of resolution, are precisely the sign that it can be elevated by grace to know separate subsisting substance [*substantia*] and separate subsisting *esse*. Thus, the abstractive power in us is seen by St. Thomas as a proportion to that in things which is most like God.[9]

Does St. Thomas abandon this doctrine of the eminence of abstractive knowing of material things when he comes to speak more particularly

9. Cf. the previous note. Cf. also *ST* 1–2.5.1.*ad* 1.

about human intellection? Not at all. For example, when teaching that the intellect directly knows the universal, and knows the singular in material things only indirectly and by a sort of reflection, he has to answer the objection that whatever an inferior power can do, a superior power can do; thus, since the sense knows the singular, all the more must this be true of the intellect. St. Thomas answers that, yes indeed, what the inferior can do, the superior can do, but in a *higher way* [*sed eminentiori modo*]. Thus, *that which* the sense knows materially and concretely (and this is to know the singular directly), *this* the intellect knows immaterially and abstractly (and this is to know the universal) (*ST* 1.86.1.*ad* 4).

The sameness here of the thing known is related to the conception of the object of knowledge as primarily *form*. Thus, when St. Thomas presents the doctrine of sensible reality, sense knowledge, and intellectual knowledge of sensible reality, he presents the whole thing in terms of *one form* and many modes of being (*ST* 1.84.1: 512a45–b7). Intellectual knowledge, one might say, is the mode of being proper to form as form.[10] Sense knowledge is not to be conceived as the grasp of the mere singularity of the singular: it is rather a grasp of form as materialized, of universal-in-particular. The property of the intellect is to "liberate" completely the form as form, even though the intellect must turn back to the imagination and senses for complete knowing of such objects, according to their own mode of being.[11]

Now let us say something about the type of abstraction which St. Thomas attributes to our knowledge of *ens*. Here we begin with a consideration of *ST* 1.85.1.*ad* 2. In this article, St. Thomas is focusing directly on the abstractive mode of our knowledge of corporeal things. Abstraction here is entirely envisaged as "from *matter.*" In the *sed contra*, Aristotle is cited to the effect that it is according as things are separable from matter that they pertain to intellect. In the body of the article, the abstraction fixed upon is abstraction from individual corporeal matter. However, in the second objection, the argument is raised that matter pertains to the very definition of natural things, and that matter is the principle of individuation: thus, natural things cannot be understood if one abstracts from the individual or particular. St. Thomas takes the occasion, in answering this objection, to present the whole panoply of intelligibilities discerned by us in material corporeal things. To answer the objection, he is obliged to distinguish between individual and common matter. It is common matter that is contained in the definitions of natural and physical things. But this very presentation of an intelligible object which itself contains matter in its intelligibility seems to constitute the invitation to

10. Cf. *De substantiis separatis*, c. 7 (Leonine ed., lines 23–40).
11. Cf. *In Post. An.* 2.20 (ed. Spiazzi/Leonine Manual, 595) and *ST* 1.84.7.

examine the interiors of our abstract notions. Thus, St. Thomas presents
a series of notions such that we watch the *materiality within* the notion
gradually "fade out." Where physicals have notions which include form
and *common sensible* matter, mathematicals abstract from common sensible matter, and even from *individual intelligible* matter: still, a mathematical notion includes within it form and common intelligible *matter.* In this
way, the stage is set for the conception of *ens* and kindred intelligibilities.
There are some items which can be abstracted *even from* common intelligible matter, such as *ens,* etc. In the explanation in the course of the
reply, "man," e.g., has been seen as not including "this flesh and these
bones" but only "(form in) flesh and bones." Sensible matter is matter as
subject to sensible qualities. "Triangle," e.g., has been seen as eliminating
(i.e. leaving out of consideration) the sort of matter which is indicated as
the subject of "hot and cold, etc.," but as including "substance as subject
for quantity": i.e. the mathematical form is the quantity, and the matter is
the substance as subject to quantity: this is the sort of "materiality" which
is left in the notion. It is obviously a diminished materiality, if matter is
most properly the substantial principle of the movable and changeable
and sensible. But the point is that the notion of *ens* leaves out of consideration even such materiality. It is a focusing on pure *form* or on *act.*
It leaves all matter out. That is why it is the principle of our intellectual-
ity.[12]

Pure form as the content of the notion of *ens* is confirmed in other
texts. I think especially of St. Thomas's explanation of the difference between such words as "stone" and "lion," on the one hand, and *"ens," "bonum," "vivens,"* and the like, on the other, such that the former type said
of God constitutes a metaphor, whereas the latter type said of God does
not constitute a metaphor. He tells us that some names signify the perfections which come forth from God in such a way that the imperfect
mode by which the divine perfection is participated by the creature is included in the very signification [*significatum*] of the name: thus, "stone"
means "something having being materially" [*aliquid materialiter ens*]. Such
names can be said of God only metaphorically. Some names signify *the
perfections themselves absolutely,* in such a way that no mode of participating

12. Abstraction is not an elimination of "content," but rather a de-materializing. It may
be imagined as a unifying of the diverse. All the points of the line become "simultaneous,"
i.e. there is no longer present the element of the need for movement, in order to go from
end to end. It is the absolute unity of the manifold which is meant by "pure form." In abstraction, the manifold loses its material diversity, but still our abstraction is a composite,
an indivisible only actually, not potentially.
    This is also why the abstract universal is a light for knowing the concrete. The return
back into things is merely return back into matter, and indeed into matter as having some
sort of proportion to the abstracted form. Cf. *ST.* 1.87.1: 540a22–36.

is included in their signification: thus *"ens,"* etc. *"Ens"* is thus taken as an expression of pure perfection.

Does "perfection" here mean form, or should one say it means *esse?* I think we should interpret it as form. The forms of things are perfections (*ST* 1.14.6: 97b17–19 and 43–46). They are even something divine.[13] What should be stressed is that in the knowledge of *ens,* form is conceived *qua* form, or *qua* act, and not *qua such* form.[14] Again, St. Thomas certainly calls *ens* a *universal form* (*ST* 1.19.6: 136b1–4).

However, there is a text in which St. Thomas, speaking very directly about the meaning of *"ens,"* says it expresses this: "something properly being actually" [*aliquid proprie esse in actu*], and the subsequent discussion is controlled by the notion of act [*actus*] (*ST* 1.5.1.*ad* 1). Does this mean we should reduce *ens* to *esse,* as though *ens* left form itself out of consideration? This is very far from St. Thomas's approach. Of course *"ens"* includes *esse* in its meaning, so much so that an *ens* which is not its own *esse* is an *ens* by participation (*ST* 1.3.4: 19a17–20). Nevertheless, St. Thomas closely associates our knowledge of *esse* with our knowledge of form: "Every *esse* . . . is considered through some form" (*ST* 1–2.85.4: 1179a30–31). We cannot imagine existence without form (*ST* 1.7.3: 39b19–22). Indeed, the very point of *ST* 1.5.1.*ad* 1 is that something is called *"ens"* primarily in virtue of substantial *esse,* not in virtue of some additional *esse.* That is, the *esse* is being conceived in the light of substance and substantial form (cf. also *ST* 1.5.4: 30a32–33, and many other passages in *ST* 1.5). It is no accident that every *esse* is considered through some form, for form precisely as form or act is the principle of *esse* (*ST* 1–2.85.6: 1181b6–11).[15]

In fact, while I have stressed that our knowledge of *ens* is an abstraction of pure form, i.e. is a conception of form entirely abstracted from matter, nevertheless it is not an *entirely simple* conception. We must apply to it the observations of St. Thomas concerning how our understanding stands vis-à-vis the *indivisible.* The proper object of our intellect comprises a certain sort of unity, i.e. is something actually undivided but potentially divisible. It is only subsequently and derivatively that we know the undivided actually and potentially. Thus, we know by priority the indivisible in the sense of the unity of the continuum, and the indivisible in the sense that the notion of man is a unity. But these are divisible into *parts.* This is also true of *ens.* Just as we know "man" as a whole, and so have a *confused*

---

13. See above, n. 8.

14. Cf. *De substantiis separatis,* c. 7 (Leonine ed., lines 91–102). Also of importance for this is *CM* 3.4 (Cathala, 384): matter is not a cause of *ens* (cf. below, chapter 8, ca. n. 6).

15. The study of form as such belongs, of course, to the domain of the metaphysician: *CP* 2.4 (Maggiòlo; Leonine Manual, 175).

knowledge already of "animal" and "rational," the parts of the notion, so we know *ens*, and so have a confused knowledge of *esse* (*ST* 1.85.8 and 1.85.4.*ad* 3).[16] But my main point here is that *esse* itself is too simple an intelligible to be known by priority by the human intellect. The notion of form I take as remaining open to that lesser indivisibility proper to the object of the human intellect.[17]

Returning to our topic that knowledge of *ens* is abstractive, we should remember that this affects its applicability to material things. We leave out of consideration the matter, but we do not view the form as existing separately. Hence, *ens* is said of *man*. The form as abstracted from the matter is said of the form as not abstracting from the matter. This is precisely because the abstraction was merely abstraction. And abstraction itself is possible precisely because matter is only matter (depends ontologically on form) (cf. *ST* 1.87.1: 540a22–36).[18] Our knowledge is a shining of the light of *ens* into the progressively darker abyss of matter and potentiality.[19]

C. 'ENS' AND OUR KNOWLEDGE OF 'ESSE'

Having stressed the abstractive cognition of *ens*, and this as the very ground of metaphysics (to use Fabro's expression), or the *seed* of metaphysics,[20] I wish in conclusion to face up to what seems to be the difficulty of the position.

---

16. The composition of something with *esse* is a composition of the type: "itself and something else," i.e. the whole thing ("itself") has the role of *component* with *esse*; cf. *Quodl.* 2.2.*ad* 1. In line with this, I say that it is primarily form which is known in *ens* (form here having the role of the whole, even though the confused knowledge of *esse* is also present). Cf. also my paper, "St. Thomas, Capreolus, and Entitative Composition," *Divus Thomas* 80 (1977), p. 368, n. 27.

17. Cf. *SCG* 1.23.2 (ed. Pera, 214): "Nothing is more formal or more simple than *esse*." Clearly, form is meant to lead toward the simplicity of *esse*.

18. See also above, n. 14.

19. Cf. *CM* 2.1 (para. 8):

Et quod quantum ad aliquas res difficultas contingat in cognoscendo veritatem ipsarum rerum ex parte earum, patet. Cum enim unumquodque sit cognoscibile inquantum est ens actu, ut infra in nono huius dicetur, illa quae habent esse deficiens et imperfectum, sunt secundum seipsa parum cognoscibilia, ut materia, motus et tempus propter esse eorum imperfectionem, ut boetius dicit in libro de duabus naturis. [That in the case of some things the difficulty as to knowing the truth about them arises from the things themselves, is clear. For since each thing is knowable inasmuch as it is *ens actu* [a being in act], as will be said below in book 9, those things which have deficient and imperfect *esse* are, just in themselves, scarcely intelligible; such as matter, movement, and time, on account of the imperfection of their *esse* (as Boethius says in the book *On the Two Natures*).]

20. St. Thomas's terms, *"seminaria,"* i.e. seed-plots (*ST* 1–2.63.1: 1038b30–31), and *"semina,"* i.e. seeds (ibid., a. 2.*ad* 3: 1040a25), suggest the movement of the generator in the thing generated: cf. *ST* 1.118.1: 700b34–44.

(1) The problem seems to be that *ens* includes in its notion *esse*, and that *esse* cannot be known through abstraction. Rather, since corporeal things have *esse* only in the concrete, only a concrete mode of knowing will be a knowledge of *esse*. Now, as so stated, the reasoning is hard to take seriously. One might as well say that the mode of the known in knowing must be the same as the mode of the known in its own being. This St. Thomas denies.[21] What abstractive knowing does not consider is the *mode of being* which both form and *esse* have in things. However, is there not a difference between form and *esse* to be considered? We can know the form without that mode of being, but can we know the *esse* if we leave out of consideration the mode of *esse*? Is not a failure to consider the *modus essendi* a failure in our consideration of *esse* itself? In short, we seem to require the non-abstractive ways of knowing so as to conceive adequately what *existence* is, i.e. to know it in its *distinction* from that with which one might confuse it.[22]

This is true. We do need the non-abstractive ways of knowing in order to answer the question: what existence is, i.e. to formulate the conclusion that a thing is not its own *esse*. We do not have that sort of knowledge of *esse* in our abstraction of *ens*. St. Thomas's care to treat separately, though in parallel, the cases of man and angel in *ST* 1.12.4.*ad* 3 emphasizes this fact.

But (2) we can also pose the problem in this way: how are we to conceive of the intellect's movements of conversion toward the phantasms, of reflection toward the singular material thing? Are these to be seen as purely automatic movements, instilled in us from on high (as we said of the first operation of the agent intellect)? Or are they to be seen as necessitating in us a "higher vantage point," neither merely of the singular, nor merely of the universal, but prior to and encompassing both? Or are we to conceive of these obviously natural operations as also themselves *sequels* to the abstractive moment of our intellectual life? Surely this last. Is not the very use of the words "indirect" and "reflection" (*ST* 1.86.1: 535b45–36a8) a solid indication that they must be conceived as in some way *products* of the abstractive moment? And must this not mean that the very nature of the abstraction, as manifested by its fruit, *ens*, is such as to instigate such a movement? I take this to mean that we must envisage the notion of *ens* as having (a) universal applicability and (b), because it is an abstraction, an absence of discontinuity with that from which it is abstracted. It is, in its own nature, apt to light up the dark recesses of matter: i.e. it is knowledge of act as act.[23]

---

21. Cf. e.g. *ST* 1.84.1.

22. I am here applying to knowledge of *esse* the doctrine of modes of knowing the intellective soul, presented in *ST* 1.87.1: 540b36ff., especially 541a18–22.

23. See above, notes 10 and 12.

Thus, when St. Thomas explains that it is by one same intellectual power that we know the objects of science and the objects of opinion, i.e. necessary things and contingent things respectively, he says that it is according to one same object-constituting aspect [*ratio obiecti*] that they are known, viz. according to the aspect of *ens* and *verum*. The intellect perfectly knows the necessaries, which have *perfectum esse in veritate:* it attains to their *quiddity,* whereby it demonstrates proper accidents concerning them. It imperfectly knows contingent things: just as they have *imperfectum esse et veritatem.* Contingents and necessaries agree in the common aspect: *ens,* which the intellect considers. The one instrument, the notion of *ens,* is used by the agent intellect[24] for its penetration into its entire field *(ST* 1.79.9. *ad* 3: 490b23–50, and cf. 1.86.3, *in toto).*

There is already present, in *ens,* a confused knowledge of *esse,* because of the proportion of *ens* to *esse.* And it is this character of *ens* which makes it the starting point of metaphysics. But it is only subsequently, through the experience of our need for the indirect, concrete ways of knowing in order to attain things as they properly have *esse,*[25] that we eventually form a notion of what *esse* is, namely a participation in the nature of the first cause lying at the upper limits of our experience of form.

24. Cf. *Quaestiones de anima* 5 (at the end of the *corpus);* still, the notion of "instrument" is least satisfactory for *ens,* of all the principles, since prior to *ens,* the agent intellect cannot be conceived as *knowing,* but only as illuminating.

25. Intellectual knowledge of things precisely *as existing* demands conversion toward the phantasm *(ST* 1.84.7: 522a10–14). Knowledge of the singular (and the object of our intellect has *esse* only in individual matter: *ST* 1.12.4) is *indirect* intellectual knowledge *(ST* 1.86.1). On the relation of our original apprehension of *ens* to the "judgment of existence" (i.e. the *intellectual* judgment), cf. Jean-Hervé Nicolas, O.P., "Chronique de philosophie," *Revue thomiste* 48 (1948), 546–547.

Chapter 4

ST. THOMAS, PHYSICS, AND THE PRINCIPLE OF METAPHYSICS

One twentieth-century school of interpretation of St. Thomas's philosophical doctrines, the "River Forest" School, holds that physics precedes metaphysics, not merely in the order of learning, but also as providing for metaphysics its proper subject of study, being as being.[1] This it does by proving the existence of immaterial reality. Thomas's commentaries on Aristotle, as well as his explicit description of intellectual development, run counter to this interpretation. I propose to show that here.

The late Fr. James Weisheipl, surely representative of the School, in a paper published in 1976,[2] was aiming to show the need for Aristotelian physics, also called "natural philosophy," and to show that it has a congeniality with modern mathematical physics. He wished to distinguish it from both mathematical science and from metaphysics. He said:

Such a natural philosophy is not only valid but even necessary for the philosophical understanding of nature itself. That is to say, there are realities in nature that are not accounted for by physico-mathematical abstraction, realities such as motion, time, causality, chance, substance, and change itself. The physicist needs mechanical causes, such as matter and force, but *the nature of causality as such is beyond mathematics*, where even final causality is out of place. *Concepts such as potency and act, matter and form, substance and accident*, quite useless to the modern physicist, are established in a realistic natural philosophy.

The aforementioned concepts are not established in metaphysics, and in this connection it is important to stress the differences between metaphysics and natural philosophy and to indicate the nature and relationship of each . . . [273, my italics]

---

1. On the School, cf. Benedict M. Ashley, O.P., "The River Forest School and the Philosophy of Nature Today," in *Philosophy and the God of Abraham*, ed. R. James Long, Toronto, 1991: Pontifical Institute of Mediaeval Studies, pp. 1–16.

2. Weisheipl, James, O.P., "Medieval Natural Philosophy and Modern Science," in *Nature and Motion in the Middle Ages*, ed. William E. Carroll, Washington, D.C., 1985: The Catholic University of America Press, pp. 261–276 [originally published in *Manuscripta* 20 (1976), pp. 181–196, under the title: "The Relationship of Medieval Natural Philosophy

He says that metaphysics has been overloaded "with innumerable problems and areas of concern that rightly belong to the natural philosopher,"[3] and he continues:

This is a perversion of metaphysics as understood by St. Thomas. [273]

A very strong condemnation, but one which is justified if the charges are
true. But are they? What sort of case does Weisheipl make in the essay under consideration?

He says there are at least two reasons why metaphysics presupposes
natural philosophy. The first is that it proves the existence of some non-
material being, and thus establishes the subject matter of a new science,
namely the science of being as such. I will return to this later.

The second reason is as follows:

. . . This is demanded by the nature of analogous concepts. Analogous concepts
are not abstracted but constructed by [275] the human mind. The prime analogue of our concept of "being," or "thing," is the sensible, material, concrete reality of things around us. The moment we realize that there is at least one thing
that is not sensible, material, and movable, we break into the realm of analogy.
From that moment on, terms such as "thing," "being," "substance," "cause," and
the like are no longer restricted to the material and sensible world. We thereby stretch and enlarge our earlier conceptions to make them include immaterial reality. Such are our analogous concepts of being, substance, potency, act,
cause, and the like. Such terms are seen in metaphysics to be applicable beyond
the realm of material and sensible realities. The prime analogue *quoad nos* of all
these concepts is material, sensible, movable being, which is the realm of the natural philosopher.

Thus, for St. Thomas, natural philosophy is prior *quoad nos* to metaphysics.
Natural philosophy establishes by demonstration that there is some being which
is not material. This negative judgment, or more properly, this judgment of separation, is the point of departure for a higher study, which can be called "first phi-

---

to Modern Science: The Contribution of Thomas Aquinas to its Understanding"]. References are to the Carroll edition.

3. One cannot help but be struck by the difference between Fr. Weisheipl's angle on
things here, and that of Thomas Aquinas in, e.g., *Commentary on the Physics* [henceforth
"*CP*"] 2.5 (ed. Maggiòlo, Rome/Turin, 1954: Marietti, 176):

. . . *to consider concerning causes as such is proper to the first philosopher* [i.e. the metaphysi-
cian]: for cause, inasmuch as [it is] cause, does not depend on matter as regards being, for in those also which are separated from matter one finds the intelligible aspect:
cause. But consideration of causes is taken on by the natural philosopher because of
some necessity: nor nevertheless is it taken on by him to consider concerning causes
save according as they are causes of natural changes. [my italics]

Of course, one sees well the abstract nature of the notion of cause by considering it as applicable to the separate entities; however, as I will show, only because such notions are abstract from the start can one raise the question of separate entity.

losophy" or metaphysics. Consequently this new study is "prior" and "first" in itself, i.e. according to nature, but it is not first *quoad nos*. [274–275]

He goes on to refer to a text in the *Commentary on the Ethics* in which Thomas gives the proper order of learning for the sciences, placing metaphysics and ethics after natural philosophy.[4]

THOMAS COMMENTING ON ARISTOTLE[5]

What is the best approach to a discussion of this theory? Spontaneously I think of such facts as that Thomas nowhere presents us with such a view of the formation of metaphysical concepts: he everywhere treats the metaphysicals as a domain unto themselves, even though they are objects first encountered by us in sensible reality. So considered, they are already analogical. Thus, when Aristotle presents the doctrine of "being" as something "said in many ways," or, as Thomas calls it, the "analogical predication" of "being," there is no appeal to immaterial being in the explanation. Rather, Thomas carefully crafts a digression presenting four modes of being, moving from the weak to the strong: viz. (1) negations and privations, (2) generation, corruption, and change, (3) inhering accidents, and (4) substance. These suffice to exhibit the analogy of being.[6] That is, for him it is not only the concepts of physics which are encountered in sensible things.[7] Of course, in knowing God and speaking of Him, we do form somewhat new concepts. The already analogical

---

4. I might underline that I am not opposing the doctrine that physics or natural philosophy is to be learned before metaphysics; my point is rather about the doctrine concerning the subject of metaphysics and how it is discovered. This does mean that I would have a different reason why metaphysics comes last in the order of learning.

5. The first "thesis" proposed by Ashley, "The School," as pertaining to the River Forest School, is this:

. . . the philosophy of Aquinas, as distinct from his theology, is best gathered . . . from the commentaries on Aristotle. [2–3]

6. *Commentary on the Metaphysics* [henceforth "*CM*"] 4.1 (ed. Cathala, Rome/Turin, 1935: Marietti, 535–543).

7. Consider especially *Summa theologiae* [henceforth "*ST*"] 1.85.1.*ad* 2: physical concepts do not abstract from sensible matter; mathematical concepts abstract from sensible matter, but not from intelligible matter:

. . . But there are certain [items] which can be abstracted even from universal intelligible matter, such as "a being," "[something] one," "potency and act," and other things of that order . . .

Thomas goes on to point out that such intelligible objects can be found existent without any matter, as is clear in the case of immaterial substance. However, this remark is not meant as a required proof of the abstractability of "a being" from all matter. There is no concept of "a being" which includes matter in the *precise target of signification (save through error)*, though all our concepts have a *mode of signifying* which derives from the materiality of the things we primarily know. See *ST* 1.13.3.*ad* 1 and 1.13.1.*ad* 2.

character of the intelligibility, "a being," makes it possible to *construct,* on the basis of the notions of being we already possess, a *somewhat* (though not altogether) *new* notion of being, which applies to the newly discovered highest cause.[8]

And again, one thinks of the actual practice of Aristotle, so carefully commented upon by Thomas, in which the metaphysician *poses for himself the question* as to the existence of any separate entity: i.e. the Aristotelian metaphysician is presented as already on the scene, and yet not knowing if there is any separate entity.[9]

A most important text for the River Forest School is mentioned by

---

8. *ST* 1.13.5 (81a38–48), and *Expositio libri Posteriorum* 1.41 (Leonine ed., t. 1*2, Rome/Paris, 1989: Commissio Leonina/Vrin, lines 161–192; ed. Spiazzi, Rome/Turin, 1955: Marietti, 363 [8]).

9. Notice, e.g., *CM* 7.1 (1268–1269), where Thomas, paraphrasing Aristotle, says that it must be asked whether the mathematicals and the [Platonic] Forms are anything other than sensible things or not, and if not, whether there are any other separable substances, and why and how: ". . . or whether there is no substance other than the sensibles." And he goes on to say that this will be determined in the twelfth book. This is quite literally in accord with Aristotle, *Metaph.* 7.2 (1028b30–31). In the *Metaphysics* itself, the question of separate entity, as to its existence, is not settled until sometime later than books 7 and 8. One can hardly claim that books 7 to 11 are merely a dialectical approach to metaphysics, at least as Thomas sees them: cf. *CM* 7.1 (1245):

> After the Philosopher removes from the principal consideration of this science incidental being [*ens per accidens*], and "being" as it signifies the true, here he begins to determine concerning coherent being which is outside the soul [*ens per se quod est extra animam*], the principal consideration of this science being about this. But this part is divided into two parts. For this science determines both concerning being inasmuch as it is being [*ens inquantum est ens*], and concerning the first principles of beings, as was said in book 6. Therefore, in the first part it will be determined concerning being [*de ente*]. In the second, concerning the first principle of being [*entis*], in the twelfth book . . .

> Ashley, in a footnote, notes ". . . the attempts of some [John Wippel and Dewan are named] . . . to show that it is possible without proving the existence of immaterial substances to make a valid judgment that *ens inquantum ens* is immaterial . . ." and says:

> . . . I would reply that such arguments at most conclude that immaterial substances are *possible,* but that is not sufficient to establish the need for metaphysics. These authors seem to start with Kant's question: "How is metaphysics possible?" . . . when for Aristotle and Aquinas it was "Is metaphysics needed?" *("Si non est aliqua alia substantia praeter eas quae consistunt secundum naturam, de quibus est physica, physica erit prima scientia,"* . . .)

He is here referring to my paper "St. Thomas Aquinas against Metaphysical Materialism," in *Atti del'VIII Congresso Tomistico Internazionale* (ed. A. Piolanti), Vatican City, 1982: Libreria Editrice Vaticana, t. V, pp. 412–434. There, I am not discussing merely the possibility of metaphysics, but its actuality. And I claim to see it as actual *even before seeing that immaterial being is possible.* Thomas, thinking metaphysically, takes the trouble to *prove the possibility* of form existing without matter. The possibility of which he is speaking is not merely logical but real, in the nature of form as form.

What is the "immaterial being" which constitutes the subject of metaphysics? I did not use the expression "immaterial being." I merely referred to "that which can be without matter." This is in accordance with how Thomas speaks about the subject of metaphysics. He says:

Benedict Ashley. It brings us back to Weisheipl's first reason why natural philosophy is presupposed to metaphysics. We read:

> But why is such a science needed or even possible? Aquinas agrees with Aristotle that natural science would be "first" philosophy if it were not for the fact that *in natural science we discover* that the First Cause of the existence and action of *ens mobile* is not itself a physical object which can be studied by the principles of natural science, and that this is true also of the human intellectual soul.[10]

This is meant to refer to *Metaphysics* 6.1 (1026a28–32) and *CM* 6.1 (1170). However, Aristotle there in fact says nothing about discoveries made by natural science. Rather, he says that if there were no separate entity, natural science would be first philosophy (as Thomas paraphrases: "first science"). Remember that "first philosophy" is Aristotle's name for what we call "metaphysics." Thus, he is saying that physics would be metaphysics if there were no separate entity. It is not said that physics discovers the existence of separate entity. What certainly could be said is that, until they discover the existence of separate entity, the thinkers who do it, though they are metaphysicians, might not be able to distinguish themselves from physicists.[11]

It is significant that in this place, Thomas sees as the principal point

---

> ... But though the subject of this science is *ens commune,* nevertheless it is said to be as a whole about those things which are separate from matter according to being and notion [*quae sunt separata a materia secundum esse et rationem*]. Because we call "separate from matter according to being and notion," not only those things which can never be in matter, such as God and the intellectual substances, but also those things which *can* be without matter, such as *ens commune.* For this would not be the case, if it depended on matter as to being.

This is to say that, when one grasps the intelligibility "being" as found in sensible things, one finds it as something different from the natural forms and the mathematicals. It includes neither sensible nor intelligible matter in its own notion. It is a metaphysical *conclusion* that form can exist without matter. It is also a metaphysical conclusion that form does exist without matter.

As for the *need* for metaphysics, Thomas, in the *Prooemium* to his *CM,* rather presents the need as based on the fact that no particular science considers the most universal things, upon which nevertheless they all depend. He says, concerning "a being," "[something] one," "potency and act":

> Such things ought not to remain altogether indeterminate, since, without them, a complete knowledge concerning those things which are proper to some genus or species cannot be had. Nor, again, ought they be treated in some one particular science: because, since each genus of beings needs them for knowledge of it, with equal justification they would be treated in any other particular science. Hence, it remains that such things be treated in one common [or universal] science; which, since it is maximally intellectual, regulates the others.

10. Ashley, "The School," p. 3. My italics.

11. I had originally written ". . . *would* not be able to distinguish themselves from physicists." However, a thinker who does not draw the erroneous conclusion that all beings are bodies might well recognize that he was doing something different from the physicists even before he has succeeded in concluding to the existence of separate entity.

that it is one and the same science which will treat of the first being and of universal being. The question at issue was whether primary philosophy is such as to treat of being universally, or whether it treats of some determinate genus. The answer is that the science that treats of the first or highest being is also the science that treats of being universally. Thomas points out that this was already established in 4.1. It is to that place we should look for the best understanding of the remark about physics and metaphysics. The early physicists provide a kind of model for the conception of *metaphysics*. Aristotle points out that the earliest physicists were seeking the causes of beings as beings. At the very moment when he wishes to show that the science which treats of the highest causes must have as its field being as being, Aristotle asks us to consider the example of the natural philosophers. Thomas comments as follows:

Here he shows that this science which is here being dealt with has "a being" [*ens*] as its subject, with this sort of argument. Every principle is the appropriate [*per se*] principle and cause of some nature; but we are seeking the first principles and highest causes of things, as was said in Book 1; they therefore are the appropriate causes of some nature. But of no other than "a being." *Which is clear from this*, that all the philosophers seeking the elements according as they are "of beings" [*"entia," lege "entium"*],[12] sought such principles, viz. the first and highest; therefore, in this science we seek the principles of "a being inasmuch as it is a being": therefore, "a being" is the subject of this science, since every science is seeking the proper causes of its own subject.[13]

Earlier in *CM,* Thomas, explaining why Aristotle speaks of such people as Thales when investigating the causes, notes:

Nor should it strike one as inappropriate, if Aristotle here touches on the opinions of those who treated merely of natural science; because, according to the ancient [philosophers] who know of no substance save the corporeal and mobile, it was necessary that metaphysics [*prima philosophia*] be natural science, as will be said in bk. 4.[14]

Once more, we see that the reference here is to book 4. The idea is that until separate entity is discovered there is no separate science of

12. The text of Aristotle which we have in the Cathala-Spiazzi edition, 296, reads:
. . . Si ergo et *entium* elementa quaerentes . . .
Since this fits perfectly with the argument of Thomas, I take it that the *"entia"* in the text of Thomas is a mistake.
13. *CM* 4.1 (533) concerning Aristotle, at 4.1 (1003a28–32).
14. Thomas, *CM* 1.4 (78), commenting on Aristotle, *Metaph.* 1.3 (983b20). Notice that the forward reference by Thomas is to book 4, not book 6, i.e. is to the place where Aristotle treats the earlier physicists as metaphysicians: cf. *CM* 4.1 (533) concerning Aristotle, at 4.1 (1003a28–32).

physics! There is, as yet, no science which confines its investigation to the particular field which characterizes Aristotelian physics, a science which does not treat things from the viewpoint of being.[15]

Still thinking about the scenario favored by Fr. Weisheipl and the River Forest School, in which we have first a sort of "pure physics" which by demonstrating the existence of separate substance provides a new "constructed" meaning for "being," one suitable for metaphysics, I would use in rejecting it, among other things, the definition of motion or change given by Aristotle, as interpreted by St. Thomas. Thomas tells us that some people have tried to define motion as "going from potency to act not suddenly." They err, positing in the definition things which are intelligibly posterior to motion itself: "going" is a species of motion or change; "suddenly" has time in its own definition: since the sudden is what takes place in the indivisible of time, the instant, and time is defined by means of motion. And he goes on:

And so it is altogether impossible to define motion by things prior and better known, save as the Philosopher here defines it. For it has [already] been said that each genus is divided by potency and act. Now, potency and act, since they are among the first differences of being [*de primis differentiis entis*], are naturally prior to motion; and it is these that Aristotle uses to define motion.[16]

My interest in this text is that it makes clear that the very definition of motion, used in the science having as its subject mobile being, uses *notions intelligibly prior* to the notion of motion. These are presented as differences of being. Obviously, being *as being* is meant. The notion of being which is being employed can hardly be conceived as limited to the mobile, since mobility is a posterior intelligible. We are witnessing the role of metaphysical considerations at the very origins of physical thought.

Or consider what Thomas says about the natures of natural science (a particular science) and metaphysics. We read:

All these particular sciences, which have just been mentioned, are about some one particular domain of being, for example, about number or magnitude, or something of that order. And each one treats circumscriptively about its own subject-

---

15. Cf. *CM* 6.1 (1147), concerning Aristotle at 1025b7–10. The text is quoted later. Thus, we see "metaphysics in embryo" regularly in the Presocratics as presented by Aristotle and Thomas. Thus, e.g., at *Metaph.* 1.3 (983b6–18), where Aristotle presents those who attempted to explain all by the material cause, it is remarkable that the issue is whether there is any such thing as coming to be and ceasing to be. They are represented as considering things from the viewpoint of being, and denying generation and corruption. This comes out in Thomas's summary at, e.g., *ST* 1.44.2, where the early philosophers are presented as holding that the substance of things is "uncreated." *ST* 1.44.2 is a history of attempts at metaphysics which are inadequate until the third stage.

16. Thomas, *CP* 3.2 (285 [3]).

domain, i.e. so [treats] of its own domain, that [it treats] of nothing else; for example, the science which treats of number does not treat of magnitude. For none of them treats of being, unqualifiedly, that is, of being in its generality [*de ente in commune*], *nor even about any particular being inasmuch as it is a being.* For example, arithmetic does not determine about number inasmuch as it is a being, but inasmuch as it is number. For to consider any being, inasmuch as it is a being, is proper to metaphysics. [italics mine][17]

In the Weisheipl scenario, physics does treat of what it talks about from the viewpoint of "being," i.e. our original concept of being. It "establishes" the concepts of act and potency, etc. It presents "the nature of causality." But as for Thomas, the above statement is quite clear. If we find, in the treatments pertaining to physical science, some approach from the viewpoint of being, this will be, not properly physical science, but a case of the physicist taking on the role of the metaphysician. Along these lines, Thomas tells us that the geometer proves his own principles by taking on the role of the metaphysician.[18]

Here is *CM* 7.11 (1525-6-7):

He [Aristotle] shows what remains besides to be determined concerning substances. And he posits that two [things] remain to be determined. The first of which is that, since it has been determined that the substance and quiddity of sensible and material things are the very parts of the species, it remains to determine whether of such substances, i.e. material and sensible, there is any substance separate from matter [*praeter materiam*], such that it is necessary to seek some substance of these sensibles other than that which has been determined, as some people say numbers existing outside matter, or something like that, i.e. species or Ideas, are the substances of these sensible things. And concerning that there must be inquiry later.

For this *inquiry* is proper to this science. For in this science we try to determine concerning sensible substances for the sake of this, that is, because of immaterial substances, because the theorizing concerning sensible and material substances in a way pertains to physics, which is not first philosophy, but second, as was established in book 4. For first philosophy is about the first substances, which are immaterial substances, about which it theorizes not merely inasmuch as they are substances, but inasmuch as they are such substances, i.e. inasmuch as they are immaterial. About sensible substance it does not theorize inasmuch as they are such substances, but inasmuch as they are substances, or even beings, or inasmuch as

17. *CM* 6.1 (1147), concerning Aristotle at 1025b7–10.
18. St. Thomas, *Expositio libri Posteriorum* 1.21 (Leonine ed., lines 75–79, concerning Aristotle at 77b3–5) (ed. Spiazzi, 177):

> ... contingit in aliqua sciencia probari principia illius sciencie, in quantum illa sciencia assumit ea que sunt alterius sciencie, sicut si geometra probet sua principia secundum quod assumit formam philosophi primi. [... it does happen in some science that the principles of that science are proved, inasmuch as that science makes use of what pertains to another science; thus, for example, the geometer proves his principles inasmuch as he assumes the role of the metaphysician.]

through them we are led to the knowledge of immaterial substances. But the physicist, conversely, determines about material substances, *not inasmuch as they are substances,* but inasmuch as they are material and [as] having in them a principle of
movement.

And because someone might believe that natural science does not theorize
concerning the complete material and sensible substances, but only about their
matters, therefore he eliminates this, saying that the physicist must consider not
only matter, but also that part which is according to reason, that is, concerning
the form. And even more about the form than about the matter, because form is
more nature than matter [is], as is proved in the *Physics,* bk. 2. [my italics]

THOMAS ON THE FORMATION OF
THE EDUCATED MIND

However, I do not think it would be very effective to take this pathway
in argument. The adversary might think it sufficient (though it is not)
to contend that all these things Thomas says about physics not treating
things from the viewpoint of being and of substance are said in the light
of the ultimate concept of being, not in the light of the original concept.
Accordingly, I see as the proper argumentative strategy that we look directly at texts of Thomas on the nature of the concept of being and its
role in the formation of the educated mind.

I will take my start from a text in Thomas's *Commentary on the Nicomachean Ethics,* on the nature of the knowability of the most universal principles. I will confirm Thomas's commitment to the position there seen
by means of texts from the *Summa theologiae* [henceforth "*ST*"] 1–2, on
the formation of intellectual virtues, and on the nature and hierarchy of
those virtues.

Our starting point, then, is a text from Thomas's *Commentary on the
Nicomachean Ethics.*[19] There we read that metaphysics is most certain, i.e.

---

19. Thomas Aquinas, *Sententia libri Ethicorum* 6.5 (Leonine ed., t. 47-2, Rome, 1969:
Ad Sanctae Sabinae, lines 102–106 (concerning Aristotle at 1141a12–17) (ed. Pirotta,
1181):

    ... existimamus quosdam esse sapientes totaliter, idest respectu totius generis en-
tium ... illa quae est sapientia simpliciter est certissima inter omnes scientias, inquantum scilicet attingit ad prima principia entium, quae secundum se sunt notissima, quamvis aliqua illarum, scilicet immaterialia, sunt minus nota quoad nos. *Universalissima
autem principia sunt etiam quoad nos magis nota, sicut ea quae pertinent ad ens inquantum est
ens: quorum cognitio pertinet ad sapientiam sic dictam, ut patet in quarto Metaphysicae.* [my
italics] [... we judge that some people are wise unqualifiedly, i.e. as regards the entire
domain of beings ... such unqualified wisdom is the most certain of all sciences, inasmuch as it attains to the first principles of beings, which just in themselves are most
known, though some of them, viz. the immaterial [things], are less known to us. *Nevertheless, the most universal principles are more known even to us, such as those which pertain to being inasmuch as it is being: knowledge of which [principles] pertains to wisdom, in that unqualified sense of the word; as is clear in Metaphysics 4.*]

more certain than any other science, inasmuch as it attains to the primary principles of beings. Though some of these principles are *less* known to us than other things, thus placing in doubt metaphysics' claim to being "most certain," nevertheless this claim is well founded, inasmuch as the most universal principles, pertaining to being as being, are *both best known in themselves and best known to us.* And these pertain to metaphysics. Obviously, if the first principles, as first known, were at first limited to corporeal being as corporeal, they would not be known as they pertain properly to metaphysics.[20] Thomas sees the principles, precisely as known first of all and to all, as having the properly metaphysical character. This does not make the beginner a finished metaphysician, but it does mean that the principles of metaphysics are precisely those very first known principles, not some newly constructed conception of being resulting from the study of physics. If we did not start with metaphysical principles, no particular science would ever provide them.

Citing one text does not provide complete assurance.[21] We should unite this statement from Thomas's *Commentary on the Nicomachean Ethics* with texts from the *ST* 1-2, so as to show that Thomas views the first

20. Ashley (p. 3) says:

> . . . According to this [River Forest] theory, since the proper object of the human intellect is *ens mobile,* being-that-becomes, the first science in the order of learning . . . can only be *natural science.*

Thomas never says, to my knowledge, and never would say, in my judgment, that the proper object of the human intellect is *ens mobile.* When he needs to underline the humble beginnings of human intellection, he uses such a formula as *"ens vel verum, consideratum in rebus materialibus,"* i.e. "a being" or "the true," considered in material things (*ST* 1.87.3.*ad* 1). This is a formula which, while indicating the mode of being which is the connatural object of the human intellect, preserves the metaphysical starting point from confusion with the notions proper to physical science.

21. Cf., for another, *Expositio libri Posteriorum* 1.5 (Leonine ed., lines 120-130; ed. Spiazzi, 50), where Thomas speaks of the first principles known to all human beings. It is these very principles of which he says:

> But of some propositions the terms are such that they are in the knowledge of all, such as "a being," "[something] one," and the others which pertain to a being precisely as a being: for "a being" is the first conception of the intellect. Hence, it is necessary that such propositions not only in themselves, but even relative to everyone, stand as known by virtue of themselves: for example that it does not happen that the same thing be and not be, and that a whole is greater than its own part, and the like. Hence, such principles all sciences receive from metaphysics, to which it belongs to consider being, just in itself [*ens simpliciter*], and those things which belong to being.

It is these propositions, *as known by everyone,* which pertain to the metaphysician. This is hardly a scenario in which "being" first has a narrow meaning, limited to the physical, and then is widened by physics proving the existence of the incorporeal. In fact, Thomas goes on to speak of propositions known by virtue of themselves, but not to all. He gives as his example here "that right angles are equals." Obviously, there are lots of such principles in each science, including metaphysics. What characterizes the group Thomas is speaking of in the text quoted above is that they are known from the start to all. These belong to metaphysics.

principles as intrinsically metaphysical, having a power which cannot possibly be the result of learning physics. We can, nevertheless, develop a doctrine as to why it is only after doing physics that one can do metaphysics.[22] This will have to do, not with the proper meaning of the first principles, but with the fact (which we will see below) that the ability to exploit such principles requires a preparation on the side of the passive principle whereby we arrive at conclusions.

I now propose to look at the line of thinking Thomas displays in the *ST* 1–2 regarding the development of intellectual virtue.[23] Metaphysics, as human wisdom, is the highest of the intellectual virtues, and our present question concerns the way this is produced in the human intellect.

The discussion begins, then, with the treatise on *habitus*,[24] the genus to which virtue belongs. We are assured that the intellect is a subject for such habits or dispositions.[25] We are also told that there is no *complete* habit inborn in the intellect, but that there is inborn the *beginning* of that habit called "the understanding of principles," the nature of the soul being such that, once it is provided with the data of sense and imagination, it immediately sees the truth of the principles.[26]

It is the next point which is of great importance: whether some habit is caused *by our acts*. Thomas carefully explains that in the agent, i.e. the being which acts, there is sometimes found only an active principle; and in such an agent there is no room for the development of a habit by its

22. Notice in *CM* 6.1 (1146), where St. Thomas is speaking of the principles and causes considered in the sciences, and explains Aristotle's having said that the causes were "more certain, or simpler":

... Those principles either are more certain for us, as in natural [objects] which are closer to sensible [objects], or else they are simpler, and prior as regards their nature, as is [the case with] mathematical [objects] ...

23. I first called attention to this line of doctrine in 1980; see chapter 3, above. See also my paper, "Jacques Maritain, St. Thomas, and the Birth of Metaphysics," *Études Maritainiennes/Maritain Studies* 13 (1997), pp. 3–18.

24. This Latin word, *"habitus,"* taken from the verb *"habere," "*to have," defies translation. It includes what we mean in English by a "habit," but also applies to such things as health and beauty, as well as to the results of training. It is one of the species dividing the category of being called *"quality."* Very often the word *"dispositio,"* i.e. "disposition," is used to convey the meaning. One might even try "set-up" or "arrangement." Thus, Thomas says:

... "habitus" conveys the meaning: some *disposition* ordered toward the nature of the thing, and toward its operation or end, in function of which the thing is well or ill *disposed* toward that [operation or end]. [*ST* 1–2.49.4 (969b7–11), my italics]

This *ST* article presents the conditions which require the existence of such qualities.

25. *ST* 1–2.50.4. It is a "subject" in the sense of something that receives and is perfected by a quality.

26. *ST* 1–2.51.1 (978b13–34). Notice that it is also said there that the individual has a natural habit, as regards the bodily organs and the corresponding sense powers, such that one person is more apt for understanding well than is another.

own action (since habits belong to things precisely as possessed of potency to several).[27] However, there are agents which contain both an active
and a passive principle of their own action (and this is the case with human beings and their actions). Thus, the intellective power, inasmuch as
it reasons concerning conclusions, has as active principle a proposition
known by virtue of itself [*per se notam*]. Hence, from such acts some habits can be caused in the agents, not as regards the first active principle,
but as regards the principle of the act which moves (or operates) upon
being moved. The said habit is formed because everything which under-
goes and receives from another is *disposed* by the act of the agent. Hence,
from the multiplied acts there is generated in the passive and moved
power a quality which is called "a habit." Thomas gives as an example the
scientific formations, i.e. the sciences, which are caused in the intellect
inasmuch as the intellect is moved by the primary propositions.[28]

A key objection points out that the habit is more noble than the acts
which precede the development of the habit: this is evident because of
the higher quality of the acts which result from the possessed habit. Thus,
since an effect cannot be more noble than its cause, the earlier acts cannot produce the habit. In answer Thomas says:

> ... the acts preceding the habit, inasmuch as they proceed from the active prin-
> ciple, proceed from a more noble principle than is the generated habit ... [*T*]*he*
> *understanding of principles is a more noble principle than the science of conclusions.*[29]

Thus, we see that the possible intellect, already naturally perfected by the
ability to understand principles, is an agent relative to itself as formable
to be adept at drawing conclusions from principles. At first, it must move
from principles to conclusion without the benefit of an ease, a mastery,
in the matter. However, this ease is eventually developed.[30] Nevertheless,

27. See *ST* 1–2.49.4.
28. *ST* 1–2.51.2 (980a4–7).
29. *ST* 1–2.51.2.*ad* 3. Notice that the habit of understanding the first principles is
caused in the possible intellect by the agent intellect: *ST* 1–2.53.1 (987a23–32).

> ... Hence, if some disposition is in the possible intellect, *caused immediately by the agent
> intellect,* such a disposition is incorruptible both on its own account and incidentally.
> Now, such are the habits of the first principles, both speculative and practical, which
> cannot be corrupted either by forgetfulness or deception: as the Philosopher [Aris-
> totle] says in *Ethics* 6 concerning prudence, which is not lost by being forgotten. [my
> italics]

30. Notice that, as regards the possible intellect itself, regarding matters of science,
one act of reason can produce the habit: one *per se nota* proposition can conquer, i.e. can
convince the intellect to assent firmly to the conclusion. In opinion and probable matter,
many acts are required. However, there is also the "particular reason," i.e. the cogitative,
memorative and imaginative powers. They are needed, and their formation requires many
repeated operations: 1–2.51.3 (980b35–981a6).

in the hierarchy of perfections, the prior condition (understanding of principles) is more noble than the subsequent one (ease in drawing conclusions from principles).

Our next point concerns the later question: is the virtue of wisdom the greatest among the intellectual virtues? The theoretical intellectual virtues are understanding of principles, science, and wisdom.[31] Wisdom is indeed the greatest, having as its object the highest cause, which is God.[32] However, an objection is raised, based precisely on what we have just seen. We read:

> ... The knowledge of principles is more noble than the knowledge of conclusions. But wisdom draws conclusions from the indemonstrable principles, upon which [the virtue of] understanding [bears], just as do the other sciences. Therefore, understanding is a greater virtue than wisdom.[33]

To this, Thomas replies:

> ... The truth and knowledge of the indemonstrable principles depends on the notion of the terms [*ex ratione terminorum*]; for, it being known what a whole is and what a part is, at once it is known that every whole is greater than its own part. But to know the notion of "a being" and "not a being" [*entis et non entis*], and of "whole" and "part," and of the other [items] that follow upon "a being," out of which as out of terms the indemonstrable principles are constituted, *pertains to wisdom;* because "a being, universally" [*ens commune*] is the proper effect of the highest cause, viz. God. And so wisdom does not merely make use of the indemonstrable principles, on which [the virtue of] understanding [bears], concluding from them, as do the other sciences; but also [it treats of them] as judging about them and as disputing against those who deny them. Hence, it follows that wisdom is a greater virtue than understanding.[34]

If we remember the idea that it is not only science, but even wisdom, that is *generated, developed,* by acts flowing from the understanding of prin-

---

31. 1–2.57.2; the *ad* 2 already makes it clear that both understanding of principles and science *depend* on wisdom, as on what is most primary in perfection.

32. 1–2.66.5:

> ... the greatness of a virtue, as to its species, is considered from the object. But the object of wisdom has priority of excellence among the objects of all the intellectual virtues: for it considers the highest cause, which is God, as is said in the beginning of the *Metaphysics.*

For the reference to Aristotle, cf. 1.2 (983a5–12) and *CM* 1.3 (64).

It must be noted that while Thomas does not generally allow that God is the subject of metaphysics, he here makes God the object of the virtue of wisdom. At *ST* 1.1.7, he tells us that the subject stands related to a science the way the object stands related to a power or habit. Of course, to consider metaphysics as wisdom is to take it in a somewhat special way.

33. 1–2.66.5.obj. 4.

34. 1–2.66.5.*ad* 4.

ciples, and that such a process of development requires that the understanding of principles be more noble than the resultant acts, we realize the implication for our own topic.

Our understanding of the terms of the first principles, precisely as prior to our knowledge of the first principles themselves, must be an intellectual event even more noble than the event which is the understanding of principles. The knowledge of the indemonstrable principles *depends* on the knowledge of the terms. Thomas's strategy here against the objection is relevant only along these lines.

Furthermore, the nobility of this event, the understanding of the terms, is directly related by Thomas to wisdom, obviously *inchoate* wisdom.[35] This means that our original and altogether first knowledge of *"ens"* is that "active principle" previously mentioned, which itself *cannot be subject to improvement.* So taken, it is not a developable item. Rather, it is the vital force for the entire development of intellectual life. And it pertains to metaphysics. The "being" which pertains to metaphysics is the "being" which we know as the very source of all intellectual operation.

Thus, I am saying that the first knowledge of *ens* is a perfect light, which will reveal itself in our lower-level intellectual endeavors, all having a somewhat secret movement toward the knowledge of God.[36] That is why, in a way, the question of knowledge of God is deceptive, as an indication of whether one is in physics or metaphysics. Already, when one undertakes one's first moral act, one has a knowledge of God.[37] However, it does not have scientific perfection.[38] We are proto-metaphysicians from the dawn of intellectual life, long before we become scientific metaphysicians.

As St. Thomas teaches, we certainly need to study physics before studying metaphysics. However, the reasons for this are not those suggested by the River Forest School.

---

35. At *ST* 1–2.63.2.*ad* 3, Thomas speaks of the naturally given beginnings of the virtues, moral or intellectual, as "seeds or principles" [*quaedam semina sive principia*].

36. Cf. *Summa contra gentiles* [henceforth "*SCG*"] 3.25 (ed. Pera et al., Rome/Turin, 1961: Marietti, 2063).

37. See *ST* 1–2.89.6.*ad* 3. I discuss this text in my paper: "Natural Law and the First Act of Freedom: Maritain Revisited," *Études Maritainiennes/Maritain Studies* 12 (1996), pp. 3–32.

38. Cf. *SCG* 3.38 in its entirety.

Chapter 5

ST. THOMAS AND THE PRINCIPLE OF CAUSALITY

INTRODUCTION

Jacques Maritain, looking back over half a century of philosophizing by Thomists, singled out as particularly remarkable Étienne Gilson's *Esprit de la philosophie médiévale* and Fr. Réginald Garrigou-Lagrange's *La philosophie de l'être et le sens commun.*[1] His interest in this latter work is not surprising when one considers his own *Sept leçons sur l'être et les premiers principes de la raison spéculative.*[2] Both books exhibit a fervent interest in and defense of the principles of identity, sufficient reason, finality, and causality.[3]

On the other hand, Étienne Gilson did not show this sort of interest in such principles. Rather, especially in "Les principes et les causes," he argued that such an interest is somewhat foreign to the type of metaphysics one finds in the writings of St. Thomas. It is not that St. Thomas would deny any of the propositions presented as first principles of speculative reason by these Thomists. It is rather that the modern interest in these propositions is symptomatic of a certain tendency to look at knowing as having some sort of independence vis-à-vis being itself. Gil-

1. See Jacques Maritain, *Le paysan de la Garonne,* Paris, 1966: Desclée de Brouwer, p. 201, n. 1. The work of Fr. Garrigou-Lagrange is actually entitled *Le sens commun, la philosophie de l'être et les formules dogmatiques,* Paris, 1909: Desclée de Brouwer.

2. Jacques Maritain, *Sept leçons sur l'être et les premiers principes de la raison spéculative,* Paris, *1932–1933:* Téqui.

3. For earlier references to Garrigou-Lagrange's book, see Maritain's *La philosophie bergsonienne,* Paris, 1948 (4th ed.): Téqui, p. 130, n. 1. This work dates from 1913, and the references to Garrigou-Lagrange are very probably original; see also Maritain's essay "La vie propre de l'intelligence et l'erreur idéaliste" (dated 1924), in *Réflexions sur l'intelligence et sur sa vie propre,* Paris, 1926 (2nd ed.): Nouvelle librairie nationale, p. 71, n. 1 (and see pp. 69–77, as regards the subject of the present essay).

son saw it as important to call attention back from the consideration of such seeming axioms to the root of all metaphysical discussion, namely, being itself.[4] In the wake of Gilson's paper, Joseph Owens published his "The Causal Proposition—Principle or Conclusion?" in which he maintained that the causal proposition, that is, some such proposition as "everything whose existence is other than its essence has its existence from something else," actually is presented by St. Thomas as the conclusion of a strict demonstration.[5] Referring expressly to Maritain's contention that the proposition "everything contingent must be caused" is a first principle of speculative reason, Fr. Owens argued that it required a demonstration.[6]

In the present paper, I propose to assemble some materials from the writings of St. Thomas which may help us form a more definite conception of the procedure in metaphysics. What kind of discussion of principles of knowledge might the metaphysician be expected to provide? Among these principles, what would count as a "principle of causality"? Such an enterprise cannot be amiss when one considers how influential the Humean view has been (i.e. that cause and effect are impossible as objects of knowledge).[7]

1. THE ARISTOTELIAN 'APORIA' AND ITS SOLUTION

Commenting on Aristotle's *Metaphysics*, book 5, St. Thomas notes the secondary meaning of the word "principle" as applying to what comes first in the order of our knowing:

4. Étienne Gilson, "Les principes et les causes," *Revue thomiste* 52 (1952), pp. 39–63:

. . . tout dépend du type de métaphysique auquel l'intellect donne son assentiment et il se peut fort bien que le Principe de causalité soit utilement explicite dans l'une alors qu'une autre n'éprouvera pas le besoin de le formuler à part. Généralement parlant, ce Principe semblera d'autant plus utile qu'une métaphysique mettra l'accent sur la nécessité formelle des preuves plutôt que sur la nécessité réelle qu'impose à l'intellect la nature même de l'actuellement existant. [p. 61]

5. Joseph Owens C. Ss. R., "The Causal Proposition–Principle or Conclusion?" *The Modern Schoolman* 32 (1955), pp. 159–171, 257–270, 323–339; cf. the same author's "The Causal Proposition Revisited," *The Modern Schoolman* 44 (1966–1967), pp. 143–151.

6. See Owens, "The Causal Proposition–Principle or Conclusion," p. 336, n. 95. Concerning the history of the controversies among Thomists in recent times as regards the principle of causality, see Raymond Laverdière, *Le principe de causalité*, Paris, 1969: Vrin.

7. See David Hume, *An Enquiry concerning Human Understanding*, ed. L. A. Selby-Bigge, Oxford, 1902 (2nd ed.): Clarendon Press, section 7, part 2:

We have sought in vain for an idea of power or necessary connexion in all the sources from which we could suppose it to be derived . . . So that, upon the whole, there appears not, throughout all nature, any one instance of connexion which is conceivable by us. All events seem entirely loose and separate. One event follows another; but we never can observe any tie between them . . . [para. 58, pp. 73–74]

But in resemblance to the order which is considered in exterior motions, there is also remarked a certain order in the knowing of things; and especially according as our intellect has some likeness of motion, proceeding discursively from principles to conclusions. *And* therefore *"principles" is said in another way: "that whence first a thing is known"*; thus, we call "principles" *of demonstration the suppositions*, i.e. the axioms and postulates.[8]

However, it is in connection with the discussions of difficulties and questions in Aristotle's book 3 that we see most reflection by St. Thomas on the metaphysician's interest in such principles. Aristotle, compiling the questions in his first chapter, asks in second place: supposing that this science is to consider the "first principles," as was said in book 1; does that mean it is to consider only the first principles of substance, or does it also pertain to this science to consider the "first principles of demonstration," for example, that this science would consider whether it comes about that one and the same thing be simultaneously affirmed and denied, or not; and similarly with the other first and self-evident principles of demonstration [*de aliis demonstrationis principiis primis et per se notis*]?[9] St. Thomas here follows Aristotle in speaking of a multiplicity of such first principles, though he gives no indication for the moment as to what he thinks the others are.

A little later, when Aristotle spells out the problem, by pointing out arguments on both sides, St. Thomas notes that Aristotle first tells us what he means by the principles of demonstration:

And he says that they are *the common* conceptions of all, *from which proceed all demonstrations*, inasmuch as (i.e.) the particular principles of the proper demonstrated conclusions have solidity in virtue of the common principles.[10]

Here, St. Thomas has replaced Aristotle's expression "common opinions" with "common conceptions," a vocabulary coming from Boethius's *De hebdomadibus*.[11] This association will be developed further later on.

Aristotle gives us here a further example of such a principle, viz. "it

---

He goes on, of course, to locate the source of our idea in the mind's experience of its own habitual anticipations:

This connexion, therefore, which we *feel* in the mind, this customary transition of the imagination from one object to its usual attendant, is the sentiment or impression from which we form the idea of power or necessary connection. [para. 59, p. 75]

8. See St. Thomas Aquinas, *CM* 5.1 (759), concerning Aristotle, *Metaph.* 5.1 (1013a14–16). Italics in our quotation indicate the words of Aristotle being explained.

9. See *CM* 3.2 (347) concerning Aristotle. *Metaph.* 3.1 (995b6–10).

10. *CM* 3.5 (387) concerning Aristotle. *Metaph.* 3.2 (996b28) (italics indicate words of Aristotle).

11. See St. Thomas Aquinas, *In librum Boetii De hebdomadibus expositio, lect. 1* (in *Opuscula theologica*, vol. 2, ed. M. Calcaterra, O.P., Turin/Rome, 1954: Marietti, nos. 14–18).

is impossible for the same thing at once to be and not to be," and St. Thomas describes it as "another principle."[12]

We should also note that at the end of his presentation here, St. Thomas sketches what will be Aristotle's answer in book 4, saying that, yes, it does belong to the philosopher to consider the axioms, inasmuch as it belongs to him to consider being in general [*ens in communi*], to which such first principles properly [*per se*] pertain. This relation to *ens* is most apparent [*maxime apparet*] in the case of the "most first principle" [*maxime primum principium*], viz. that it is impossible for the same to be and not to be.[13] This last remark is important as indicating that one principle is more obviously related to *ens* than another, even though both are first principles of demonstration.

If we turn now to St. Thomas's book 4, *lectio* 5, we find not only a presentation of Aristotle's doctrine that it is for metaphysics to consider generally *all* the principles of demonstration (and not merely the absolutely first), but also, and more important, a digression by St. Thomas so as to make clear the doctrine at issue. We should notice that Aristotle himself relates the type of propositions he has in mind to the practice of the mathematicians. He says he is speaking about what in mathematics are called "axioms." The relation to mathematics is made, St. Thomas tells us, because mathematical sciences have more certain demonstrations, and make a more obvious use of such *per se nota* propositions, reducing all their demonstrations to such principles.[14]

St. Thomas's digression is intended to clarify the link between the science that treats of substance as such and the science that treats of the first principles of demonstration. In order to do so, he primarily considers what constitutes a first principle of demonstration, i.e. that it is known to all, because it is about the most common things. And this is then related to metaphysics as treating of the common terms.

---

12. *CM* 3.5 (387) concerning Aristotle. *Metaph.* 3.2 (996b29–31):

Et exemplificat de primis principiis maxime sicut quod necesse est de unoquoque aut affirmare aut negare. Et aliud principium est quod impossibile est idem simul esse et non esse.

13. *CM* 3.5 (392):

Hanc autem quaestionem determinat Philosophus in quarto huius; et dicit, quod ad philosophum potius pertinet consideratio dignitatum, inquantum ad ipsum pertinet consideratio entis in communi, ad quod per se pertinent huiusmodi principia prima, ut maxime apparet in eo quod est maxime primum principium, scilicet quod impossibile est idem esse et non esse. . . .

14. *CM* 4.5 (588) concerning Aristotle, *Metaph.* 4.3 (1005a19–21):

Appropriat autem ista principia magis mathematicis scientiis, quia certiores demonstrationes habent, et manifestius istis principiis per se notis utuntur, omnes suas demonstrationes ad haec principia resolventes.

Thus, he begins by telling us that those propositions are known by virtue of themselves [*per se notae*] which are immediately known, upon the terms out of which they are composed being known (and for this he refers us to *Posterior Analytics*, book 1).[15] This immediate knowing happens in the case of those propositions in which the predicate is included in the definition of the subject, or in which the predicate is the same as the subject.[16] St. Thomas then points out that it happens that a proposition be *per se nota* in itself but not to all. Some people may be in ignorance of the definition of the predicate and of the subject. (And here he cites Boethius's *De hebdomadibus*, as to the existence of propositions *per se notae* only to the wise.) Those propositions are *per se notae* to all whose terms fall into the conception of all [*in conceptionem omnium cadunt*], i.e. which occur to the mind of anyone who thinks (it seems to me that St. Thomas means by "all" all minds rather than all things, in view of the reason he goes on to give). These terms are *the common ones* [*communia*], since our knowledge proceeds from common things to proper things (for this, he refers us to *Physics*, book 1).[17] Thus, those propositions are first principles of demonstration which are composed of common terms. Such terms are "whole" and "part" which yield the principle: "a whole is greater than its part"; and "equal" and "unequal," yielding: "what are equal to one and the same thing are equal to each other." And the same idea holds for similar cases. It is because the philosopher, i.e. the metaphysician, is the one to whom it belongs to consider such common terms that it belongs to him to consider these principles.

St. Thomas concludes the digression by pointing out the type of handling such propositions receive from the metaphysician. He does not demonstrate them, but rather treats of the notions of their terms, saying what is a whole and what is a part. St. Thomas does not say anything about why such treatment is required.[18]

---

15. See St. Thomas Aquinas, *Expositio libri Posteriorum* 1.7 (67 [8]), concerning Aristotle, 1.3 (72b24) (the third number in the reference to St. Thomas is to the paragraph in ed. R. M. Spiazzi, O.P., Rome/Turin, 1955: Marietti; cf. ibid., 1.5 (50 [7]), concerning Aristotle at 1.2 (72a15–19).

16. We might underline how constant St. Thomas is concerning this feature of first principles of demonstration. They are in the *first* mode of *per se* predication: see *In Post. An.* 1.10 (84 [3]), concerning Aristotle, 1.4 (73a34–37). Still, it should also be noticed that in any demonstration one of the premises must be in the *fourth* mode of *per se* predication (the predicate expressing some sort of *cause* of the subject): see *In Post. An.* 1.13 (111 [3]).

17. See St. Thomas Aquinas, *CP* (ed. P. M. Maggiòlo, O.P., Turin/Rome, 1954: Marietti; Leonine manual) 1.1 (6–8). For my use of the word "thing," in the expression "common things," see St. Thomas, *In Post. An.* 1.20 (171 [5]): "Philosophia enim prima est de communibus, quia eius consideratio est circa ipsas res communes, scilicet circa ens et partes et passiones entis."

18. *CM* 4.5 (595):

From all of this, then, we see the metaphysician as treating of a multiplicity of such principles, composed of common terms, and having the predicate included in the definition of the subject. Exploration of St. Thomas's other writings only serves to confirm and somewhat expand this doctrine. Thus, some texts stress the order to be found among the multiplicity of such first principles, an order which corresponds to the order of objects in human intellectual apprehension.[19]

2. THE PRINCIPLE OF CAUSALITY

I propose for discussion, not as the only causal principle, but certainly as a causal principle, the proposition: "an effect depends on its cause." This is not a principle simply invented in imitation of "a whole is greater than its part," for the purposes of the present reflections. We find St. Thomas using it at important moments. Thus, in *ST* 1.2.2, when explaining the possibility of demonstrating the existence of God, he makes it the basis of the argument. We read:

> ... philosophi erit considerare de omni substantia inquantum huiusmodi, et de primis syllogismorum principiis. Ad huius autem evidentiam sciendum, quod propositiones per se notae sunt, quae statim notis terminis cognoscuntur, ut dicitur primo Posteriorum. Hoc autem contingit in illis propositionibus in quibus praedicatum ponitur in definitione subiecti, vel praedicatum est idem subiecto. Sed contingit aliquam propositionem quantum in se est esse per se notam, non tamen esse per se notam omnibus, qui ignorant definitionem praedicati et subiecti. Unde Boetius dicit in libro de Hebdomadibus, quod quaedam sunt per se nota sapientibus quae non sunt per se nota omnibus. Illa autem sunt per se nota omnibus, quorum termini in conceptionem omnium cadunt. Huiusmodi autem sunt communia, eo quod nostra cognitio a communibus ad propria pervenit, ut dicitur in primo Physicorum. Et ideo istae propositiones sunt prima demonstrationum principia, quae componuntur ex terminis communibus, sicut totum et pars, ut Omne totum est maius sua parte; et sicut aequale et inaequale, ut Quae uni et eidem sunt aequalia, sibi sunt aequalia. Et eadem ratio est de similibus. Et quia huiusmodi communes termini pertinent ad considerationem philosophi, ideo haec principia de consideratione philosophi sunt.–Determinat autem ea philosophus non demonstrando, sed rationes terminorum tradendo, ut quid totum et quid pars et sic de aliis. Hoc autem cognito, veritas praedictorum principiorum manifesta relinquitur.

On this last point, cf. *CM* 3.5 (392):

> ... philosophus non considerat huiusmodi principia tamquam faciens ea scire definiendo vel absolute demonstrando; sed solum elenchice, idest contradicendo disputative negantibus ea, ut in quarto dicetur.

For a modern example of a defense of "a whole is greater than its part," see Charles De Koninck, "Random Reflections on Science and Calculation," *Laval théologique et philosophique* 12 (1956), pp. 96–100 (against Bertrand Russell). See also *CM* 11.4 (2208 and 2210): the study of quantity as quantity is proper to the metaphysician.

19. See especially *ST* 1-2.94.2:

> In his autem quae in apprehensione hominum cadunt, quidam ordo invenitur. Nam illud quod primo cadit in apprehensione est ens ... [1225b6–9].

... from any effect it can be demonstrated that its proper cause exists, if, that is, the effects of that [cause] are better known to us; because, since *effects depend on the cause*, if the effect is posited, the cause must exist by priority [*praeexistere*].[20]

This consideration thus commands the entire discussion of the five ways.

Elsewhere in the same work, speaking of the need for every creature to be conserved in its being by God, he once more makes our proposition the principle of the argument:

... the being [esse] of every creature depends on God ... For every effect depends on its cause, according as it is its cause ... [21]

Still, concerning the proposition itself there is no discussion in these passages. It is simply used as a principle, and in fact is understood within the confines of efficient causality, not as applying to all the types of causal relation.

Fortunately, on at least one occasion, St. Thomas provides us with a brief study of the proposition. This is in the slightly earlier *De potentia* presentation of God's conservation of creatures. Here is the passage which interests us:

... For it is necessary that *an effect depend on its cause.* For this belongs to the notion of effect and cause;[22] which manifestly appears in formal and material causes. For, any material or formal principle being subtracted, the thing immediately ceases to be, because such principles enter into the essence of the thing.—But it is necessary that there be the same judgment concerning efficient causes as concerning formal or material [causes]. For the efficient cause is cause of the thing according as it induces the form or disposes the matter. Hence, there is the same dependence of the thing with respect to the efficient cause as there is with

---

20. *ST* 1.2.2:

Ex quolibet autem effectu potest demonstrari propriam causam eius esse, si tamen eius effectus sint magis noti quoad nos; quia, cum *effectus dependeant a causa,* posito effectu necesse est causam praeexister. [my italics]

21. *ST* 1.104.1 (ed. Ottawa, 622b36–38):

Omnis enim effectus dependet a sua causa secundum quod est causa eius.

22. See also St. Thomas, *CP* 1.1.5 [5]:

... causae autem dicuntur ex quibus aliqua dependent secundum suum esse vel fieri ...

In this text, St. Thomas is aiming to say what precisely is said by the word "cause" as distinct from "element" and "principle." He goes on to say that Aristotle seems to be using "element" for the material cause, "principle" for the efficient cause, and "cause" for the formal and final cause: the reason?

... per "causas" autem videtur intelligere causas formales et finales, a quibus maxime dependent res secundum suum esse et fieri ... [ibid.]

He is commenting on Aristotle at *Phys.* 1.1 (184a11–12).

respect to the matter and the form, since it is through one of them [i.e. the matter or the form] that it [i.e. the thing] depends on the other [i.e. the efficient cause].—But it is necessary that there be the same judgment concerning final causes as concerning the efficient cause: for the end is a cause only inasmuch as it moves the efficient cause to act: for it is not first in being [*esse*], but only in intention. Hence, where there is no action, there is no final cause . . .[23]

What is of interest here especially is the *gradual* presentation of "an effect depends on its cause." We have, it would seem, three different levels of judgment in the matter. It *appears manifestly* [*manifeste apparet*] [24] as regards the formal and material causes. If we take away either of them, the thing no longer has being. The reason for this is that matter and form are parts of the essence, enter into the essence. The essence, as St. Thomas said in the *De ente*, is that through which and in which a being [*ens*] has being [*esse*].[25] We see how directly we have to do here with what

23. *DP* 5.1:

Effectum enim a sua causa dependere oportet. Hoc enim est de ratione effectus et causae: quod quidem in causis formalibus et materialibus manifeste apparet. Quocumque enim materiali vel formali principio subtracto, res statim esse desinit, cum huiusmodi principia intrent essentiam rei.—Idem autem iudicium oportet esse de causis efficientibus, et formalibus vel materialibus. Nam efficiens est causa rei secundum quod formam inducit, vel materiam disponit. Unde eadem dependentia rei est ad efficiens, et ad materiam et formam, cum per unum eorum ab altero dependeat. De finalibus autem causis oportet etiam idem esse iudicium quod de causa efficiente. Nam finis non est causa, nisi secundum quod movet efficientem ad agendum; non enim est primum in esse, sed in intentione solum. Unde et ubi non est actio, non est causa finalis, ut patet in III *Metaph.*

24. Joseph Owens, in "The Causal Proposition–Principle or Conclusion," p. 160, n. 1, after speaking of the controversy concerning the causal proposition as having its beginning in Hume's separating two components of the Lockean idea of effect, namely "beginning to exist" and "operation of some other being," goes on:

This background restricts the controversy to efficient causality, and rightly so. The causality of the intrinsic causes, material and formal, is self-evident once these components of a thing are distinctly grasped, while the final cause and the exemplar cause exercise their causality through the efficient cause. The difficulty lies in showing how a thing necessarily contains a relation to an efficient cause which produced it, even though that efficient causality, except in the cases of one's own conscious activity, is not immediately evident.

On the one hand, Fr. Owens's difficulty is not the one presented by Hume, since Fr. Owens thinks he has immediate evidence of the efficient causality which he exercises in his own conscious activity. On the other hand, his position is very different from that of St. Thomas, for whom the efficient causality of sensible bodies is evident:

. . . sensibiliter apparet aliqua corpora esse activa . . . [*ST* 1.115.1]

But above all it seems to me wrong to cut off the discussion from formal causality. The *DP* text shows this. Charles De Koninck, *The Hollow Universe*, London, 1960: Oxford University Press, p. 100. n. 1, appreciates the necessity of beginning any critical discussion of causality with the material and formal causes.

25. *De ente* c. 1, lines 50–52 (*Opera omnia*, t. 43. Rome, 1976: Editori di San Tommaso):

Sed essentia dicitur secundum quod per eam et in ea ens habet esse.

we mean by "a being [*ens*]." As St. Thomas says elsewhere, "something is called 'caused' because it has a cause of its being [*esse*]"[26] and "a cause is that upon which the *esse* of something else follows."[27]

"Effect" here is the thing, and "cause" means the thing's own form, or the thing's own matter.[28] To say that an effect depends on its cause is first of all to say that the being of a thing depends[29] on its form.[30]

This dependence is so immediate that, if there is a problem here, it is to see it as dependence at all. We see the need for the form in such a strong way that we scarcely see any duality. That is, from the point of view of the primacy of sense cognition for human beings, we are better off where causes are sensibly diverse things. We are better off the more "extrinsic" the cause is. Thus, in *Metaphysics* 7.17, Aristotle argues that the form is cause of being, because to say what a thing is, is really to say "why is the wood a house," where the answer might be "because of the activity of the builder" or "for the sheltering of a family." That is, he assimilates formal causality to efficient or final causality, where the duality of cause

26. St. Thomas, *In Post. An.* 2.7 (471 [2]), concerning Aristotle *Post. An.* 2.8 (93a4–7):
. . . propter hoc enim dicitur aliquid causatum, quod habet causam sui esse. Haec autem causa essendi aut est eadem, scilicet cum essentia ipsius rei, aut alia. Eadem quidem, sicut forma et materia, quae sunt partes essentiae: alia vero, sicut efficiens et finis: quae duae causae sunt quodammodo causae formae et materiae, nam agens operatur propter finem et unit formam materiae.

27. St. Thomas *CP* 2.10 (240 [15]):
. . . cum causa sit ad quam sequitur esse alterius. . . .

It should not, of course, be thought that it is the *esse* which is the caused thing: it is the subsisting thing, the composite, the thing that has *esse*, which is caused: cf. *ST* 1.45.4c. and *ad* 1; *ST* 1.3.7.*ad* 1.

28. From the properly metaphysical viewpoint, matter is quite secondary: see our paper, "St. Thomas Aquinas against Metaphysical Materialism," in *Atti del'VIII Congresso Tomistico Internazionale. V–Problemi Metafisici* (Studi Tomisticci 14), Citta del Vaticano, 1982: Libreria Editrice Vaticana, especially pp. 428–434. Nevertheless, in the order of human learning it is quite important. Cf. De Koninck, *The Hollow Universe*, p. 100, n. 1:
. . . once we have defined cause as "that upon which something depends in being or becoming," the notion of the material cause is the most obvious and certain, such as the wood of a wooden table; then that of form, e.g. the shape of the table: and any critical discussion of causality should begin with these.

29. Even the word "depends" supposes *understood* the cause/effect situation of the beings we know. One can see this in St. Thomas's *CM* 5.13, where he is commenting upon Aristotle's presentation of the notions of priority and posteriority. Thus, in para. 950, the first way in which something is prior to another "in being" (*in essendo*) involves the notion of dependence (*ratione . . . dependentiae*): "those are called 'prior' which can *be* without others and those [others] cannot be without them"; and in para. 953, all modes of priority and posteriority are said to be reducible to this one. The reason for this reducibility:
For it is clear that the prior do not *depend* on the posterior, the way the converse [is true]. Hence, all prior [things] can in some way *be* without the posterior [things] and not conversely.

30. See *ST* 1.75.6 (445b2–6); 1.50.5 (321a8–14).

and effect is more evident.[31] But St. Thomas is here speaking from the viewpoint of intellect as first of all grasping the quiddity of a thing.[32] The first intelligible conception of what is in fact causal dependence is the dependence of a thing on its matter and on its form (on its form primarily). That is, just as the first conception of all is *ens*, so the first conception of a cause is of form: "... 'a being' conveys no causal stance except that of the formal cause ..."[33] Notice that we are here considering the order of being, not the order expressed most properly by the word "cause." We know that, according to St. Thomas, it is the final cause which is first in the order of causality as such: the final cause is the cause of the causality of all the other causes, and the good is prior to being in the order of causality.[34]

"An effect depends on its cause" thus is first of all expressive of the unity of a being composed out of matter and form. The proposition expresses a *per se* unity, that of a substance itself. Still, it does more than that. It expresses dependence and priority. It means that if one were to

31. See Aristotle, *Metaph.* 7.17 (1041a25–b9). It seems to me the reduction of form to agent and end is important in this passage, even though in another way, "logically," it is the agent and end which are assimilated to the form ("what the thing is").

32. See *ST* 1.85.8 (534b5–14); 1.85.6 (532b39–42); 1.85.5 (531b12–19).

33. See *ST* 1.5.2 *ad* 2:

Ens autem non important habitudinem causae nisi formalis tantum, vel inhaerentis vel exemplaris; cuius causalitas non se extendit nisi ad ea quae sunt in actu.

34. See *ST* 1.5.2 *ad* 1:

Bonum autem, cum habeat rationem appetibilis, importat habitudinem causae finalis, cuius causalitas prima est, quia agens non agit nisi propter finem, et ab agente materia movetur ad formam; unde dicitur quod finis est causa causarum. Et sic in causando bonum est prius quam ens, sicut finis quam forma . . .

I do not believe that St. Thomas proceeds in the order he does in *DP* 5.1 merely because of intelligibility for us (as one might think from what De Koninck says, as quoted above, n. 28). Metaphysics, at least as far as it is the knowledge of being (as distinguished from its being knowledge of the first or highest substances: see *CM* 3.4.384), belongs to the domain wherein intelligibility for us and absolute intelligibility coincide: see Thomas Aquinas, *Sententia libri Ethicorum Aristotelis* 6.5 (Leonine ed., t. 47-2, Rome, 1969: Ad Sanctae Sabinae, lines 102–106 (concerning Aristotle at 1141a12–17) (ed. Pirotta, 1181):

. . . existimamus quosdam esse sapientes totaliter, idest respectu totius generis entium . . . illa quae est sapientia simpliciter est certissima inter omnes scientias, inquantum scilicet attingit ad prima principia entium, quae secundum se sunt notissima, quamvis aliqua illarum, scilicet immaterialia, sunt minus nota quoad nos. *Universalissima autem principia sunt etiam quoad nos magis nota, sicut ea quae pertinent ad ens inquantum est ens: quorum cognitio pertinet ad sapientiam sic dictam, ut patet in quarto Metaphysicae.* [my italics] [Cf. above, chapter 4, n. 19]

The causality of form is a more intelligible object, absolutely, than the causality of agent or end. The reason is that the viewpoint of being is absolutely prior to that of cause. See, for this line of thinking, *ST* 1.82.3.*ad* 1 (503b19–24); 1.13.11.*ad* 2; 1.13.11c. (89a31–b4); 1.16.4 (116b43–49); 1-2.66.3; 2-2.174.2.*ad* 3 (2282b6–9). Just as the word and the notion "virtue" is more properly applied to moral virtue, and yet intellectual virtue is a more noble and intelligible reality, so I would suggest that the formal cause is less properly called "a cause" than the final, but is a more noble and intelligible item than the efficient or final cause as such.

take away the form or the matter, one would no longer have that thing. The being of the thing, the *esse* of the thing is being considered, and is being seen as following from the matter and the form.[35]

We could say that the proposition "an effect depends on its cause," taken as referring to the composite of matter and form as having its being by virtue of the form, envelops the entire domain of discussion of Aristotle's *Metaphysics* 7: i.e. is it a *"per se"* proposition? Is the essence altogether identical with the thing whose essence it is? In things composed out of matter and form, one has neither pure logical identity nor a mere *"per accidens"* unity.[36] In a way, the form is related to the matter *per accidens,*[37] though in another way they are *per se* one and "a being."[38]

We should remember that the being [*esse*] which the composite has by virtue of the form is neither a *per accidens* accident nor a property (a *per se* accident). It belongs to the domain of substance; it is the act of the essence.[39] Thus, the triad of matter, form, and *esse*[40] included in the signification of "an effect depends on its cause" (within the limits which we are presently giving it) does not break down the *per se* unity. Still, we are expanding the domain of substance so as to consider the really existing

35. See *CM* 4.2 (558); also 9.11 (1903).

36. See *CM* 7.11 (1535–1536); also *ST* 3.2.6.*ad* 3; *Quodl.* 2.2.2.*ad* 1.

37. See *CM* 7.2 (1290), concerning Aristotle at 1029a25:

Sicut enim formae sunt praeter essentiam materiae, et ita quodammodo se habent ad ipsam per accidens, ita negationes formarum. . . .

38. See *CM* 8.5 (1767), concerning Aristotle at 1045b16–23:

Unde simile est quaerere quae est causa alicuius rei, et quae est causa quod illa res sit una: quia unumquodque inquantum est, unum est, et potentia et actus quodammodo unum sunt. Quod enim est in potentia et actus quodammodo unum sunt. Quod enim est in potentia, fit in actu. Et sic non oportet ea uniri per aliquod vinculum, sicut ea quae sunt penitus diversa. Unde nulla causa est faciens unum ea quae sunt composita ex materia et forma, nisi quod movet potentiam in actum . . .

See also St. Thomas, *In De anima* 2.1 (234) (concerning Aristotle at 412b6–9) [in ed. A. M. Pirotta, O.P., Turin, 1936: Marietti]:

Ostensum est enim in octavo Metaphysicae quod forma per se unitur materiae, sicut actus eius: et idem est materiam uniri formae, quod materiam esse in actu. Et hoc est etiam quod hic dicit, quod cum unum et ens multipliciter dicatur, scilicet de ente in potentia, et de ente in actu, id quod proprie est ens et unum est actus. Nam sicut ens in potentia non est ens simpliciter, sed secundum quid, ita non est unum simpliciter sed secundum quid: sic enim dicitur aliquid unum sicut et ens. Et ideo sicut corpus habet esse per formam, ita et unitur animae immediate, inquantum anima est forma corporis.

39. Cf. *DP* 5.4.*ad* 3 (presented below in chapter 9, n. 30); and also *Quodl.* 12.4.1 [6] (presented below in chapter 11, n. 57).

40. See St. Thomas, *Quaestiones disputatae de anima* q. 6, lines 229–240 (*Opera omnia,* t. 24, 1. Rome/Paris, 1996: Commissio Leonina/Cerf. Ed. B.-B. Bazan):

In substantiis enim ex materia et forma compositis tria invenimus, scilicet materiam, et formam, et tertium esse, cujus quidem principium est forma. Nam materia ex hoc quod recipit formam participat esse. Sic igitur esse consequitur ipsam formam, nec tamen forma est suum esse cum sit ejus principium. Et licet materia non pertingat ad esse nisi per formam, forma tamen, in quantum est forma, non indiget materia ad

substance, the concrete individual or supposit.[41] In this line of thinking one could go so far as to say that "an effect depends on its cause" is nothing less than a realistic principle of identity (substantial unity).[42]

Let us pass on to the second level of judgment, that concerning efficient causes. It is necessary that the judgment be the same concerning them, as concerning material and formal causes. What is interesting here is the *derivation*. We are dealing with the proposition "an effect depends on its cause." One might think that with something so obvious no commentary is needed. On the contrary, we are asked to consider the nature of efficient causality itself. "The efficient cause is a cause according as it induces the form or disposes the matter." Our vision of the *efficiens* as a cause is seen to derive from our vision of matter and form as causes. Only inasmuch as something comes to be associated with the originally seen dependence for being does it get the status of a cause. It is only through dependence on form that the thing has dependence on the efficient cause.

Clearly, St. Thomas sees a *problem* as regards the efficient cause, a problem which (a) does not exist for the material and formal causes, and which (b) the latter can help to resolve. This problem can only be a *seeming dissociability* of effect from cause, a seeming non-dependence of effect on cause, a possibility for the mind to lose sight of the causal relation. This seeming dissociability can have its source only in the key difference between the efficient cause and the material and formal causes, viz. that cause and effect for efficient causality are substantially diverse.[43] The remedy is to focus on the *notion* of efficient cause as that which induces the form. It is only insofar as one grasps a thing *as source of form for another thing* that one grasps it *as* efficient cause. And this is actually to see *the depending of the thing on its form* "stretched out," as it were, beyond the confines of the thing, to another thing.

What this means is that efficient causality is a different grade of intelligible object than is formal causality. Efficient causality is a relation be-

---

suum esse cum ipsam formam consequatur esse; sed indiget materia cum sit talis forma quae per se non subsistit.

[This text is discussed below, chapter 11, n. 9.]

41. See texts referred to in n. 36.

42. See *CM* 4.2 (561):

Sicut enim partes entis sunt substantia, quantitas, et qualitas, etc., ita et partes unius sunt idem, aequale, et simile. Idem enim unum in substantia est. Aequale, unum in quantitate. Simile, unum in qualitate. Et secundum alias partes entis possent sumi aliae partes unius, si essent nomina posita.

43. I leave aside the secondary case where the substance is productive of its own accident (i.e. property): see *ST* 1.77.6.

tween substances, and a real relation. That is, it has the ontological status of an accident, not a substance. As such, it requires for its intelligibility the presence, in its notion, of things outside its own "essence."[44] It must be presented with the *proper subject* to which it belongs, and the proper term of the relation.[45] The proper subject of efficient causal dependence is the dependent being as a dependent being, and this is seen in the vision of the substantial composite, with its essential causes, the matter and the form. The term of the relation is the other thing *as source of the form* of the dependent being. The proposition "an effect depends on its cause," understood as expressing the relationship of the effect of the efficient cause to the agent, signifies this vision.

Thus, the proposition has the kind of *per se* character it can have, considering that the quiddity on which it is based is an accident, not a substance. The subject is "an effect," meaning the effect of an efficient cause. Such a term signifies a relation in a subject, i.e. it says "a thing depending on another"; and the predicate merely predicates the definition "depends on another." An effect depends on its cause. One might say: "one being depends on another, and then the former is called 'an effect' and the latter 'its cause.'" However, this formulation would seem to *leave out* the proper character of the effect, as a composite of matter and form. Composition out of matter and form[46] is included in the notion of the effect. Thus, the efficient causal meaning of the principle is not *dissociable* from the formal causal meaning. The two meanings do not exist side by side, each independent of the other. One can only *add* the efficient causal meaning to the formal causal meaning. One can only *extend* the originally seen dependence of the thing from inner cause to outer cause.

3. THE PROBLEM OF HUME

The responsibility of the metaphysician for discussing the causal principle becomes indubitable when the principle is attacked. The most famous such attack in modern times is that of Hume.[47] The depth of

---

44. See St. Thomas, *CM* 7.4, in its entirety, concerning Aristotle, 1030a17–1031a14; see especially *CM* paras. 1340 and 1352.

45. See *ST* 3.2.7.*ad* 2:

. . . ratio relationis, sicut et motus, dependet ex fine vel termino, sed esse eius dependet a subiecto.

Cf. also *ST* 1.28.2 and *DP* 8.2.

46. In accordance with the text of St. Thomas being discussed (*DP* 5.1), I limit myself to the case of material substances: see *ST* 1.87.3.*ad* 1.

47. See David Hume, *A Treatise of Human Nature*, ed. L. A. Selby-Bigge, Oxford, 1888: Clarendon Press, I.III.III (pp. 78–82).

Hume's denial must be appreciated. He eliminates "cause" and "effect" as names of intelligible objects. He does not question the naturalness and appropriateness of the thoroughgoing certitude that things arise and can only arise through causes. He rather says that the source of the certitude is not knowledge, because causal connection is not a possible object of knowledge.[48] Furthermore, we must focus on the source of the strength of the Humean conviction. How can he be so sure of the impossibility of cause/effect being an object of knowledge? The source, I would say, is our appreciation of the diversity of one being from another. The key doctrine of Hume is that an effect is quite distinct from its cause. *The effect is not the cause.*[49] This is, of course, quite true, and most unambiguously true as regards efficient causality, which is the target of Hume's critique. However, it is taken as implying that from the idea of the effect, one can never arrive at a cause. One can envisage the effect without envisaging the cause.[50] Indeed, what would it be to envisage a connection? Hume stresses the "loose" character of all events, a looseness extending to every perception with respect to every other perception.[51]

48. See Hume, in *The Letters of David Hume,* ed. J. Y. T. Greig, Oxford, 1932: Clarendon Press, 1, 187: ". . . I have never asserted so absurd a Proposition as that *anything might arise without a cause:* I only maintained that our Certainty of the Falsehood of that Proposition proceeded neither from Intuition or Demonstration: but from another source" (quoted by Owens, "The Causal Proposition–Principle or Conclusion?," p. 170, n. 35). On the impossibility of causal connection as an object of knowledge, see Hume, *Treatise* I.III.XIV (p. 161): "Now nothing is more evident, than that the human mind cannot form such an idea of two objects, as to conceive any connexion betwixt them, or comprehend distinctly that power or efficacy, by which they are united." Ibid. (p. 166): ". . . the simple view of any two objects or actions, however related, can never give us any idea of power, or of a connexion betwixt them. . . ." I must admit that it seems to me that on Humean grounds we can hardly be said to have certainty of the falsehood of the proposition: something might arise without a cause. If anything, we would have certainty that it is not a proposition at all, not an intelligible discourse. No use of the word "cause" would seem to me acceptable, except as illustrative of unintelligibility. This I would say is because I regard the word "cause" as involving in its meaning the attribution of real intelligible connexion to objects (see ibid., p. 168). Hume's redefining of "cause" seems to me quite beside the point.

49. See Hume, *An Enquiry concerning Human Understanding* IV.I (para. 25, p. 29):

For the effect is totally different from the cause . . .

And ibid. p. 30:

. . . every effect is a distinct event from its cause.

50. See Hume, *Treatise* I.III.III (pp. 79–80):

. . . as all distinct ideas are separable from each other, and as the ideas of cause and effect are evidently distinct, 'twill be easy for us to conceive any object to be non-existent this moment and existent the next, without conjoining to it the distinct idea of a cause or productive principle. The separation, therefore, of the idea of a cause from that of a beginning of existence, is plainly possible for the imagination; and consequently the actual separation of these objects is so far possible, that it implies no contradiction nor absurdity . . .

51. See above, n. 7. See also *Treatise,* Appendix (pp. 634–636), especially:

What can one say to the Humean? It is true that an effect is not its cause. This is part of the truth expressed by the causal principle itself. An effect depends on something else, i.e. another thing. However, is an effect conceivable without its cause?

Suppose that the term "an effect" is taken to mean the effect of an efficient cause. Then it is naming primarily the *relation* by which one thing depends on another.[52] Looked at from the viewpoint of quiddity, looked at "logically" if one will, its whole notion is formed in function of the cause, i.e. that toward which it orders the thing which is the effect. Thus, if we mean by "the effect" the very relation to the cause, it cannot be conceived without the cause.[53] However, there are two things to note about this conception. One is that the name of any predicamental accident signifies primarily the accident itself, and only secondarily the subject of the accident, i.e. the substance in which it inheres.[54] Thus, already, on this basis, the thing which is the effect, the thing which has order through the accidental relation, is somewhat out of the picture, when one says: "an effect depends on its cause." One is not speaking to any great extent about what sort of thing is characterized as an effect. In this way, we already see some truth in the Humean contention that one can dissociate the notions of effect and cause. It is rather that effect gets split up into an item associated with cause and an item dissociated from cause. And one

---

... there are two principles, which I cannot render consistent [with, I take it, a satisfying theory of personal identity]; nor is it in my power to renounce either of them, *viz. that all our distinct perceptions are distinct existences*, and *that the mind never perceives any real connexion among distinct existences* [p. 636, his italics].

And again: ibid., I.IV.V (p. 233).

52. See St. Thomas. *DP* 7.9.*ad* 4. I have been taking it for granted that "effect of efficient cause" signifies primarily a relation, for this corresponds to St. Thomas's doctrine, especially *CM* 5.17 (1003–1005 and 1026–1029). One of the three modes of relation is of the measurable to the measure, not according to quantity, but measure of *esse* and *veritas* (1003). He explains:

Ordinatur autem una res ad aliam . . . secundum esse, prout esse unius rei dependet ab alia, et sic est tertius modus . . . [1004]

[One thing is ordered to another . . . as to being, inasmuch as the being of one thing depends on another; and this is the third mode [of relation].

He comes back to this doctrine in 1027, at the end:

. . . ab eo quaelibet res mensuratur, a quo ipsa dependet.

[. . . anything whatsoever is measured by that on which it depends.]

Notice that this is quite a distinct conception from action and passion as relatives (or, as said, of the relatives based on quantity).

53. This is the sense of "an effect depends on its cause" (an effect must have a cause, presupposes a cause, since they are correlatives) which Hume rightly (at least in a way) says cannot resolve the question: is a thing which begins to exist, an effect?

54. See St. Thomas, *CM* 5.9 (894), where he criticizes Avicenna for not having seen this point.

might make this same point starting from the side of the substance. A substance must be considerable without considering any accident (that is not to admit that any substance other than God can *be actually* in dissociation from all accidents).[55]

However, secondly, we must note a special feature of relation, which distinguishes it from other types of accident. The other types of accident, such as quantity and quality, include the substance in which they inhere in the proper quidditative notion of the accident. Quantity is the quantity *of the* substance, quality the quality *of the* substance. Relation, on the other hand, is a type of notion peculiarly devoid of quidditative content of its own. Its intrinsic notion is the "toward," faced entirely toward its term, its goal, and more associated with the thing it relates than inherent in or conceived as "of" the thing it relates. A real relation *is inherent* in the thing it relates, but its quidditative content does not include that inherence.[56] This means that, more than in the case of any other sort of accident, it is true of relation, and so of the relation which is signified by "an effect," that it says nothing about the thing in which it is. Thus, in this way also, Hume's contention makes sense, that one can think of an effect without thinking of its cause. That is, "relation to a cause" says peculiarly little about what kind of thing it is to which it properly belongs.

Still, we have not as yet addressed the question (is an effect conceivable without its cause?) in the most appropriate way. We have stayed at the level of form or quiddity, considered quite abstractly. While the object of the intellect is form, quiddity, or nature, the intellect (and not merely the senses) knows also the being actually (the *esse*) and the mode of *esse proper* to the nature. As St. Thomas says:

... the intellect knows the stone according to the intelligible *esse* which it has in the intellect, but nevertheless it [also] knows the *esse* of the stone in [its, the stone's] proper nature.[57]

This it knows first of all in its operation of composing and dividing.[58] However, it does not merely *encounter* the sensible existence of things,

55. See St. Thomas, *Quodl.* 10.2.1:

... de re aliqua possumus loqui dupliciter: uno modo secundum quod est in rerum natura; alio modo secundum quod est in consideratione nostra. Primo modo accipitur substantia rei cum omnibus suis dispositionibus et operationibus, quia sine his substantia non invenitur in rerum natura; sed secundo modo potest accipi substantia absque suis dispositionibus, quia consideratio substantiae non dependet a consideratione suarum dispositionum.

56. See St. Thomas, *ST* 1.28.2 (188a38–b15); and ibid., *ad* 2: also *Quodl.* 11.2.1 and *CM* 4.1 (539–543).

57. See *ST* 1.14.6.*ad* 1 (98a20–24).

58. See *ST* 1.14.14 *ad* 2:

but conducts itself *as intellect* with respect to such existence, i.e. discerns, to the extent possible, *what* existence is, and *what is* the proper mode of existence of the sensible natures. As St. Thomas says:

> ... the sense knows *esse* only under the aspect of the here and now, but the intellect apprehends *esse* absolutely and according to all time.[59]

In fact, there is a sequence of intelligible objects natural to the human intellect, according as there is a unity and sequence of intelligible features to be found in things. A form has its proper mode of being. When one has grasped the form, one grasps, secondly, its mode of being as *proportionate to the form.*[60]

Thus, first, we note the primacy for intellection of the grasp of quiddity or specific nature as such. This is the *"ens"* which is the object of the intellect. Such form or essence is anything but existentially neutral. It is *intrinsically* "principle of being" [*principium essendi*].[61] Through it, *esse* is

---

> ... compositio enuntiabilis significat aliquod esse rei ... [Ottawa ed. has "aliquid," seemingly a misprint].

See also *ST* 1.16.1.*ad* 3:

> ... esse rei, non veritas eius, causat veritatem intellectus ...

and *ST* 1.16.2:

> nam in omni propositione aliquam formam significatam per praedicatum, vel applicat alicui rei significatae per subiectum, vel removet ab ea.... quando iudicat rem ita se habere sicut est forma quam de re apprehendit, tunc primo cognoscit et dicit verum. Et hoc facit componendo et dividendo.

59. See *ST* 1.75.6 (445b31–34).
60. See *ST* 1.85.5 (531b12–21):

> ... intellectus humanus non statim in prima apprehensione capit perfectam rei cognitionem: sed primo apprehendit aliquid de ipsa, puta quidditatem ipsius rei, quae est primum et proprium obiectum intellectus: et deinde intelligit proprietates et accidentia et habitudines circumstantes rei essentiam. Et secundum hoc necesse habet unum apprehensum alii componere et dividere ...

Concerning the mode of being of the form or nature, see *ST* 1.5.5:

> ... praeexigitur autem ad formam determinatio sive commensuratio principiorum, seu materialium, seu efficientium ipsam: et hoc significatur per modum ...

Concerning the knowing of matter only according to its proportion to form, see *ST* 1.87.1 (540a31–36):

> ... intellectus manifestum est quod, inquantum est cognoscitivus rerum materialium, non cognoscit nisi quod est actu: et inde est quod non cognoscit materiam primam nisi secundum proportionem ad formam ...

61. See *ST* 1–2.85.6 (1181b4–11):

> ... corruptiones et defectus rerum sunt naturales, non quidem secundum inclinationem formae, quae est principium essendi et perfectionis, sed secundum inclinationem materiae, quae proportionaliter attribuitur tali formae secundum distributionem universalis agentis ...

See also *ST* 1.75.6 (445b2–6):

already known "in principle." Secondly, this principle is applied to the consideration of things as sensed and imagined, that is, to things as they exist. Thus, the intellect sees the existence of the thing as flowing from the principle, i.e. sees formal causality, and sees the unity of the principle with the mode of being, sees the "fit." Thus, St. Thomas can say:

> There are many modes of being of things. For there are some [things], the nature of which has being only in "this individual matter": and of this mode are all corporeal [things] . . .[62]

This is a universal, necessary judgment about the mode of being proper to a certain sort of nature. It is an assessment of the *per se* unity of the concrete substance. It sees the nature as "at home" in the concrete, the principle of being of the concrete, and so as presupposing the individual matter; indeed, as presupposing even the efficient cause.[63]

I am going into this issue because it seems to me that the proposition "an effect depends on its cause" belongs properly to the same order of discourse as the statements about the mode of being proper to corporeal things. This order of discourse coincides, I suggest, with what St. Thomas calls, when commenting upon Aristotle, the consideration of "being as it is divided by act and potency," which consideration is wider than that which focuses on being as divided by the categories. The latter is a division of perfect being, whereas the former includes both the perfect and the imperfect.[64] "An effect depends on its cause" expresses, first of all,

---

Esse autem per se convenit formae, quae est actus. Unde materia secundum hoc acquirit esse in actu, quod acquirit formam; secundum hoc autem accidit in ea corruptio, quod separatur forma ab ea.

62. See *ST* 1.12.4 (64b13–17):

Est autem multiplex modus essendi rerum. Quaedam enim sunt, quorum natura non habet esse nisi in hac materia individuali; et huiusmodi sunt omnia corporalia . . .

63. See above, n. 60, *ST* 1.5.5. It seems to me that, for this doctrine of our conception of the mode of being proper to corporeal natures, *CM* 7.11, the entire *lectio*, is of interest. The conception of the common matter, included in the species or quiddity of the thing, is a kind of bridge, intelligibly, from the substantial form to the individual matter. We might also remember that the nature and the mode of being together constitute a *per se* unity: see *ST* 1.29.1 (192a20–21): "Substantia enim individuatur per seipsam . . ." For our knowledge of the modes of being of forms, we should remember *ST* 1.84.1 (512a45–b7), and also *Qq. de anima* 20, *ad* 1ᵐ *sed contra* (ed. Robb, p. 262): sense knowledge also constitutes a medium for the intellect in forming its conception of things existing concretely. And see also Cajetan's commentary on *ST* 1.84.7 (521b44–522a14), to be found in the Leonine ed. of *ST, ad loc.*

64. See St. Thomas, *CM* 5.9 (889):

. . . distinguit [Aristoteles] ens, quod est extra animam, per decem praedicamenta, quod est ens perfectum . . . dividit ens per potentiam et actum: et ens sic divisum est communius quam ens perfectum. Nam ens in potentia, est ens secundum quid tantum et imperfectum . . .

the dependence of the composite of matter and form with respect to its form. It expresses, secondly, the dependence of the composite of matter and form on the source of the form. It expresses, thirdly, the dependence of the composite of matter and form on the goal which the agent, the source of the form, has in view. All of these things come into sight precisely inasmuch as one views things from the viewpoint of *esse;* as St. Thomas says: "Something is called 'caused' because it has a cause of its *esse*."[65]

Can one conceive of the effect without the cause? This question primarily means: can one think of the effect *as having being* without the cause *having being*? Can one think of the composite of matter and form without the form? (Or, can one think of the matter having being without the form?)[66] And can one think of the composite of matter and form as existing without an efficient cause?[67] To the extent that one has caught sight of the existing thing as a composite, i.e. as distinct items which nevertheless are so proportioned one to another as together to constitute a

---

One is talking about the *proportion* of the contingent to the necessary, one is using the *light* which the necessary throws on the contingent: an effect depends on its cause, or act is prior to potency. See *ST* 1.87.1 (quoted above, n. 60); also *ST* 1.86.3 and 1.79.9.*ad* 3. See also *CM* 9.5 (1826–1829), on the role of *proportion* in the grasping of act and potency.

65. See above, n. 26.

66. See *DP* 4.1; *ST* 1.66.1; *Quodl.* 3.1.1:

Omne enim quod est actu: vel est ipse actus, vel est potentia participans actum. Esse autem actu [read: actum] repugnat rationi materiae, quae secundum propriam rationern est ens in potentia. Relinquitur ergo quod non possit esse in actu nisi in quantum participat actum. Actus autem participatus a materia nihil est aliud quam forma; unde idem est dictu. materiam esse in actu, et materiam habere formam. Dicere ergo quod materia sit in actu sine forma, est dicere contradictoria esse simul; unde a Deo fieri non potest.

67. It is precisely the negative answer to this question which leads St. Thomas to an ultimate conclusion of the divine conservational causality, in the text which has constituted our starting point in this paper: *DP* 5.1, and its parallels (*ST* 1.104.1, etc.). This doctrine of our appreciation of the need for a cause necessarily involves our grasping of form as form, i.e. as something which according to its own nature transcends the material individual. In contrast to form so seen (i.e. in its proper amplitude or ontological wealth), it is then seen, according to its presence in matter, as diminished form, secondary form, form derived from form existing in a higher mode of being: see *ST* 1.3.8:

Tertio, quia nulla pars compositi potest esse simpliciter prima in entibus; neque etiam materia et forma, quae sunt primae partes compositorum. Nam materia est in potentia, potentia autem est posterior actu simpliciter . . . Forma autem quae est pars compositi, est forma participata; sicut autem participans est posterius eo quod est per essentiam, ita et ipsum participatum; sicut ignis in ignitis est posterior eo quod est per essentiam.

We see how the sensible experience of fire as "at home" in one thing and as merely "present through the influence" in the next thing leads us to the notion of derivative form. See also our paper referred to in n. 28, as well as our paper "St. Thomas, Joseph Owens and Existence," *New Scholasticism* 56 (1982), pp. 399–441.

kind of *per se* unit, one is seeing the need for the causes. One is seeing the dependence.[68]

To return to Hume, perhaps we could say that the problem he poses occurs because he requires that all intellectual knowledge be in the purely quidditative order, whereas cause and effect are intelligible objects but not the intelligible objects that occur first in our order of objects.

---

68. Hume, *Treatise* I.III.III (ed. cit., p. 79), speaking of the proposition "whatever begins to exist must have a cause of its existence," says:

> . . . all certainty arises from the comparison of ideas, and from the discovery of such relations as are unalterable, so long as the ideas continue the same. These relations are *resemblance, proportions of quantity and number, degrees of any quality, and contrariety;* none of which are imply'd in this proposition. *Whatever has a beginning has also a cause of existence.* That proposition therefore is not intuitively certain. [his italics]

See St. Thomas, *De substantiis separatis* c. 7, lines 47–52 (*Opera omnia*, t. 40, Rome 1969: Ad Sanctae Sabinae):

> Manifestum est autem quod cum ens per potentiam et actum dividatur, quod actus est potentia perfectior et *magis habet de ratione essendi;* non enim simpliciter esse dicimus quod est in potentia, sed solum quod est actu. [my italics]

I would say that the conception of "whatever begins to exist" includes the conception of the not-being *of the thing:* and that this conception necessarily involves that of the thing's being in potency (see *ST* 1.14.9). Thus, I see the Humean proposition as a consideration of degrees of a quality, taking quality in the large sense of a communicable formal perfection; it amounts to saying that that which in its own nature is a being in potency has actual being only from another. It is the discerning of a necessary relation or proportion between intelligibles. See also above, n. 52, on measure and the measurable.

Chapter 6

ST. THOMAS AND ANALOGY
The Logician and the Metaphysician

INTRODUCTION

The late Charles De Koninck, certainly someone to be revered,[1] said that "analogy is primarily a logical problem, to be used eventually in analogical naming by the metaphysician . . ."[2] Ralph McInerny, in many works over the years, and most recently in *Aquinas and Analogy*, has undertaken to spell this out.[3] It is then with considerable hesitation that I propose a criticism of the latter's position.

McInerny's book takes the form of a rejection of the system of analogical naming proposed by Cajetan, together with a proposal for a much simpler approach. Because Cajetan used in an important way, among other texts of Thomas, a lengthy reply to an objection in *Sent.* 1.19, McInerny's first chapter consists largely in a rereading of this text, in order to show, against Cajetan, that it is not a classification of types of analogy of names at all, but merely a proof that consideration of named things

---

1. Cf. Plato, *Theaetetus* 183e. Concerning De Koninck, cf. my entry: "Charles De Koninck," in *The Oxford Companion to Canadian Literature,* ed. William Toye, Toronto/New York, 1983: Oxford University Press.

2. "Metaphysics and the Interpretation of Words," *Laval théologique et philosophique* 17 (1961), pp. 22–34, at p. 33. Cf. Hyacinthe-Marie Robillard, O.P., *De l'analogie et Du concept d'être,* Montréal, 1963: Les presses de l'Université de Montréal, pp. 218–219:

> . . . rappelons que le présent Traité [Cajetan's *De nominum analogia*] est un traité de *Logique.* Sans doute, en effet, métaphysiciens, théologiens, scientistes mêmes, font-ils usage de l'analogie, mais ils n'en dissertent point; du moins, s'ils se permettent à l'occasion d'en discuter et d'en fixer les règles, ils ne le font qu'à leurs risques et périls, s'engageant dans une discipline étrangère à leur spécialité. L'analogue, en effet, comme le genre, l'espèce etc. est un être de seconde intention, une construction de l'esprit qui intéresse, immédiatement, le Logicien . . .

3. McInerny, Ralph, *Aquinas and Analogy,* Washington, D.C., 1996: The Catholic University of America. References to this work will be in the body of my text, simply noting the page number.

from the viewpoint of their being is incidental to analogy of names, properly so called.

It is not my purpose to defend Cajetan in this matter. However, I do wish to affirm that the *Sent.* 1.19 text, a text which was used very effectively by Johannes Capreolus to combat the metaphysical errors of Duns Scotus and Peter Auriol,[4] is truly meant as a classification of types of analogy of names.

I am quite happy to say that the analogy of names pertains to logic. For example, we see Thomas treat the modes of unity presented in *CM* 5.8 (876–880): numerical, specific, generic, and *analogical*, as a logical presentation, i.e. in function of logical notions [*secundum intentiones logicales*]. Analogy is thus presented as one of the logical *intentiones*.[5] Nevertheless, I wish to discuss the idea of logic and the relation of logic to metaphysics (and, to a certain extent, to other sciences of things).

METAPHYSICS AND LOGIC

Logic exists because of the difference between the mode of being of material things in their own nature and the mode of being which those same things have in human intellection. Like all knowers, we consider things according to the being which they have in reality, i.e. outside of knowledge, but unlike some knowers we are also able to consider things according to the being which they have in the mind, and to *compare* the thing as found in the two modes.[6] It is in this comparison that we form the notions of "genus" and "species," "individual," etc., which Thomas calls the "logical notions."[7]

However, logic itself, as a science,[8] is of modest extent. It pertains to the general introduction to the sciences. It is to be taught before the sci-

---

4. Capreolus, *Defensiones theologiae divi Thomae Aquinatis*, 1.2.1 [ed. C. Paban and T. Pègues, Turonibus, 1900: Alfred Cattier, t. 1, pp. 117–144] asks whether God is intelligible for us in the state of the way (i.e. in the present life). The ninth conclusion is that by the same concept by which the wayfarer conceives of the creature it can conceive of God, though the name signifying that concept is not said univocally of God and of the creature. Cf. 124b–125a for the use of the *Sentences* text. On Capreolus's use of the text, cf. my paper: "Does Being Have a Nature? (Or: Metaphysics as a Science of the Real)," in *Approaches to Metaphysics*, ed. William Sweet, Dordrecht, Holland, 2004: Kluwer Academic Publishers, pp. 23–59.

5. Thomas is there commenting on Aristotle, *Metaph.* 5.6 (1016b31–1017a3).

6. Cf. *ST* 1.14.6.*ad* 1; 1.16.4.*ad* 2; 1.16.2; 1.84.1. Thomas accuses Plato of failing to appreciate the possibility of our having a mode of knowing of material things different from the mode of being proper to the things themselves (*ST* 1.84.1): this suggests why in a Platonism metaphysics and logic would tend to be identified.

7. Cf. *Sent.* 1.2.1.3 (ed. Mandonnet, p. 67); also, *CM* 4.4 (572–577, especially 574); and 6.4 (1233). Cf. also *De ente et essentia*, c. 3 (Leonine ed., lines 73–119).

8. Cf. *CM* 4.4 (577), concerning the "demonstrative part of logic" (not to be confused with dialectic as demonstrative (576)).

ences which bear upon things, and it teaches the method common to all. As such, it has an extremely limited outlook. We are accustomed to the idea of such sciences as mathematics and physics being contrasted with metaphysics, in that the two former are particular sciences, cutting out some part of being and treating of it.[9] So also, but even more so, the science of logic is of limited outlook, being meant to consider the points of method common to all rational undertakings. Each special science of things has its own peculiarities of method, and these are to be treated when the sciences themselves are taught, toward the beginning of the presentation of the science.[10] Thus, Aristotle, in *Physics* 2, presents the nature of physics in contrast to mathematics, and also to metaphysics.[11]

Whose responsibility is the doctrine of method in the special science? To the extent that it requires the comparison of diverse sciences, it is the responsibility of the metaphysician. One of the main arguments for the existence of metaphysics is the need for a science which considers the principles common to all the sciences.[12]

Indeed, this is so much the case that the principles of some sciences are simply given to that science by the metaphysician. St. Thomas gives the example of geometry which obtains from metaphysics the definition of magnitude, its subject genus.[13] This is also the case with logic. Whose

---

9. Cf. *CM* 7.1 (1147). On the limits of physics as compared to metaphysics, cf. above, chapter 4.

10. *CM* 2.5 (335):

[Aristotle] shows what is the appropriate method of seeking truth; and . . . firstly he shows how man can know the appropriate method in the quest for truth . . . He says . . . that diverse people seek the truth by virtue of diverse methods, therefore it is necessary that a man be instructed in what way [*per quem modum*] in each of the sciences [*in singulis scientiis*] the things said are to be taken [*sint recipienda ea quae dicuntur*].

And because it is not easy for a man to grasp two things at once, but rather while looking toward two he can grasp neither, it is absurd for a man simultaneously to seek science and the method which is appropriate to science. And because of this one ought to learn logic previously to the other sciences, because *logic treats of the common method of proceeding in all the other sciences*. However, *the method proper to each of the sciences ought to be treated in the individual sciences, toward the outset.* [My italics.]

11. Cf. *CP* 2: Thomas presents the whole of book 2 of the *Physics* as treating of "the principles of natural *science*": cf. 2.1 (ed. Maggiòlo, 141), and we get such questions as how the physicist and the mathematician differ (2.3) and on the basis of which sorts of cause the physicist demonstrates: cf. 2.5 (176). At 2.4 (175), we see a contrast between the physicist's interest in form and the metaphysician's interest in form.

12. Cf. *CM* prologue: without a knowledge of the things metaphysics teaches, one cannot fully know the things proper to a genus or species; metaphysics is described as maximally intellectual and thus *regulative* of all the sciences. In *CP* 1.1 (4), we are taught that Aristotle's *Physics* is placed at the beginning of the study of natural science, just as *first philosophy*, i.e. metaphysics, is placed before *all* of the sciences; this is because it treats of what is common to beings as such.

13. Cf. *CM* 6.1 (1149); the geometer receives from the metaphysician the answer to the question: what is magnitude? i.e. the very essence of the "subject genus" of the science of geometry; the example is not in Aristotle, but is supplied by Thomas.

responsibility is it to define the genus, the species, and, we can add, the analogue? Aristotle is explicit, and Thomas takes no exception to his doctrine on this point. *To investigate genus and species is proper to the metaphysician, since they pertain properly to being as being.*[14]

Accordingly, when Thomas writes his short overall view of the metaphysical world, the *De ente et essentia*, he spends a good part of it discussing genus and species, finding this crucial for the presentation of essence in material substances, but also explaining what is to be said concerning the divine essence in this regard, and how genus and species are found in separate substance and in accidents.—What is proper to the notion of the genus, as found in material things, is its being a name for the whole, but one derived from the (common) matter. This tie of the genus to matter is crucial for Thomas's treatment of "body" as an analogical name, metaphysically speaking, when used in common for the corruptible and the incorruptible (i.e. celestial) body.[15] In the subsequently inserted disputed question found in *Sent.* 1.2,[16] on *ratio* in things, we see the importance of genus and species having a foundation in things, if they are to be distinguished from chimeras from the viewpoint of truth.[17]

But all of this is beyond the ken of the logician, who receives the doctrine of genus and species from the metaphysician. The logician's outlook is limited to things from the viewpoint of their mode of being in the intellect.[18] Indeed, his outlook, even about logical *intentiones*, does

14. Cf. *CM* 4.4 (587), concerning Aristotle at 4.2 (1005a13–18):

[The metaphysician] . . . considers the prior and the posterior, genus and species, whole and part, and others things of this sort, because these also are accidents of that which is inasmuch as it is that which is [*accidentia entis inquantum est ens*].

15. On this, cf. *CM* 10.12 (2137 [2]; and 2138–2142; and 2145). This doctrine figures in an important way later in this essay.

16. *Sent.* 1.2.1.3. This item is a disputed question, probably written about 1265–67, and inserted by Thomas in his *Sent.;* cf. James Weisheipl, *Friar Thomas D'Aquino, His Life, Thought, and Work*, Garden City, N.Y., 1974: Doubleday, p. 366 and p. 359. See especially A. Dondaine, O.P., "Saint Thomas et la dispute des attributs divins (I *Sent.*, d. 2, a. 3): authenticité et origine," *Archivum Fratrum Praedicatorum* 8 (1938), pp. 253–262.

17. Concerning logic, I have noted Aristotle's statement that it is the metaphysician who considers what genus and species are. In this respect, I would refer not only to *De ente et essentia* 2 and 3 (and especially 2, wherein we get the definitions of the genus and the species), but also to *De substantiis separatis* c. 6 (Leonine ed., lines 74–77; ed. Spiazzi, 70), where, in criticizing the position of Gebirol, Thomas says that it does away with *the principles of logic*, doing away with the true notion of the genus and the species and the substantial difference, inasmuch as it changes all into the mode of accidental predication. Now, no particular science really provides the definition of its principles, not even logic. It seems to me clear that it is the metaphysician who provides the logician with the definitions of the principles. But the logician accepts them only in a limited way, by mere "logical consideration."

18. It is true that he is closer, in treating of names, to the concept's relation to things themselves than is the mere grammarian. Cf. *In Peryermenias* 1.2 (Leonine ed., lines 49–55, in t. I* 1, 1989: Commissio Leonina and Vrin):

not coincide with that of the metaphysician, who considers beings as be-ings.[19]

Let us recall the occasion in the *Metaphysics* in which Aristotle argues that a universal cannot be a substance, because a substance is not "said about something." Thomas introduces the obvious possible objection that what is proper to substance is, rather, that it cannot be "*found in something.*" Being "*said of* something" is attributed to secondary sub-stance in Aristotle's own *Categories*. Thomas's reply is of interest:

> . . . But it is to be said that the Philosopher is speaking in accordance with logical consideration [*secundum logicam considerationem*] in the *Categories*. Now, the logi-cian [*logicus*] considers things inasmuch as they are in the reason [*res secundum quod sunt in ratione*]; and so he considers substances inasmuch as according to the intellect's grasp [*secundum acceptionem intellectus*] they lie under the intention of universality [*subsunt intentioni universalitatis*]. And thus, as regards predication, which is an act of reason, he says that they are predicated "of a subject" [*de sub-jecto*], i.e. of a substance subsisting outside the soul. But the primary philosopher considers things [*de rebus*] according as they are beings [*entia*]; and so in his con-sideration "being *in* a subject" and "being *about* a subject" do not differ. For here "being said of a subject" [*dici de subjecto*] is taken as regards that which is in itself some thing and is present in an actually existing subject [*quod est in se aliqua res et inest alicui subjecto existenti in actu*]. And it is impossible that this be a substance. For thus it would have being *in* a subject. Which is against the notion of sub-stance, [a point] which is had even in the *Categories*.[20]

The logician hears something of what the metaphysician says, but cannot be concerned with the whole of it.

Thus, we can expect that logic itself will provide only a rather super-ficial account of genus or species, and that the application of such *inten-tiones* in this or that science, including metaphysics, will require a special treatment.—So also, the account of *analogy* given by logic cannot be ex-pected to do the job that a metaphysician will do, either as presenting logic with its principles or as explaining their application in metaphysics itself.

There is another extremely important feature of the relation between the *intentiones* of logic and the science of metaphysics which should be

---

. . . But because logic is ordered toward knowledge to be obtained concerning things [*de rebus sumendam*], the signification of vocal utterances, which is immediately relat-ed to the very conceptions of the mind [*inmediata ipsis conceptionibus intellectus*], per-tains to its principal consideration, whereas the signification of letters, inasmuch as it is more distant [from our conceptions], does not pertain to its consideration, but rather to the consideration of the grammarian . . .

19. Cf. *CM* 4.5 (591), concerning the limited outlook the physicist has regarding the first principles of demonstration.

20. *CM* 7.13 (1576), concerning Aristotle at 7.13 (1038b15–16).

considered. It is mentioned by Thomas in connection with Boethius's definition of the person. An objector, criticizing the Boethian definition, viz. "an individual substance of a rational nature," points out that "individual" is not the name of a thing outside the mind, but is rather a logician's consideration; not the name of a *"res,"* but merely of an *"intentio";* and yet the person is a *real* thing. Boethius's definitional procedure is thus, he claims, unsuitable.

Thomas replies, explaining carefully the meaning of "individual" in the definition. We read:

> . . . because substantial differences are not known to us, or else are not named, it is necessary sometimes to use accidental differences in place of substantial [differences], for example, if someone were to say: "fire is a simple, hot, and dry body"; for proper accidents are the effects of substantial forms, and reveal them. And similarly the names of logical notions [*intentiones*] can be accepted in order to define real things [*res*], inasmuch as they are accepted *in the role of some names of real things which* [*names*] *have not been invented.* And thus this name "individual" [*individuum*] is inserted in the definition of the person in order to signify the mode of subsisting, which belongs to particular substances [*modum subsistendi qui competit substantiis particularibus*].[21]

That the logical intention called "analogy" is used in this way by Thomas is clear. For example, consider *ST* 1.4.3, whether some creature can be like God. This is obviously a metaphysical question, a question about the intrinsic being of creatures. The notion of likeness involves community of form. The question is answered on the basis of the doctrine that every agent causes something like itself, so that in any effect there must be a likeness of the form of the agent. Degrees of such likeness are sketched, and it is true that logical notions of species and genus are used to describe these degrees of likeness, but clearly this is a use of logical notions as stand-ins for metaphysical conceptions. Ultimately one reasons to the case of the divine agent as "not contained in any genus." Here *the similarity of the effect to the cause* is called "according to some sort of analogy" [*secundum aliqualem analogiam*]. Notice that we proceed from the species to the genus to the analogously one. Thomas explains what he means:

> . . . as being itself is common to all [*sicut ipsum esse est commune omnibus*]. And in this way those things which are from God are assimilated to him inasmuch as

---

21. *ST* 1.29.1.*ad* 3. In *DP* 9.2.*ad* 5, on the same point, we have:

. . . "individual" is inserted into the definition of the person in order to signify the individual mode of being [*ad designandum individualem modum essendi*].

At *Sent.* 1.25.1.1 [ed. Mandonnet, p. 601], the discussion of Boethius's definition of "person," note how different is Thomas's handling of *"individua"* than in *ST* 1.29.1 and *DP* 9.2; in the *Sent.* it is still merely the name of an *intentio.*

they are beings [*inquantum sunt entia*], as to the first and universal principle of being in its entirety [*totius esse*].

And one could cite many prominent texts in this line.[22]

I notice in McInerny's conclusion, "The Point of the Book," that he says:

My second thesis is that Thomas never speaks of the causal dependence in a hierarchical descent of all things from God as analogy. That is, terminologically speaking, there is no analogy of being in St. Thomas. [162]

McInerny is surely in error on this point. Thomas uses logical terms as stand-ins for metaphysical terms.

THOMAS'S 'SENTENCES' ANALOGY PRESENTATION

The text which McInerny interprets, *Sentences* 1.19.5.2.*ad* 1,[23] occurs in a discussion of the point: whether all things are true [*vera*] by virtue of the uncreated truth [*veritate increata*]. Thomas's general answer will be that, just as there is the one divine *esse*, the efficient exemplar cause by virtue of which all things *are*, and yet each thing has its own *esse* by which formally it *is*, so also there is one divine truth by which all are true, as by an efficient exemplar cause, and yet there are the many truths in created things by which formally they are called "true." In the *ad* 2 it is clear that it is the created *things*, taken in their own being, which are viewed as measures of our intellect and so are viewed as formally containing "truths."[24]

The first objector, holding that only in God himself is there truth [*veritas*], bases his argument on the doctrine of the preceding article, that "the true" [*verum*] is said analogically. Using the standard model of "healthy," he argues that this means that truth is found only in God, and that other things are called "true" by reference to God.[25] Thomas replies:

. . . it is to be said that something is said according to analogy in three ways [*aliquid dicitur secundum analogiam tripliciter*]: either according to notion only and not according to being [*secundum intentionem tantum et non secundum esse*]: and this is when one notion [*una intentio*] is referred to several [things] through priority

22. Cf. e.g. *Sent.* 2.1.1.1 [ed. Mandonnet, pp. 12–13]: the *"natura entitatis,"* by which is meant the act of being, is one *"secundum analogiam"* in all creatures, with a unity sufficiently real to imply the unity of the first principle of all, i.e. the Creator.

23. Mandonnet, p. 492.

24. Mandonnet, pp. 492–493. Thus the doctrine is significantly different from that in *ST* 1.16.6 (118a49–b19); there, there is no formal truth *(veritas)* in things. See my paper: "Is Truth a Transcendental for St. Thomas Aquinas?" *Nova et Vetera* [English edition] 2 (2004), pp. 1–20.

25. Mandonnet, p. 491.

and posteriority, which nevertheless has being only in one: for example, the notion of health [*intentio sanitatis*] is referred to the animal, the urine, and the diet in diverse measures [*diversimode*], according to priority and posteriority; not nevertheless according to diverse being, because the being of health is only in the animal.

Or else, [something is said according to analogy] according to being and not according to notion [*secundum esse et non secundum intentionem*]; and this occurs when many things are taken as equal [*parificantur*] in the notion [*in intentione*] of something common, but that common item does not have being of one intelligible character [*esse unius rationis*] in all: as for example, all bodies are taken as equal in the notion of corporeity [*in intentione corporeitatis*]; hence, the logician [*logicus*], who considers only notions [*intentiones tantum*], says that this name "body" is predicated of all bodies univocally; however, the being of this nature [*esse hujus naturae*] is not of the same intelligible character [*ejusdem rationis*] in corruptible and incorruptible bodies; *hence, for the metaphysician and the physicist, who consider things according to their being, neither this name, "body," nor any other [name] is said univocally of corruptibles and incorruptibles,*[26] as is clear from *Metaph.* 10, text 5, from [both] the Philosopher and the Commentator.[27]

Or else, [something is said according to analogy] according to notion and according to being [*secundum intentionem et secundum esse*], and this is when they are not taken as equal either in the common notion [*in intentione communi*] or in being; the way, for example, "a being" is said of substance and accident; and in such [cases] it is necessary that the common nature [*natura communis*] have some being in each of those things of which it is said, but differing according to the intelligible character [*rationem*] of greater or lesser perfection.

And similarly I say [*dico*] that "truth" and "goodness" and all such [items] are said analogically [*dicuntur analogice*] of God and creatures. Hence, it is necessary that according to their being all these be in God and in creatures according to the intelligible character [*secundum rationem*] of greater and lesser perfection; from which it follows, since they cannot be according to one being [*esse*] in both places, that there are diverse truths [*diversae veritates*].[28]

In this, it is quite clear that all three classifications are cases of *analogy*. The middle one is univocity, not analogy, for the logician, but is not univocity, indeed is analogy, for the metaphysician and the physicist. More is included in the metaphysician's notions of univocity and analogy than in the logician's notions of these *intentiones*.

The point of the objector was that since analogy was on the scene, one should conceive of it on the model of "healthy," and thus conclude that there is not truth in the creatures called "true." Thomas could have

---

26. These italicized words are omitted from the Latin and from the English translation by McInerny in his presentation on p. 6.

27. For examples of this sort of analogy, and the denial of its univocity, cf. *SCG* 1.32 (285) and *DP* 7.7.*ad* 6.

28. Mandonnet, p. 492.

answered this by merely distinguishing between type 1 and type 3. That is, he could have said that there are two sorts of analogy, one which is merely causal and one which is more essential (somewhat as he will reply to the objector in *ST* 1.13.6.*ad* 3). Instead, he deliberately set out a threefold classification, and one in which the middle member makes the remarkable point that there is a type of term which a logician sees as univocal and a metaphysician sees as analogical. Of course, the middle position does help to make us think about the roles of *esse* and *intentio*, and the *ratio* that the common item has according to *esse*. But is there truly a systematic unity here? We will see that there is.

Again, our interest is not in the question: did Cajetan read this text well? Nor: did Cajetan speak well about analogy? It is rather: what has McInerny done with the above text? Is he reading it as Thomas meant it?

THE MCINERNY READING OF THE 'SENTENCES' TEXT

Having sketched my idea of Thomas's view of the difference between the logician and the metaphysician, and presented the key text for our present purpose, I come to how McInerny reads *Sent.* 1.19. His argument for its interpretation focuses on the *second* mode, which he holds is *not meant as a sort of analogy of names at all*. He even regards it as *showing* that the distinctions the reply mentions as between the first and third modes are *incidental* to analogy as such.

At p. 11, McInerny thinks he has shown that there is something wrong with Cajetan's division of analogy into types, based as it is on the text of 1.19. But, posing an objection to his own procedure, he asks whether Cajetan is not justified in using in the way he does a text which begins with the words:

. . . something is said according to analogy in three ways . . .

He then gives us his own reduction of Thomas's reply to its essential message:

The response to the objection comes down to this. The feature *secundum esse* of things named healthy analogously is *per accidens* to their being named analogously. Other things named analogously have a different feature *secundum esse*. If some analogous names have feature X and other analogous names do not, feature X is accidental to their being analogous names. To underscore this point, Thomas notes that you can find the same variation *secundum esse* in univocal terms. [p. 11]

The last sentence refers to the second mode passage, held by McInerny to be about "*univocal* terms"!

This is a remarkable rewrite of the answer to an objection. In doctrine, I might suggest, it apes such a text as *ST* 1.26.1.*ad* 3, on whether God has beatitude. The objector there argues that beatitude is the *prize* for virtue, and that neither merit nor prize befits a God. Thomas answers:

. . . to be the prize for virtue *happens* to beatitude or felicity inasmuch as someone *acquires* beatitude; just as to be the terminus of generation *happens* to a *being* inasmuch as [the being] issues forth from potency into act. Hence, just as God has being, though he is not generated, so also he has beatitude, though it is not merited.

That is, Thomas knows how to make this sort of argument. One should wonder, say I, why he did not simply make it where McInerny wants to read it.[29]

McInerny wants us to reduce analogy to the issue of "*secundum intentionem.*" Thus, he says:

There can be inequality, a relation *per prius et posterius*, both *secundum intentionem* and *secundum esse*. The FORMER is what is in play when we talk of a term being used analogously. [p. 12, my small caps]

Now, of course, this is true for McInerny, the logician. Thomas Aquinas's *explicit* point is that this is not true for the metaphysician or the natural philosopher. *They* say that the issue of "*secundum esse*" difference regarding a term such as "body" makes this an *analogous* term.

If we take the presentation of his argument from the beginning, I regret to note that what we first see, on p. 6, is that McInerny, aiming to quote the crucial text of Thomas, *inadvertently leaves out the key passage in the middle case concerning the metaphysician and the physicist.* (For clarity on this, in quoting the passage earlier, I used italics to show the exact passage.) This is alarming, since so much of McInerny's argument discourages the reader from seeing such things as univocity and analogy as having a peculiarly metaphysical interest. They are the proper preserve of the logician, he tells us.—Still, this is just a very bad typographical error (one, nevertheless, which carries over from the Latin to the English translation, given in the footnote!).

When he goes on to discuss what Cajetan has done with the text, McInerny provides his own analysis. He claims that the logician in the text is the dialectician, not the logician in the sense of the thinker who gives a

---

29. This point of McInerny's, that the distinctions in *Sent.* 1.19 are *per accidens* as regards analogy of names, runs through his whole book. Thus, after telling us (erroneously) that Thomas does not use the terminology of "analogy of being," he says that, if he had, he would have made it clear that whether or not there is the same order in the *things* named, as regards their being, as there is in the *names* used about the things, is *per accidens,* having nothing intrinsically to do with the analogy of names or the analogy of being. [p. 162]

definition of "genus" and "named univocally" and "named analogically." [p. 8] This in itself is not clear to me. The basis for the discussed difference concerning "body" is the doctrine that the genus is a name for a thing taken from the side of the matter. The reason why "body" is different from a genus such as "animal" is that the things called "animals," though they have natures which are ordered according to more perfect and less perfect, nevertheless have at bottom the same sort of matter: the genus has a foundation in reality which is one. In the case of "body," the matter of the corruptible is of a different order than that of the incorruptible. Hence, the genus "body" is called "logical," in the sense that it does not have the sort of foundation in reality that genera of generable and corruptible things have.—All of that sort of theory seems to me to pertain to the metaphysician (and the physicist), not to *any* logician. It has to do with that conception of the logical notion which includes the notion's foundation in reality. That is, it has to do with the *full* definition of those logical notions, not the sort of definition of them which satisfies the logician.[30]

I notice also that McInerny tells his reader that the metaphysician, faced with the "dialectician" calling "body" univocal, calls it "equivocal." [p. 9] He seems not to want to let the reader face the fact that Thomas has said that this middle item is a case of something being "said according to analogy"!

McInerny actually uses the (in this aspect, regrettable) doctrine of Cajetan, that the middle case is true of *any* genus, even e.g. "animal," in order to argue that Thomas is not really teaching us about types of analogy at all in the text.[31] We read:

30. On this, cf. *CM* 10.12 (2137 [2]; and 2138–2142; and 2145). In 2142 we read:

... But no matter what genus be taken, it is necessary that corruptible and incorruptible be [intrinsic] to its notion. Hence, it is impossible that they communicate in any genus. And it is reasonable that this happen. For there cannot be one matter of corruptibles and incorruptibles. But *the genus, physically speaking,* is taken from matter. Hence, it was said above that those things which do not have matter in common are generically diverse. But, *logically speaking,* nothing prevents their agreeing in *genus,* inasmuch as they agree in one common notion [*in una communi ratione*] whether of substance or of quality or of something of that sort.

Obviously, it is the word "genus" which is *differently defined* by the physicist and by the logician. Hence arise two different "ways of speaking." And we can expect the same thing with the word "analogy."

31. Cf. Thomas de Vio Cajetan, *De nominum analogia,* c. 1, in *De l'analogie et Du concept d'être,* ed. Hyacinthe-Marie Robillard, O.P., Montréal, 1963: Les presses de l'Université de Montréal, para. 15 (corresponds to para. 5 in the edition of Zammit and Hering): "Omne enim genus, analogum hoc modo appelari potest . . ." McInerny refers to this text on p. 9, n. 4. Cf. Armand Maurer, "The Analogy of Genus," *The New Scholasticism* 29 (1955), pp. 127–144, who notes that "[of late] the consensus of opinion . . . is that the analogy of genus is not in the long run a true metaphysical analogy." [p. 127] Fr. Maurer does not, himself, join this consensus. One should note, nevertheless, that his expression "analogy of genus" is itself somewhat Cajetanian by suggestion.

... the second member of Thomas's division of things said according to analogy makes it clear that inequality *secundum esse* is irrelevant to what is meant by
an analogous name, just as inequality *secundum esse* is irrelevant to the univocal
character of generic terms. In short, Thomas is noting that there are inequalities,
orderings *per prius et posterius,* among things talked about that do [10] not affect
our way of talking about them . . . [9–10]

This is not true. The second member is a member of a group, each of
which is a case of things said according to analogy. In that second member, though the logician sees only univocity, the metaphysician, Thomas
is telling us, sees analogy *in the names.* This is because his mode of consideration of things is different from that of the logician. The metaphysician incorporates into the meaning of the *name* of the thing differences
in the mode of being of the things given the common name. For him,
"body" has two different meanings, as used of the natures of corruptible
and incorruptible substances. A genus such as "animal," *pace* Cajetan and
McInerny, is quite a different case.

Unless one thinks that Thomas is criticizing the metaphysician here,
accusing him of a mistake (obviously this is not so), this is what is being
said.

But we must not miss how far McInerny is willing to go in defense of
his thesis. On p. 13, still attempting to explain to us the threefold analogy text in the *Sentences,* he tells us:

Why, then, does Thomas introduce these three accidental conjunctions with the
remark that something is said according to analogy in three ways? It is already
clear that he cannot be taken to mean that there are three kinds of analogous
name. When analogy is used to speak of a kind of naming, there is an inequality, an order *per prius et posterius,* among the intentions it signifies. Thus, when
there is inequality *secundum esse,* the term "analogy" can be used to refer to it.
Then we can say that talk of inequality can conjure up three different states of affairs *(aliquid dicitur secundum analogiam tripliciter).* Sometimes (1) there is inequality of meaning (and thus an analogous name), but the denominating quality is
not multiplied in the things named so that it exists in them equally or unequally.
Sometimes (2) there is inequality among things named univocally. We might put
this as "proper inequality," or "specific inequality," or "*inaequalitas secundum rationes proprias.*" Finally, sometimes (3) there is a conjunction of order and inequality
among a plurality of notions of a common term *and* unequal, more or less perfect, existence of the denominating quality in the things talked about. [p. 13]

If this is to be read as an answer to the question with which it begins, we
must think that Thomas really meant to speak of three ways in which
inequality is found (thus, McInerny's remarkable rewrite: ". . . talk of *inequality* can conjure up three different *states of affairs*" [!]). McInerny, in
his eagerness to convince us, even begins composing a Latin text that

Thomas should have supplied us with: *"inaequalitas secundum rationes pro-prias"!* But Thomas Aquinas did not say that. He said "analogy," and even "something is *said* according to analogy . . ."

To accept the "explanation" of McInerny, we must understand the middle item, the (2), as using "analogy" in a different sense: not about *naming,* but about inequality in the *being* of the things named. But this is an explanation which *flies in the face of the text.* The text does not say that the thing is spoken of univocally, but that what is being spoken of does not have the equality which the univocal way of naming (all that is seen by the logician) might lead one to believe it had. It says:

. . . for the metaphysician and the physicist, who consider things according to their being, neither this *word* [*nomen*] "body," nor anything else [i.e. any other name or word], is *said* univocally of corruptibles and incorruptibles . . .

Clearly, we are speaking about how people understand *words.* The *logicus* understands them in one way and the metaphysician and physicist in an-other.—This is quite against the McInerny reading.

Coming back to McInerny's argument to show that the threefold divi-sion in *Sent.* 1.19 is not a division of kinds of analogy, I would say that if we grant him his conception of defining the genus, the species, analogy, etc., then what he says will follow. But we should not do so. The very text of 1.19, in the part on the middle mode, tells us that one thinker has a different conception of "univocity" than the other has: they agree that there is only one *intentio,* but they differ as regards the importance of the difference in the case. It is not enough, according to the metaphysician, to have one *intentio* for *univocity.* One must have the same kind of mat-ter.[32]—Or, if one will, we can say that the two do not speak one language as regards what is "one notion." But the reason they do not is that they

---

32. McInerny says:

The question must arise as to whether the *logicus* of the present text has a different conception of univocal or equivocal terms from the philosopher. Surely they agree on what such terms mean but disagree as to whether the things being talked about can provide a *ratio communis* which is found equally in them.

I say: no, they speak different languages; hence, the need to qualify the word "genus" with the mode of consideration being used. For example, in *ST* 1.66.2.*ad* 2 we read:

. . . si genus consideretur physice, "corruptibilia et incorruptibilia non sunt in eodem genere," propter diversum modum potentiae in eis, ut dicitur 10 *Metaph.* Secundum autem logicam considerationem, est unum genus omnium corporum, propter unam rationem corporeitatis. [. . . if the genus is considered physically, "corruptibles and in-corruptibles are not in the same genus," because of the diverse mode of potency in them, as is said in *Metaph.* 10. However, according to logical consideration there is one genus of all bodies, because of the one notion of corporeity.]

And cf. *ST* 1.88.2.*ad* 4.

have no agreement, either, on what "notion" means. "Being based on the matter" pertains to the *notion* of a genus, according to the metaphysician, but this is not in the *"notion"* of the genus, according to the logician. The net result is that the logician never has the last word, not even on "genus" or "univocity" or "analogy of names."[33]

CONCLUSION

Let us consider one last time the objection to which Thomas is replying. The objector wanted to locate truth in God alone, all other things being called "true" relative to God. His middle term was that it had already been established that "true" is said analogically concerning those things in which there is truth. This led him to introduce the model of "healthy" and to conclude that truth is in God alone. Obviously Thomas could have answered that in some cases of things said analogously what the objector says applies, but other cases exist in which what is said analogously is found in all the things spoken of, though according to more and less. Had he deigned to explain why this difference exists, he could have spoken of modes of causality.[34] If he were McInerny, he would have gone on to say that whether or not the nature is found in all the things said by analogy is *per accidens* to analogy as such. Why did he rather give what has all the appearance of wanting to be a taxonomy of analogy of names?

Why does Thomas answer the way he does? What is the lesson being taught by the answer? It is a little system, certainly mnemonically helpful, in terms of *intentio* and *esse*. It bears upon analogy, because that was the point of the objection, the objector's middle term. And it bears upon cases of analogy *precisely as regards having a multiplication of the quality in being, or not*. It is an argument that it is ONLY IN ONE SORT of analogy that one does *not* have the quality *distributed in the many things*.

Are these cases merely *per accidens* as regards analogy? No. It is the metaphysician who defines analogy, and does so in terms of *the foundations in reality* for the modes of discourse. Thus, for example, we read in Thomas's paraphrase of Aristotle in the *Nicomachean Ethics:*

Thus, therefore, he says that "good" is said of many things, not in function of meanings altogether different, as happens in those which are equivocals by

---

33. I note that *CP* 7.7 (ed. Maggiòlo, 936 [9]) contrasts the "abstract consideration of the logician or the mathematician" with the "concrete conception of the physicist making applications to matter" [*concretam rationem naturalis ad materiam applicantis*] (a text referred to by Maurer, "The Analogy of Genus," n. 16).

34. Cf. the reply in *ST* 1.13.6.*ad* 3.

chance, but inasmuch as all goods depend on one first source of goodness or inasmuch as they are ordered to one end. For Aristotle did not think that that separate good is the idea and *ratio* of all goods, but the source and end.

Or else they are all called "good" according to analogy, that is, the same proportion, as sight is the good of the body and intellect is the good of the soul.

He prefers this third mode for this reason, because it is taken in function of goodness inhering in things, whereas the first two modes [were taken] in function of a separate goodness, on the basis of which something is not *named so properly*.[35]

We see here the interest of the metaphysician in the *real* foundation for naming: naming is more truly *naming* when the foundation in reality is *fuller*.

It is "dialectical" or "logical" to reduce analogy to the issue of *intentio* alone. This McInerny has done, but only by misreading the text. Thomas, in the passage on threefold analogy is not, in the middle item, merely interested in teaching us the difference between the logician and the philosopher. He is interested in *grading analogies from the viewpoint of being*. McInerny, looking at the whole thing from the viewpoint of the logician, does not see any point in looking at the analogy of names from the viewpoint of being. But that is to be expected. The metaphysician conceives of different modes of analogy as based on *the sort of real foundation* the logical intention has. We might say that it "happens" to the logician that he still recognize analogy in the third type, this being because it does have a *"secundum intentionem"* dimension to it. What we should expect, however, is that he will not recognize it as significantly different, *qua* analogy, from the first type. And this is, of course, what happens to McInerny.

35. Thomas, *Sententia libri Ethicorum* 1.7 [Leonine ed., lines 198–213, concerning Aristotle at 1.6 (1096b26–29)]; cf. Pirotta ed., 95–96.

Chapter 7

THE IMPORTANCE OF SUBSTANCE

What separates us irreparably from [modern science] is the Aristotelian (and common sense) notion of Substantial Form . . . Descartes rid nature of it. They understand nothing anymore since they forgot Aristotle's great saying that "there is no part of an animal that is purely material or purely immaterial." It is not the word "philosophy," it is the word "nature" which separates us from our contemporaries. Since I do not have any hope of convincing them of the truth (which yet is evident) of hylomorphism, I do not believe it is possible to propose our hypothesis to them as scientifically valid. [Étienne Gilson, Sept. 8, 1971, in a letter to Jacques Maritain][1]

1. *Étienne Gilson, Jacques Maritain, Correspondance,* 1923–1971, ed. Géry Prouvost, Paris, 1991: Vrin, p. 250 (letter of Gilson, Sept. 8, 1971):

Ce qui nous en sépare irréparablement est la notion aristotélienne (et de sens commun) de la Forme Substantielle . . . Descartes en a dépeuplé la nature. On ne comprend plus rien depuis qu'on a oublié la grande parole d'Aristote, qu'il n'y a "aucune partie d'un animal qui soit purement matérielle ou purement immatérielle." Ce n'est pas le mot philosophie, c'est le mot nature qui nous sépare de nos contemporains. Comme je n'espère pas les convaincre de la vérité (pourtant évidente) de l'hylémorphisme, je ne crois pas possible de leur proposer notre hypothèse comme scientifiquement valide.

Maritain had written to Gilson September 3 (the letter is in the same collection, pp. 247–248) praising Gilson's book *D'Aristote à Darwin et retour* published that year. However, in a postscript he had questioned Gilson's view that like the doctrine that each species is the object of a special divine creation, Darwin's doctrine of the progressive formation of living things which had been brought about of itself was another "indemonstrable theology." Maritain asked:

Don't you think . . . that the philosopher can legitimately hold for most probable the idea that the creative act was accomplished [by God] through time by evolution, whereas the coming on the scene of the human species was the object of a special creation in the case of the first human being (as, subsequently, for every human individual), the creation of the spiritual soul?

This is what Gilson refers to as "our hypothesis" concerning evolution. Gilson's quotation from Aristotle is in *Parts of Animals* 1.3 (643a25).

INTRODUCTION

Our reason for speaking about science, philosophy, and theology, here at this Summer Institute,[2] is surely to provide ourselves with as high quality access to the being of things as is possible. All three, science, philosophy, and theology, aim to say something about reality, and the clearer the task assigned to each, the better off we are.

Since this is a Thomistic Institute, I need not apologize for taking as my guide Thomas Aquinas. Nevertheless, I will be looking to him as a guide in philosophy, as distinct from theology. What I hope to do is highlight the principles of metaphysics, inasmuch as they tend to be obscured by the very prominence of present-day science. In fact, my concern is with features of science which invite the scientist to take himself for the metaphysician, sometimes unbeknownst to himself.

Since science is vast, I will focus mostly on a discussion connected with evolution. The shape which such discussions take can raise doubts about the being of things.

I say, "about the *being* of things," using the word "being" in order to be as general as possible. In my title, I used the word "substance." It is a fact that the vocabulary for the discussion of being has been difficult and complicated from the start. The one Greek word, *"ousia,"* has had to be translated by many Latin forms, giving us such English words as "essence" and "substance," accompanied by such outriders as "quiddity," "form," and "nature." When I put "substance" into my title, I was really thinking of *"ousia."* I want to talk about things as having "essences" (the targets of universal definitions) and as being "substances" (particulars instantiating such essences).

THE PERENNIAL PRESOCRATIC

Our knowledge of the world of corporeal things takes various forms. St. Thomas distinguished three possible approaches, i.e. physical, mathematical, and metaphysical.[3] The former two are specialized, focusing on particular aspects of the reality which confronts us. Neither considers the being of things, as such. As Thomas teaches, only metaphysics considers even this or that particular thing from the viewpoint of being.[4] When we

2. This paper was originally read at the (July) 1997 Thomistic Institute, University of Notre Dame.

3. *ST* 1.85.1.*ad* 2.

4. Consider what Thomas says about the natures of particular sciences (among which, physics or natural philosophy) and metaphysics [*CM* 6.1 (1147), concerning Aristotle at 1025b7–10]. We read:

come upon a physicist or a mathematician (or a combination of both) making entirely universal claims, we can be sure that, in fact, that scientist (knowingly or unknowingly) has taken on the task of the metaphysician.[5]

Of course, nothing prevents one person from performing diverse tasks. What is desirable is that one do whatever one does with full awareness of the requirements of the undertaking. We have a history of thought wherein we see that metaphysics was at first practiced by people under the spell of physics or mathematics. It took centuries of philosophical experience to circumscribe the endeavor of the particularizing sciences, thus liberating metaphysics from certain erroneous judgments.[6]

That history of thought, and of metaphysics in particular, is sketched in the first book of the *Metaphysics* of Aristotle. In undertaking to present metaphysics, Aristotle sees himself as having many predecessors, even though they represent the infancy of the science. (Let's call metaphysics a "science.") For example, when he proposes a science of that which is, considered precisely as that which is, his argument is that it was the causes and principles of that which is, as such, that the earlier cosmologists were seeking. It is the precise target of their quest that he puts forward as his model.[7]

All these particular sciences, which have just been mentioned, are about some one particular domain of being, for example, about number or magnitude, or something of that order. And each one treats circumscriptively about its own subject-domain, i.e. so [treats] of its own domain, that [it treats] of nothing else; for example, the science which treats of number does not treat of magnitude. For none of them treats of being, unqualifiedly, that is, of being in its generality [*de ente in communi*], *nor even about any particular being inasmuch as it is a being*. For example, arithmetic does not determine about number inasmuch as it is a being, but inasmuch as it is number. For to consider any being, inasmuch as it is a being, is proper to metaphysics. [italics mine]

5. Along these lines, Thomas tells us that if the geometer proves his own principles, he does so by taking on the role of the metaphysician. Cf. *Expositio libri Posteriorum* 1.21 (Leonine ed., lines 75–79, concerning Aristotle at 77b3–5) (ed. Spiazzi, 177):

. . . contingit in aliqua sciencia probari principia illius sciencie, in quantum illa sciencia assumit ea que sunt alterius sciencie, sicut si geometra probet sua principia secundum quod assumit formam philosophi primi.

6. The "perennial Presocratic" could be said to be the theme of Étienne Gilson's *The Unity of Philosophical Experience,* New York, 1937: Scribners.

7. Aristotle, *Metaph.* 4.1 (1003a26–32):

. . . Now since we are seeking the first principles and the highest causes, clearly there must be some thing to which these belong in virtue of its own nature. If then those who sought the elements of existing things [Greek: *ton onton*] were seeking these same principles, it is necessary that the elements must be elements of being not by accident but just because it *is* being. Therefore it is of being as being that we also must grasp the first causes.

Yet these budding metaphysicians, the early natural philosophers, had to advance slowly, from discovery to discovery, as regards the possibilities of causal explanation. True, Aristotle sees something of a causality along the lines of what he calls "matter" in such a thinker as Thales. Still, think of the erroneous metaphysical judgment, common to all the early thinkers, Thales included, that nothing comes to be or ceases to be.[8]

Aristotle, like Plato before him,[9] rejoices in the coming of Anaxagoras, with his presentation of a cause which is both source of movement and source of goodness and beauty in things, viz. a cosmic intelligence. There is already a suggestion that what has the nature of the good must be a cause. Yet we do not have final causality here, i.e. the causal role proper to the object of appetite, but merely a good agent.[10]

With Socrates and Plato we do have definition and the causality of form in a preliminary way. Still, Aristotle tells us that none of his predecessors really spoke of the causes as they deserve to be spoken of. And, in particular, the physical philosophers err in not seeing the causal role of substance and essence.[11]

It is with Aristotle that we have physics assigned a particular task, leav-

---

Aristotle, *Metaph.* 1.3 (983b1–6), speaks of the thought of his predecessors in a similar vein:

> ... let us call to our aid those who have attacked the investigation of being [*episkepsin ton onton*] and philosophized about reality [*peri tes aletheias*] before us. For obviously they too speak of certain principles and causes; to go over their views, then, will be of profit to the present inquiry, for we shall either find another kind of cause, or be more convinced of the correctness of those which we now maintain.

8. *Metaph.* 1.3 (983b8–18 and especially 984a31–33).

9. Plato, *Phaedo* 97b–99d. The entire passage, 95b–102a, in which Socrates recounts his disappointment with the doctrines of the natural philosophers, his admiration for and disappointment with Anaxagoras, and his own eventual solution concerning the cause of being, is fundamental for the consideration of "perennial Presocratism."

10. *Metaph.* 1.3 (984b8–22) and 1.7 (988b6–11).

11. Aristotle reviews and criticizes the causal views of all his predecessors, and eventually he concludes at *Metaph.* 1.10 (993a11–16):

> ... It is evident, then, even from what we have said before, that all men seem to seek the causes named in the *Physics,* and that we cannot name any beyond these; but they seek these vaguely; and though in a sense they have all been described before, in a sense they have not been described at all. For the earliest philosophy is, on all subjects, like one who lisps, since it is young and in its beginnings.

Concerning the formal cause in particular, notice *Metaph.* 1.7 (988a34–b1):

> The essence [*to ... ti en einai*], i.e. the substantial reality [*ten ousian*], no one has expressed distinctly. It is hinted at chiefly by those who believe in the Forms ...

Especially regarding the physical philosophers, cf. 1.8 (988b28–29):

> ... they err in not positing the substance [*ten ousian*], i.e. the essence [*to ti esti*], as the cause of anything ...

ing it to metaphysics to discuss causality as such[12] and all the things that pertain to being as such.[13]

But why rehearse these famous moments in the history of the human mind? The reason is that we must not allow ourselves to view this history as achieved once and for all. There is another aspect of the human situation which is well described by Plato in the *Sophist*. I refer to the passage about the battle like that between the gods and the giants.[14] This is a battle about what it is to "be," a battle which is "always" going on.[15] On the one side are those who identify "being" with "being a body" or "being sensible"; on the other side are those who identify "being" with the invisible, the intelligible, the incorporeal, the immobile, i.e. certain forms which are ever the same. Plato says that we need a doctrine of being which somehow can include both.[16]

My point, then, is that *the Presocratics are always with us*. We do not have to look far to find positions taken which resemble those reported by Plato and Aristotle. We need to rehearse the history because rehearsing the

---

12. Thomas, *Commentary on the Physics* [henceforth "*CP*"] 2.5 (ed. Maggiòlo, Rome/Turin, 1954: Marietti, 176), explaining Aristotle at 2.3 (194b16–23):

   ... firstly, he shows the necessity of determining about the causes ... [for] to consider concerning causes as such is proper to the first philosopher [i.e. the metaphysician]: for cause, inasmuch as [it is] cause, does not depend on matter as regards being, for in those also which are separated from matter one finds the intelligible aspect: cause. But consideration of causes is taken on by the natural philosopher because of some necessity: nor nevertheless is it taken on by him to consider concerning causes save according as they are causes of natural changes. [my italics]

Of course, one sees well the abstract nature of the notion of cause by considering it as applicable to the separate entities; however, only because such notions are abstract from the start can one raise the question of separate entity.

13. Thomas Aquinas, *CM* 7.11 (1526) commenting on *Metaph.* 7.11 (1037a10–16):

   ... in this science [i.e. metaphysics or "first philosophy"] we try to determine concerning sensible substances ... for the sake of immaterial substances; because theorizing concerning sensible and material substances in a way pertains to physics, which is not first philosophy, but second, as was established in book 4.

   For first philosophy is about the first substances, which are immaterial substances, about which it theorizes not merely inasmuch as they are substances, but inasmuch as they are *such* substances, i.e. inasmuch as they are immaterial. About sensible substance it does not theorize inasmuch as they are *such* substances, but inasmuch as they are *substances,* or even beings, or inasmuch as through them we are led to the knowledge of immaterial substances.

   But the physicist, conversely, determines about material substances, *not inasmuch as they are substances,* but inasmuch as they are material and [as] having in them a principle of movement. [my italics]

14. Plato, *Sophist* 246a–249d.

15. Ibid., 246c.

16. Ibid., 249d. Notice that in their "tamed" form, the giants hold rather that to "be" is well circumscribed as the ability to act upon another or be acted upon by something, thus *dunamis:* 247d–e.

history may serve to awaken contemporary Presocratics from their dogmatic slumber.

When I speak of "contemporary Presocratics," I think of someone as distinguished in physics as Stephen Weinberg.[17] Weinberg is an elementary particle physicist, a Nobelist, and in a recent book he presents the idea of a final or ultimate physical theory, together with speculation on the likelihood of arriving at it. He certainly does not present himself as a philosopher, and, indeed, comments on how little philosophy has to do with genuine scientific work. He stresses that his own interest is in physics. However, much that he says in his book is, I would say, the proper business of the metaphysician. He is attempting to put on display for as wide a readership as possible the nature of physical science. He seeks to show it as moving toward greater and greater unity of vision. He wishes to communicate something of the intrinsically interesting character he finds in such vision. In this attempt, he is obliged to propose certain conceptions of the explanation of things, what it is to answer the question "why?" He also must face up to a certain human dissatisfaction with the sort of explanation he thinks is available, and to persuade the reader that such dissatisfaction is unreasonable.

After dealing with the issues of complexity and historical accident as they affect the nature of scientific explanation, Weinberg moves to the problem of "emergence." He says:

. . . As we look at nature at levels of greater and greater complexity, we see phenomena emerging that have no counterpart at the simpler levels, least of all at the level of the elementary particles. For instance, there is nothing like intelligence on the level of individual living cells, and nothing like life on the level of atoms and molecules. The idea of emergence was well captured by the physicist Philip Anderson in the title of a 1972 article: "More is Different." The emergence of new phenomena at high levels of complexity is most obvious in biology and the behavioral sciences, but it is important to recognize that such emergence does not represent something special about life or human affairs; it also happens within physics itself. (39)[18]

Here, the point is still that such a phenomenon does not entail the rejection of the explanatory power of the physical laws Weinberg has in mind.

17. Stephen Weinberg, *Dreams of a Final Theory*, New York, 1993: Pantheon.
18. The notion of "complexity" should be scrutinized. It is a "material causality" approach. It is a treatment of parts as material parts. For example, the word "item" or the word "time" is more complex than the word "act" or the word "cat." The insight that a more complex being is somehow "higher" on the scale of beings is not altogether wrong. In the realm of material things, the simpler things are not able to perform all the operations that the more complex perform. Still, there is a simplicity of form as form, and thus, as we mount in a scale of immaterial being, simpler is better. Cf. *ST* 1.77.2.

He presents first the case of thermodynamics, as a domain within physics itself:

... even though thermodynamics has been explained in terms of particles and forces, it continues to deal with emergent concepts like temperature and entropy that lose all meaning on the level of individual particles. (41)

Coming to biology, he continues to maintain the fundamental role of the standard model of elementary particles, but he allows that the scientists in the disciplines that speak in terms of the emergent phenomena are asking questions peculiar to themselves:

... scientists use languages that are special to their own fields ... [I]t is ... a reflection of the sort of question we want to ask about these phenomena. Even if we had an enormous computer that could follow the history of every elementary particle in a tidal flow or a fruit fly, this mountain of computer printout would not be of much use to someone who wanted to know whether the water was turbulent or the fly was alive. (43)

Weinberg merely insists that all the things such scientists talk about "work the way they do because of the underlying quantum mechanics of electrons, protons, and neutrons." (44) He says (speaking of chemists, but by implication of all such scientists):

... I see no reason why chemists should stop speaking of such things as long as they find it useful or interesting. (43)

He clearly thinks that his objects of interest are more "fundamental," but obviously the word "fundamental" is as ambiguous as the word "why."

He brings this discussion of emergence to a climax with the case of "consciousness," by which he means specifically *human* consciousness. He admits he finds this issue "terribly difficult," but envisages coming to an understanding of "objective correlatives to consciousness" in terms of physics. It "may not be an explanation of consciousness, but it will be pretty close." (45)

What I find about this discussion of emergence is that it constitutes a move from potency to act, from material preparations to a new form or actuality. The reason these other scientists have these proper objects of interest is that the objects are interesting just in themselves. In the line of final causality, they give meaning to the existence of the electrons, protons, and neutrons.

What he himself is talking about sounds like something in the line of Aristotle's material cause. He says:

... Indeed, elementary particles are not in themselves very interesting, not at any rate in the way that people are interesting. Aside from their momentum and spin, every electron in the universe is just like every other electron—if you have seen one electron, you have seen them all. But this very simplicity suggests that electrons, unlike people, are not made up of numbers of more fundamental constituents, but are themselves something close to the fundamental constituents of everything else. It is because elementary particles are so boring that they are interesting; their simplicity suggests that the study of elementary particles will bring us closer to a fundamental study of nature. (58)

The simplicity Weinberg is speaking of seems to be that of fundamental constituents in the *potential* sense, items that are "ready to be anything." In themselves, they offer little distinctive character to the observing mind.[19]

I would say that we should go back and consider the idea of emergence: "more is different." This "more" is obviously not the material "more," i.e. merely juxtaposing identical items. As Weinberg says: see one electron, you have seen them all. So taken, more is not different. No, the "more" in question in emergence is the formal "more." Add a difference and you have a new kind of thing. In this line, Aristotle said that "the forms of things are like numbers": just as the addition of a unit gives a new number, so the addition of a difference gives a new species.[20] This is most obviously true at the level of life, but it seems to have application, too, in fundamental physics; as Weinberg said, there is a sort of "emergence" there.

Now it is just this variety which many of us would like to understand, and the primary notion Weinberg provides is "accident." Obviously, from the viewpoint of fundamental particle physics, there is nothing else to say. However, there is good reason to think that these unities, the tree, the spider, the dog, the human being, also have the status of "universals," even if their appearance here or there in physical reality has the authentically accidental character Weinberg speaks of. And if so, then they too can serve as principles for a "reductionist" program, in which what Weinberg sees as fundamental will appear as "instrumental."[21]

What should engage our wonder? Why does Weinberg himself call

19. Of course, a true particle would not be merely a building block, but would have a nature of its own. I am speaking only of Weinberg's line of thinking. Cf. William A. Wallace, "Are Elementary Particles Real?," in *From a Realist Point of View: Essays on the Philosophy of Science,* Washington, D.C., 1979: University Press of America, pp. 187–200. It is significant that Weinberg thinks what he should be after is "fundamental constituents." This means that he looks to some elementary *kind of thing* as what is fundamental. That is, he has not the idea of primary matter in the Aristotelian sense, and so his ontology is really mechanistic, which is to say that he sees all forms as accidental.

20. Aristotle, *Metaph.* 8.3 (1043b32–1044a14); Thomas, *CM* 8.3 (ed. Cathala, 1722–1727).

21. See the criticism of the Presocratics by Aristotle, *De gen. et corr.* 2.9 (335b30–336a12).

certain questions, particularly that about "an interested God" "our *deepest questions*"?[22] If the object of intellect is universal being, then the more a thing has the aspect of being, the more fittingly it elicits wonder. Weinberg is right in claiming that it is interesting to trace things back to their first principles. Where he is weak is in the narrowness of his conception of principles.

He tells us:

... we think that by studying quarks and electrons we will learn something about the *principles* that govern everything. (61, his italics)

He italicized "principles" but I would stress his "govern" and "everything." He wants to talk about all things, and in that he is a budding metaphysician. He uses what he might call a "slippery" word, viz. "govern." It certainly is said in many ways, and obviously is not meant by him to express conscious purpose.

I come back to my main point. Weinberg seems to me to be at a Presocratic stage of metaphysics.

Weinberg is an elementary particle physicist, but one interested in "final theories" and "deepest questions." Another scientist with philosophical interests is the biologist Michel Delsol. A few years ago, an issue of *Laval théologique et philosophique* was dedicated to discussions of the synthetic theory of evolution.[23] Delsol was particularly prominent in the presentation.[24] He contended that the synthetic theory is quite adequate to explain evolution, including the passage from non-life to life. He expressly featured the issue of the development of the human eye, so well-known as a Darwinian problem.

Delsol held that the synthetic theory is the entirely satisfactory scientific explanation of life as we know it. Those who say otherwise, he assures us, simply do not have the expertise. However, he also contended that there is another whole dimension to human questioning, viz. the metaphysical.

As making room for the metaphysician beyond the biologist, Delsol can hardly be described as "Presocratic." However, his confidence in the

---

22. *Dreams,* p. 245:
   ... Will we find an interested God in the final laws of nature? ... [P]remature as the question may be, it is hardly possible not to wonder whether we will find any answer to *our deepest questions,* any sign of the workings of an interested God, in a final theory. I think we will not. [my italics]

23. *Laval théologique et philosophique* 50 (1994), pp. 3–143, is a "dossier" presented under the title: "La théorie synthétique de l'évolution."

24. Michel Delsol, Philippe Sentis, Roger Payot, Régis Ladous, and Janine Flatin, "Le hasard et la sélection expliquent-ils l'évolution? Biologie ou métaphysique," *Laval théologique et philosophique* 50 (1994), pp. 7–41.

explanatory power of the synthetic theory, as regards the passage from non-life to life, puts him at odds with another scientist I wish to mention, one who has made something of a splash recently, the biochemist Michael Behe. In his book *Darwin's Black Box*,[25] subtitled *The Biochemical Challenge to Evolution,* he argues that while evolution need not be rejected altogether, it cannot account for the origin of the cell in living things. Behe presents the cell as what he calls "an irreducibly complex system," and holds that such a system cannot come into being one step at a time. Since the evolutionary explanation requires one step at a time, it cannot be the answer to the question: "whence comes life?" Behe holds that the obvious answer to that question is mind.[26] He does not consider this answer as one outside the bounds of science, since it is the only answer to an altogether scientific question.

Behe begins his book by explaining what he means by "evolution." We read:

In its full-throated biological sense . . . *evolution* means a process whereby life arose from non-living matter and subsequently developed entirely by natural means. That is the sense in which Darwin used the word, and the meaning that it holds in the scientific community. And that is the sense in which I use the word *evolution* throughout this book.[27]

He aims to present the progress made by biochemistry since the mid-1950s. His question is whether the theory of evolution has been made unacceptable by this progress (3). He says:

For more than a century most scientists have thought that virtually all of life, or at least all of its most interesting features, resulted from natural selection working on random variation. [4]

Behe makes it clear that he does not doubt that the universe is billions of years old, and he finds "the idea of common descent (that all organisms share a common ancestor) fairly convincing . . ." (5).

As I said, Behe does not altogether reject evolution. Once even one

---

25. Michael J. Behe, *Darwin's Black Box: The Biochemical Challenge to Evolution,* New York, 1996: The Free Press. Cf. also his op-ed article, "Darwin Under the Microscope," *New York Times,* Oct. 29, 1996, written on the occasion of Pope John Paul II's statement that evolution is "more than just a theory." Also his "The Sterility of Darwinism," *Boston Review,* February/March 1997. The *Boston Review* website has a collection of articles in this connection.

26. Notice the way Behe sums up his line of thinking:

. . . The irreducibly complex Rube Goldberg machine required an intelligent designer to produce it; therefore the irreducibly complex blood-clotting system required a designer also. [218]

27. Behe, p. xi. His italics.

cell is given, evolution could be the answer to much development. He says:

Although Darwin's mechanism—natural selection working on variation—might explain many things, I do not believe it explains molecular life. I also do [6] not think it surprising that the new science of the very small might change the way we view the less small. [5–6]

He regales us with chapter after chapter of information on the complexity and functionality of living cells. He also mentions various candidates for explaining the origin of this complexity. The first candidate is, of course, Neo-Darwinism (24). At the beginning of his chapter entitled "Intelligent Design" (ch. 9, 187–208), he has made his case against Darwinism as an answer to the question of the origin of "complex biochemical systems." He notes a few attempts to provide different answers, which he also finds unsatisfactory.

Then Behe comes to his own solution, intelligent design. He says:

. . . To a person who does not feel obliged to restrict his search to unintelligent causes, the straightforward conclusion is that many biochemical systems were designed. They were designed not by the laws of nature, not by chance and necessity; rather, they were *planned*. The designer knew what the systems would look like when they were completed, then took steps to bring the systems about. Life on earth at its most fundamental level, in its most critical components, is the product of intelligent activity. [193][28]

He immediately stresses that this is not some special religious view:

28. Notice that not every appeal to intelligence is truly a case of "finality." It may be more the needed agent of a technique, rather than the true causality of the good as such. Thus, in the treatment of Anaxagoras in the *CM*, Thomas speaks of:

. . . the cause of the good, which indeed is the final cause, though it was not proposed by them save incidentally, as will be clear later. [*CM* 1.5 (97)]

The later place Thomas has in mind we find at *CM* 1.11 [177]. He says:

. . . Those who said that the cause is intellect or love posited them as causes as [being] something good. For they said that such things are causes that things are in a good condition. For the cause of the good can only be the good. Hence it follows that they posited that intellect and love are causes in the way that the good is a cause.

But "the good" can be understood in two ways. In one way, as the final cause, inasmuch as something is done for the sake of some good. In the other way, in the mode of the efficient cause, as we say that the good man does what is good. Therefore, these philosophers did not say that the aforementioned causes are good, such that for the sake of them [*horum causa*] something of beings is or is made, which pertains to the idea of final cause; but that from the aforementioned items, i.e. intellect and love, there issued forth some movement toward the being and becoming of things, which pertains to the idea of efficient cause.

And in 179, Thomas explains that this is to touch upon the final cause merely incidentally. I had thought that this might be true of Behe, too; but it may simply be that he abstracts somewhat from the question.

The conclusion of intelligent design flows naturally from the data itself—not from sacred books or sectarian beliefs. Inferring that biological systems were designed by an intelligent agent is a humdrum process that requires no new principles of logic or science. [193]

It is at this point that he sets out the look of designed things, and then calls attention to the fact of our concluding that a designer is at work.

Notice that Behe says:

There is no magic point of irreducible complexity at which Darwinism is logically impossible. But the hurdles for gradualism become higher and higher as structures are more complex, more interdependent. [203]

Behe shows that intelligent design need not be the only explanation for the way things are. It may be one of the explanations, together with evolution over centuries, etc. He is also very careful to say that it can only be invoked when the evidence is right.

He then makes a very interesting move. He presents intelligent design as a new *scientific* response to certain definite givens. He says:

The discovery of design expands the number of factors that must be considered by science when trying to explain life . . . Unlike Darwinian evolution, the theory of intelligent design is new to modern science, so there are a host of questions that need to be answered and much work lies ahead. For those who work at the molecular level, the challenge will be to rigorously determine which systems were designed and which might have arisen by other mechanisms. [230]

And:

. . . Since the simplest possible design scenario posits a single cell—formed billions of years ago—that already contained all information to produce descendent organisms, other studies could test this scenario by attempting to calculate how much DNA would be required to code the information (keeping in mind that much of the information might be implicit) . . . [231][29]

Behe sees the introduction into science of intelligent design as a theory as "a useful tool for the advancement of science in an area that has been moribund for decades." [231]

Thus, he is proposing that this is the only acceptable *scientific* answer to a certain problem. I stress "scientific" because, even in the blurb on

29. Obviously, there are many questions to be asked about the possibilities present in an original cell: is this a doctrine of substantial potentiality, of seminal plans, or what? Notice that St. Thomas, *ST* 1.65.4 (400a32) calls the ideas [*species*] of natural kinds in the angelic intellect "seminal plans" [*seminales rationes*]. And *ST* 1.73.1.*ad* 3 (431b17–22) tells us that if new species of animals arise from the interbreeding of already given species, these pre-existed in some *active* causal powers from the beginning.

the dust jacket of the book, James Shapiro is quoted as saying that "Behe selects an answer that falls outside of science . . ." That is not how Behe describes what he is doing.[30]

Weinberg I call a "Presocratic." Delsol and Behe differ as to the origin of life. Behe is proposing what he regards as the only available scientific explanation. He is reliving the experience of Anaxagoras, but with infinitely better observational opportunities.

Delsol thinks that Neo-Darwinism can account for life. He wrote before Behe, but one may be forgiven for thinking he might reject the Behe approach.

Delsol's reasons for thinking there is room for a "metaphysical" discussion of the same reality seem very largely to depend on his not being ready to account for the human mind other than as the product of a mind. In this connection, he speaks of "the logic of things," but that, healthy as it is, needs spelling out.

Both Delsol and Behe are impressed by the possibilities they see as provided from the outset in the life of the cell, or in even more elementary things. I would say their views would be well completed by recourse to Charles De Koninck's views on the "cosmos" and on the "indetermination" of nature.[31]

---

30. I might note a review of Behe's book: H. Allen Orr, "Darwin v. Intelligent Design (Again)," *Boston Review,* December 1996/January 1997, pp. 28–31. This is in tone very hostile, using the word "screed" to characterize the work. Rhetoric aside, it claims to have an answer to Behe at the level of evolutionary theory. However, judging from the examples and from the description of the theory, Orr is working with the *adjusting* of *already given* irreducibly complex systems. Now, Behe's claim is that the only explanation for the original existence of an irreducibly complex system is mind. He quite explicitly rejects the claim that the *changes* in such systems are exclusively the result of mind. Thus, I would say that Orr is quite off the mark.

Long after writing the last remark, I have had the benefit of seeing Behe's own most interesting reply to Orr: cf. Michael J. Behe, "The Sterility of Darwinism," *Boston Review,* February/March 1997.

31. I refer to these below. But cf. De Koninck, Charles, "*Le cosmos* (1936)–Extrait," *Laval théologique et philosophique* 50 (1994), pp. 111–143. De Koninck says that we hesitate to apply to the whole of nature a principle which Thomas presented: that the way of generation is from the less to the more perfect, with man coming last. He refers to *DP* 4.2, and he says:

> And if we do not seem able to follow the Angelic Doctor, is it not because we have excluded from the universe the efficient and sufficient cause moving the cosmos and pushing it upwards? Our timorous attitude is only too easily explained. Since Suarez we have resolutely put a plug on the world's top side: we wish to explain everything in nature by means of intracosmic causes. Suarez, in denying the apodictic value of the arguments presented by Saint Thomas for demonstrating on strictly rational lines the existence of pure spirits, cut every essential link between the cosmos and the created spiritual universe. Let us add to that his hybrid notion of prime matter, and we arrive logically at the barbarous creationism of our philosophy manuals. It is obvious that if we sterilize the world from its outset, nothing more can come forth. Creationism, which from all angles opens the world directly on God, passing to one side of the

However, De Koninck's argument for the need in the material world for causality by a separate substance, a purely spiritual agent, takes its start from the analysis of movement in terms of act and potency. That is an ontological analysis, one that finds its roots in an approach to reality from the viewpoint of being. So also, the Gilsonian call (referred to at the outset) for hylomorphism, the conception of things as composites of substantial form and prime matter, itself is an approach to change in the light of the notion of substance. Thus, the primary point I wish to insist on today is the importance of substance and our grasp of things from the viewpoint of substance.[32]

SUBSTANCE, INDIVISIBILITY, IMMOBILITY

Reality consists primarily of beings, and indeed, of substances.[33] There are many substances, differing from one another in kind, and differing from one another numerically within one kind. The intellectual grasp of these substances in their diversity and multiplicity is the starting point of metaphysics.[34] Substances are not all that there is. There are all the things-which-happen-to-substance or things-that-are-found-in-substances

---

universal hierarchy, implicitly rejects what is essential to the universe: unity of order. [129]

De Koninck says that since Suarez the Scholastics abandon more and more the ontological study of nature. They think that scientific explanations replace the philosophy of nature. The philosophers concentrate only on notions of interest to the theologians. Cosmic repulsion may explain the expansion of the universe, and the theory of genes explain mutations, but none of that is an explanation of why anything is in motion.

32. It is notable that in his *CP* 1.1 (4 [4]), in order to explain Aristotle's presentation of the *Physics* at the very beginning of all the physical works, Thomas asserts that prior to all the sciences one locates "first philosophy," in which one determines concerning those things which are common to that which is, as such [*communia enti inquantum est ens*]. While in the order of human learning one should learn physical science before metaphysics, nevertheless at the more mature level one's curriculum should give metaphysics the priority.

33. The following twelve paragraphs are an adaptation from my paper, "Something Rather than Nothing, and St. Thomas' Third Way," *Science et Esprit* 39 (1987), pp. 71–80, at p. 77.

34. Thomas Aquinas, *De substantiis separatis*, ch. 6 (Leonine ed., in *Opera omnia*, t. 40, 1969), lines 88–129:

... [Gebirol's] position does away, indeed, ... with the principles of first philosophy, taking away unity from singular things, and consequently the true entity and diversity of things ...

And also *De veritate* 5.2.*ad* 7:

... the necessity of the mentioned [absolutely first] principles follows upon the divine providence and disposing: for from this [fact], that the things have been produced in such a nature, in which they have determinate being [*esse terminatum*], they are distinct from their negations: from which distinction it follows that the affirmation and the negation are not simultaneously true; and from this principle there is necessity in all other principles, as is said in *Metaphysics* 4.

—there are "accidents" and movements and so on.[35] However, all these others have being only in dependence upon substances. If other beings do not "flow" from the substance in which they have being, then they "flow" from some other substance which is thus "influencing" the substance in which they are found. All the things that are depend for their existence on substances.[36]

What sort of thing is substance? What are some of the characteristics by which we recognize it, discern it, and keep from confusing it with other things? It is difficult to present because it is *so well known* and it is on it as basis that questions of "recognition" (even, "how will I recognize substance?") are posed, understood, and answered. To ask for "identifying marks" is to know already what "identity" is. Now, identity is a notion which expresses *unity,* and not mere unity as to quantity (the "same" size), as "equality" does, or mere unity as to quality, as "similarity" does (two white things look "the same"), but unity in *substance* (things are truly "identical," unqualifiedly "the same," when they are one substance). We see how we depend on substance to make sense, and employ its notion in various watered-down ways to talk about everything else.[37]

Substance, along with "a being," belongs to the domain of what all naturally know. Metaphysical reflection can only serve to render that knowledge less subject to impediments, freer from the influence of our various lesser habitual cognitive stances. Among these, physics, because of its proximity to metaphysics (physics is "second philosophy," relative to metaphysics being "first"),[38] is very likely to cause confusion. Although and even because physics is developed (by Aristotle) in accordance with and under the rule of substance, so that its principles are the matter and the form in the order of substance, physics can act as a smoke screen between the real and metaphysical reflection.

Thus, it is in physics that the doctrine of matter and form as parts of substance is first presented (first, speaking of pedagogical order).[39] How-

35. Thomas Aquinas, *CM* 4.1 (ed. Cathala, 540–543). Thomas there presents four "modes of being," beginning with the weakest, the least, and moving toward the strongest. The four are (1) negations and privations, (2) generations and corruptions and movements, (3) inhering accidents, and (4) substances. See above, chapter 2, ca. n. 17.

36. On the primacy of substance among beings, cf. Thomas, *CM* 7.1 (1246–1259). On the causal "flow" of all beings from substances, cf. *ST* 1.77.6. The whole of *SCG* 3.97 should be read.

37. Cf. Thomas, *CM* 7.4 (1331–1334), concerning the fact that all the categories participate in the mode of entity proper to substance, viz. being a "what" [*quid*]. On identity as substantial unity, cf. *CM* 4.2 (561).

38. I use the word "physics" here to encompass all interest in the mobile as such. Cf. Thomas Aquinas, *CM* 7.11 (1526–1527), quoted above, n. 13.

39. Thomas teaches (*CP* 1.12 [ed. Maggiòlo, 107 (10)]) that to prove through a reason [*"per rationem"*] that in all natural production there must be a subject pertains to metaphysics; that is why, in the *Physics* 1.7 (190a31–190b11), Aristotle proves it merely by induction.

ever, our vision of substance, in physics, remains tied to the problems of
mutual influence, through action and passion, proper to the physical interest. That is why, for example, in the ancient doctrine of the elementary substances, fire and water were seen as *contraries*, one to the other, a
view ultimately requiring correction (or interpretation) by the metaphysician—since a substance, as such, has no contrary. A substance, as such,
simply *is*, absolutely. We have to purge our vision of substance of influ-
ences coming from the "mobility" setting. [See Addendum 1]

Approaches to being and substance always oblige us to talk about
something at least conceptually slightly different. To talk about "indivisibility" is to shift the discussion at least into the domain of unity. The beings that we know most readily are composites, and we easily see that it
is one and the same thing to preserve one's being and to preserve one's
unity. Remember the biblical incident of Solomon and the two women
both claiming the one baby. The real mother refuses to take half a baby.
Half a baby is no baby at all.[40]

Many issues requiring insistence on the indivisible character of substance could be mentioned. There is need for a theory of elements and
how they persist in the resultant substance.[41] There is need for a theory
of parts and how they unite in a substantial whole.[42] There is need for
a doctrine of substantial identity throughout a lifetime of metabolism.[43]
There is need for a discussion of the substantiality of cadavers.[44]

One of the reflective occasions provided by St. Thomas which seems
to me very helpful for fixing our attention on substance and its primacy occurs in the *De potentia* discussions of God's conservational causality.
Thomas's doctrine is that creatures would not remain in being were it
not for God's conservational causality. The objectors see some efficient
causes other than God as simply establishing things in being in such a
way that the effect no longer needs the efficient cause: the house builder
builds a house which has no need of him later; why not envisage God's
role that way.[45] The objector I am especially interested in is rejecting a
distinction employed by Thomas between a "cause of coming to be" and
a "cause of being." This is a distinction exemplified by the difference between the house builder (who causes the coming to be of the house, but
not its constantly remaining in being) and the natures of cement, stones,
and wood, which are receptive of and conservative of composition and

40. 1 Kings 3:16–28.
41. *ST* 1.76.4.*ad* 4.
42. *CM* 7.16 (1631–1636). This touches on the important question of survival of parts
of living things when separated.
43. Thomas, *In De generatione* 1.17 (118).
44. Thomas, *In* De generatione 1.8 (60 [3]), concerning Aristotle at 1.3 (318b1–14).
45. *DP* 5.1.obj. 4.

order, the form of the house (thus the being of the house depends on those natures).[46]

The idea (and it is indeed Thomas's) would be to explain the need for God as conserver by claiming that the proximate causes of things, the lower agents, are merely causes of coming to be, not causes of being. That is why one can take them away and still have the effect. However, God is a cause of being, and so must "stay around" and conserve things even once they have been produced.

The objector says that using this distinction, in such a way as to make lower agents mere causes of coming to be, puts one in the camp of Plato and Avicenna, and against Aristotle. Aristotle taught that it is forms in matter which cause forms in matter. Thus, since something, inasmuch as it is cause of *form*, is cause of *being*, to say that the lower causes (corporeal causes) do not cause *being* but only coming to be, is to say that they do not cause *form*. Hence, one is holding that the forms in matter must come from separate forms (the Platonic position) or that they come from the "giver of forms" (the Avicennian position).[47]

Thomas replies that since corporeal agents can act only by producing changes, and since nothing is changed except by reason of matter, the causality of corporeal agents can extend only to those things which are in some way in matter. The Platonists and Avicenna did not posit that forms are educed from the potency of matter, and so they were forced to say that natural agents merely *dispose matter*: the introduction of forms was from an incorporeal principle. If we say (as Thomas *does* say) with Aristotle, that substantial forms are educed from the potency of matter, then natural agents will not be merely the causes of the dispositions of matter, but even *the causes of the substantial forms*. However, Thomas qualifies this as follows:

. . . but just so far and no farther, viz. that the forms are educed from potency into act. Consequently, the natural agents are principles of being as regards beginning to be [*essendi principia quantum ad inchoationem ad esse*], and not as regards being, absolutely [*et non quantum ad ipsum esse absolute*].[48]

Obviously, Thomas's distinction between "cause of becoming" and "cause of being" is not the same as that of Avicenna. However, it is a distinction which must be maintained because, in our very consideration of mobile substances, we see that substantial being, as such, lies beyond the order of motion and change. As Thomas says in the body of the same article:

46. Cf. *ST* 1.104.1 (622b43–623a4).
47. *DP* 5.1.obj. 5.
48. *DP* 5.1.*ad* 5.

... Since the being of form in matter [*esse formae in materia*], speaking of this just in itself, implies no movement or change, except, if one will, *per accidens*, and since no body brings to actuality anything except "the moved" ... therefore it is necessary that the principle on which form as such depends be some incorporeal principle.[49] [See Addendum 2]

The metaphysical vision grasps the integrity of the whole, the indivisible, the "being of form in matter." The importance of totality[50] and indivisibility[51] for the grasp of substance needs stressing.

Notice that while we are dealing with the very same matter and form which is talked about in (Aristotelian) physics, they are now seen as ingredients and principles of substance, rather than as principles of movement. We grasp substance first, and develop the substantial but subordinate notions of "form" and "matter" in order to respect the substantiality of the movable and changeable thing.[52]

The metaphysician directs our attention to substances, as lying beyond generation and corruption. Substance is not the terminus of generation, except *per accidens*. It is rather what simply is (even though it has been generated). Form, the principle of substantial being, is recognized as form, in part, because it is the unity, *through time*, in spite of changes in things, of something recognizable. And by "being" [Latin *esse*] we mean the actuality of a substance, the *remaining one* in the midst of change.[53] When generation and corruption reveal the ontological status of the substances most immediately known to us as "possibles with respect to being and not being" (to use the language of Thomas's "Third Way")[54] and so as caused, our only recourse, in order to explain why there is anything at all, is to admit there is a higher kind of substance, necessary being. (And inasmuch as that too can be found in a caused instance, we are eventually led to uncaused necessary substance.)

The metaphysical habituation of the mind, the relentless return to

---

49. *DP* 5.1. See my paper, "St. Thomas, Joseph Owens and Existence," *New Scholasticism* 56 (1982), pp. 399–441. Fr. Owens conceives of the substantial being of movable things as intrinsically a "flux," ignoring the *per accidens* aspect of such being's being measured by time. Charles De Koninck strikes me as tending in this same direction: cf. e.g. his "Thomism and Scientific Indeterminism," in *Proceedings of the American Catholic Philosophical Association* (1936), Washington, D.C., 1937: The Catholic University of America Press, pp. 58–76, at pp. 60–61.

50. *ST* 1.76.8 (461b39–43 and 462a8–11).

51. *ST* 1.85.8 (534b22–31); 1.76.3 (454a24–48); 1.76.4.*ad* 4 (457a3–16).

52. For the point that it is the same matter which is considered by the physicist and by the metaphysician, cf. *CM* 7.2 (1285); for the difference in outlook of the two, cf. 7.11 (1526), cited above at n. 13.

53. Even this expression is inadequate, since it suggests rest, i.e. absence of motion; the being of substance, as such, is beyond both motion and rest.

54. *ST* 1.2.3 (14a44–b15), the "third way" of proving the existence of a God.

substance and that-which-is as principles of judgment of all experience, requires long practice. Physics, on the one hand, is an invitation and disposition toward the metaphysical, but it is also a source of possible "forgetfulness of being," as it already was for Thales.[55]

To repeat, both the Aristotelian physicist and the metaphysician are interested in the analysis of natural changeable substances into form and matter. The physicist locates in matter and form the *principles* of the movements or changes (and rests) found in things. The metaphysician, on the other hand, keeps his eye fixed on substance as a primary *unit* or "indivisible." He then *sizes up* the "ingredients" or components of composite substance, from the viewpoint of being. It is *the composite* which properly *has* being (and so it is what we mean primarily by "a being").[56] As such, it is called "the *subsisting* thing." The matter, just in its own nature, is *a being, potentially* or is *a being in potency.* Form is that by virtue of which the matter has definiteness and being. It is the composite which *is.*[57]

We must dwell on the (intellectual) vision we can have of *the existing substance,* if we are to come to a truly philosophical understanding of these questions. I *imagine* the existing substance by imagining *a bear* coming at me in the forest. It is the *"one,"* *independent* of *me,* which I encounter in the bear. It is not just the bear's movements, but the *unity of source* of those movements. It is not even the bear's being *source of movement* which I wish to point out, though from the strictly practical point of view, i.e. my own safety, that is what counts; also, that is what interests the physicist. But for the metaphysician, it is the *one*[58] which is *at* the source. I might

55. Thales depreciated the being of sensible substances in their *variety,* inasmuch as he held that nothing comes to be or ceases to be.

56. See Thomas Aquinas, *ST* 1.45.4:

... [the act of] being belongs properly to *subsisting things,* whether they be simple, as are separate substances, or composite, as are material substances. For, to that [sort of item] it belongs properly to be, which *has* being, and that is what is subsisting in *its own* being. Forms, on the other hand, and accidents, and other items on that level, are not called "beings" as though to say that *they themselves are,* but rather because in function of them *something* is; for example, whiteness is called "a being" for this reason, that in function of it *the subject* [i.e., e.g., the dog] is white. Hence, according to Aristotle, an accident is more properly said to be *"of* a being" rather than simply "a being."

This text speaks of "form" as something that does not subsist; however, we eventually reason to the existence of subsisting forms.

57. *CM* 8.1 (1687), concerning Aristotle at 8.1 (1042a24–31).

58. Thomas, at *ST* 1.11.1, raises the question: whether "one" adds anything to "a being." He replies:

... "one" does not add on, over and above "a being," some real thing, but merely the negation of division. For "one" signifies nothing else but "an undivided being"; and from that very fact it is apparent that "one" is interchangeable with "a being." For every being either is simple or composite. But what is simple is undivided both actually and potentially. But what is composite does not have being [*esse*] so long as its parts are di-

kill the bear, but what I am pointing to is just *what is there* until I kill it.

We have a strong tendency to reduce things to a *mechanical* character. We have a tendency toward a *particle* theory, i.e. to think of each distinctive being as made up of "a lot of little beings (substances!)." The bear, one might say, is an assemblage of "molecules" or some other sort of small item. "Mr. Smith is a bundle of events."[59] This kind of picture is a formula for permanently setting aside the being of things, a technique for evading "substance."

If we are to have a grasp of substance, we must allow the *unity* of substance to *dominate* the multiplicity of parts. We can see something of this in Thomas Aquinas's discussion of the human soul, in which he is teaching that the soul is the *substantial form* of the body. He is asked whether the soul is *in every part* of the body. What he says applies, not merely to the human soul, but to any and every substantial form relative to the body in which it is:

... if the soul were united to the body merely as a source of movement, then one could say that it was not in every part of the body, but only in one part, by means of which it moved the others. But because the soul is united to the body as its form, it is necessary that it be in the whole of the body and in every part. For it is not an *accidental* form of the body, but rather the *substantial* form.

Now, the substantial form is not merely the perfection of the whole, but of every part whatsoever. For since the whole is constituted out of the parts, a form of the whole which does not give being [*esse*] to each of the parts is [merely the sort of] form which is *composition* and *order,* as for example the form of a house: and such a form is an *accidental* form.[60] But the soul is a *substantial* form; hence, it is necessary that it be the form and the "act," not merely of the whole, but of every part. Thus, if the soul withdraws, just as the thing is no longer called "an animal" or "a human being," save equivocally, the way one says such things of a *pictured* animal or of *the statue* of an animal, so also this is the case as regards a hand or an eye, or flesh and bone ...[61]

vided, but [only] after they constitute and compose the composite. Hence, it is evident that the *being* [*esse*] of anything whatsoever consists in *indivision.* And thus it is that each thing, just as it protects its being, so also it protects its unity.

This is to say that "a being" and "a unit" are two words for the very same thing. The word "one" or "unit" adds a notion not expressed by the word "a being"; "one" says "being" but adds "undivided." "Undivided" is a negative notion, viz. the negation of "division." Thus, using the word "one" does not say any real thing more than "a being": it adds a mere negation.

59. Concerning this view as presented by Bertrand Russell, cf. Charles De Koninck, *The Hollow Universe,* London, 1960: Oxford University Press, pp. 60–69.

60. Cf. *CM* 7.2 (1277).

61. *ST* 1.76.8 (461b5–26). I should note that Thomas goes on to say:

... A sign of this is that no part of a body has its proper operation, given the removal of the soul; whereas nevertheless everything which retains its species retains the operation of the species.

In fact, this is only the first moment in Thomas's reflection on soul and substantial form. Not only is the soul in every part of the body, but the *whole* soul is in *every* part. We should not leave this aside, not only because it helps liberate us from mere imagination, but because Thomas provides some helpful distinctions about totality. He says:

And that the whole [soul] is in every part [of the body] can be considered from this, viz. that since a whole is what is *divided* into parts, in accordance with three [sorts of] *division*, there is threefold totality.

For there is a whole which is divided into quantitative parts, such as the whole line or the whole body.

And there is also a whole which is divided into the parts of the notion and of the essence: as the defined [item] is analyzed into the parts of the definition, and the composite [is analyzed] into the matter and the form.

But the third whole is the potential [whole], which is divided into the parts of the power [*virtutis*].[62]

Now, these distinctions are applied:

Now, the first mode of totality does not pertain to forms, save perhaps by association [*per accidens*]; and [even then] only to those forms which have an *indifferent* relation to the quantitative whole and to its parts. For example, whiteness, as regards its own [proper] character, stands equally as regards being in the whole surface or being in any part of the surface; and so, if the surface is divided, the whiteness is divided by association. However, the [sort of] form that requires diversity in the [quantitative] parts, such as is soul, and especially soul [as found] in perfect animals, does not stands equally as regards the [quantitative] whole and the parts; hence, it is not divided by association, i.e. through the division of the quantity. Thus, therefore, quantitative totality cannot be attributed to soul, either on its own account or by association.

But the second [sort of] totality, which is seen in function of perfection of notion and essence, belongs to forms properly and on their own account [*per se*].

And similarly, the totality of power [belongs to form as such], because form is the principle of operation.[63]

The diversity of totalities is now illustrated by consideration of the form which is whiteness. Thomas says:

If, therefore, one inquires about *whiteness*, whether it is as a whole in the whole surface and in its every part, one must distinguish. Because if mention is made of *quantitative* totality, which whiteness has by association, then the "whole" [of the

Obviously, present-day transplant surgery raises a question here. The answer required by the nature of substance is that which we find in Thomas, *In De generatione* 1.8 (60 [3]), concerning Aristotle at 1.3 (318b1–14). There are incomplete or imperfect forms, as one moves from the living thing to its degenerate states.

62. *ST* 461b33–45.
63. *ST* 461b46–462a13.

whiteness] is not in every part of the surface. And the same thing is to be said regarding totality of power: for the whiteness which is in the whole surface can *affect* sight *more* than [can] the whiteness which is in some part [of the surface]. But if mention is made of the totality of the species and the essence, then the whole whiteness is in every part of the surface.[64]

We see how these distinctions help us to "zero in" on the nature and role of *form precisely as such.*

Lastly, we have the application to the *soul.* We continue:

But because the soul does not have quantitative totality, either on its own account or by association, as has been said, it suffices to say that *the whole soul is in every part of the body as regards totality of perfection and essence; but not according to totality of power. Because it is not in every part of the body in function of every [one of] its powers; rather, in function of sight, it is in the eye, in function of hearing, in the ear, etc.*

Nevertheless, it is to be noted that, because the soul requires diversity of parts, it does not stand related to the whole [body] and to [its] parts in the same way; rather, [it stands related] to the whole primarily and of itself, as to its proper and proportionate perfectible [item]; whereas [it stands related] to the parts secondarily, inasmuch as the parts have an order toward the whole.[65]

I know of no substitute for this sort of analysis, if one is truly to grasp the sort of being which the substantial form, and particularly the souls of perfect animals, have. Thomas clearly does not want to say that substantial form and even soul in some less complex animals does not have the sort of relation to quantity which he sees in whiteness. However, someone like Behe is saying that life as such requires a complexity, i.e. a diversity of parts. Thomas, I think, would draw the conclusion that soul as such, i.e. substantial form in living things, does not have quantitative totality even by association. However, the general lesson is that we should have our eye on the sort of "perfection," "totality," "being all there" which pertains to form as such, if we are to see things, animate or inanimate, from the viewpoint of substance.

Thus, if we are to see well what is meant by "substance," we must keep it at a distance from our *images* of "sensible things." I would insist very much on the need to base all philosophizing on "sensible, natural things": metaphysics must begin with *that-which-is* [Latin: *ens*], as found in sensible things. Still, it must be said that *substantial natures* and *substantial being* are not *objects of sense*, are not "sensible."[66] Or rather, they are only

64. *ST* 462a13–25.
65. *ST* 462a26–42.
66. See Thomas Aquinas, *In De generatione* 1.8 (62 [5]):

. . . no substantial form is essentially [*per se*] perceptible to sense, but only to intellect, whose object is *the "what it is"* [*quod quid est*]; rather, the forms which are essentially perceptible to sense are qualities of the third species [of qualities], which for that reason

"sensible" if this word is used in a *wide* sense, to include *what immediately occurs* to the *intelligence* on the basis of experience of sensible things in sense cognition. We *see* and *hear* that-which-is-colored and that-which-is-sounding, a particular sensible unity. But the *substance* "dawns on" the mind, the intellect, because of such sensible experience.

The substance, as such, is not even really *imaginable*. Rather, we "get the point" of experience. Here is a passage from Thomas Aquinas on the meaning of the word "intellect," which, I would say, could be taken as a guide in these matters:

> ... The word "intellect" suggests a *deeply penetrating* knowledge: the Latin word *"intelligere"* suggests "reading the interiors." And this is quite clear to anyone considering the difference between *intellect* and *sense:* for sense-knowledge has to do with *exterior sensible* qualities; whereas intellective knowledge penetrates right to the *essence* of the thing: for the object of the intellect is *what the thing is* ... Now, there are many sorts of thing which are "hidden inside" [as it were], regarding which it is necessary that human knowledge "penetrate to the interior," so to speak. Thus, *"within"* the accidents lies hidden the substantial nature of the thing; *"within"* words lie hidden the meanings of words; *"within"* likenesses and symbols lies hidden the symbolized truth; and effects *lie hidden* in causes, and vice versa. Hence, with respect to all these cases, one can speak of "intellect."[67]

I am saying these things because I want to encourage an awareness of the problem of *penetrating* the sensible real with genuine metaphysical perspicacity. We find such items as substantial form difficult to grasp. Still worse is matter. Some of the things said about these items are strange. But part of the problem is that we have not seen, at the outset, how strange is sensible substance itself. It is a target of the *mind*, the mind "reading the interior" of sensible phenomena.

It is the metaphysician's business to "double back" on what seem to be *natural* concepts and judgments in order to show that they are not *all* "flat earth" errors.[68] We surely do conceive of things as many in kind and in number. Philosophers (or scientists) *very early on* proved unable to accept this.[69] Aristotle's work, in part, is aimed at honoring the original nat-

---

are called "experienceable" [*passibiles*], since they inscribe impressions [*passiones*] on the senses, as is said in the *Categories* ...

67. *ST* 2–2.8.1. See also *ST* 2–2.180.5.*ad* 2:

... human contemplation, as found in the present life [as distinct from life after death], cannot be without images [in the imagination], because it is connatural to man that he see intelligible conceptions in images, as Aristotle says in *De anima* 3.7 (431a16). Nevertheless, intellectual knowledge does not come to rest in the images themselves, but in them it contemplates the purity of intelligible truth.

68. Cf. Lawrence Dewan, "Laurence Foss and the Existence of Substances," *Laval théologique et philosophique* 44 (1988), pp. 77–84, at pp. 82–84.

69. This is true of thinkers like Thales, inasmuch as he views everything as substantially the same, but it reaches most alarming extremes in the Eleatics, who reject all variety. Cf.

ural judgment. We ourselves can exploit various advances in observational technique to confirm it.[70] While far from admitting that the natural judgment is a mistake, we do, nevertheless, insist that, for its well-being, it needs the advantages of reflection.

Both essence and substance are objects of natural intellectual knowledge, though not equally so.[71] First of all, *prior* to our intellectual knowledge, and *cause* of our intellectual knowledge[72] is sense-knowledge, a vital process of memories and *reasoned*, i.e. *comparative* experience, which has its climax in a perception of the universal-in-the-particular. Human sense has as its object, not merely the singular in its singularity, but somehow the universal-in-the-singular, e.g. "this man" or "this animal."[73] This is to say that the human sensorium is quiddity-oriented. The *anthropos* is by nature *onto-centric*.[74]

Aristotle, *Metaph.* 1.5 (986b10–987a2); 1.3 (984a29–b4); *Phys.* 1.2–3 (184b25–187a10).

70. I think of the knowledge of cell life presented by someone like Behe.

71. I leave discussion of the difference for another occasion.

72. The causality exercized by the phantasm is described in *ST* 1.84.6 (520b11–19), as "the matter of the cause" [*quodammodo . . . materia causae*] of intellectual knowledge. Now, the relevant causality is that applied by an object to a passive cognitive power. At *ST* 1.77.3 (466a31–33), it is characterized as *"principium et causa movens."* Thus, one might say that the phantasm is the matter of the moving cause, in the sense that the object of a passive power is a moving cause. I do not think it need or should be characterized merely as "material causality."

73. Thomas Aquinas, *Expositio libri Posteriorum* II.20 (Leonine ed., in *Opera omnia*, t. 1* 2, Rome and Paris, 1989: Commissio Leonina/Vrin, at lines 258–271):

. . . it is evident that it is the singular that is sensed, properly and through itself, but nevertheless the sense is in some measure also of the universal: for it knows Callias not merely inasmuch as he is Callias, but also inasmuch as he is *this man*, and similarly Socrates inasmuch as he is *this man*. And thence it is that, such a grasp by sense being already in existence, the intellective soul can consider man in both. But if the situation were such that the sense apprehended only that which there is of particularity, and in no way apprehended along with that *the universal nature in the particular*, it would not be possible that from the apprehension of sense [*ex apprehensione sensus*] universal knowledge be *caused* in us. [my italics]

Cf. Thomas, *Sentencia libri De anima* (in *Opera omnia*, t. 45/1, Rome/Paris, 1984: Commissio Leonina/Vrin), 2.13 (lines 191–220). The human "cogitative" power is contrasted with the lower animal's "estimative" power. The human inner sense power participates in something of the intellective:

. . . the cogitative apprehends the individual as existing under the common nature [*ut existentem sub natura communi*], which happens to [the cogitative] inasmuch as it is united to the intellective, in the same subject; hence, it knows this man inasmuch as he is this man, and this tree inasmuch as it is this tree; but the estimative does not apprehend some individual according as it is under the common nature, but only as it is the terminus or principle of some action or passion, as the sheep knows this lamb not inasmuch as it is this lamb, but inasmuch as it is nurse-able by it, and this grass inasmuch as it is its food . . .

Cf. also T. G. R. Bower, "The Object in the World of the Infant," *Scientific American* 225, no. 4 (October 1971), pp. 30–38.

74. On the power of discernment or comparison as running all through our cognitive life, cf. Thomas Aquinas, *Sentencia libri De anima* 2.27 (in *Opera omnia*, t. 45/1, Rome/Paris, 1984: Commissio Leonina/Vrin), *in toto* but esp. lines 229–236.

It is such a sensitive life which is properly disposed for intellection. And intellection is a continuation of that cognitive life of *comparison*, of reasoning, of seeing where something *leads*. That cognitive life is intellection when it moves *beyond experience*. This is true of all intellection, but most of all of intellection at its height, the cause of all intellection, knowledge of "a being" and "substance." The absoluteness of those objects requires that such knowledge be visions of "where experience *leads us to*" or "*points us to.*"

In a remarkable passage in *De malo* 6, a discussion of the existence of human free choice, we are presented with the following argument against saying that man has free choice:

... The principle of all human knowledge is the senses: therefore, man can know something only to the extent that either it or its effect falls under sense. But the [supposed] power itself, having a stance vis-à-vis opposites [i.e. the power of free choice], does not fall under sense; and in the effects of that power which *do* fall under sense, two contrary acts are not to be found existing simultaneously, but rather we always see that determinately one act always actually occurs. Therefore, we cannot judge that there is in man any active power having a stance vis-à-vis opposites.[75]

To this Thomas replies as follows:

... the beginning [or principle] of all human knowledge is from the senses, and nevertheless it is not necessary that whatever is known by man be subject to sense, or be known immediately through a sensible effect. Because the intellect itself has intellective knowledge of itself through its own act which is not subject to sense; and similarly, [the intellect] has intellective knowledge of the interior act of the will, inasmuch as through the act of the intellect the will is in a way rendered operative [literally: moved] and in another way the act of the intellect is caused by the will ... [and so the intellect understands the act of the will] as an effect is known through its cause and a cause through its effect.—*Nevertheless, even if we grant that the power of the will having a stance vis-à-vis opposites could not be known except through a sensible effect, still [the adversary's] argument does not follow. Because just as the universal, which is always and everywhere, is known by us through singulars which are here and now, and primary matter, which is in potency to diverse forms, is known by us through the succession of forms which nevertheless are not simultaneously in matter, so also the power of the will having a stance vis-à-vis opposites is known by us, not indeed by the opposite acts existing simultaneously, but because they succeed one another successively from the same source.*[76]

This reply reveals a conception of intellect and its relation to sense which is worlds apart from what is often called "empiricism."

---

75. Thomas Aquinas, *Quaestiones disputatae de malo* 6.obj. 18 (in *Opera omnia*, t. 23, Rome/Paris, 1982: Commissio Leonina/Vrin, lines 166–176).
76. *De malo* 6.*ad* 18 (Leonine ed., lines 641–664). My italics.

I say it is the *absoluteness* of the objects, "a being" and "a substance," which require the work of intellect. This is because the more absolute an object is, the less it is being taken as engaged in motion and change.

ESSENCE AND EVOLUTION

To complete this meditation on the importance of essence and substance, I wish to look at some of the things Charles De Koninck said about species in his presentation of cosmic evolution.[77] [See Addendum 3] This is important because many people would say that the very notion of a "species" is questionable[78] and that Aristotelian substantial form is an idea which can be blamed for thousands of years of intellectual (and seeming natural) stasis.[79]

What interests me most in De Koninck's study is the conception of the forms and essences of material things.[80] He presents a view of these "absolutes" as being very weak absolutes. The texts I think of in St. Thomas that help see where De Koninck is going are such as *ST* 1.11.4.*ad* 3, on diverse substances or essences as having diverse powers of effecting unity; *SCG* 2.68 (cited by De Koninck) on the greater unity of higher form;[81] the doctrine of "partial form" in the *In De caelo*,[82] and the general doc-

---

77. Charles De Koninck, "Le problème de l'indéterminisme," in *L'Académie Canadienne Saint-Thomas d'Aquin* (Sixième session, 9 et 10 octobre 1935), Québec, 1937: Typ."L'Action Catholique," pp. 65–159. De Koninck published a shorter study on the general idea of indeterminism, "Thomism and Scientific Indeterminism," in *Proceedings of the American Catholic Philosophical Association* (1936), Washington, D.C., 1937: The Catholic University of America Press, pp. 58–76. In this (p. 68, n. 20), he refers us to the Québec item for more detail. Subsequently he published "Réflexions sur le problème de l'Indéterminisme," *Revue thomiste* 43 (1937), pp. 227–252 and 393–409. I would like to have used some material from the recently published "*Le cosmos* (1936)–Extrait," *Laval théologique et philosophique* 50 (1994), pp. 111–143. However, I call attention to this important paper, which presents evolution as requiring the causality of an extra-cosmic pure spirit. The footnotes in what follow are mine, not De Koninck's, unless indicated.

78. Michel Delsol, "Où mène la biologie moderne? Questions aux théologiens et aux philosophes," *Laval théologique et philosophique* 52 (1996), pp. 339–353: the second section is entitled "The Disappearance of the Notion of Species." The idea is that the picture of the species as something well defined is to be abandoned: pp. 340–341.

79. Cf. e.g. David L. Hull, "The Effect of Essentialism on Taxonomy–Two Thousand Years of Stasis," *British Journal for the Philosophy of Science* 16 (1965), no. 60, pp. 314–327, and no. 61, pp. 1–18.

80. I set aside for another time discussion of the general conception De Koninck has concerning the philosophy of evolution, particularly as presented in "Le cosmos."

81. *SCG* 2.68 (para. 6; ed. Pera, 1453 [c]), where Thomas concludes:

. . . But something is not less one [if composed] out of intellectual substance and corporeal matter than out of the form of fire and its matter, but perhaps more [one]: because the more a form conquers matter, the more a unit [*magis unum*] is effected out of it and matter.

82. *In De caelo* 1.6 (63 [6]).

trine of hierarchy of form in Thomas.[83] I would say that De Koninck is explaining the oft-repeated doctrine that natural forms are "educed from the potency of matter," being present in matter not actually but potentially.

What then is De Koninck's conception? He tells us that Thomas distinguishes between necessary forms and contingent forms. De Koninck says:

> . . . Those forms are necessary which are entirely determined, and which constitute, [123] just by themselves essences—the pure spirits; and the forms which determine their matter sufficiently so as to be inseparable from it—[the forms] of the celestial bodies in an outmoded astronomy and those of men in the definitive future state of our universe. The forms of corruptible beings are contingent.[84] Among these beings, we distinguish those which are entirely corruptible *secundum totum et secundum partem;* and those which are only in part [corruptible],—such as men in the present state of the world. Thus, we obtain forms that are absolutely contingent, and forms which are contingent *secundum quid.* Natural beings are contingent because there is in them a real potency for not-being: prime matter. [122–123]

I take it that in the above he is calling the human soul a *secundum quid* contingent form, i.e. contingent "in a certain respect." He goes on to explain his conception of contingent form:

> Precisely what do we mean by the contingency of the form? Indeed, the form is not contingent because its co-principle is for it a potency toward not-being; the composite is corruptible because its form is contingent. It is the contingency of the form which is the intrinsic reason for the precariousness and the uncertainty of its [the composite's] existence. That is why we can conceive of a form which would not be contingent, in spite of its union with matter—the human form after the resurrection, where the composite is incorruptible.[85]

And he continues, underlining indetermination:

> The upshot is then that the form is contingent because it is not sufficiently determined in itself. Indeed, it is the lack of determination and the incapacity to individuate itself which call for matter[86] and which are the ultimate cause of the essen-

83. See especially *SCG* 3.97 in its entirety.

84. I would underline that this is true of them, not as form, but as *such* form. See my paper, "St. Thomas Aquinas against Metaphysical Materialism," in *Atti del'VIII Congresso Tomistico Internazionale,* t. 5, Vatican City, 1982: Libreria Editrice Vaticana, pp. 412–434.

85. Notice here that he has this idea of the human soul in the present state as in a measure "contingent." This is a recognition of the essential incompleteness of the human form. His eye is on the composite.

86. Cf. *CM* 5.10 (905):

> . . . matter is included in the first mode [of substance, i.e. particular substance], because particular substance does not have it that it be *substance* and that it be *individual* in material things, save by virtue of matter [*ex materia*]. [my italics]

tial complexity of mobile being. The existence of cosmic essence will be complex in its way, i.e. successive and continuous.[87] Indeed, the nature of existence is measured by the nature of essence. *Quantum unicuique est de forma, tantum inest ei de virtute essendi.*[88] If the form is not necessary, its existence cannot be totally assured.

Having thus focused on the ontologically hierarchical character of form, he goes on:

This need for matter which is the form [*qu'est la forme*] introduces into it [the form] an irreducible obscurity. Of the cosmic form[89] there cannot be a distinct idea, [an idea] independent of the idea of the composite; even the separated human form implies a relation to matter. And the matter which enters into this idea is not determined save as also signifying determinability relative to an infinity of other forms. A non-subsistent form is not a quiddity in the strict sense. This is to say that the different sub-species, such as the canine species and that [125] of the elephant, cannot be absolutely opposed, as are the individual-species which are the pure spirits; this is also to say that their definition will include the notion of matter, i.e. the possibility of an infinity of other sub-specific forms which can be drawn forth from matter. If they were determined in the matter, there would be of each one of them an idea independent of matter; and it [matter] would not be pure potency; there would be *latitatio formarum*, or else all the forms would come along *ab extrinseco.* [125–126][90]

I must say that, reading the above, I was not sure why De Koninck was speaking of "sub-species." This comes out much more clearly in his slightly later *Revue Thomiste* article, wherein he is much more explicit regarding "natural species" as distinct from "sub-species." There he says:

. . . the different natural forms are not contingent from every angle. The contingency only affects the sub-species; but since the sub-human natural species are only realized in sub-species, the importance of this contingency is appreciable.

Let us suppose, to illustrate this idea, a finite intelligence contemplating the world at the moment when there was in it no thing actually alive. This in-

87. Here, I would note that the *esse* of temporal things is only *per accidens* measured by time; but it is measured by time. Cf. *Quodl.* 4.3.2 [5], summarized below in Addendum 2.

88. De Koninck gives no reference for this, but it is doctrinally the same as what is said in *In De caelo* 1.6 (Spiazzi 62 [5]): each thing is, i.e. has being, through its form; hence, just so much and for so long each thing has of being, viz. just as great as is the power of its form. Cf. also *ST* 1.42.1.*ad* 1, on the quantity of power of being and operation as flowing from the quantity of power of the form. [I have more recently found the exact reference: *DP* 5.4.*ad* 1.]

89. This means the sort of form which we find in the world of generation and corruption.

90. On these two positions concerning form, see *ST* 1.45.8; "*latitatio formarum,*" i.e. the forms are "hidden" in the matter, considers the forms as already actual but "lying low"; obviously, the coming of forms from outside also views them as having complete being. Thomas's doctrine is that higher, i.e. spiritual, beings employ movement and change to exercize causality upon composite, i.e. material, agents, which bring form out of the potency of matter into act: cf. *ST* 1.65.4.*ad* 2.

telligence could foresee infallibly the coming of man into this world and also all that conditions absolutely the determination of matter in view of the human composite: it foresees the plant and the brute, but it is impossible for it to foresee all the concrete ways in which the natural species will be realized. These species, which are *quasi-genera* relative to the sub-species, are certain, *a priori*, because they constitute irreducible degrees of being: there is no intermediary between "being," "living," "knowing," and "understanding." Besides, the absolute character of this gradation finds its foundation in the idea of man whose soul is formally sensitive, vegetative, and form of corporeity. Because the soul of man is all that, not merely eminently but formally, these degrees of being are susceptible to being distinctly realized outside of him. The inorganic, the plant, and the animal are species-limits and [are] certain. But it is impossible that the proper determination of the sub-species which realize in a particular way these natural species participate in this certitude. Otherwise, the ways in which the animal and the plant can be realized would be determined in advance in matter; or, again, the matter included in the idea of man would signify explicitly all and the only possible forms: this is to say that there would not only be an idea of matter, but determinate ideas.[91]

He goes on to say that all sub-species were at a given moment future contingents. Thus, "cow" as "cow" is "philosophically indefinable." Its determinate truth is *a posteriori*. And:

The fixity of sub-human forms is thus only a counterfeit fixity. We are naturally metaphysicians: hence, the need to see the necessary and to assimilate, in the present case, the cosmic hierarchy to the series of whole numbers or to the immobile series of pure spirits, though there exists between them only an analogy.[92]

I am sure you see why I wished to qualify the meditation on substance in itself with these observations, so interesting from the viewpoint of evolution.

Coming back to the Québec paper, we see that De Koninck is able to convey the unforseeability of just what particular forms will emerge as nature moves toward its goal:

91. De Koninck, *Revue thomiste*, p. 234. In the Québec article, in a footnote (and again, one much more intelligible when one has read the *RT* article) he says:

... By existent varieties I mean the sub-species included within the limits of absolute natural species. Note nevertheless that a sub-species which constitutes in fact a limit of a natural species is never the absolute limit of this natural species. It tends towards a limit which is to be found at infinity. In the last analysis, the absolute character of natural species is founded on matter as essentially ordered towards its ultimate act, towards its last end—the human form, which is formally and in eminent fashion, at once sensitive, vegetative, and the form of corporeity. [p. 125, n. 1]

What he seems to mean is that the absolute lower forms are likenesses of what we see in the highest form of matter, and that it is matter, as calling for that highest form, which calls for forms which possess that sort of likeness.

92. *Revue thomiste*, p. 235.

Thus, the existent varieties are analogous to the cuts made in a continuum which are determinately true only *a posteriori*. Consequently, the determination which is a material form is something yet to be made [*est à faire*], precisely as determination. If it were entirely made in advance, then generation, for example, would be a pure launching into existence of a form already determined in the matter. [124–125]

We go on, now, to consider the field of species. We are told:

Two neighboring angelic forms are infinitely close in that they admit no intermediary species; they are also infinitely distant in that a transition from one species to the other is impossible, because they do not have in common a physical genus; they are absolutely heterogeneous. Natural sub-species, on the contrary, are infinitely close by their common natural genus; infinitely distant by the real possibility of an infinity of other intermediate sub-species. Thus, the vegetal realm has no absolute extreme limits. Between the most perfect of plants that exist and the lowest of animals, there is the possibility of an infinity of more perfect plants and of less perfect animals, even if this infinity is incompossible, from the viewpoint of existence. [126]

And at last we come to some remarkable conceptions of the "natural species" and the "sub-species":

. . . Natural species should be conceived of as zones of probability. No natural and individual form is an absolute type of a sub-species, nor [is] any sub-species [an absolute type] of its natural species. "The dog," "the carrot" are statistical entities like "the Frenchman" or "the Englishman." None of the elements exhausts the essence of its class. (That is why racism, which erects nations as absolute entities, and its contrary, atomism, are forms of determinism. The satirical poet is right to say:

All men are fools, and, despite all their care, Differ among themselves only as to more or less.

Because the reasonable man also is only a statistical entity.) [126–127]

It is hard to say what to attribute to form, and what to attribute to matter here. And what is meant by a "statistical entity"? This makes it seem as though it is the truly statistical mode of knowing which gets at the specific real. Have we lost the property of form here? Perhaps not. Rather, it might be said that form only comes into its own in intellectual consideration.[93] The sensible real is only potentially intelligible. As Thomas says:

93. *ST* 1.75.5 (444a6–11):
. . . the intellective soul knows some thing in its nature absolutely, for example, the stone inasmuch as it is a stone, absolutely. Therefore, the form of the stone, absolutely, according to its proper formal character, is in the intellective soul . . .

. . . the intelligible in act is not something existing in natural reality, as far as the nature of sensible things is concerned, which do not subsist outside of matter.[94]

De Koninck is challenging us to take seriously the form as perfection of matter, and even as only a partial perfection of matter, matter which is open to an infinity of such partial perfections.

Here, we get an important point as to what De Koninck means to say about nature and its evolutionary process. He tells us:

The higher one climbs in the hierarchy of species, the more the forms become necessary and consequently intelligible. *Quanto magis distant a materia, tanto magis necessariae.*[95] But only the human form will have an existence which is totally assured, by the fact that it is spiritual and that its duration [*sa durée*], leaving aside the time which it involves by its union with matter, is eviternal. [128]

The idea is constantly to give us more and more a sense of the nature of corporeal forms, as having something of determination and something of indetermination.

Obviously, De Koninck is giving us an interpretation of Thomas's doctrine. The merit of it, as I see it, quite aside from modern interests in evolution, is the extent to which it adds to the intelligibility of "educing form from the potency of matter." Is his argument compelling? His contention is that if the "sub-specific" forms were determinate, we would find ourselves in a doctrine of "hiddenness of forms" or else in a doctrine which gives a definite idea or ideas of matter. Yet he allows his hypothetical observer to foresee, not only the human form, but even the "natural forms" or "quasi-genera." The question then is: if one can foresee any form at all, without ruining the doctrine of "educing from the potency of matter," why cannot one posit that one can see all forms within the "zone" of the natural forms? I suppose the answer must lie in the need to preserve the indetermination, the infinity of possibilities, which such matter has.[96]

What is clear is that De Koninck helps us see the many levels of form which Thomas really has in mind. And that is all to the good.

94. *ST* 1.79.3.*ad* 3.

95. The Latin is not from St. Thomas. De Koninck is speaking of the cosmic forms, and so cf. such texts as *ST* 1.76.1 (449b37–450a5), or *ST* 1–2.85.6 (1181b4–27) on forms as aiming at incorruptibility.

96. On the infinity of forms to which matter is in potency, cf. *CM* 1.12 (198) and *ST* 1.7.2.*ad* 3. [A later note: as De Koninck rightly said, however, the matter is for the sake of the form; thus, the indetermination must find its ultimate explanation in that mode of form which requires a matter having indeterminacy. In *ST* 1–2.85.6, on whether death is natural, we learn that form is essentially the principle of being, that any particular sort of form tends to perpetuate its being, but that among the forms of material things, only the human form is of such a nature as to necessitate perpetual being. We also see there that the matter, whence comes corruption, makes a needed universal, i.e. cosmic, contribution to the situation.]

I have never heard any public discussion of this doctrine of De Koninck's (perhaps I have just not been in the right place at the right time), but I think it merits exploration.

Addendum 1

For this issue, cf. Thomas, *CP* 5.3 (ed. Maggiolo, #663–664) and *In* 'DE CAELO' 1.6 (ed. Spiazzi, #67). In the latter, we are told:

... there is not something contrary to substance, which is maximally evident in animals and plants (similarly, neither is there anything contrary to shapes and to relations. . . .)

And:

... nothing is contrary to substance as regards the composite, nor as regards the matter, nor as regards the substantial form: nevertheless, there is something contrary to it as regards the proper disposition to such a form, as for example fire is said to be contrary to water by the contrariety of the hot and the cold. And such contrariety is required in all those things which are generated and corrupted. And the contrariety of the movements according to the heavy and the light follow upon such contrariety. . . .

In the former, Thomas seems to have trouble with the above line of thinking. There, he at first had put that solution this way:

... fire is the contrary of water in function of active and passive qualities, which are the hot and the cold, the wet and the dry; but not as regards substantial forms. For it cannot be said that heat is the substantial form of fire, since in other bodies it is an accident in the genus of quality. For what is in the genus of substance cannot be an accident for something.

This he forthwith rejects:

But this answer has an obvious difficulty. For it is evident that the proper affections are caused by the principles of the subject, which are the matter and the form. If, therefore, the proper affections of fire and water are contraries, since the causes of contraries are contraries, it would seem that the substantial forms are contrary. Furthermore, in *Metaph.* 10.8 [1058a11–22); *CM* 10.10 (2122–2123)], it is proved that every genus is divided by contrary differences; but the differences are taken from the forms, as is established in book 8 of the same work [*Metaph.* 8.2 (1042b10–1043a29), and *CM* 8.2 *in toto*]; it would seem, then, that there is contrariety in substantial forms.

[664 (5)] Therefore, it is to be said that the contrariety of the differences, which is in all genera, is seen as regards the common root of contrariety, which is excellence and deficiency, to which opposition all contraries are reduced, as is had in the first book of this present work. For all differences dividing a genus stand in this relation, that one of them is in the role of the abundant, and the other in the role of the deficient relative to the first. For which reason Aristotle says in *Metaph.* 8 that the definitions of things are like numbers, whose species vary by addition and subtraction of unity [Aristotle, *Metaph.* 8.3 (1043b34–1044a11); Thomas, *CM* 8.3 (1722–1727)]. Nevertheless, it is not necessary that in every genus there be contrariety according to the proper intelligible character of this or that species; but merely according to the common character of excellence and deficiency.

For since contraries are [items] which are maximally distant [from each other], it is necessary that in any genus [where] there is found contrariety, there be found two terms maximally distant, in between which fall all those things which are of that genus.

Nor will [even] that suffice for there to be movement in the genus, unless from one extreme to the other it happens that one continuously proceed.

Therefore, in some genera these two conditions are lacking, as is clear in the case of numbers. For though all the species of number differ according to excellence and deficiency, nevertheless one cannot take two extremes maximally distant in that genus; for one can take a minimum number, viz. duality, but not a maximum. Similarly, there is no continuity between the species of number: because any species of number is formally perfected by unity, which is indivisible and not continuous with another unity.

And it is similar, also, in the genus of substance. For the forms of diverse species are different from each other according to excellence and deficiency, inasmuch as one form is more noble than another; and for that reason, from diverse forms diverse passions can be caused, as it was objected. Nevertheless, one specific form as regards its proper intelligible character is not contrary to another.

First of all, [this is] because in substantial forms one does not find a maximum distance between some two forms, such that from one of them one does not come [to the other] in an orderly way save through intermediaries; but rather matter, when it is deprived of one form, can indifferently receive diverse forms without order. Hence, Aristotle says in *De generatione* 2, that when from earth comes fire, it is not necessary that it undergo a transit through intermediate elements.

Secondly, because, since the substantial being of anything whatsoever is in some indivisible, one cannot find continuity in substantial forms, such that there be a continuous movement possible from one form into the other in function of the remission of the one and the intensification of the other.

Hence, Aristotle's proof, by which he proves that in substance there is no movement because there is no contrariety there, is demonstrative, and not merely probable, as the Commentator [Averroes] seems to imply. Still, it is true that it can be proved by another argument that movement is not in [the genus of] substance; which [argument] he presented earlier: viz. because the subject of substantial form is a being only in potency [*ens in potentia tantum*].

Addendum 2

Closely linked to this doctrine of the absoluteness of substantial being, to be dissociated from the motions it may involve, is the teaching of *Quodl.* 4.3.2 [5] (Leonine *Opera omnia,* t. XXV.2, Rome/Paris, 1996: Commissio Leonina/Vrin, p. 325), that by a miracle it is possible for God to restore to existence the numerically same substance which has ceased to exist, whether it has been corrupted or even annihilated, whereas it is impossible to restore movements once interrupted.

The reason is that some things, such as movement and time, have within the notion of their very unity the continuity of duration, so that any interruption is directly contrary to their numerical unity. To restore the being of such an item is thus intrinsically contradictory. But permanent things (and this is primarily the case of a substance) are such that their unity does not have in its notion continuity of duration, save *per accidens,* inasmuch as their being is subjected to motion: so taken, their being is one and continuous in accordance with the unity and continuity of time. And because the natural agent cannot produce such things without movement, thus it is that the natural agent cannot restore such things in their numerical identity, if they have been returned to nothing, or if they have been substantially corrupted. But God can restore such things without movement, because it is in his power to produce the effect without the intermediate causes, and so he can restore them in their numerical identity, even if they have been reduced to nothing.—The *Quodlibet* 4 is dated at Easter, 1271.

Addendum 3

De Koninck ("Le cosmos") says:

And if we do not seem able to follow the Angelic Doctor, is it not because we have excluded from the universe the efficient and sufficient cause moving the cosmos and pushing it upwards? Our timorous attitude is only too easily explained. Since Suarez we have resolutely put a plug on the world's top side: we wish to explain everything in nature by means of intra-cosmic causes. Suarez, in denying the apodictic value of the arguments presented by Saint Thomas for demonstrating on strictly rational lines the existence of pure spirits, cut every essential link between the cosmos and the created spiritual universe. Let us add to that his hybrid notion of prime matter, and we arrive logically at the barbarous creationism of our philosophy manuals. It is obvious that if we sterilize the world from its outset, nothing more can come forth. Creationism, which from all angles opens the world directly on God, passing to one side of the universal hierarchy, implicitly rejects what is essential to the universe: unity of order. [129]

De Koninck says that since Suarez the Scholastics abandon more and more the ontological study of nature. They think that scientific explanations replace the philosophy of nature. The philosophers concentrate only on notions of interest to the theologians. Cosmic repulsion may explain the expansion of the universe, and the theory of genes explain mutations, but none of that is an explanation of why anything is in motion. He says:

... none of that can explain the simple displacement of a material point from the ontological point of view. And to do that, one cannot have direct recourse to the general notions of metaphysics—we must find appropriate causes. If I have a headache because God wills it, that does not prevent my attributing it to a too long evening, and [does not prevent] its being removable by an aspirin. [129]

And he continues:

Now, I say that no intra-cosmic cause can provide for me an ontological explanation of the movement of the moon, not that the movement of the moon interests me particularly in philosophy of nature, but it is the movement of an inorganic phenomenon, and it is as such that I consider it. [130]

Chapter 8

ST. THOMAS, METAPHYSICS, AND FORMAL CAUSALITY

I. THE PROBLEM OF THE CAUSES

As I have elsewhere had occasion to remark, St. Thomas Aquinas's *Commentary on the Metaphysics of Aristotle* can, if carefully controlled, provide precious indications of how a Thomistic metaphysics ought to be constructed.[1] In the present paper I wish to expose and to some degree explore one such indication. Aristotle, in *Metaphysics* 3, presents problems which the metaphysical inquirer ought to have in mind, so that in his thinking he will aim at a definite goal and thus will be able to see when the task has been truly accomplished.[2] The first problem presented is whether the consideration of the four types of cause pertains to one science or to many and diverse sciences. This question presupposes what had been said in the introductory books, namely that the sought-after science of wisdom would be knowledge of the first and highest causes. St. Thomas also relates it to the last words of Book 2, which raise the same issue. And this, says St. Thomas, is to ask whether it belongs to one science, and especially to this one, to demonstrate by means of all the causes, or rather is it the case that diverse sciences demonstrate from diverse types of cause. St. Thomas sees this problem raised in first place because it deals with the very method[3] of the science itself. Aristotle had said in Book 2 that before undertaking to learn a science, one ought to be clear about its method.[4]

1. Cf. my article, "Being *per se*, Being *per accidens* and St. Thomas' Metaphysics," *Science et Esprit* 30 (1978), pp. 169–184. Henceforth I will refer to St. Thomas's *Commentary on the Metaphysics of Aristotle* as *"CM,"* citing book, *lectio,* and the paragraph number from the Cathala-Spiazzi edition, Rome/Turin, 1950: Marietti.
2. Cf. *CM* 3.1 (340–341) and Aristotle, *Metaph.* 3.1 (995a34–62).
3. The Latin word is *"modus."* I use "method" somewhat reluctantly to translate this word. Method, as involving the notion of pathway, would be more the *"ordo"* of the science. *Modus* is a more qualitative conception.
4. *CM* 3.2 (346).

After giving a list of the problems, Aristotle undertakes to spell them out as problems one by one. Our question, on the method of the science, is discussed by St. Thomas in *lectio* 4. St. Thomas, in all his discussions of the problems of Book 3, concludes each one with a brief statement of the solution eventually taught by Aristotle later in the *Metaphysics*. Needless to say, these brief presentations of the Aristotelian conclusions make most interesting reading. However, the presentation as regards the first problem is of special interest because St. Thomas tells us that Aristotle never expressly answers it. He says one can gather the answer from what Aristotle says in various places, and he proceeds to explain what he has gathered to be the answer:

For he determines in Book 4 that this science considers *ens* inasmuch as it is *ens:* and so it belongs to it to consider the primary substances, and not to natural science, because above mobile substance there are other substances. But every substance either is *ens* through itself, if it is form alone, or else, if it is composed out of matter and form, it is *ens* through its own form; hence, inasmuch as this science undertakes to consider *ens*, it considers most of all the formal cause. But the primary substances are not known by us in such a way that we know about them what they are, as can in a way be had from those things which are determined in Book 9: and thus in the knowledge of them the formal cause has no place. But though they are immobile according to themselves, nevertheless they are the cause of motion of other things after the manner of an end; and therefore, to this science, inasmuch as it undertakes to consider the primary substances, it especially pertains to consider the final cause, and also in a way the moving cause. But [it pertains to it to consider] the material cause, according to itself, in no way, because matter is not universally[5] a cause of *ens*, but rather of some determinate kind, i.e. mobile substance. But such causes pertain to the consideration of the particular sciences, except perhaps that they are considered by this science inasmuch as they are contained under *ens*. For in that way its consideration extends to all things.[6]

This then is the basic statement from which we take our start. In order to bring out its decisive features, we will note our disagreement with the discussion of it found in James C. Doig's book *Aquinas on Metaphysics*.[7] Doig discusses it principally in his comparison of the doctrine of St. Thomas in *CM* 4.1, on metaphysics as the study of *ens* inasmuch as it is *ens*, with what Avicenna, Averroes, and St. Albert had taught.[8] Since both Aver-

5. The text reads *"convenienter,"* i.e. suitably. I am conjecturing the reading: *"communiter,"* i.e. universally. Concerning this doctrine about the limited, particular nature of matter's causality, cf. St. Thomas, *De substantiis separatis,* c. 7 (Leonine ed., lines 91–102).

6. *CM* 3.4 (384). For *"ens"* (that which is), we retain the Latin.

7. James C. Doig, *Aquinas on Metaphysics,* The Hague, 1972: Martinus Nijhoff. We will make references to this work in the body of our text, by page.

8. It is to be noted that in his *ex professo* review of *CM* 4.1, Doig (pp. 102–110) omits all

roes and Albert had looked on the doctrine of Aristotle at this point as a reply to the first problem posed in Book 3, Doig is led to speak of it. But since, in *CM* 4.1, St. Thomas makes no reference whatsoever to this issue, Doig is obliged to look back to where St. Thomas treats it, viz. in Book 3.

Doig presents Averroes as saying that metaphysics treats of the formal and final causes only (p. 127). He then presents Albert as saying the same thing (p. 128), on the basis of Albert's *Metaphysica* 4, tr. 1. However, he notes that Albert also attributes to metaphysics the study of the efficient and material causes as well; this is inasmuch as metaphysics studies all beings (among which are efficient and material causes) (p. 129, using texts from Albert, *Metaph.* 3, tr. 2).

Doig goes on to contrast St. Thomas with these positions. He says that, in his presentation of *CM* 4.1, he has already mentioned that Thomas earlier in *CM* "explained that metaphysics studies all four causes" (p. 129). Now he turns to *CM* 3.4, St. Thomas's *ex professo* treatment of Aristotle's first problem. Doig stresses the importance of the question at issue:

Obviously, the answer given to the difficulty will completely determine the science of metaphysics: the object, the method, the relationship to the other sciences—all is affected. (p. 130)

He points out that Aristotle has given no answer in Book 3, but he never alludes to the fact that, for St. Thomas, Aristotle *never* explicitly answers the question. St. Thomas says he has been able to gather a solution from doctrines in various parts of the *Metaphysics*.[9] Doig speaks about how elaborate St. Thomas's treatment is, but when he comes to tell us what the doctrine is, he says:

As Albert, so Thomas too says that all four causes are studied. As both Averroes and Albert, Thomas says that to study being as such means above all to study the formal cause; yet unlike his predecessors, Thomas does not hold that one studies especially form because the form is the principle of our knowledge; rather one studies form because beings have their perfection from the formal cause . . . And finally, Thomas parts company with Averroes, but joins Albert, in nothing [read: noting][10] that metaphysics studies the material cause due to the fact that some beings are material. (p. 131)

As he goes on, Doig examines the merits of Albert's and Thomas's diverse reasons for metaphysics' study of the formal cause. He says that

---

mention of St. Thomas's paragraphs 540–543, on the reduction of all the things Aristotle has mentioned to four modes of being [*modi essendi*]. One would have thought this would have some importance.

9. *CM* 3.4 (384). Doig (p. 132, n. 3) does quote the Latin text as part of a larger whole.

10. Doig's book abounds in scribal errors.

Thomas's reason goes deeper than Albert's (which is supposed to be that the knowledge of the formal cause gives us the greatest knowledge of a thing), implicitly explaining Albert's reason. Thus, Doig continues:

... because the form of a thing is the source of what the thing is. Thus Thomas says, we study the formal cause of being as such. As Thomas indicates, Book Γ (IV) explains that it is the metaphysician who studies being as such, and not the natural philosopher, since some beings are not natural, that is not material. Now it would follow from this—and this is Thomas's point—that to study what all beings have in common is to study the formal cause ... only by studying what is common to all substances (namely form) can one study being as such. (pp. 132–133)[11]

In his resumé (pp. 139–140) Doig unites the materials from *CM* 3.4 and 4.1. He says:

Metaphysics studies all four causes: the formal cause because the form is the source of a thing's perfection; the final cause, because first substances are to be studied and they are the final causes of other beings; the efficient cause, again because one studies first substances; the material cause, because some beings are material.

The first thing to be noted (we intend to speak only of St. Thomas and St. Albert, not of Averroes) is that in treating of this first Aristotelian problem, Doig has failed to use the *third* tractate of Albert's *Metaphysica* 3. In tr. 2, used by Doig, Albert presents a first discussion of the problems. Tr. 3 is a second, more ample treatment of the same problems, and is written entirely in the "digressive" mode, i.e. dispenses with the paraphrase format in favor of a more comprehensive discussion.[12]

In tr. 3, the first chapter is on the first problem. In the course of presenting the difficulty, Albert introduces the opinion of Avicenna that

11. Doig postpones (at p. 134) his remarks on the efficient and material causes, and the reasons given by St. Albert and St. Thomas concerning them, until his chapter 5. Concerning the efficient cause, cf. pp. 202–210. At p. 202 Doig asks: "As a philosopher did Albert prove God was cause of being?" He does not refer to, and seems entirely unaware of, Albert, *Metaphysica*, bk. 5, tr. 1, c. 3 (ed. Cologne 16/1, p. 213, lines 60–75), where there is a proof of the first efficient (and creative) cause of being, prior to all moving causality (the whole of 213.33–214.56 should be noted). Doig (p. 202), in beginning his own reply to his question, says of Albert: "If he did, he has certainly left no trace of his proof in his exposition of Book Λ." This does not seem correct. At bk. 11, tr. 2, c. 1 (ed. Cologne, 16/2, 482.39–71), on Aristotle at 1071b4–6, Albert takes the single sentence of Aristotle as a complete argument and spells it out, just in itself. This is not an argument from motion, but from substance, generation, and corruption. And it seems to prove a cause of being. Cf. my paper, "The Distinctiveness of St. Thomas' Third Way," *Dialogue* 19 (1980), pp. 201–218; and more fully, cf. "The Interpretation of St. Thomas's Third Way," in *Littera, sensus, sententia*, Studi in onore del Prof. Clemente J. Vansteenkiste, O.P., ed. A. Lobato, O.P., Milan, 1991: Massimo.

12. Cf. Albert, *Metaphysica*, bk. 3, tr. 3, c. 1 (ed. Cologne, 16/1, 138.7–16).

cause and caused are a division proper to *ens*, and so belong properly to the first philosopher: and so Avicenna says that the knowledge concerning all the causes belongs *only* to the first philosopher.[13]

Albert further wonders why Aristotle, in Book 1, first inquired into the number and sorts of cause, and then, in Book 2, showed that they were finite, and now here asks whether all this is really his task or not. The implication is that the question must have something else in mind than the study of *causes as beings.*

Albert accordingly judges "without prejudice to a better opinion" that the knowledge of causes can be inquired into by one same science in three ways: (1) as something sought and eventually concluded to (we may suppose, as in Book 1), and (2) as part of the subject, or the subject, concerning which something is concluded (we may suppose, as in Book 2, where it was shown that the causes are finite), and (3) as a means or principle, through which one concludes that which one concludes concerning the subject or part of it. Now, says Albert, in this present question, we are not asking about the causes in the first or second way, though Avicenna's argument seems to suggest that we are. Here, the issue is solely about the third way. Albert says that this was the way he treated it earlier, in tr. 2, in accordance with Aristotle's own intention.[14]

In his ultimate resolution of the problem, Albert says that since the mathematician considers things conceived with matter according to being [*esse*] and separate from matter according to notion [*ratio*], and the efficient and final causes are causes of *esse* rather than of *ratio*, neither the efficient nor the final cause is used in mathematics. But in metaphysics [*in divinis*] there is consideration especially of *esse*, and the principles of *esse* are prior to *esse mobile*, and *all* the kinds of cause are principles of *esse*. Thus, the metaphysician demonstrates through all the kinds of cause. Though the cause "whence motion" and the matter and the end seem to be principles of the mobile as mobile, nevertheless there is an immobile cause "whence motion"; and there is a matter not determined through the subject of change and motion, but rather through this, that it itself is constituting the foundation of that which is [*fundans ens*], and individuating and standing under entity [*individuans et substans entitati*]: and these roles are prior to the subject of motion, since only that which is founded [*fundatum*] and an individual and something standing under is subject to change and motion, but the converse is not true, i.e. that every founded and individuated thing, every intrinsically substantive thing [*substans in*

13. That the study of causality as such is proper to the metaphysician is taught by St. Thomas, *CP* 2.5 (ed. Maggiòlo, Rome/Turin, 1954: Marietti, 177).

14. Cf. Albert, *Metaphysica*, bk. 3, tr. 3, c. 1: in *ed. cit.*, concerning Avicenna, cf. 138.66–72; on Aristotle's order of procedure, cf. 139.1–9; on the three ways, cf. 139.10–23.

seipso], is subject to change and motion. And Albert continues by presenting the properly metaphysical conception of the final cause.[15]

Thus, Albert has made the genuine meaning of the question: what kinds of cause does the metaphysician use in order to demonstrate his conclusions. And to the question as so understood, he gives as the proper answer: all four causes. And he has provided this answer by presenting properly metaphysical modes of all four causes. Whereas in the earlier presentation, in tr. 2, he brought in the material cause through using what he has in tr. 3 described as the first two ways of understanding the question,[16] here in tr. 3 he brings matter in in the way that the question is really meant.[17]

We are now in a position to appreciate St. Thomas's treatment of the problem. The first thing to determine is how he understands the problem. And he is quite explicit from the start:

Therefore he [Aristotle] says that the first query is . . . whether the consideration of the four causes, according to the four kinds, pertains to one science, or to many and diverse. And this is to ask whether it belongs to one science, and especially to this one, to demonstrate from all the causes, or rather do diverse sciences demonstrate from diverse causes.[18]

Again, at the beginning of the *lectio* in which he discusses the argumentative treatment of the problem, he says:

First he [Aristotle] argues concerning the consideration of this science, as to the causes through which it is demonstrated.[19]

Accordingly, St. Thomas's presentation of what he has gathered together and constructed as "Aristotle's answer" is to be read in the light of

---

15. Ibid., 139.65–96.
16. Cf. Ibid., bk. 3, tr. 2, c. 1 (ed. Cologne 16/1, 113.58–65). Albert uses the language of Avicenna here.
17. Cf. nevertheless Albert at bk. 3, tr. 3, c. 2. The problem is, in part, if both the physicist and the metaphysician demonstrate with all the causes, will not both have equal right to the title: "wise man"? The answer is that the metaphysician is the wise man. He primarily demonstrates with the ultimate end and the first formal substance and quiddity. And we read: "And though first philosophy demonstrates through the cause which is moving principle, nevertheless it then considers the first unmoved mover, which, through its own form which it has substantially within itself, acting toward form, makes substance known: as one knows the house from the form of the housebuilder as housebuilder, and the healthy (man) from the form of the healing doctor, as healer.–And if it uses matter in demonstrating, again it invokes it as related through proportion to form, which is in it [matter] confusedly, because otherwise it would not be a principle of knowing something. And thus it is clear how the first philosopher relates use of the mover and matter to the form and the end . . ." (ed. Cologne, 16/1, 141.47–59).
18. *CM* 3.2 (346).
19. *CM* 3.4 (369).

his quite definite understanding of the question. Thus, we cannot accept Doig's judgment: "As Albert, so Thomas says that all four causes are studied" (p. 131). What we read in St. Thomas is:

Causam autem materialem secundum seipsam nullo modo . . .[20]

The science of metaphysics considers the material cause, as such, in no way. The reason is that matter is not universally[21] a cause of *ens,* but is a cause of some determinate genus, namely mobile substance. Such causes pertain to particular sciences, not to metaphysics.

Following this, in the text of St. Thomas, comes the *"nisi forte"* remark. Of course, one can say that such causes, i.e. particular causes, are considered by this science inasmuch as they are contained under *ens:* in that way, metaphysics talks about all things.

This last remark is clearly outside the proper mode of the question— i.e. by what causes does the metaphysician demonstrate? We have dropped into the Avicennian (or an even more remote) treatment of the question.

What emerges here is quite a definite opposition between St. Thomas and St. Albert. Both are very clear on the sense of the question. St. Albert provides a notion of a strictly metaphysical material cause. St. Thomas quite definitely refuses to accept it. Albert proposes a matter prior to the subject of change, a cause of *esse.* St. Thomas will have none of it.

Now what about Doig's treatment of St. Thomas and St. Albert on the formal cause? First, we might note that St. Albert does not limit himself to saying that the formal cause is primary because it is the principle of knowledge. He says that the reason for its being principle of knowledge is that it is the principle of substance as substance, and of *"ens in eo quod ens."*[22] Albert says he himself has often said this, and one of the places to which we are referred by the editor shows us Albert, in the very act of paraphrasing Aristotle, including the reason why form gives more knowledge, viz.:

For though someone may know the same thing in many ways, we say indeed that he more fully knows who through demonstration says that thing in its own formal *esse,* what the thing itself is according to substance, which is the "what" and the "on account of what," than he who does not know such substantial *esse* of the thing.[23]

Doig at least once uses the following formula to express what he sees as the deeper reason stated by St. Thomas for the study of form in meta-

20. *CM* 3.4 (384).
21. Cf. above, n. 5.
22. Albert, *Metaphysica,* bk. 3, tr. 2, c. 1 (ed. Cologne 16/1, 113.54–56).
23. Ibid. (113.27–31).

physics: ". . . because the form is the source of what the thing is" (p. 132).
Now, this is very close to Albert as quoted above.

Indeed, what one might wonder about in Doig's presentation is the
way he treats St. Thomas. He constantly *paraphrases* St. Thomas on the
reason for the study of form in metaphysics; thus, "one studies form because beings have *their perfection* from the formal cause" (p. 131); "because the form is the source of *what a thing is*. Thus Thomas says, we
study the formal cause of being as such" (132);[24] "because the form is the
source of a thing's *perfection*" (p. 140, also p. 335).

Let us look at what St. Thomas says. He begins his gathering of Aristotle's position by a reference to Book 4:

For he determines in Book 4 that this science considers *ens* inasmuch as it is *ens:*
and so it belongs to it to consider the primary substances, and not to natural science, since above mobile substance there are other substances.[25]

Here, then, we have metaphysics and "two things" to consider, so to speak,
viz. *ens* and primary substances.

Next, St. Thomas settles the question of the cause used to demonstrate, as regards the consideration of *ens:*

But every substance either is *ens* through itself, if it is form alone, or else, if it is
composed out of matter and form, it is *ens* through its form; hence, inasmuch as
this science undertakes to consider *ens*, it considers most of all the formal cause.[26]

St. Thomas gives no reference here, probably because it is too clear that
this is the doctrine of Books 7 and 8.[27]

The argument of St. Thomas is clear also. The cause (hence the repeated use of "through" [*per*]) of *ens* is *form:* i.e. if a thing itself is *form*,
then it is *ens through* itself, and if a thing is a composite of matter and
form, then it is *ens through* form. Thus, a survey of the modes of *ens* (simple and composite) reveals the universal *causality* of form vis-à-vis *ens*.[28]

24. What St. Thomas says is that every substance is *ens* through form, i.e. form is the
cause of *ens*. I call it "paraphrasing" to say "form is cause of *what a thing is*." Doig does immediately add: "we study the formal cause of being as such," and if he takes this as the *primary* statement of St. Thomas, he is right. But his "thus" makes it look as though form is
cause of *ens* because form is cause of what a thing is. This is not true. Rather, form is cause
of what a thing is because form is cause of *ens*.

25. *CM* 3.4 (384).

26. Ibid.

27. Cf. especially Aristotle, *Metaph.* 7.17 (1041b25–28) and 8.2 (1043a1–12), as regards the causality of form in composite substances; and 8.6 (1045a36–67) (cf. *CM* 8.5:
1762–1764), as regards the role of form in substances which are form alone.

28. If this picture contains any difficulty (and I do not consider it a major difficulty), it
is in the notion of the "through itself," which gives a cause-effect or dual schema to what
is one. Cf. St. Thomas, *ST* 1.39.2.*ad* 5: the formal cause as such does not imply diversity of
cause and effect.

Doig's account of this passage (quoted above, ca n. 11) I find inadequate. St. Thomas is not speaking about the mere *community* of form ("... what is common to all substances ...") but about the community of form's *causal* role vis-à-vis *ens* inasmuch as it is *ens*.

Thus, two features of Doig's presentation here seem objectionable: (a) he loses sight of the importance of the notion of cause in his account of St. Thomas's solution, and (b) he substitutes some other item for St. Thomas's *"ens."* St. Thomas does not say in the solution that form is cause or source of a thing's *perfection*, or of *what the thing is*. He says that the form is the cause of *ens*.

It is our intention in the rest of this paper to follow out to some extent this doctrine of metaphysics as using the formal cause especially, insofar as metaphysics is *considerativa entis:* as this can be seen in *CM* 7 and 8. But before leaving the solution to the first problem, let us note the brief remarks made about the final and moving causes. St. Thomas (in the text quoted above, ca n. 6), having dealt with metaphysics as *considerativa entis,* then directs his attention to the other target of metaphysical investigation established in Book 4, namely the primary substances: and the point is that we cannot know them in such a way as to know what they are. He says that this is had *in a way* [*aliqualiter*] from Book 9.[29] Going on to say, then, that accordingly formal causality has no place in metaphysics as it undertakes to consider the primary substances [*considerativa primarum substantiarum*], St. Thomas puts the main insistence on the final cause of motion, just as one finds in Aristotle's Book 12, though once again St. Thomas does not bother to give a reference.[30] The addition concerning the moving cause "in a way" [*aliqualiter causam moventem*] could hardly be more cryptic.[31]

It is clear enough from what we have seen that St. Thomas's position is that metaphysics makes no use of the material cause for demonstration, and that as *considerativa entis* metaphysics is primarily knowledge through *formal causality*. This at any rate is St. Thomas's interpretation of Aristotle. One would expect, then, that this view of Aristotle's metaphysics would be readily apparent in St. Thomas's reading of *Metaphysics* 7 and 8, in

29. One would think St. Thomas must mean ca. 9.10 (1051b17–1052a11), but in his comments on this, at *CM* 9.11 (1904–1919), one would gather more that we *do* know the *quod quid est* of simple substances. Cf. 1905: "Quicumque enim non attingit ad quod quid est rei simplicis, penitus ignorat ipsam ..." (and cf. 1915); 1916: "... patet quod secundum sententiam Aristotelis humanus intellectus potest pertingere ad intelligendum substantias simplices ..." (cf. also 1912: "sed oportet ut intelligantur si mente attingantur ...").

30. Cf. Aristotle, *Metaph.* 12.7 (1072a26–30); and *CM* 12.7 (2519–2522 and 2528).

31. St. Thomas is here probably hinting at creative causality. The sliding from the moving cause to the divine mode of agency is a subtle process: cf. e.g. *CM* 7.17 (1660–1661).

which *ens is* considered as divided by the categories.[32] Our aim, then, in what follows is to consider *CM* 7 and 8 from this point of view.

II. THE PROCEDURE IN BOOKS 7 AND 8

Questions of order are very important for St. Thomas.[33] Here in *CM*, if we ask for the order of Books 7 and 8, we find quite a definite approach different from that of, e.g., Albert the Great.[34] The point of doctrine which St. Thomas exploits to the maximum in presenting Books 7 and 8 is the distinction between the merely logical mode of consideration, and the mode of consideration which penetrates to the *proper* principles of things: let us call the latter the "philosophical" or even the "existential" consideration.[35] Thus, if we look at the introduction to Book 8, we read:

After the Philosopher has determined in Book 7 concerning substance, in the logical mode, i.e. considering the definition, and the parts of the definition, and other such things which are considered according to reason [*secundum rationem:* following reason, or in the *domain* of reason], in this Book 8 he intends to determine concerning sensible substances through proper principles [*per propria principia:* through the *things' own* principles], applying what were inquired above logically to those substances.[36]

This is St. Thomas's general picture, one which he takes the trouble to repeat in the very same paragraph when he begins the word by word paraphrase of Aristotle. Thus, he says:

Therefore, he [Aristotle] says, firstly, that since many things have been said in Book 7, according to logical consideration, about substance, it is *necessary* to *syl-*

32. *CM* 7.1 (1245–1246 and cf. 1269). We by no means wish to neglect book 9, but we are inclined to think it belongs to a more comparative, less absolute, mode of consideration of *ens,* one already pointing us toward the primary substances. Cf. St Thomas, *CP* 2.10 (ed. Maggiòlo, 240) as well as *CM* 5.9 (889). For an indication of the importance of book 9 in St. Thomas's metaphysical schema, see our paper, "The Number and Order of St. Thomas' Five Ways," *Downside Review* 92 (1974), especially pp. 11–17.

33. Cf. our just mentioned paper, at p. 1. Also of interest in this regard are the remarks of St. Albert, *Metaphysica,* bk. 3, tr. 3, c. 1 (ed. Cologne 16/1, 139.1–9), concerning the order to be found (or not found) in Aristotle's procedure: who should be more orderly than the wise man? Doig, p. 240, speaking of "the numerous explanations of the connection between the various books, and even of the connections between the parts of individual books," judges that "points concerning method made in this regard are of little use in an attempt to grasp the metaphysics at work in Aquinas' mind when he wrote." The reader will see by our procedure how strongly we disagree with this.

34. Cf. below, n. 89, concerning St. Albert's opinion.

35. Such nomenclature is justified by the way St. Thomas speaks at, e.g., *CM* 7.17 (1658).

36. *CM* 8.1 (1681).

logize from those things which have been said, so that what have been said according to logical consideration will be applied to existing natural things.[37]

The words we have in italics represent what St. Thomas is working with in Aristotle. One can see that St. Thomas is taking it upon himself to contrast the two books on the basis of the modes of consideration.[38]

This contrast is carried over into what comes next in Book 8, namely Aristotle's review of what has been seen about substance and his proposal of what remains to be seen. St. Thomas divides Aristotle's presentation of substances so that Aristotle is first speaking about "substances existing in reality" [*quae dicuntur substantiae in rerum natura existentes*].[39] Some of these all admit, viz. sensible substances. Some are proposed by a few people, viz. the Platonic Ideas and the mathematicals. The other division of substance is "according to the viewpoint of the notion" [*secundum rationis acceptionem*].[40] One of these is the quiddity or "what it is" of the natural thing. The other is the substance in the doctrine that genus is more a substance than species, universal more than singular (which doctrine ties in with the argument concerning the Ideas).

This division having been made, St. Thomas understands Aristotle's statement of what has been done and what remains to be done in accordance with it. In Book 7 we have had the complete discussion concerning substance and notions [*de rationibus et de substantia*], i.e. the quiddity has been discussed, and the universal has been shown not to be substance. It remains to discuss substances existing in reality [*substantias . . . quae in rerum natura existunt*].[41] The ones posited by a few will be discussed in the last books (13 and 14, presumably). Now (in the present Book 8), we will discuss those substances which all admit are, i.e. the sensible ones [*quas omnes confitentur esse;*[42] this is *esse* as *in rerum natura subsistere*].[43] Enough

---

37. Ibid.
38. It need hardly be said that our procedure of italicizing the words of Aristotle in St. Thomas's paraphrase is highly approximative. Nevertheless, it serves to give the general picture of the commentator at work. The words I have in italics represent what St. Thomas is working with in Aristotle, with the exception of the word *"itaque"* in *"Ex his itaque dictis syllogizare oportet"* (at 691, in the Latin Aristotle of the Cathala-Spiazzi edition of *CM*). That this word was actually in St. Thomas's text seems indicated by the rubrics at *CM* 7.3 (1306). I mention this word only because it is barely conceivable that St. Thomas is giving it the sense of *"ita"*: "From the things so said . . ." This would be an opening to introduce the theme of the diverse modes of speaking and considering, as distinguishing the two books.
39. *CM* 8.1 (1683).
40. *CM* 8.1 (1684).
41. *CM* 8.1 (1685).
42. Ibid.
43. *CM* 8.1 (1683). Henceforth, we will sometimes make references to *CM* directly in the text.

has been said to show the importance of this distinction between logical and concrete or existential consideration for the *Metaphysics* as read by St. Thomas. Let us now look at the way St. Thomas uses the distinction in various stages of *CM* 7 and 8. We should note first of all that St. Thomas had already announced that he understood the distinction between 7 and 8 in the way we have just seen. He did so at 7.3, in explaining for the first time the order of procedure in treating of sensible substances. He says:

... it is divided into two parts. In the first he determines concerning the essence of sensible substances by means of logical and common notions [*per rationes logicas et communes*]. In the second part, through the principles of sensible substances, in Book 8, where it says: *"Ex his itaque dictis syllogizare oportet."*[44]

Now, here, St. Thomas divides Book 7 (i.e. the remaining larger part, for he is now at Aristotle's 7.4) into two parts:

The first part is divided into two. In the first he shows us of what sort is the essence of sensible substances. In the second, he shows that this sort of essence has the role [*ratio*] of principle and cause, there [where it says] "Quod autem oportet."[45]

Thus St. Thomas sees Aristotle's 7.17, corresponding to his own *lectio* 17, the last *lectio* of the book, as a distinct step in Book 7.

And indeed, if we look at the beginning of *lectio* 17, we find a most interesting assessment of what has already been done and of what there remains for Aristotle to do. St. Thomas says:

The Philosopher, in the beginning of this Book 7, was promising that he would treat of [that] substance of sensible things which is the "what is being" [*quod quid erat esse*],[46] which he made known logically [*logice notificavit*], showing that those things which are predicated by virtue of themselves [*per se*] pertain to the "what the thing is" [*quod quid est*]: from which [procedure] it was not yet manifest what is the substance which is *quod quid erat esse*. Now, this substance the Platonists said was the universals, which are separated species: which Aristotle disproved immediately above. Thus, it remained, that the Philosopher himself show what in reality [*secundum rem*] is the substance, which is *quod quid erat esse*. And with a view to showing this, he lays down as a preliminary [*praemittit*] that the substance, which

44. *CM* 7.3 (1306). On the significance of the world "principles" in this statement, see below, ca n. 107.

45. The text of Aristotle, as commented upon by St. Thomas, at 7.17 (1648) actually has *"quid,"* not *"quod."*

46. We will generally leave in Latin this Aristotelian formula. On its Aristotelian sense, cf. J. Owens, *The Doctrine of Being in the Aristotelian Metaphysics,* Toronto, 1963 (2nd ed.): Pontifical Institute of Mediaeval Studies, pp. 180–188.

is *quod quid erat esse*, has the role of principle and cause: and that is the intention of this chapter.[47]

Here, then, once more, we have the characterization of Book 7's treatment, and most explicitly of its positive part, as a logical presentation. And it is made perfectly clear that St. Thomas regards what Aristotle has so far done as falling short of *knowledge of the real*. The chapter 17 itself is assigned the doctrine that the substance as *quod quid erat esse* is a principle and a cause, just as St. Thomas said in 7.3 (1306). And we see that this is regarded as a kind of preliminary point, preparatory for the treatment of the *reality* of quidditative substance.

But there is more here which pertains to our study, in the word-by-word presentation of Aristotle. St. Thomas says:

He therefore says firstly that now that it has been shown that nothing of things said universally is substance, as the Platonists held, *let us say what* in truth *must be called "substance,"* viz. which is *quod quid erat esse, and of what sort* this substance is: whether, that is, it is form, or matter, or something like that; and this, I say, let us say *inserting* or announcing, *as it were,* a *starting point other* than that logical starting point, by which we entered, at the beginning of Book 7, into the investigation of the aforesaid substance . . . And he adds what that other starting point is by which one is to enter into the proposed inquiry, saying that *from here one is to proceed* toward the manifestation of the aforementioned substance, that we know that in the *substance* itself there is [or: it is] some *principle and some cause.*[48]

Here we see that the new starting point is not regarded as logical, and that its positive content is that in the substance (the composite, apparently), it (the reality which is, or which lies behind, the quiddity) is a principle and a cause. One can see to what extent St. Thomas's procedure constitutes a definite interpretation by considering that for St. Albert, at this point, not only has chapter 17 been treated as part of the treatise on substance as non-universal (although as a kind of return to the truth at the end of it),[49] but we read this:

Therefore, let us begin by saying that, certainly, of the composite sensible substance, which is the "this something," there is some principle and some cause which is the quiddity of it. And though we showed this above through the definition, nevertheless now, in order that the doctrine be more certain, we will show the same thing through the natural question about anything whatsoever, and

47. *CM* 7.17 (1648).

48. Ibid. The italics represents the text of Aristotle. It is to be noted that Doig, who gives much prominence to "the logical method" in his reconstruction of St. Thomas's metaphysics (cf., e.g., pp. 306–311), never cites or refers to this paragraph of *CM*.

49. Cf. Albert, *Metaphysica*, bk. 7, tr. 5, c. 8 (ed. Cologne 16/2, 383.73–384.3).

these two manifestations are logical. Hence, therefore, it will be clear that such substances have some substance [as] principle and cause.[50]

Albert has favored the *"iterum"* in Aristotle's text,[51] thus understanding that the quiddity has *already* been shown *as principle and cause*. And while he says this was done by means of the definition, he regards the novelty of the present moment, not as the very doctrine of "cause and principle," as in St. Thomas, but in the technique of using the doctrine of natural questions. Moreover, almost as if he meant to contradict the text of St. Thomas's *CM*, he says that this second approach, like the first, is *logical.*[52]

Turning back to St. Thomas, we have now seen that for him Book 7 differs from Book 8 in that the former uses logical consideration while the latter treats of the principles proper to existing substances. And we have seen that 7.17 marks a transition to the new mode of consideration, seemingly by shifting the approach from definition to causality. However, we must now look further at Book 7, for while globally we can say it employs logical consideration, this is not the whole story for St. Thomas.

The most telling passage for the study of the situation is *CM* 7.11 (1535–1536). Aristotle, at an earlier point in Book 7, had concluded that the quiddity, and the thing whose quiddity it is, are identical, and even notionally identical. Non-identity of these means that one is faced with mere *ens per accidens.*[53] However, now, at *Metaph.* 7.11 (1037a33–b7), Aristotle says that things which include matter do not have identity of quiddity and thing. In explaining this change of doctrine, St. Thomas says that the earlier doctrine was true for the logical consideration of *quod quid erat esse*. Here, at 7.11, Aristotle has "descended to the natural principles which are the matter and the form, and showed how they are diversely related to the universal, and to the particular which subsists in nature." And so, explains St. Thomas, Aristotle excludes from his previous judgment of identity of quiddity and thing "material substances existing in reality" [*substantias materiales in rerum natura existentes*].[54]

From this we can see that Book 7, though for St. Thomas it is dominated by the logical consideration, is not entirely uniform, but involves the introduction of the *real principles of things* (matter and form) as well.

50. Ibid., 384.10–20.

51. The Latin of Aristotle at 1041a6, in the Cologne ed. of Albert, 383.82, reads: "Quid autem oportet dicere et quale quid substantiam, iterum, aliud tamquam principium facientes, dicimus . . ." The word "iterum" does not figure in Albert's paraphrase, but it seems to be reflected in the idea that the doctrine has already been taught.

52. We presume that Albert's *Metaphysica* was written not much later than 1262–1263 (cf. B. Geyer, in ed. Cologne 16/1, p. viii), and thus antedates *CM* in all probability (cf. J. A. Weisheipl., *Friar Thomas D'Aquino*, Garden City, N.Y., 1974: Doubleday, p. 379).

53. Cf. our paper concerning this notion, mentioned in n. 1.

54. *CM* 7.11 (1536).

Let us now examine the procedure of "logical consideration," together with some statements of St. Thomas about it, to get a better idea of what is meant. We should begin with *CM* 7.3 (1308–1309). Paraphrasing Aristotle, St. Thomas says:

He says firstly that one must speak first of sensible substances, and *quod quid erat esse* must be shown first in them: *therefore, first we will* say *some things logically* about that which is *quod quid erat esse*. For, as was said above, this science has some affinity with logic, because of the generality of both. And so the logical mode is proper to this science, and from it it fittingly begins. But he says he is going to speak more in a logical way about the "what the thing is," inasmuch as he investigates what *quod quid erat esse* is, starting from the mode of predicating [*ex modo praedicandi*]; for this properly pertains to logic.[55]

If we look back at *CM* 4.4 (572–577), concerning Aristotle, *Metaph.* 4.2 (1004b17–26), we are told, in quite a long development by St. Thomas, that the dialectician and the philosopher cover the same field, but that the dialectician does so with less than scientific knowledge, treating things on the basis of their existence in notions, and not on the basis of the principles intrinsic to things themselves. The reason that the two cover the same field is that the intelligible roles [*intentiones intelligibiles*] which the dialectician studies coincide in extent with the beings of nature [*entia naturae*] which the philosopher studies, because all the beings of nature fall under the consideration of reason. Examples of the intelligible roles are genus and species. St. Thomas explains that dialectic, called "tentative" by Aristotle, does have a demonstrative phase, i.e. it has a science of the use of intelligible roles for arriving at probable conclusions about the real. However, use of this science, as it takes place in the sciences of the real, is probable, not demonstrative, procedure: it is not scientific knowledge of the real.[56]

It is clear, then, that in metaphysics, to the extent that we have genuinely to do with the use of logical consideration, while we have what St. Thomas calls a way of beginning particularly suitable for metaphysics, we do not have scientific metaphysical procedure.[57]

Now let us consider the actual use of the logical consideration which begins the metaphysical study of substance as quiddity. We might re-

---

55. The italicized words, except for the first and last instances of *"quod quid erat esse"* represent the text of Aristotle.

56. *CM* 4.4 (576–577). Again, it is notable that Doig makes no use of these paragraphs; perhaps they have to do with the disappointment he expresses concerning 572–577 generally (cf. p. 251, n. 1). St. Thomas in this passage does not go into the question of why there is the diversity between things in reason and things in reality; cf., on this, *CM* 1.10 (158).

57. It is notable that nothing is said as to *why* one begins this way.

mark that, in *CM* 7.3 (1308), quoted above ca n.55, St. Thomas speaks as though *"quod quid erat esse"* ("quiddity" for short) names something which might be considered logically, or might be considered philosophically. That is, the very term "quiddity" is not seen as exclusively pertaining to the logical consideration of substance. And this is true also in *CM* 7.17 (1648), quoted above ca n. 47. On the other hand, at *CM* 8.1 (1683–1684), discussed above ca nn. 39–40, the quiddity of the natural thing is classified as substance "according to the viewpoint of the notion" [*secundum rationis acceptionem*], and is contrasted with really existing substance [*substantiae in rerum natura existentes*].

Here is St. Thomas paraphrasing Aristotle as actually carrying out the logical consideration:

> But this firstly is to be known concerning the *quod quid erat esse*, that it is necessary *that it be predicated according to itself* [*secundum se*]. For those things which are predicated according to accompaniment [*per accidens*] of something do not belong to its *quod quid erat esse*. For by *"quod quid erat esse* of something" we mean this, viz. that which can fittingly be replied to the question posed by "what is it?" But when we ask about something: "what is it?" we cannot suitably reply the things which are in it according to accompaniment; as, when it is asked "what is a man?," it cannot be answered that it is "white" or "seated" or "musical." And thus none of the things which are predicated according to accompaniment of something pertain to the *quod quid erat esse* of that thing: *for "to be musical" is not "for you to be."*[58]

One can see how little in the above comes directly from Aristotle and how much is St. Thomas's presentation of Aristotle's logical consideration. It is to be noted that the term *"quod quid erat esse"* is from the start associated with the question: "what is it?" (which will be used in 7.17 in approaching quiddity as principle and cause).

St. Thomas at this point undertakes to explain Aristotle's use of *"esse"* with a dative, as in *"tibi esse,"* "for you to be." He says:

> But it must be known that in all the following, by the expression "being this" [*hoc esse*] or "being for this" [*huic esse*], he means the *quod quid erat esse* of that thing: for example, "being for man" [*homini esse*] or "being man" [*hominem esse*]: he means that which pertains to the "what is man."

And then he continues with the paraphrase:

> Now, *that which is "being musical,"* i.e. the very "what musical is," *does not pertain to what you are.* For if it be asked: "what are you?" it cannot be replied that you are

---

58. *CM* 7.3 (1309), on Aristotle at 1029b13–15. The words in italics (excepting all but the first *"quod quid erat esse"*) are Aristotle.

musical. And therefore it follows that "to be musical" is not "for you to be"; because those things which belong to the quiddity of the musical are outside your quiddity, though "musical" is predicated of you. And this is *because you are not musical according to yourself,* that is, because "musical" is not predicated of you according to itself, but according to accompaniment. *That* therefore pertains to the "what it is" of you *which you are according to yourself,* that is, because it is predicated of you according to itself and not according to accompaniment: as, of you is predicated according to itself "man," "animal," "substance," "rational," "sentient" [*sensibile*], and other things of this sort, which all pertain to the "what it is" of you.[59]

We are engaged in speaking of real things, but we are considering them as they are exhibited through predication. The focus is on predicates and how they are predicated, even though it is the *things* spoken of that one wishes to know. Obviously such a procedure implies confidence that these discussed differences in modes of discourse reflect differences in things themselves.

What is the general effect of the logical consideration of substance as quiddity, in that portion of Book 7 which most unquestionably involves logical consideration, viz. *CM* 7.3–5?[60] We should note that, for St. Thomas, the target of attention in Books 7 and 8 is the formal natural principle, the substantial form. The study of quiddity is seen as an approach to the substantial form.[61] The latter is distinguished from the concrete composite: it has some kind of real distinguishablity.[62] With the recourse to quiddity, or *per se* predication, we have before us a distinction between a thing and what that thing is. Our discourse takes separately the two, the thing as subject and the "what the thing is" as predicate. Moreover, what is exhibited in this way is the *unity* of such a predication. What is predicated is the very thing itself, i.e. thing and quiddity are one *in notion,* and not merely by accompaniment of some sort.[63] In this way, we are able to contrast what has a quiddity, a true definition, with such realities as fall short of this sort

59. Ibid., on Aristotle at 1029b15–16.
60. We say this most unquestionably involves logical consideration because, starting with 7.6, we enter into a discussion of *generation,* which extends to 7.8 inclusively; St. Thomas says nothing to exclude this from logical consideration, but it can hardly be seen as the pure article, considering that in the next section, 7.9–12, which returns to the topic of definition, we are told that Aristotle has "descended to the natural principles which are the matter and the form . . ." It is constantly the introduction of the natural principles (as in discussions of generation) which constitutes diminution of the logical consideration.
61. See below, ca n. 83.
62. I take it that form does not *really* enter into the discussion of substance until *matter's* existence has been established (through motion, generation, and corruption). That is, first comes substance, then generation and corruption reveal matter (cf. *CM* 8.1: 1689), and then one sees that the *substantial principle* must have the nature of *form* (i.e. something analogous to the shape of the statue, but in the order of substance) (cf. *CM* 7.2: 1277).
63. *CM* 7.5 (1375).

of unity and self-containment. There is no quiddity in the categories other than substance, or at least only quiddity in a secondary sense.[64]

A notable feature of this discussion is that while at the beginning, with the talk about what can be predicated of "you" *per se,* one might think one was dealing with a predication such as "Socrates is a man," in fact, in the fully developed logical consideration, the individual is not in the picture. The subject is the *definitum,* properly so called, i.e. the species. "Man" and "man is a rational animal": these are the objects of logical consideration.[65] But once one descends to the material individual, one is no longer having to do with the sort of unity one observed in "man is a rational animal." The thing and its quiddity are no longer identical. Thus, in *CM* 7.9–12, our attention is turned from the unity of definition with *definitum* to the compositeness of definition, and indeed to this as a kind of springboard to a consideration of the non-definable singular (locus of the "parts" which are not "parts of the definition")[66]—i.e. the logical consideration itself is used as a means of directing attention beyond mere logic.

In general, the logical consideration serves to display the unity or self-identity proper to substance. Moreover, it displays this unity as a unity of *things,* fully conceivable realities such as we commonly name in subjects and predicates. It seems to be above all the need to take account of *matter* which forces the revision of this picture, and thereby forces us to the proper conception of substantial form (not a fully conceivable reality, not a predicable thing; not even a predicable thing taken abstractly, like "humanity") as cause of the unity which is indeed found in sensible substances as they actually exist.[67]

Let us look now at the *philosophical* consideration, in some of those passages in which St. Thomas is contrasting it with the logical. We will begin with St. Thomas's treatment of the passage (Aristotle, *Metaph.* 7.3: 1029a20–27) wherein, in order to answer those who make substance primarily or even exclusively matter, Aristotle says what matter really is. In St. Thomas, we find:

Because the aforesaid argument showing that matter alone is substance seems to have proceeded from ignorance of matter . . . therefore he [Aristotle] conse-

---

64. Cf. especially *CM* 7.4 (1331–1341). The key notion in these discussions is that of *per se* unity: cf. 1340. And this in turn suggests that behind all the discussion of definition is substance as caught sight of in the theatre of generation and corruption: cf. *CM* 6.2 (1179). It is, therefore, we believe, regrettable that Doig, in his meticulous exposition of *CM* 4.2 (at pp. 110–120), on the fact that the study of *ens is* also the study of unity, omits all mention of paras. 551–552, which use generation and corruption to establish the sameness of *ens* and *unum.*

65. Cf. *CM* 7.11 (1536); also, 7.5 (1378).

66. See below, ca n. 92.

67. On the distinction between form and quiddity, see below, ca n. 88.

quently says what matter is according to the truth of things, as declared in *Physics*, Book 1. For matter in itself cannot sufficiently be known, except through motion; and its investigation seems to pertain especially to the natural scientist. Hence the Philosopher accepts here, concerning matter, those things which were investigated in physics, saying: *"But I say matter* is *that which according to itself,* that is, considered according to its own essence, *in no way* is either *what,* i.e. substance, *or quality,* or *anything of* the *other genera by which ens* is divided or *determined."*[68]

St. Thomas thus bears down hard on the point that matter can be sufficiently known only through motion, and that Aristotle is here depending on what he has said in the *Physics.* And he continues:

And this appears primarily through motion. For it is necessary that the subject of change and motion be other, speaking essentially [*per se loquendo*], than either of the termini of motion: as is proved in *Physics* 1. Hence, since matter is the first subject standing under not merely motions, which are according to quality and quantity and the other accidents, but even [under] the changes which are according to substance, it is necessary that matter be other, according to its own essence, than all substantial forms and their privations, which are the termini of generation and corruption; and not merely that it be other than quantity and quality and the other accidents.[69]

All this St. Thomas has *inserted* in his insistence that it is through motion alone that a sufficient knowledge of the essence of matter can be had. Nothing in the text of Aristotle demanded this clarification: on the contrary, as we are about to see.

St. Thomas goes on:

And yet, for all that [*Attamen*], the Philosopher [i.e. Aristotle] does not prove the diversity of matter from all forms through the route of motion, which proof indeed is by the route of natural philosophy, but through the route of predication, which is proper to logic, which in Book 4 of the present work he says is akin to this [present] science.[70]

St. Thomas seems here somewhat taken aback by Aristotle's procedure. He goes on to explain Aristotle's argument, which supposes a real distinction between subject and predicate. St. Thomas has to relate this to what he calls "denominative" or "concretive" predication, rather than univocal, essential predication. But it is clear that for St. Thomas, Aristotle's doctrine really depends on the physical argument.[71]

To this it should be added that later (Aristotle, *Metaph.* 8.1: 1042a32–b8) we have matter actually presented by means of the doctrines of the

---

68. *CM* 7.2 (1285). The italics are the Aristotle text.
69. *CM* 7.2 (1286).
70. *CM* 7.2 (1287).
71. *CM* 7.2 (1288–1289).

Physics, and St. Thomas once more insists: "From this argument of Aristotle, it is clear that substantial generation and corruption are the starting point for coming to a knowledge of first matter."[72] Thus, the procedure of Aristotle in *Metaph.* 7.3 is seen by St. Thomas as provisional at best. Furthermore, while we found in the foregoing no explicit formula such as "philosophical consideration," nevertheless we did have the contrast between Aristotle's logical procedure and the other procedure, the only one which gives "sufficient knowledge" of matter.

Having looked at the text of *CM* 7.2 on matter, let us look again at *CM* 7.11 (1535–1536). What we mean to focus upon is what characterizes the properly philosophical consideration. Previously Aristotle had not excluded material substances from his judgment that quiddity and thing are identical. St. Thomas points out that the quiddity is what is signified by the definition,[73] and that the individual is not defined.[74] Thus, individual matter, which is the principle of individuation, lies outside the quiddity. But, says St. Thomas:

> . . . it is impossible that the species be in reality [*in rerum natura esse*] unless in "this individual." Thus, it is necessary that any real thing [*res naturae*], if it have matter which is part of the species, which pertains to the "what it is," also have individual matter, which does not pertain to the "what it is." Hence, no real thing [*res naturae*], if it has matter, is the very "what it is," but is that which has it: as Socrates is not humanity, but is that which has humanity. But if it were possible for there to be a man composed of body and soul, who was not "this man" composed out of "this body" and "this soul," nevertheless he would be his *quod quid erat esse,* though he had matter. [1536] But though man outside the singular does not exist really [*non sit in rerum natura*], he does exist in notion [*est, tamen, in ratione*], which pertains to logical consideration. And so above, where he [Aristotle] considered logically concerning *quod quid erat esse,* he did not exclude material substances, that in them also the "what it is" be identical with that to which it belongs. For common "man" [*homo communis*] is identical with his "what it is," logically speaking. But now, after he has descended to the natural principles which are the matter and the form, and has shown how they are diversely related to the universal, and to the particular which subsists in nature [*particulare quod subsistit in natura*], he excepts here from that which he said above had "what it is" identical with thing, material substances existing in reality [*substantias materiales in rerum natura existentes*]. But it remains that those substances which are forms alone subsisting [*formae tantum subsistentes*] do not have something through which they are individuated, which is outside the notion of the thing or of the species signifying "what it is." And in them it is true unqualifiedly that any of them is its *quod quid erat esse.*[75]

72. *CM* 8.1 (1689).
73. Cf. also *CM* 7.5 (1378).
74. Cf. also *CM* 7.10 (1493–1496); but also 7.15 (1617–1618).
75. *CM* 7.11 (1535–1536).

What Aristotle has done, in moving, "descending," from logical to philosophical consideration, is to introduce the natural principles, the matter and the form, and to show how they stand with respect to the universal, and to the particular which subsists in nature. Just as later, at 7.17, when St. Thomas wishes to exemplify what it would be finally to say what in reality the quiddity is, he says: "whether it be form, or matter, or something like that,"[76] so also here we have the reference to matter and form. Similarly, when we come to Book 8, which St. Thomas presents as the major shift to philosophical consideration, we see that we are to consider the substances through their own principles, matter and form.[77] And earlier, in *CM* 4.4, it was the mark of the proper demonstrative sciences of the real, both "philosophy," i.e. metaphysics, and the other particular sciences, that in their study of real things [*de rebus naturae*] they use the principles of things, whereas the tentative dialectic, or logical consideration associated with the science of the real, made use of principles "outside the nature of things" [*extranea a natura rerum*].[78]

The field of consideration of the philosopher is given, here in 7.11, as the *res naturae*, that which exists *in rerum natura*, as distinguished from that which "is, in notion." It is the same contrast, between *ens naturae* and *ens rationis*, that we saw in 4.4.[79] The issue is not materiality as such, nor even individuality, but ultimately whatever conditions prevail as regards *being in reality*. Again, this agrees with 7.17: the philosopher considers the existence of *things*, the truth of *things*,[80] and agrees with 7.13, where it is said that the metaphysician, who considers things as *entia*, brings the conditions of actual existence into his discourse.[81]

It is to be noted also, concerning 7.11, that when St. Thomas speaks of "*res naturae*" and "*in rerum natura existens*," the word "nature," while it may very well relate to motion, is not meant to limit the consideration to the things studied properly by the physicist, the natural philosopher. What is meant is the field of beings outside the mind, whether material or immaterial, as is shown by the conclusion concerning subsistent forms. These are *res naturae*. Still, the reference to nature, with its association with motion, is not accidental. For us, motion is the route to knowledge of actuality.[82]

---

76. See above, at n. 48.
77. *CM* 8.1 (1686 and 1681).
78. *CM* 4.4 (574–577). Notice also, in 7.2 (1280): "principia *rei*."
79. Above, ca n. 56.
80. *CM* 7.17 (1658): "... existentiam *rei* ... existentiam quaerit *rerum* ... secundum *rei* veritatem ..."
81. *CM* 7.13 (1576): "Hic enim accipit dici de subiecto, quod est *in se aliqua res* et inest alicui subiecto *existenti in actu*."
82. Cf. *CM* 9.3 (1805–1806).

Lastly, we should reflect that the metaphysical judgment involved here in Book 7 was that a thing and its quiddity are identical. Using the logical consideration, Aristotle showed this in a probable way, concerning all *entia per se*. Once matter and form began to make their presence felt, the judgment had to be revised, so as to exclude material substances in their real existence. From a metaphysical point of view, the probable judgment will find verification unqualifiedly only with the bringing on the scene of subsisting form.

We have said enough as to the philosophical point of view as contrasted with the logical. The general idea of St. Thomas's reading of Books 7 and 8 is a movement of the mind, from the mind as taking things on its, the mind's, own terms, to a greater and greater submission to things themselves. This is brought about primarily through the consideration of motion, generation, and corruption.

Professor Doig has remarked that "Aristotle ends by rejecting the entire discussion of the logical investigation, but Thomas does not (p. 280, n. 1)." This hardly does justice to the situation. Whatever be the truth about Aristotle, St. Thomas makes it a major point that the logical consideration is inadequate, does not give us the real quiddity, and requires completion by the properly scientific metaphysical treatment.

III. ST. THOMAS AND SUBSTANTIAL FORM

Thus far, we have seen that the science of metaphysics, as *considerativa entis*, is primarily demonstrative by means of the formal cause. We have also seen that, in his reading of the main treatment of material beings as beings in Aristotle's *Metaphysics*, St. Thomas saw the movement of the discussion as starting with logical consideration and ending with philosophical consideration, i.e. with the presentation of the proper principles of sensible substances, the matter and the form and their unity. Clearly, since matter is in no way a cause of beings as beings, the primary consideration of Book 8 is of substantial form as cause of being. However, as we have also seen, the movement of Books 7 and 8 is not abrupt. Already, in Book 7, there is something of the philosophical consideration. What we wish to do in this section is to provide a few notes on St. Thomas's reading of Books 7 and 8 as a gradual manifestation of the formal cause.

a) Substantial Form the Target

It is remarkable that already, at the beginning of Book 7, St. Thomas sees the primary interest of Aristotle as bearing upon substance in the sense of subject.[83] Then, in the subject, it is the substantial form which is to be the chief target of investigation.[84] St. Thomas also speaks of it as the particular form [*forma particularis*].[85] It is this which is presented at the very beginning, albeit in barest outline, as the cause of *ens:* matter is not constituted as a being actually [*ens actu*] except through form; thus, form is the "because of which [*propter quod*]."[86] And already we note, even in what is a rather "physical" discussion by Aristotle (*Metaph.* 7.3: 1029a1–9), a phenomenon we will be studying in more detail in a moment, namely St. Thomas's careful distinction between form and species. Aristotle is using the bronze statue to convey what he means by matter, form, and composite. Concerning the form, St. Thomas seems to have read: "the shape, as the form of the species," and he is quick to paraphrase: "that is, giving the species." The shape is the form, and the form gives the species. St. Thomas is distinguishing between form, the physical principle, and species, the effect of the form found in our intellectual conception of the thing (the species, as we will see, is a composite of form and matter, taken universally).[87] That is, St. Thomas is already eager to distinguish what pertains more to logical consideration, the species, from what pertains to metaphysics in its properly scientific character, the substantial form.

While there is some ambiguity in the treatment of the division at *CM* 7.2 (1297 and following), the "third division" spoken of should be *particular form*. The parts of the third division should be sensible substances and non-sensible substances, i.e. forms in matter and forms subsisting by themselves. What is to be determined concerning sensible form is the *quod quid erat esse*, the quiddity and essence of the thing (1299). At 1302, it is clear that we are after *"formae sensibiles"* which are *"formae in materia,"* as less remote from sense than the separate entities, and so more knowable for us. But, again, we see that even our road to the substantial forms of sensible things must pass through such non-entities or near nonentities as accidents, motion, and privations (1304).

In fact, what we learn least about here is why we are going to study the quiddity (cf. 1299). It seems to be somewhat different from substance as subject, to judge by the list given in 1270–1274. It is to be noted that

83. *CM* 7.2 (1274), concerning Aristotle at 1028b37–1029a1. While the Latin of Aristotle in the Cathala/Spiazzi ed. has: *"Propter quod 'PRIMUM' de hoc determinandum est,"* and this is identical with the *translatio media* text in Albert, *Metaphysica* (ed. Cologne 16/2, 322.83), St. Thomas makes no mention of the *"primum."* He speaks rather as though substance as subject is what the investigation not merely begins with, but is mainly about.

84. *CM* 7.2 (1296).
85. *CM* 7.2 (1276–1277).
86. *CM* 7.2 (1278).
87. See below, ca n. 97.

here at the outset, before we enter into the full logical consideration (it would seem), *quod quid erat esse* is explained (1275) as something which does not fall into the order of predicaments except as formal principle. Thus, it sounds like "humanity," rather than "rational animal." It will be taken as "rational animal" in the full-fledged logical consideration (*CM* 7.5: 1378).

It remains that, in the light of St. Thomas's 7.2, we are prepared for a study of substantial form. We are not going to be altogether puzzled to find quiddity as the target in 7.3, since we have been forewarned in 1299. But we cannot be altogether content. Thus, St. Thomas himself, at *CM* 7.13 (1566–1567), when explaining the list of modes of substance given by Aristotle at *Metaph.* 7.13 (1038b1–8), says that while at the beginning of Book 7 (i.e. 7.3: 1028b33–1029a2) Aristotle divided the subject in three, viz. the matter, the form, and the composite, here in 7.13 he uses *quod quid erat esse* in place of *form,* "because it is *now* clear that the *quod quid erat esse* stands on the side of form" (1567). Hence, it cannot have been all that clear where we are now, i.e. at 7.3, where, expecting a treatise on form, we get one on quiddity.

b) Form and Species

While the study is of quiddity, we are quickly obliged to turn our attention toward things in the concrete. Already in *CM* 7.6–8, on generation, this is so. However, the passages to which I wish to call attention are in 7.9–11, which we have seen St. Thomas himself describe as a descent from the logical consideration into the natural principles.[88] In those passages we shall look at St. Thomas's (previously mentioned) careful distinction between the species or quiddity, and the substantial form. This care of his has the effect of keeping before the mind the secondary and derivative character of the issues in Book 7 (to 7.16). Beyond the quiddity lies the substantial form, which is the real target of our metaphysical quest.

At the very beginning of this section of *CM,* i.e. in 7.9, St. Thomas explains the distinction between quiddity and substantial form. He has already presented the problem which Aristotle has proposed (and to which we will refer later), but before coming to Aristotle's solutions, he introduces a lengthy note to the reader. Concerning the definitions of things, and their essences, he tells us, there are two opinions. Some say that the essence of the species is the form itself: e.g. that the entire essence of man is the soul. Thus, the words "humanity" and "soul" are understood

88. See above, ca n. 54.

to name exactly the same *thing:* it is called "form of the part" inasmuch
as it perfects the matter and makes it to be actually; and it is called "form
of the whole" inasmuch as through it the whole thing is given a place in
a species. And thus these people maintain that no parts of the matter are
posited in the definition indicating the species, but rather only the formal principles of the species. Averroes and others seem to hold this view.[89]
This opinion, says St. Thomas, seems to be against the intention of Aristotle. Above, in Book 6, he said that natural things have sensible matter
in their definitions. Nor can it be said that natural substances are defined
by that which is not of their essences: substances do not have definition
by addition (i.e. of things external to the precise thing defined), but only
accidents are so defined, as was said earlier in the *Metaphysics.* Hence, it
remains that sensible matter is part of the essence of natural substances,
not only as regards individuals, but even as regards the very *species:* for definitions are given, not of individuals, but of species.—Here we see that St.
Thomas does not depend on his reading of *Metaph.* 7.10–11 for his position, but on much clearer previous statements of Aristotle.[90]

Thus, he continues, there is another opinion, followed by Avicenna,
according to which the "form of the whole," which is the very quiddity
of the species, *differs* from the "form of the part," as a whole from a part:
for the quiddity of the species is a composite out of matter and form, but
not, nevertheless, out of "this form" and "this individual matter." Out of

89. Albert the Great seems to be among those who identify form and quiddity, to judge
by his *Metaphysica* bk. 7, tr. 1, c. 1 (ed. Cologne 16/2, 316:28–41). Since this passage is
Albert's view of the distinction between book 7 and book 8, we quote at length: "Furthermore, the principles of substance are matter and form, and especially form is the principle of substance, and it is necessary that this [the form, as principle of substance] be
determined in two ways: in one way, according as it is the entire being [*totum esse*] of first
substance and its quiddity, which is signified by the definition; and it is necessary that we
inquire concerning substance in this way in this seventh book of this first philosophy. But
it is to be considered in another way inasmuch as it is a certain form and nature considered in itself, diverse from matter, which is the other part of the composite, as the soul is
the form of man and not predicated of him, and in this way it is also called 'quiddity' by some,
speaking broadly but improperly. And in this way we will consider form in the next book,
which is the eighth book of this first philosophy." The form and the quiddity seem to be
the same *thing* here. At ibid. bk. 8, tr. 1, c. 1 (389.9–21), we seem to have the same position, and the sameness is rather explicit: ". . . ostendemus eandem substantiam ad quam
refertur diffinitio, esse formam et actum et naturam diffiniti . . ." (389.14–15). At bk. 8, tr.
1, c. 3 (391.46–61), however, we seem to be going to treat of form as predicable (391.60).
As regards the division of the two books, Albert's distinction between form as quiddity and
form as form or nature or act contains no suggestion of St. Thomas's contrast between
logical consideration and consideration of the proper principles of things; in St. Albert,
there seems to be none of the diminishing of the ontological status of quiddity which is
implied in St. Thomas's classifying of it as substance "from the viewpoint of reason" (*CM*
8.1: 1684).

90. *CM* 7.9 (1468). The point that the individual is not defined, it is true, is taken from
a clear *subsequent* statement of Aristotle (7.10: 1036a2–5).

these, the individual, e.g. Socrates or Callias, is composed. This is the opinion of *Aristotle* here, says St. Thomas. Aristotle brings in this opinion (St. Thomas must mean: in a clear way) in order to exclude the opinion of Plato concerning the Ideas. Plato said that the species of natural things are existing by themselves without sensible matter, as though sensible matter were not in some way part of the species. Thus, once it is shown that sensible matter is part of the species in natural things, it is shown that it is impossible for the species of natural things to be without matter: as man without flesh and bones, etc.

Here, St. Thomas seems to be referring to what Aristotle says in 7.11, where the argument is to the point that not only in natural things, but even in mathematicals, there is a matter in the definition. Cf. Aristotle at 1036b22–30. It is of some importance to pinpoint just where Aristotle so expresses himself according to St. Thomas, since in other places in the discussion (e.g. *Metaph.* 7.10: 1036a13–25) St. Thomas sees Aristotle as favoring neither opinion over the other (*CM* 7.10: 1498–1500). St. Thomas will, in general, interpret the discussion according to what he sees as the opinion of Aristotle, i.e. the distinction between form and quiddity of the species.

Since St. Thomas has himself called attention so explicitly and deliberately to this distinction, let us see how it shows up in his presentation of Aristotle. The phenomenon is difficult to present because of the instability of the vocabulary, as used by the two authors. The Latin Aristotle often has *"species"* where St. Thomas will wish to interpret by using the word *"forma."* St. Thomas, on the other hand, uses *"species"* for the quiddity as a whole. Again, Aristotle reserves, for the most part, the word "matter" to refer to what belongs to the individual as such, whereas St. Thomas, exploiting some few remarks of Aristotle, makes constant use of a distinction between common matter and individual matter.

Before looking at the texts we might recall the problems which Aristotle is facing in this part of *Metaphysics* 7. Whereas the earlier presentation of substance and definition had focused upon the thoroughgoing unity of definition and *definitum,* the present section (Aristotle's chapters 10–12) considers definition as *composite* discourse, as a formula composed of parts, e.g. "rational animal." And the problem is that there does not seem to be thoroughgoing correspondence between the parts of the *definition* and the parts of the *thing defined.* Sometimes the parts of the thing *are* parts of the definition (as letters occur in the definition of a syllable), and sometimes they are not (the semicircle is not part of the definition of the circle). Another problematic feature of the same situation is that some parts are prior to the whole (as letter to syllable) or at least simultaneous (as the heart or brain to the animal), and some are posterior (as finger to animal, and semicircle to circle).[91]—One of the results of the exploration of the situation so presented is that we see an ambiguity in our speech between two meanings of such words as "the circle," and so are led to distinguish two targets of attention in thought—"the circle" as the *definable* thing, and "the circle" as the *concrete* thing.[92] Another result is that we come to see that even within the definable reality as such, there is *composition*, there are parts, there is the structure of "this in this" (as form in matter).[93]

We will look first at *CM* 7.10. We should note, in 1482, the reason given by St. Thomas for Aristotle's having to repeat and clarify the already given solution. Aristotle has not shown how the parts are prior and posterior, nor again has he distinguished the universal composite from the particular composite, nor also the *species from the form.*

Then, commenting on Aristotle at 1035b27–33, St. Thomas says:

Nevertheless, it must be known that this composite which is animal or man can be taken in two ways: either as universal or as singular. As universal: as "man" and "animal." As singular: as "Socrates" and "Callias." And so he [Aristotle] says that *man and horse and what so [ita] are in singulars, but* said *universally,* as "man" and "horse," *are not substance,* i.e. are not form alone, *but* are *a certain whole-together* [*simul totum quoddam*] composed *out of determinate matter and determinate form;* not indeed as singularly, but *universally.* For "man" says something composed out of soul and body, but not out of this soul and this body. But *"the singular"* says something composed *out of the ultimate matter,* i.e. individual matter . . .[94]

The universally signified species are not "substance," says Aristotle, and St. Thomas quickly identifies this "substance" as the substantial form. Then, in the next paragraph, where Aristotle might very well seem to be distinguishing various types of part, i.e. 1035b31–33, St. Thomas rather interprets this as a distinction of matters. He says:

Thus, *therefore,* it is clear that matter *is part of the species.* But *"species"* we here *understand* not as form alone, but as *quod quid erat esse.* And it is clear also that matter is a part *of that whole which is out of the species and the matter,* i.e. the singular [whole], which signifies the nature of the species in this determinate matter. For matter is a part of the composite. But the composite is both the universal and the singular.[95]

Once again, St. Thomas has Aristotle including matter in the quiddity, and setting it off carefully from the "form alone." Then, subsequently,

91. Cf. *CM* 7.9 (1460–1466).
92. Cf. *CM* 7.9 (1480–1481) concerning Aristotle at 7.10 (1035b1–3).
93. Cf. Aristotle, *Metaph.* 7.11 (1036b22–24) and *CM* 7.11 (1517).
94. *CM* 7.10 (1490). The italics are the text of Aristotle.
95. *CM* 7.10 (1491). Aristotle in italics.

the quiddity or species is coupled with further matter to constitute the singular.

Later in 7.10, commenting on the fact that the definition is of the universal only, St. Thomas explains that by the definition a thing is supposed to be *known;* and it is clear that when they are absent, individual things are not known, even though we still possess the definitions. Thus, the definitions do not bear directly on the individuals. And the reason for this is that matter, which is the principle of individuation, is according to itself unknown, and is known only through *form,* from which the *notion of the universal is taken.* And so singulars are not known in their absence except through universals.—Here, we see the distinction between form and universal (i.e. species) maintained: the form is the principle of the universal.[96] We shall see more of this in a moment.

Still in 7.10, St. Thomas goes on to paraphrase and comment on the few words of conclusion of Aristotle at 1036a12–13. He says:

He [Aristotle] concludes, *therefore,* that *it has been said how things stand concerning whole and part, and* concerning *prior and posterior,* i.e. of what is the part a part, and how it is prior and how posterior. For the parts of the individual matter are parts of the composite singular, but not of the species, nor of the form. But the parts of the universal matter are parts of the species, but not of the form. And because the universal is defined, and not the singular, therefore the parts of the individual matter are not placed in the definition, but only the parts of the common matter, together with the form or the parts of the form.[97]

Here again, we see how the analysis keeps the form clearly in view at all times, in distinction from the species. We might notice also that the form itself is conceived by St. Thomas as susceptible to having parts.

We move now to *CM* 7.11. For our present purposes, 1529–1532, wherein St. Thomas is commenting on Aristotle at 1037a21–33, is all of interest. Aristotle is recapitulating what he has done since the beginning of Book 7. If, in the interests of brevity, we begin at 1037a24, we have Aristotle saying:

And that in the notion of the substance, what so are parts, as matter, will not be included. For neither are they parts of that substance, but of the whole. But of this there is in a way a notion and there is not. For, with matter, there is not. For that is indeterminate. But according to the first substance, there is, as of man the notion of the soul. For the substance is the species, which is within, out of which and the matter the whole substance is said.[98]

96. Cf. *CM* 7.10 (1495–1496).
97. Ibid. 1497. Aristotle in italics.
98. In the Cathala-Spiazzi edition of *CM,* the Aristotle text 639. The text of Aristotle St. Thomas is using is close enough to this to give the reader the picture of St. Thomas's commenting which I wish to convey. Obviously, the mere putting into English forces the addition of words here and there.

And here is St. Thomas's presentation:

Also, it has been said *that in the notion of the substance*, i.e. of the form, *are not placed the parts* which are parts of the substance *as matter, because* such [parts] *are not parts of that substance*, i.e. of the form, *but* parts *of the* composite *whole*.

[1530] *Of which* composite, *in a way there is a definition*, in a way *there is not*. *For if it be taken with matter*, i.e. individual [matter], *there is no* definition of it, for singulars are not defined, as was shown above. *For* which the reason is that *such* individual matter is an unfinished [*infinitum*] and *indeterminate* something. For matter is not finished except through form.

But the composite taken *according to the first substance*, i.e. according to the form, *has* a definition. For the composite taken in [its] species [*in specie*] is defined, not according to the individual. [1531] But just as the individual is individual through the matter, so each thing is placed in its species through the form. For man is not man because he has flesh and bones but from this, that he has rational soul in flesh and bones. Whence it is necessary that the definition of the species be taken from the form, and that in the definition of the species be placed only those parts of matter in which the form is primarily and principally. *As the notion of man* is that which is *of the soul*. For from this, man is man, that he has such a soul. And because of this, if man is defined, it is necessary that he be defined through the soul, and that nevertheless in his definition be placed the parts of the body in which primarily is the soul, such as the heart or the brain, as he said above.

[1532] *For the* very *substance* of which matter is not a part *is the species*, i.e. the form, *which is within* the matter, *out of which* form *and the matter the whole substance is said*, i.e. is determined and defined . . .⁹⁹

The reader can see how relentlessly St. Thomas maintains the distinction between species and form, with the idea that the species includes matter, and that thus matter is part of the definition. Even where the text of Aristotle has "species," St. Thomas does not hesitate to say it means "form."

The result of all this is that St. Thomas keeps a firm hold on the distinction between logical consideration, to which properly the species belongs, and philosophical consideration, to which belong matter and form as principles of the composite substance. The species is the individual composite taken universally. The real ground for so taking it is the particular form.

c) Form and Causality

We have done enough to illustrate how St. Thomas, even within *CM* 7, keeps in view the distinction between quiddity and form, between "substance according to reason" and "substance as it exists."¹⁰⁰ We wish now

99. *CM* 7.11 (1529–1532). Aristotle in italics.
100. Cf. *CM* 8.1 (1683–1684).

to reconsider the second clear step toward the real principles of things noted by St. Thomas himself in his interpretation of Aristotle, viz. the "new beginning" in 7.17.

Why is this such a new beginning? We have seen that it is a beginning other than the logical one, and that it consists precisely in saying that *within* the *substance,* there is a *principle,* a *cause.*[101] While from our point of view (that of interest in the substantial form) the word "in" or "within" is highly interesting,[102] nevertheless it is the notion of cause and principle which St. Thomas seems to be regarding as innovative here. Thus, he divides 7.17 into the two points: that the quiddity is cause and principle; and what sort of cause and principle it is (1649). This point was mentioned at the beginning of Book 7, but our treatise has been dominated by quiddity as definition.[103] From this point of view, the quiddity seems to stand *by itself* in a sort of intelligible sphere. Its notional separability is exploited to the utmost, and rather than appear as cause or principle, it seems more to appear as substance itself, with the particular as something more like an attendant shadow than as an effect.

That the new approach, the causal, is new is illustrated in a way by the mode of exemplification now employed. Typical is the house and its construction.[104] We are in the domain of events, of generation and corruption. Even though it is the *intrinsic* cause which mainly interests us, it is by the consideration of the assembling and disassembling of things that we catch sight of the causal contribution.[105] Generation as an approach to *ens* as *ens* has been present in the background all along.[106] Now it is coming forward.

The challenge for the formulator of this doctrine is to put the notion of cause to work even *within* substance. This is a challenge because it would seem that substance involves simplicity whereas causality involves composition. Thus, as regards substance, one sees the problem presented in 7.17, that it does not *appear* to be a cause at all: this is presented by means of the *simplicity* of the question which inquires about the substance, viz. "what is it?" (1662–1668). And yet there is already the clue, in the way the mere logician speaks about causes generally, i.e. "because of *what* is A B?" Thus the "what" is used to name what are manifestly causes,

101. Cf. above, at n. 48.
102. Cf. *CM* 9.5 (1828). Form is *in* matter.
103. Cf. *CM* 7.5 (1378).
104. Cf., e.g., *CM* 7.17 (1657, 1658, 1659, 1660, 1666).
105. Cf. *CM* 7.17 (1672–1674).
106. Cf. especially *CM* 6.2 (1179); and cf. 7.1 (1256); even 4.1 (540–543): the realm of *ratio* is put in last place, though this is not quite what is said. For the way we have a hint of this even as the ground of definition itself, cf. 7.4 (1339–1340).

namely the agent and the end, and this suggests that the true "what," i.e. the substance, has the nature of a cause (cf. 1656–1661).

That causality involves composition is brought out in *CM* 7.17 (1649–1655): that causal inquiry is always about a duality: why A is B. The picture of the quiddity (still considered as that which corresponds to the question: "what is it?") as cause already brings in the role of *matter* (1667–1668). And one might well wonder what more there is to say about the quiddity as cause—a sort of "influence" of form on matter. And yet St. Thomas designates the considerable passages of 7.17 which remain (i.e. 1672–1680) as treating of *what sort* of cause or principle quiddity is. The problem seems to be that once one *locates* the causality of the quiddity as *intrinsic*, one runs the risk of confusing its proper causal contribution with that of the matter. Thus Aristotle calls our attention to the mode of unity which is unqualified unity. And he points out that such a unit is not merely its elements, but that inasmuch as one can have the elements and not have the unit, it is seen that there is "something else" within the unit. This something else cannot be conceived as an element, that is, as a cause after the manner of *matter* (1675–1677). Rather, it is the principle and cause of being (1679).

We should note, at this point in *CM*, on the very threshold of Book 8, and with the very words of Aristotle, the way St. Thomas insists upon the need to locate this sort of substance (i.e. the cause of being), not just anywhere, but in *natural* things:

Therefore, he [Aristotle] says that *because some things* are *not substances*, as is particularly clear in the case of artifacts, *but whatever are according to nature*, as regards being, and *constituted by nature*, as regards becoming, are true *substances*, *it will be manifest* that *this nature* which we have sought is *substance in some*, viz. in natural, things, and not in all. *Which* nature, also, *is not an element, but* the formal *principle . . .* (1680)

We come strongly to the viewpoint of nature and generation.

d) Book 8

Lastly, in this section, we will consider a few aspects of Book 8. One is the use St. Thomas makes of the word *"principium."* We have already seen that St. Thomas regards the move to Book 8 as a move "toward existing natural things" [*ad res naturales existentes*].[107] He says that here Aristotle intends to treat of them "through their own principles" [*per propria principia*], which, as we have also seen, is the procedure of the philosopher

---

107. *CM* 8.1 (1681).

in his scientific or demonstrative phase.[108] The word *"principium"* is repeated surprisingly often in St. Thomas's presentation of Aristotle here in Book 8. Thus, we read:

> ...here the Philosopher begins to treat of sensible substances by inquiry into their *principles*.
>
> And it is divided into two parts. In the first, he determines concerning the matter and the form, which are the *principles* of sensible substances. In the second, concerning their union with each other.
>
> Regarding the first point he does two things. First he shows that matter is *principle* of sensible substances. Secondly he shows the same about form. (*CM* 8.1: 1686)

Then, at the beginning of the next *lectio,* we read:

> After the Philosopher has sought out the *material principle* in sensible substances, here he inquires into the *formal principle*...
>
> ...First, he investigates the differences in sensible things, which demonstrate the *formal principle*... (*CM* 8.2: 1691–1692)

And, in the next *lectio:*

> After the Philosopher has sought out the *principles* of sensible substance, showing that the sensible substance is composed out of matter and form, now he intends to determine concerning *the material and the formal principles*, inquiring as to those things which are to be considered about each.
>
> And it is divided into two parts. In the first he inquires as to those things which are to be considered about the *formal principle*. In the second, those things which are to be considered about the *material principle*...
>
> And because Plato most especially touched upon the *formal principle*, therefore he determines concerning the *formal principle* according to those things which Plato held. Thus, the first part is divided into two parts.
>
> In the first he determines concerning the *formal principle* by comparison with the Ideas. In the second, by comparison with numbers. (*CM* 8.3: 1703–1704)

At this point, as St. Thomas begins his explanations, this insistence on the full formula is left aside. However, as we begin the next *lectio* (4), *"principium formale"* and *"principium materiale"* (especially) come in for extraordinarily heavy use, extending right into the commentary (cf. 1729–1732). And, lastly, they are used once again in the introduction to the last *lectio* (*CM* 8.5: 1755).

This use of *"principium"* corresponds, it seems to us, not only to the "new beginning" we saw in 7.17, with quiddity now taken as formal prin-

---

108. Cf. *CM* 4.4 (577).

ciple of being, but also to the idea that we are now working with existing natural substance. The hope is to avoid the picture of form as a substance in its own right, a picture so much encouraged by the definitional approach. St. Thomas is here very much in accord with the doctrine he expressed earlier, in the part of Book 7 dealing with quiddity and generation:

> Matter and form . . . are not substances, except insofar as they are the principles of composite substance.[109]

Thus, also, here in 8.1, in explaining the division of substance into matter, form, and composite, and their status as substances, the composite appears to get the primary role:

> But the composite out of these is said to be substance as *separable unqualifiedly*, that is, capable of existing by itself separately in reality; *and of it alone* there is *generation and corruption*. (1687)

St. Thomas thus paraphrases the Latin Aristotle's *"separabile simpliciter"* [separable unqualifiedly] with the unusually explicit formula: *"separatim per se existere potens in rerum natura"* [capable of existing by itself separately in reality]. And our inclination is to see the reference to generation and corruption (which, of course, is in Aristotle) as a way of pointing out that this is the thing which is, in the primary sense of "is."[110]

We see this aspect of the situation still more evidently when we consider that in Book 8 the first step is the presentation of the *material* principle. It is arrived at through the consideration of substantial generation and corruption. As St. Thomas says:

> From this argument of Aristotle it is apparent that substantial generation and corruption are the starting point for coming to the knowledge of prime matter. (*CM* 8.1: 1689)

Clearly then, it is of substance as caught sight of with the help of generation and corruption that we have to do here.

We saw at the outset that matter is not a cause of beings as beings. However, it is only inasmuch as we distinguish between matter and form, as a composition *found* in existing substances, that we can have the duality required to see the *causality* of form. And in 8.2, we have the presentation of form, by means of the differences found among things. Aristotle's approach to the question by using Democritus, and the subsequent use of examples in artifacts and natural things, puts us very much

---

109. *CM* 7.6 (1386).
110. Cf. *CM* 7.1 (1256) and 6.2 (1179); also 4.2 (551–552).

into the more "physical" realm. Nevertheless, the definitional approach is mixed in as well.[111] Thus, we find St. Thomas paraphrasing Aristotle as follows:

He shows how the aforementioned differences are related to substances; and he says: *from the foregoing it is* now *clear that in the aforementioned* differences is *to be sought that which is the* formal *cause of being* [causa formalis essendi] *of any of the aforesaid*, of which they are the differences, *if* things are such that the formal *substance* [substantia formalis] or "what it is" *is the cause of* any *being* [causa cuiuslibet essendi], as was shown in Book 7. For the aforesaid differences signify the form and the "what it is" of the aforementioned things. However, *none of the aforesaid* differences is *substance, nor anything near* to substance (as pertaining to the genus of substance). *But the same proportion* is found in *them* as is found in substance. [1697] *For just as in* the genus of *substance*, the difference, which is predicated of the genus, and comes to it for the constituting of the species, is compared to it as act and form, so *also in the other definitions.*[112]

Here, St. Thomas is impelled to add:

But[113] one ought not to understand that the difference is the form, or that the genus is the matter, since the genus and the differences are predicated of the species, but the matter and the form are not predicated of the composite; but this is said because the genus is taken from that which is material in the thing, while the difference is taken from that which is formal. For example, the genus of man is "animal," because it signifies "something having a sentient nature"; which [sentient nature] indeed stands materially toward the intellective nature, from which is taken "rational," which is the difference of man; but "rational" signifies "something having an intellective nature." And thus it is that the genus has the differences potentially, and that the genus and the difference are proportionate to the matter and the form, as Porphyry says. And for that reason also it is said here that *the act*, that is, the difference, *is predicated of the matter*, i.e. the genus; and similarly in the other genera. (1697)

St. Thomas, as he indicates by the paraphrase quoted first, would have liked Aristotle to say that "the *difference*, which is predicated of the *genus*, . . . is compared to it as act and form . . ." But what he finds in the text is that "that which is predicated of the *matter is act.*" That is, Aristotle said that the act is *predicated* of the matter. He is, in St. Thomas's eyes, mixing a way of speaking which pertains to the logical, definitional, or predicational approach, with the considerations (matter, and act or form) proper to the philosophical approach. St. Thomas puts first in his paraphrase what he would like to have found, then explains the situation

---

111. Cf. Aristotle at 8.2 (1042b25–1043a26) and St. Thomas, *CM* 8.2 (1694–1701).
112. *CM* 8.2 (1696–1697). Aristotle in italics (approximately).
113. The text here has *"enim,"* but we are reading *"autem."*

to the reader, and lastly introduces the actual text. He painstakingly distinguishes the factors pertaining to the two domains.

St. Thomas is determined not to confuse what pertains to logical consideration with the knowledge of the proper principles of the existing natural thing. In insisting that he is speaking about the principles, St. Thomas never allows them to be envisaged as mere duplicates of the subsisting thing.

Besides the scrupulous use of *"principium,"* another important point in Book 8 is the key role of the notion of matter for the conception of form as cause of being. Besides the already mentioned fact that we begin the discussion with matter, this point can perhaps be heightened by a brief consideration of *CM* 8.3 (1713). There the Platonists are complimented for having said that the house is not stone *and composition,* as though the house were constituted out of these as out of parts of matter. If this were so, i.e. if the form were one of the parts of matter, it would *depend* on matter. And we see that this is false, says St. Thomas, because the composition and the mixture, which are the formal principles [*formalia principia*], are not constituted out of the things which are composed or are mixed, just as neither is anything else formal constituted out of its matter, but rather the *converse*. Being-a-threshold is constituted by position, which is its form, and not vice versa.

The point that the form is the cause of being is seen to the extent that the ontological indetermination of matter is seen. It must be grasped as the character of the effect as an effect, so that the form will be the cause of being. And it is the development of the notion of matter in the light of generation and corruption which brings about the vision of the required dependent nature. Thus it is seen that form is truly the cause, within the *ens*, of nothing short of its being *ens*.[114] It is not at all necessary to have a form capable of separate existence, in order to see that the form is the cause of being. It is only necessary to grasp the ontological character of matter, and to see form, then, as something quite *distinct*. Even a form whose being is so inseparable from matter that it cannot be conceived without matter[115] nevertheless appears as cause of being of the whole composite.

Lastly, concerning the final *lectio* of Book 8, in which the union of the material and formal principles is presented, we should note to what extent we have once again the problems of definition, as presented in Book 7, mixed in with the presentation. Of course, the same mixture was found in Book 7 itself: e.g. in *CM* 7.11, we had the same sort of pre-

---

114. Cf., on the relation of form, taken as form, to matter, St. Thomas, *De substantiis separatis*, c. 7 (Leonine ed., lines 91–102).

115. Cf. *CM* 7.9 (1477).

sentation of the solution in natural things (1516–1519), then in mathematicals (1520–1522), as we have here in 8.5: i.e. natural things in 1759, mathematicals in 1760, and separate entity in 1762.

But this very mixture in the Aristotelian text suggests the extent to which St. Thomas's insistence on the move from logical to existential consideration as the movement of the *Metaphysics* is an interpretation, and probably involves a certain ingredient of what "ought to be found in Aristotle," in St. Thomas's judgment.

Chapter 9

ST. THOMAS, METAPHYSICAL PROCEDURE, AND THE FORMAL CAUSE

INTRODUCTION

St. Thomas Aquinas, in his *Commentary on Aristotle's Posterior Analytics*, often showed his interest in the way the doctrine of the *Analytics* applies to the science of metaphysics.[1] Fr. Joseph Owens in his interpretations of St. Thomas's metaphysical thought has reflected this interest of Thomas.[2] In the present paper I will be concerned with one feature of Fr. Owens's interpretation, viz. his rejection of the view that St. Thomas's *esse*, i.e. the aspect of being or existence found in things, has the role of a property of the nature.

It will be remembered that Aristotle's schema of scientific demonstration includes a subject of inquiry (which is a composite), the principles of this subject (i.e. the parts into which the subject is analyzed), and the property or attribute of the subject (which is seen to belong necessarily to the subject, because it belongs necessarily to the principles of the subject).[3]

For Fr. Owens, the principle of metaphysics as a scientific endeavor is the aspect of being, i.e. the existence of sensible things, which existence we grasp through the act of judgment. Just as the Aristotelian philosophy of nature has as principles of its subject the matter and the form in the order of substance, so the subject of metaphysics, beings as beings, would

---

1. Cf. *In Post. An.*, 1.41 (ed. Spiazzi, 361–363); also 1.17 (146–147). All references are to Thomas Aquinas, unless otherwise indicated.

2. Cf. Joseph Owens, "The 'Analytics' and Thomistic Metaphysical Procedure," *Mediaeval Studies* 20 (1964), pp. 83–108. I have in mind, also, his *Elementary Christian Metaphysics*, Houston, Tex., 1985: Center for Thomistic Studies [reprint of the volume published by Bruce, Milwaukee, 1963]. It will be referred to here as "ECM."

3. Cf. *In Post. An.*, 1.41 (361–364), concerning Aristotle, A. Po. 1.28 (87a37–38).

have as principles essence and existence.[4] Of the two, "being is absolutely primary."[5] Now, I have no wish to underplay the necessity of explor-
ing both these targets of metaphysical attention, existence and essence.
My concern is more about the "shape," so to speak, that the exploration
should take. It is no accident that the focus of St. Thomas's treatise *De
ente et essentia* is *essence*. It is not (I suggest) as if someone had been having
trouble with that particular topic and had asked Thomas for a little en-
lightenment. Rather, the *De ente* exhibits the *appropriate focus* for a fundamental metaphysical treatment. It studies and presents essence, because
essence is *the* principle of the science of beings as beings.

We have to have a kind of double optic in metaphysics, with essence
(or form) and existence as the targets. The question is about the proper
roles of these two. I would call the role of essence the causal role. *Esse* has
the causal role only in God (I mean, of course, God's being causal with
respect to other things), and there it has that role because it has the status of essence. "Essence" expresses an ineluctable ontological contribution which in creatures cannot be that of *esse*. Such a contribution is conceivable only because *both* essence and *esse* in creatures presuppose the
divine causality.

I would take as expressive of the general vision I am promoting the
words of St. Thomas in the *De ente:*

Of substances, some are composite and some are simple, and in both there is essence; but in simple [substances there is essence] in a truer and more noble degree, according as, also, they have more noble being [*esse*]: for they are the cause
of those which are composite, at least [this is true of] the first simple substance
which is God.[6]

That is, the study is of essence. Essence is found most truly of all in God
(how far we are from a doctrine in which "God has no essence"!).[7] We
grade essence by the grade of *esse* the thing exhibits (since essence is
that through which and in which a being [*ens*] has being [*esse*]),[8] and we
grade that *esse* by the efficient causal hierarchy. The efficient cause has
more noble *esse* than its effect.[9]

---

4. ECM, pp. 303 and 141.
5. ECM, p. 127.
6. *De ente et essentia*, ch. 1 (Leonine ed., lines 58–63): my translation.
7. Concerning this doctrine, cf. *De ente,* ch. 5 (line 5).
8. *De ente,* ch.1 (lines 50–52): "Sed essentia dicitur secundum quod per eam et in ea
ens habet esse."
9. Cf. Avicenna, *Liber de philosophia prima (Metaph.)* 6.3 (ed. S. Van Riet, p. 309, lines
81–82, and 77; also p. 319, line 11).

AN OBJECTION

The claim that *esse* has the role of property or attribute in the Aristotelian demonstrative scheme as applied to metaphysics seems to be rejected by Fr. Owens. He says:

> . . . being, if caused, comes through efficient causality and not through formal causality. In the exercise of formal causality the being of the nature is presupposed. Its being is prior to any formal causality exercised by the nature and so cannot be the result of the formal causality. Being, therefore, cannot present itself as a property of the nature. As a predicable, it is an accident and not a property.[10]

Fr. Owens is here making an argument which resembles some things St. Thomas says. However, what St. Thomas rules out is that form or nature be the *efficient* cause of its own being.[11] He does not rule out its being cause of its being. Thus, at *Summa theologiae* (hereafter, *ST*) 1.3.4 we read:

> . . . it is impossible that being [*esse*] be caused *only* by the essential principles, for no thing *suffices* to be cause of its own being, if it has caused being. [my italics]

Here, St. Thomas leaves room for a causal contribution on the part of the essential principles vis-à-vis the very *esse* of the thing.

I believe that Fr. Owens's use of the word "exercise" provides us with a clue to what I take to be his difference from St. Thomas. If formal causality were something a form or nature *exercised,* then one would have to envision the form or nature as having *esse* in order to perform the exercise. Exercise, i.e. actions and efficient causality, presupposes subsisting things, things having *esse,* as agents.[12] Formal causality, however, consists in a *specification,* not an exercise.[13] Form and *esse* are *given together,* by virtue of another thing, the efficient cause. In speaking of formal causality *within* the caused thing, one is merely spotlighting the distinctive roles of the items in the metaphysical analysis. Formal causality is a priority in the order of intelligibles in the caused thing. What one is saying in attributing a *priority* to form over existence is that the influence of the efficient cause on the caused thing will be the *existence* of the caused thing only inasmuch as the efficient cause also provides *form* for the caused thing,

---

10. ECM, p. 73.

11. Cf., e.g., *De ente,* ch. 4 (lines 131–135).

12. Cf. *ST* 1.75.2 (ed. Ottawa, 440b48–51); also, *ST* 1.77.1.*ad* 3.

13. On specification and exercise, cf. *ST* 1–2.9.1; cf. also *ST* 1.48.1.*ad* 4 (ed. Ottawa, 304b22–28), on "agere . . . formaliter": this can be attributed even to privations.

whereby that thing *appropriates* the influence. This is because "existence" names a thing's *own* act.[14]

St. Thomas himself seems to have no difficulty in viewing *esse* as the effect of form (as long as an outside efficient cause is posited). Thus, for example, he can argue:

. . . Just as *esse* is first among effects, so also it corresponds to the first cause, as the proper effect [of the first cause]. But *esse* is through form and not through matter. Therefore, the first causality of forms is to be attributed most of all to the first cause.[15]

In this text, St. Thomas is setting aside any idea that formal variety, as a feature of created reality, has its ultimate origin in causes operating at a merely secondary level. God himself must be the author of the formal distinction in things. But the argument draws this conclusion by pointing out that God is author of *esse,* and that *esse* is *through* form. Thus God must, to be source of *esse,* be source of form.

Somewhat akin to the foregoing text is a remarkable reply to an objection in the *De potentia.* What is at issue is whether the substance of God is being itself [*ipsum esse*]. The objector says:

. . . that which is signified after the manner of an effect does not befit the first substance, which has no principle. But *esse* is such: for every being [*ens*] through the principles of its essence has *esse.* Therefore, the substance of God is unsuitably said to be *esse.*[16]

Here, the objector is aiming to consider *esse* as to what typically characterizes it as a target of metaphysical attention. And his contention is that it has, universally, the role of an effect, a result. To show this, he employs what might be called *the* expression of fundamental ontology; every *ens* through the principles of its *essentia* has *esse.*

St. Thomas, in replying, is careful to preserve the position that *esse* indeed follows from the various causes. He does not say, as Fr. Owens says, that *esse* cannot be the result of formal causality. Rather, he replies:

. . . according to the order of agents is the order of ends, such that to the first agent there corresponds the ultimate end, and proportionally in [due] order to the other agents the other ends . . .

Therefore, *esse,* which is the proper effect and end in the operation of the first agent, must have the place of the ultimate end.

14. This is what St. Thomas means when he insists that *esse* is the act of the *essence* (and *thus* cannot be a *per accidens* addition). Even if it were as "other" as a predicamental accident, it would have to be a property. As it is, it is *even more one* with the thing than a property: cf. *DP* 5.4.*ad* 3, quoted below, at n. 30.
15. *SCG* 2.43 (ed. Pera, 1200; para. 8).
16. *DP* 7.2.obj. 10.

Now, the end, though it is first in intention, nevertheless is last in operation, and is the effect of the other causes. And so created *esse* itself, which is the proper effect corresponding to the first agent, is caused by the other causes, although the first cause causing *esse is* the first principle.[17]

One sees here how, instead of putting aside the essential principles as causes of *esse*, St. Thomas explains their ontological role as instruments, so to speak, within the caused *ens*, of the highest (efficient) cause. *Esse* is seen as flowing from the essence, just as a genuine contribution to victory is made by the mere individual soldier, and a genuine contribution to the common well-being is made by the mere army commander. Mere form (i.e. form which is other than *esse*) can be principle of *esse*.

FORMAL CAUSALITY

Does the doctrine of formal causality apply only when one is speaking of composites of *matter* and form? Is the proper doctrine of formal causality expressed by the formula: "form gives being to matter" [*forma dat esse materiae*] ?[18] While such a situation is more readily grasped by us, and has great importance for St. Thomas's presentation of fundamental ontology, its ultimate service to metaphysics is to isolate the peculiar roles of form and *esse* in any finite being. As long as form is seen as that by which the agent's influence is *appropriated* to the effected thing, form is "resulting" in *esse*, and so is causal.

Thus, we see that in his *Commentary on the Metaphysics*, replying to the question: by virtue of what causes does metaphysics demonstrate, Thomas answers:

... every substance either is a being [*ens*] through itself, if it is form alone, or else, if it is composed out of matter and form, it *is ens* through its form; hence, inasmuch as this science undertakes to consider *ens*, it considers most of all the formal cause.[19]

The argument is clear: the cause (hence, the repeated use of "through" [*per*]) of *ens* is form: i.e. if a thing is itself form, then it is *ens through* itself, and if a thing is a composite of matter and form, then it is *ens through*

17. *DP* 7.2.*ad* 10 (in part).
18. This formula, which can be found, e.g., in *De ente*, ch. 4 (lines 41–50), seems, as a formula, to stem from Ibn Gebirol, *Fons vitae*, IV, 10 (cf. ed. Clemens Baeumker, *Beiträge GPM*, Band I, Heft 2–4, p. 234, lines 13–14). The irony of the situation is that Gebirol (who does embrace the doctrine himself) put it in the mouth of the student who wishes to use it to argue that form can exist without matter, and Gebirol goes on to reply that this is impossible because form is precisely the unity of the matter. Thomas Aquinas makes his own (in the *De ente*, and elsewhere) the argument of Gebirol's student against Gebirol.
19. *CM* 3.4 (ed. Cathala, 384); and cf. chapter 8 above, at n. 26.

form. Thus, a survey of the modes of *ens* (simple and composite) reveals the universal *causality* of form vis-à-vis *ens*.

In the same context, St. Thomas tells us that the metaphysician makes no demonstrative use of the material cause, since it is not a cause of *ens* in its entire community, but only a cause of mobile being. Now, clearly, if formal causality obtained only inasmuch as form gives being *to matter,* the same limitation to mobile being would apply to formal causality.[20]

In another work, St. Thomas makes clear that in the case of formal causality, a thing can be cause of *itself.* He says:

> . . . the prepositions "out of" [*ex*] and "from" [*de*] do not signify the formal causal relationship, but rather the efficient or material causal relationships. Now, these latter causes are always distinct from that of which they are the causes: nothing is its own matter, nor is anything its own active principle. Still, something is its own form, as is clear regarding all immaterial things.[21]

Hence, we are not wrong in seeing *causality* in the form which is through itself an *ens.*

However, as it seems to me, we should keep firmly in mind still another doctrine of St. Thomas, if we are properly to understand formal causality, viz. that "it is for this reason that something is said to be 'caused,' i.e. because it has a cause of its being [*esse*]."[22] If form is cause of itself, and cause of its being *ens,* this is because, in finite things, it gives to itself what is other than itself, namely its own *esse.*

That *esse is* the *per se* result of form as form in no way compromises the doctrine that form, in all beings other than the first, *participates* in *esse,* and stands related to *esse* as potency to act. Rather, formal causality, in finite things, consists precisely in the potency to *esse.* To say that form is potential relative to *esse* does not mean that form as form, just in itself, *can be or not be.* As St. Thomas says, one should not be deceived by the

---

20. *CM* 3.4 (384), and cf. chapter 8 above.

21. *ST* 1.39.2.*ad* 5.

22. *In Post. An.,* 2.7 (471). We should notice the argument of St. Thomas here; he says:

> The reason for this, viz., that it is the same thing to know "what it is," and to know the cause of the very "is it?" is this: that it is necessary that there be some cause of "the thing is" [*rem esse*]: for something is called "caused" because of this, viz., that it has a cause of its *esse.* Now, this cause of being [*essendi*] either is identical with the essence of the thing itself, or is other than it. Identical indeed, as form and matter, which are the parts of the essence; but other, as the efficient cause and the end: which two causes are in a way the causes of the form and the matter: for the agent operates on account of the end, and unites the form to the matter.

The point here is that all causality is of *esse,* and all causality is in a way reducible to the causality of *esse* by essence: that is why to know "what the thing is" is to know the cause of "the thing exists."

equivocation of the word "potency." Not all potencies are to opposites (as to being and not being). Some potency is entirely to *esse* and not to *non esse*.[23]

CONCLUSION

What is the importance of the insistence that *esse follows* upon form as such? I would say that it pertains to the doctrine that metaphysics treats of beings as being [*ens secundum quod ens*],[24] where *"ens"* signifies what is most profoundly a thing's *own*. In a genuine doctrine of being, one must be speaking of what is wholly *at home* in the thing.[25]

This is in line with the predominance in Thomas Aquinas's metaphysical vision of the absolutely necessary being of creatures. In the overwhelming majority of creatures, intrinsic absolute necessity of being prevails.[26] And even contingency, as to substances, is a case of "failing *eventually*," i.e. "always working, until one day . . ."[27] Thus, it pertains to the very intelligibility of *ens* that it have as differences the necessary and the contingent (or possible), and recognition of this is required if one is to grasp God as cause of beings as beings, with the sublimity which this involves. Thus, we read:

. . . that-which-is, inasmuch as it is that-which-is [*ens inquantum ens est*], has God himself as its cause: thus, as that-which-is is subject to divine providence, so also are all the properties [*accidentia*] of that-which-is inasmuch as it is that-which-is, among which are the necessary and the contingent . . .[28]

And:

. . . the divine will is to be understood as standing outside the order of beings [*ut extra ordinem entium existens*], as a cause pouring forth that-which-is in its entirety

23. *CP,* 8.21 (ed. Maggiòlo, 1153).
24. *CM* 4.1 (529–530).
25. This seems to me to be the sense of St. Thomas's criticism of Avicenna, at *CM* 4.2 (558), which argues that *ens* is said *per se* of the thing [*res*], as naming the very *same thing*, because though it is named *"ens"* from *esse*, and *esse* indeed is other than the essence, yet *esse* is something of the essence's *own*. The name *"ens"* is not being applied in virtue of a merely outside influence, but in virtue of something which is, as it were, constituted *through* the essential principles. This point holds even though *esse* itself, in caused things, transcends the form, and is the influence of what is proper to a higher nature; cf. *Quodl.* 12.5.1 (presented in the Conclusion of chapter 11, below).
26. *SCG* 2.30 (first three paragraphs). On the question of number, cf. *ST* 1.50.3 and 1.112.4.*ad* 2.
27. Cf. *CM* 6.2 (1188), and my paper: "Being *per se*, Being *per accidens*, and St. Thomas' Metaphysics," *Science et Esprit* 30 (1978), at pp. 174–175. Cf. also *In De caelo*, 1.20 (ed. Spiazzi, 258), and my "The Distinctiveness of St. Thomas' 'Third Way,'" *Dialogue* 19 (1980), at pp. 203–205.
28. *CM* 6.3 (1220; cf. also 1222).

[*totum ens*] and all its differences. Now, the possible and the necessary are differences of that-which-is . . .[29]

To an objector who argues that creatures cannot last forever, because no accidental unity can last forever, and the act of being [*esse*] is accidentally united to the creature, Thomas replies:

. . . *esse* is not called an "accident," as if it were in the genus of accident, speaking of the *esse* of the substance: for it is the act of the essence. Rather, [it is called an "accident"] by a certain similarity: because it is not part of the essence, as neither is an accident [part of the essence]. If, nevertheless, it were in the genus of accident, nothing would prevent its lasting interminably: for *per se* accidents inhere in their substances necessarily, and thus nothing prevents them inhering perpetually. Accidents, however, which inhere in their subjects *per accidens* in no way endure forever, according to nature. But the substantial act of being of the thing [*ipsum esse rei substantiale*] cannot be something of that order: because it is the act of essence.[30]

Clearly, *esse* is too intimately united to the thing to be even a predicamental accident, let alone a predicable accident, i.e. a *per accidens* associate. If it were an accident in the predicamental sense, it would have to be a property. However, its mode of unity with the thing is greater than that. It is the act of the *essence*. If the Aristotelian demonstrative schema limps at all as regards form and *esse*, it is that *esse* is too intimate to form to be a mere property.

---

29. *In Perih.* 1.14 (ed. Spiazzi, 197); cf. also *ST* 1.48.2 (ed. Ottawa, 305a41–45) and 1.22.4.*ad* 3.
    30. *DP* 5.4.*ad* 3.

Chapter 10

ST. THOMAS, FORM, AND INCORRUPTIBILITY

Anyone reading the later writings of St. Thomas Aquinas, for example the *Disputed Questions on the Soul*, can have no doubt as to the importance accorded, in the argument for the incorruptibility of the human soul, to the doctrine that existence is the inseparable associate of form. It is remarkable, then, that in his early *Commentary on the Sentences of Peter Lombard*, the discussion of the human soul's incorruptibility makes no mention whatsoever of such a doctrine. This situation calls for investigation.[1]

Let us begin by recalling the elements of the argument for incorruptibility as found in the mature writings. One premise is that the soul is form having its own existence independently of the corporeal composite: the rational soul is *subsisting* form. The other premise is that form, by its very nature, is inseparable from existence: existence accompanies form, just because of the sort of thing form is: the rational soul is subsisting *form*. It is this latter premise which will occupy us here. In passing, we might note that these elements correspond fairly closely to the ultimate argument of Plato's *Phaedo* (which St. Thomas did not know directly): in the face of Simmias, who wonders whether the soul is not a harmony, it is argued that the soul is a subsisting thing; in the face of Cebes, wondering whether this subsisting thing might not eventually cease to exist even though it outlasts the body, it is argued that the soul has the nature of something indissociable from life or existence.[2]

---

1. Cf. St. Thomas Aquinas, *Quaestiones de anima*, q.14 (ed. James H. Robb, Toronto, 1968: Pontifical Institute of Mediaeval Studies, pp. 200–201). Though Robb, p. 36, dated these questions 1268–1269 (at Paris), R.-A. Gauthier has argued convincingly that they are more likely a preparatory exercise for the corresponding questions of *Summa theologiae* 1, and thus should be dated 1266–1267 (at Rome): cf. R.-A. Gauthier, O.P., "Quelques questions à propos du commentaire de St. Thomas sur le De anima," *Angelicum* 51 (1974), p. 452, n. 44bis. For the *Sentences*, cf. *Scriptum super libros sententiarum* 2.19.1.1 (ed. P. Mandonnet, Paris, 1929: Lethielleux, pp. 481–483).

2. Cf. Plato, *Phaedo* 91c–107a.

In its developed state, St. Thomas's premise concerning form runs as follows:

It is manifest that that which belongs to something according to itself is inseparable from it. But being [*esse*] belongs to form, which is act, through itself: thus, matter, according to precisely this, acquires being-actually [*esse in actu*], viz. that it acquires *form;* according to precisely this does corruption take place in it, viz. that *form* is separated from it.[3]

We should notice that while the doctrine leads to genuine incorruptibility only where one has to do with *subsisting* form, nevertheless it is a general doctrine of the nature of form as form, and one arrived at by observation of the role of form in corporeal, perishable things.

In the early *Commentary on the Sentences,* we find a firm theological stand as to the fact that the human soul is a substance not depending on the body, that it is multiplied according to the multiplication of individual bodies, and that it survives the destruction of bodies, nor does it pass into other bodies. However, as to the philosophical doctrine supporting this view, the article argues merely that the human soul has its own being [*esse absolutum*], i.e. does not depend on the body for its *esse.* Thus, it is not corrupted upon the corruption of the body. No mention is made of the nature of form and what it tells us about the subsisting soul. We have a doctrine here which responds to Simmias but not to Cebes.[4]

The closest St. Thomas comes here to discussing the relation between form as form and being is in the answer to an objection. The objector has argued that as form of the body, the soul has one being [*unum esse*] with the body, and so must perish with the body. The objector envisages someone replying that the soul is both form and substance, and at death it ceases to be form but continues as substance. He counters that either the soul is essentially form, and then what he has said holds, or else it is only accidentally form: which leads to the absurd result that man is only

---

3. St. Thomas, *Summa theologiae* [henceforth "*ST*"] 1.75.6 (ed. Ottawa, 425a54–66):

Manifestum est enim quod id quod secundum se convenit alicui, est inseparabile ab ipso. Esse autem per se convenit formae, quae est actus. Unde materia secundum hoc acquirit esse in actu, quod acquirit formam; secundum hoc autem accidit in ea corruptio, quod separatur forma ab ea.

Notice that the argument continues:

Impossibile est autem quod forma separetur a seipsa. Unde impossibile est quod forma subsistens desinat esse. [445b7–9]

Some people, seeing the proposition: "form cannot be separated from itself," have thought that the argument is based on simplicity. The truth rather is that it is based on the nature of form, and its relation to existence.

4. St. Thomas, *Sentences* 2.19.1.1, the body of the article and *ad 2* (ed. Mandonnet, pp. 481–483).

accidentally something one. St. Thomas replies, first, that it is right to say that the soul is not form in exactly the same way as other (material) forms; since the soul has its own being, it does not have being through the being of the composite, though the composite has being through the being of the soul. He then goes on to say that the two terms "form" and "substance" apply to the same thing, but according to two diverse considerations. That thing, the soul, remains after the body, not precisely from the fact that it is *form*, but from the fact that it has its own being [*esse absolutum*], i.e. is a subsisting substance.[5]

Here, we find no interest on St. Thomas's part in the notion of form as form for furthering the doctrine of incorruptibility. Nothing he says is *opposed* to the later doctrine: he does not say that form as form *must* disappear or *tends* to disappear with the body. He says simply that it is not "as form" that the soul has the capacity to remain after the body.

It is remarkable that in the discussion of angels in *Sentences*, book 2, there is no discussion of their incorruptibility. This surprises since such a doctrine figures in the text of Peter Lombard being commented upon. The angels are described as "indissoluble and immortal."[6] Albert the Great in his commentary provides at least brief comment.[7] St. Thomas himself, later in his career, will consider the question of the angels' incorruptibility as one which even an elementary questionnaire for beginners in theology ought to contain.[8] One has very much the impression that St. Thomas did not feel philosophically at ease with this issue of incorruptibility at the beginning of his academic career.

The *Sentences* date from 1252 to 1256. By the time he writes *Summa contra gentiles* 2.55 (dated ca 1261),[9] St. Thomas already has the fully de-

5. Ibid., obj. 3 and 4 (p. 479) and the replies (pp. 483–484); especially:

. . . non enim ex hoc quod est forma habet quod post corpus remaneat, sed ex hoc quod habet esse absolutum, ut substantia subsistens . . .

With this text is to be associated St. Thomas, *Sentences* 1.8.5.2, *ad* 5 (ed. Mandonnet, p. 231):

Dico igitur, quod animae non convenit . . . habere esse absolutum, inquantum est forma; sed inquantum est similitudo Dei.

6. Peter Lombard, *Sentences* 2, dist. 3 (in St. Thomas's commentary, ed. Mandonnet, p. 80):

Quod [angeli] spiritus erant, quod indissolubiles et immortales erant, commune omnibus et aequale erat.

7. Cf. Albert the Great, *Sentences* 2, dist. 3, a, art. 2 (ed. Paris, t. 27, p. 63a and 64a–b); also, dist. 3, c, art. 11 (p. 78a–b).

8. Cf. St. Thomas, *ST* 1.50.5, and also the prologue for the whole *Summa theologiae* in which the aim is stated: to avoid needless questions lest beginners be confused.

9. For the dates, cf. James Weisheipl, O.P., *Friar Thomas D'Aquino*, Garden City, N.Y., 1974: Doubleday, pp. 358–360. Henceforth we will use *"SCG"* for *Summa contra gentiles*.

veloped argument. To what extent can we discover something about the process of St. Thomas's thinking between *Sentences* 2 and *SCG* 2? One obvious item to consider is the *Question on the Immortality of the Soul.*[10] Discovered in this century, this document has recently been published in a good edition. While the few scholars who have spoken of it have tended to date it later than *SCG* 2, I will suggest that it is an earlier work.

The main response in the *Question* is rather long (quite normal for a *quaestio disputata*), and is taken up for the most part with the premise that the human soul is incorporeal and subsisting (fairly parallel to *ST* 1.75.2). The premise which interests us, viz. that such a being is incorruptible, is rather briefly presented, using the argument that corruption being the outcome or terminus of a movement, only beings subject to movement are corruptible, and only bodies are subject to movement. The response then goes quickly on to consider at some length the problem presented by the position that the possible intellect is not a part of the soul at all.[11]

However, the doctrine upon which we are focusing does occur in the *Question.* The fifth objection to the soul's incorruptibility is that everything composite has a possibility of dissolution, and that the soul has at least the composition of "that which is" [*quod est*] and "that by which it is" [*quo est*]. St. Thomas's reply begins on the entirely defensive note that the composition which is found in the soul is not grounds for concluding to its corruptibility. It is not a composition out of matter and form, but out of *quod est* and *quo est.* He then explains what he means by such a composition, the explanation first introducing *esse* as what is meant by "*quo est,*" and then presenting the hierarchy of beings: God, created immaterial substances, and substances composed of matter and form, in the light of the doctrine of *quod est* and *esse.* At the point of speaking of substances composed of matter and form, St. Thomas asserts that *esse* attends upon form of itself, so that the material substance only loses *esse* inasmuch as matter is separated from form. It is quickly pointed out that such separation from *esse* cannot even be conceived with respect to a substance which is pure form. The conclusion is no longer merely defensive. It is that a substance which is form alone cannot possibly be corruptible. Thus, the actual accomplishment of the reply goes far beyond what was

10. Cf. Leonard A. Kennedy, "A New Disputed Question of St. Thomas Aquinas on the Immortality of the Soul," *Archives d'histoire doctrinale et littéraire du moyen âge,* 45 (1978), pp. 205–208 (introduction) and 209–223 (text).

11. St. Thomas, *Quaestio de immortalitate animae* (ed. Kennedy, p. 217):

Non enim potest corrumpi per se, cum per se non moveatur. Nihil enim movetur nisi corpus, nec aliquid per se corrumpitur nisi moveatur, cum corruptio sit terminus motus.

announced in its first sentence. It ends up being the doctrine which as we have said will become paramount.[12]

Both doctrines used in the *Question,* that on form and *esse* and that on only bodies being subject to movement and corruption, appear in *SCG* 2.55, but that on form is given a very prominent place in the chapter. It is the second argument presented, and the first argument in the chapter falls in with it very closely.[13] The argument from movement and corruption comes in seventh place.[14] While such positioning in an *SCG* chapter proves nothing by itself, when added to the general picture it suggests that the *Question on the Immortality of the Soul* represents an earlier stage of St. Thomas's reflection than *SCG* 2.55.[15]

Let us now present more fully that general picture. To do so, we will look first at *Quodlibet* 10.3.2 and then at the *De ente et essentia.* The *Quodlibet* asks about the incorruptibility of the rational soul, and is generally

12. The objection (ed. Kennedy, p. 209) runs:

5. Preterea. Ubicumque est aliqua compositio, ibi est possibilitas ad dissolutionem. In anima est aliqua compositio, saltem ex quo est et quod est. Ergo est dissolubilis et non incorruptibilis.

The reply (ed. Kennedy, p. 219):

Ad v dicendum quod compositio que est in anima non potest esse ratio corruptibilitatis. Non enim est composita ex materia et forma, sed ex quo est et quod est, sive ex esse et quod est, quod idem est, nam ipsum esse est quo unumquodque est. Hanc autem compositionem inveniri oportet in omnibus preter Deum, in quo solo idem est sua substantia et suum esse. In substantiis autem immaterialibus sed creatis, aliud est esse et substantia rei. Sed substantia subsistens in esse est ipsa forma. In materialibus autem substantiis est compositum ex materia et forma: esse autem est per se consequens formam. Unde substantia materialis non amittit esse nisi per hoc quod materia separatur a forma. Que quidem separatio nec intelligi potest in substantia que est forma tantum. Nihil enim potest a seipso separari. Unde impossibile est quod substantia que est forma tantum sit corruptibilis.

13. The first two arguments in *SCG* 2.55 differ inasmuch as the first bases the inseparability of form from *esse* on form's being that through which the substance is the proper receiver of *esse,* whereas the second uses to the same effect the doctrine of *per se* sequence. These two approaches differ only inasmuch as the former brings more into the picture how the formal cause presupposes an outside agent: cf. St. Thomas, *ST* 1.104.1 *ad* 1, and *SCG* 2.54 (para. 5; ed. Pera, 1291). For the background of this doctrine of form as constituting the proper subject of *esse,* notice Avicenna, *Liber de philosophia prima,* tr. 2, c. 4 (ed. Simone Van Riet, Louvain/Leiden, 1977: Peeters/Brill, pp. 98.47–99.64).

14. St. Thomas, *SCG* 2.55 (para. 8; ed. Pera, 1304). We might note that this argument is not to be found even as an auxiliary in *ST* 1 or *Qq. de anima* (where there are four *sed contra* arguments given).

15. In the *Compendium theologiae,* the doctrine of form and *esse* is used in 1.74, and then that chapter is related to the rational soul in 1.84. No use or mention is made of the movement/corruption argument. I have elsewhere argued that the *Compendium* should be dated (at least the main part: *De fide*) between the *SCG* and the *ST* 1. Cf. my "St. Thomas and the Divine Names," *Science et Esprit* 32 (1980), p. 26, n. 22. This is also the opinion of the Leonine editor (H.-F. Dondaine), in *Opera omnia,* t. 42, Rome 1979: Editori di San Tommaso, p. 8.

dated at Christmas 1258.[16] Its main response has some differences and some resemblances in pattern with the *Question*. It includes at the end a lengthy discussion of the problem of whether the intellect is substantially one with the human soul, and so in this way is similar to the *Question*. However, it begins with the discussion of corruptibility and takes some time over it, before moving on to what is the main discussion in the *Question*, viz. the soul having being of its own because it has an operation of its own. The argument that the soul cannot be subject to corruption on its own account is this:

Only those things can be corrupted on their own account which are composed of matter and form having a contrary: which cannot be [the case of the soul] unless it is an element or [composed] out of the elements, as the ancient philosophers held, which positions are disproved in *De anima* 1.[17]

This is not the argument from corruption as terminus of movement, the argument featured in the *Question*, though it belongs to the same "physical" genre, one might say. The main point to note is that there is no mention whatsoever in the *Quodlibet* of the doctrine of form and *esse*.

We turn now to the *De ente et essentia*. In so doing, we turn away from Thomas's direct consideration of the problem of the soul's incorruptibility, our purpose being to note a hint of development in his general ontology, revealed in his early discussions of created intellectual substances. There is a change in St. Thomas's approach to the ontology of the soul and the angel between his *Sentences* 1 and 2, and his *De ente et essentia*. In the *Sentences*, in order to ascend to the level of immaterial beings, he points out that to quiddity as quiddity, it belongs neither to be composite nor to be simple: either may be the case.[18] In the *De ente*, in order to make the same move, St. Thomas rather argues that since form is the cause of being of matter [". . . *forma dat esse materie* . . ."], therefore form can exist without matter. It happens to some forms that they cannot be without matter, according as they are distant as to ontological perfection from the first principle which is the first and pure act.[19] Thus, we see St. Thomas showing an increased interest in form as exhibited in material things, as presenting a nature to which being belongs. He no longer has

16. Cf. Weisheipl, *Friar Thomas*, p. 127: "According to Mandonnet's chronology, about which there has been little discussion . . ." In any case, it belongs to the first Parisian professorship.

17. St. Thomas, *Quodlibet* 10.3.2 (ed. R. Spiazzi, Rome/Turin, 1949: Marietti, 200):

Per se quidem corrumpi non posset nisi esset composita ex materia et forma contrarietatem habente: quod esse non potest, nisi esset elementum aut ex elementis, ut antiqui philosophi posuerunt, quorum positiones in I *De anima* reprobantur.

18. Cf. St. Thomas, *Sentences* 1.8.5.2 (ed. Mandonnet, p. 229); also 2.3.1.1 (ed. Mandonnet, p. 87).

19. St. Thomas, *De ente et essentia*, c. 4.42–56 (*Opera omnia*, t. 43):

the outlook, which we noted earlier in this paper, that it is not "as form" that the soul is able to exist independently of the body, but "as substance" or "as resembling the first cause."[20] Rather, to be form is to have a resemblance to the first cause; to require matter in order to exist is to fall somewhat short in the very line of being a form. This *De ente* doctrine of form's natural independence of matter, precisely inasmuch as form is cause of being of matter, is to be found throughout the rest of St. Thomas's career, and nowhere more forcefully than in the *De substantiis separatis* written near the end of his life.[21]

Is this interest in the form/*esse* association to be related primarily to the doctrine of Boethius in his *De trinitate:* "All being is from form" [*"omne esse ex forma est"*]?[22] It is unfortunate that Thomas Aquinas, in his early *Expositio super librum Boethii De trinitate,* discontinued work just at the point where Boethius begins to talk about the relation between form and *esse.*[23] However, the tendency of the Boethian text is toward an identification of form and *esse,* and it could easily be read (and was read by some) as support for a doctrine of composition of matter and form in all subsisting things other than God.[24] Thomas, on the other hand, is the proponent of the doctrine of created *subsisting forms.* While the Boethian

---

Quecumque enim ita se habent ad inuicem quod unum est causa esse alterius, illud quod habet rationem cause potest habere esse sine altero, sed non conuertitur. Talis autem inuenitur habitudo materie et forme quod forma dat esse materie, et ideo impossibile est esse materiam sine aliqua forma; tamen non est impossibile esse aliquam formam sine materiam. Sed si inueniantur alique forme que non possunt esse nisi in materia, hoc accidit eis secundnm quod sunt distantes a primo principio quod est actus primus et purus. Unde ille forme que sunt propinquissime primo principio sunt forme per se sine materia subsistentes . . .

20. Cf. above, n. 5.

21. St. Thomas, *De substantiis separatis,* c. 7.91–102 (*Opera omnia,* t. 40):

Amplius, cum actus naturaliter sit prior potentia et forma quam materia, potentia quidem dependet in suo esse ab actu et materia a forma, forma autem in suo esse non dependet a materia secundum propriam rationem, ut actus [alternative reading]; non enim priora naturaliter a posterioribus dependent. Si igitur aliquae formae sint quae sine materia esse non possunt, hoc non convenit eis ex hoc quod sunt formae sed ex hoc quod sunt tales formae, scilicet imperfectae, quae per se sustentari non possunt sed indigent materiae fundamento.

Cf. St, Thomas, *CP* 1.15 (ed. P. Maggiòlo, 135 [7]):

. . . omnis forma est quaedam participatio similitudinis divini esse, quod est actus purus; unumquodque enim in tantum est actu in quantum habet formam.

22. Cf. Boethius, *De trinitate* II (in *The Theological Tractates,* ed. H. F. Stewart and E. K. Rand, Harvard University Press/Heinemann, 1953 [originally 1918]: Cambridge, Mass./ London, lines 19–56, especially line 21): "Omne namque esse ex forma est."

23. Cf. St. Thomas, *Expositio super librum Boethii De trinitate,* ed. Bruno Decker, Leiden, 1959: Brill, Expositio capituli secundi (p. 160, n. 3).

24. Notice the use of Boethius's doctrine (from the same *De trinitate* passage) that simple form cannot be a subject (*"forma simplex subiectum esse non potest"*) to support Gebirol's doctrine: St. Thomas, *ST* 1.50.2. obj. 2; also, at *ST* 1.77.1 *ad* 6, Thomas limits the validity of that proposition of Boethius concerning form to the case of God.

passage should not be ignored, the more proximate background for St. Thomas's doctrine of form and *esse* is, I would say, Avicenna's *Metaphysics*, where Avicenna considers at some length how form *gives* (Latin: *dat*) being to matter, form doing so under the influence of an external cause. I have presented this background in detail in a previous paper.[25] However, at that time I was ignorant of the literary source, so to say, of the *formula:* "forma dat esse materiae," used by Thomas in the *De ente* presentation. I have since found it in Solomon Ibn Gebirol's *Fons vitae*.[26] The irony of the situation is that Gebirol (who does embrace the doctrine himself) puts it in the mouth of the student who wishes to use it to argue that form can exist without matter, and Gebirol goes on to reply that this is impossible because form is precisely the *unity* of the matter. Thomas Aquinas makes his own the argument of Gebirol's student against Gebirol.[27] Thomas's doctrine is not identical with that of Avicenna, but Avicenna has certainly provided Thomas with much food for thought.

The *De ente* appears to me to be later than *Sentences* 2, dist. 3.[28] *Quodlibet* 10 is generally placed chronologically after the *De ente*.[29] In the *Quodlibet*, as we have seen, there is no use of the form/*esse* relationship as regards the proof for incorruptibility. This must await, it would seem, the occasion of a reply to an objection in the *De immortalitate animae* to come into use,[30] and comes to dominate the scene once and for all in *SCG* 2.55.

25. Cf. my paper: "St. Thomas Aquinas against Metaphysical Materialism," in *Atti dell'VIII Congresso Tomistico Internazionale*, vol. 5, Vatican City, 1982: Libreria Editrice Vaticana, esp. pp. 424–430.

26. Cf. Avencebrolis (Ibn Gebirol), *Fons Vitae*, ed. Clemens Baeumker, Münster, 1895: Aschendorff (Beiträge zur Geschichte der Philosophie des Mittelalters, Band I, Heft 2–4), at IV, 10 (ed. cit., p. 234, lines 13–14): "(Discipulus.) Postquam forma dat esse materiae, cur non habebit esse per se?" These pages of the *Fons Vitae* (pp. 234–237) constitute an important background for Albert the Great, *Metaphysica*, lib. 1, tr. 4, cap. 2 (ed. Cologne, t. 17, p. 48ff.).

27. Cf. above, n. 19.

28. Cf. my paper, mentioned above in n. 25, at p. 424.

29. Cf. above, n. 16, concerning the *Quodlibet*, and Weisheipl, *Friar Thomas*, pp. 78–79, concerning the *De ente*. It is clear that the sole reason for placing the *De ente* chronologically prior to Thomas's becoming "Regent Master" is the testimony of Tolomeo of Lucca. For an idea of the fragility of this testimony, cf. Antoine Dondaine, "Les 'Opuscula fratris Thomae' chez Ptolémée de Lucques," *Archivum Fratrum Praedicatorum*, 31 (1961), pp. 142–203. Tolomeo wrote his testimony some forty years after the death of St. Thomas, when in his mid-seventies (cf. p. 172). He is obviously quite wrong in much of his chronological information. It is true that the information concerning the *De ente* is contained not only in the less reliable summary of St. Thomas's life (ed. Dondaine, p. 150, lines 4–8), but also in the notably precise (cf. Dondaine, p. 172) list of works (cf. p. 152, lines 79–80: *"Tractatus de ente et essentia, quem scripsit ad fratres et socios nondum existens magister . . ."*). However, the expression *"nondum existens magister"* is to be found *not at all* in the document which Dondaine presents as Tolomeo's source (cf. p. 181, n. 31, and p. 184, no. 31). It appears thus to be an addition by Tolomeo himself, and one is left to wonder what value it has.

30. The posteriority of the *De immortalitate animae* relative to the *Quodlibet* seems clear. An especially interesting point of comparison, as regards the subject of this paper, relates

Thus, St. Thomas appears to have been searching for an adequate premise for his doctrine of incorruptibility. He first tried what we may call physical arguments: the relation between contrariety and the elements, the nature of corruption as something terminating a movement. At about the same time, he was working on the ontology of created intellectual substances, and this work he eventually applied to the problem of the soul's immortality.

What encouragement would he have had in the work of previous writers to make this application? Albert the Great in his *Commentary on the Sentences* singles out for praise the argument of Avicenna, which distinguishes between corruption of a thing of itself [*per se*] and through association [*per accidens*]. In the *per se* corruptible, one must find potency toward not-being [*non-esse*], a potency arising from the composition out of contraries. The soul, to be corruptible in such a way, would have to have simultaneously actual existence [*actus existendi*] and the potency for not

---

to the objection: either the soul is only accidentally the form of the body (thus compromising the unity of the human being), or else it is essentially form of the body, and thus cannot exist without matter. The form inasmuch as it is form (*"forma inquantum est forma"*), says the objector. cannot exist without matter. St. Thomas replies that the soul is essentially the form of the body, and when the body is destroyed, it is not destroyed as regards that by virtue of which it is form: rather, it merely ceases to be "form in act": ". . . *anima secundum suam essentiam est forma corporis, nec destructo corpore destruitur anima quantum ad id secundum quod est forma, sed solum desinit esse forma in actu"* (*ad* 4). In the *De immortalitate animae*, we have a parallel in obj. 2 and its reply. It is the language of the reply which strikes me as a clear advance over the *Quodlibet:* "Though upon corruption of the body, the form as forming actually does not remain, still the form remains as that which has (or: as having) the formative power": *"Corrupto autem corpore, forma, ut formans in actu si non remaneat, remanet tamen forma ut formativam virtutem habens . . ."* (ed. Kennedy, p. 218). I must warn the reader, however, that the general conception of St. Thomas's advance which I am envisaging is at best a hypothesis. Thus, on the same point as the above, there is a reply to an objection in the *Qq. de anima* 14. *ad* 10, which is at bottom a return to the "neutrality" of quiddity position found in the *Sentences* (cf. above, ca. n. 18). Thus, St. Thomas says: ". . . though the soul by its essence is form, nevertheless something can belong to it inasmuch as it is *such* form, namely *subsisting* form, which does not belong to it inasmuch as it is form: just as understanding does not belong to man inasmuch as he is an animal, though man is an animal according to his own essence." One sees how, in this line of thinking, form is given the indifference of a logical genus, with the differences "subsisting" and "non-subsisting," making it "such" in different ways. The case I am making throughout this paper rests on the prevalence, in St. Thomas's thinking, of a view expressed succinctly in *De immortalitate animae ad* 17, viz. that "form" and "act" are among the things predicated analogically of diverse things: ". . . *forma et actus et huiusmodi sunt de hiis que analogice predicantur de diversis."* (ed. Kennedy, p. 222) This is to say that the nature of form as form is found more truly in the higher, more perfect realizations. Thus, already in the *De ente*, instead of the *Sentences'* "neutrality" of quiddity approach, we are told that essence is found in a *truer* and nobler mode in simple as contrasted with composite substances: *"in utrisque est essentia; sed in simplicibus uerioni et nobiliori modo . . ."* (cap. 2.59–60). It is this approach which makes possible St. Thomas's position on the immortality of the soul, as well as his position on the unnaturalness of death (*ST* 1–2.85.6) and the type of argument he uses for the existence of immaterial form in *De substantiis separatis* (Leonine ed., cap. 7, lines 92–110).

existing. It cannot have both of these from one source within itself: there is never the same principle of existence and non-existence. *Existence is from the form*, while the principle of corruption is the composition out of contraries. Thus, to be corruptible, the soul must be such a composite, i.e. must be composed out of contraries, the hot, the cold, the wet, the dry, and the form: thus, it is a body, or the harmony of a body, both of which were disproved in Aristotle's *De anima* 1.[31]

This presentation of Albert's has the interesting feature of actually involving both the doctrine of composition out of contraries, which we saw used in St. Thomas's *Quodlibet* 10, and the doctrine of the form as pure principle of existence: the ultimate solution focused upon by St. Thomas.[32] However, Albert uses this doctrine of form and existence to show only that a corruptible soul would have to include both matter and form. He does not attempt to apply the doctrine of form as principle of existence to the soul just by itself. Rather, the positive doctrine of incorruptibility for Albert has its focus on the soul's being the image and likeness of the first cause. This is quite explicit in his treatise *On the Nature and Origin of the Soul*, dated at the beginning of the 1260s.[33] It remains his posi-

31. Albert the Great, *Sentences* 2, dist. 19, a, art. 1 (ed. Paris, t. 27, pp. 328b–329c):

Una est ratio Avicennae, quae melior est omnibus aliis . . . Si anima corrumpitur . . . per se, cum secundum Philosophiam nihil corrumpitur per se, nisi quod habet potentiam ex compositione contrariorum ad non esse, oportet animam simul habere actum existendi ut nunc, et potentiam non existendi: aut secundum idem, aut secundum diversa. Non secundum idem; quoniam numquam idem est principium existentiae [*I add:* et non existentiae]: quia existentia est a forma, et principium corruptionis est compositio ex contrariis: ergo habebit hoc a diversis: ergo habet in se compositum ex contrariis, scilicet calido, frigido, humido, sicco, et formam: ergo est corpus, vel harmonia corporis: et utrumque horum improbatum est a Philosopho in primo *De anima*.

Cf. also Albert, *De homine* (i.e. *Summa de creaturis* 2), q. 61, a. 2, arg. 24 (ed. Paris, t. 35, pp. 526b–527a). Albert's *Sentences* 2 was put in final written form about 1246, and the *De homine* about 1242: cf. James A. Weisheipl, "The Life and Works of St. Albert the Great," in *Albertus Magnus and the Sciences*, ed. J. Weisheipl, Toronto. 1980: Pontifical Institute of Mediaeval Studies, p. 22. Cf. also R.-A. Gauthier, "Preface" to *Sentencia libri de anima*, in St. Thomas, *Opera omnia*, t. 45/1, Rome/Paris, 1984: Commissio Leonina/Vrin, pp. 256*–257*.

32. It is interesting to note the different forms the statement of the relation between form and existence takes in Albert's various presentations of Avicenna. In the *Sentences*, we have: *"existentia est a forma"*; and in the *De homine*: *"Esse quod est actu, a forma est actu: et esse quod potest non esse, a materia potest non esse."* (References in the previous note.) In the *De anima*, 3.3.13 (ed. Cologne, t. 7/1, p. 225.63–64), dated 1254–1257 (cf. Weisheipl, "Life and Works," p. 35), we read: *". . . actus existendi est a divino et optimo, quod est forma eius quod vere est . . ."* (the terms *"divino et optimo"* are an allusion to Aristotle, *Phys.* 1.9 [192a17]). In the *De natura et origine animae*, tr. 2, cap. 2 (ed. Cologne, t. 12, p. 21.57–58), dated by B. Geyer (ibid., pp. ix–x) between 1258 and 1262–1263, we read: *". . . actus permanendi est secundum formam, quae dat esse et permanere secundum actum . . ."*

33. Albert, *De natura et origine animae*, tr. 2, c. 6 (ed. Cologne, t. 12, p. 25.77–91):

Et sic in scientia *De anima* superius quidem induximus demonstrationem, quod anima non destruitur pereunte corpore, per hoc quod ipsa essentialiter est imago et simili-

tion to the end.[34] It is true that in that treatise he teaches that the rational soul is not a composite of matter and form: he says it is "more truly form" than any other natural form, and this being more truly form is immediately linked to its being more separate from matter and closer in nature to the first cause.[35] Thus, one would be tempted to conclude that the root of the rational soul's incorruptibility is its being pure form. Still, in the same work, in discussing whether the rational soul is simple or composite, while Albert assures us that it is not a composite of matter and form, and says that is why Aristotle does not say the soul is a "this something" [*hoc aliquid*] and why Aristotle says it is "form absolutely" [*forma absolute*], nevertheless Albert is not quite satisfied with this last statement. It is better to say [*melius dicitur*] that the rational soul is an intellectual nature composed out of that which is [*quod est*] by its own nature intellectual, and that by which there is [*quo est*] the perfection of intellect. He does not seem happy with the conception of the spiritual creature as pure subsisting form. This is very probably why he never put forward the type of argument for incorruptibility which we find in St. Thomas.[36]

Avicenna himself comes much closer than Albert to saying what St.

---

tudo causae primae et similitudo lucis intellectuum caelestium, non educta de materia generabilium per qualitates corporeas operantes. Haec enim demonstratio fuit per causam; nulla enim causa est permanentiae animae nisi ea quae dicta sunt. Huius autem causae effectus sunt et propria convertibilia cum ipsa: esse separatum, esse ex se causam operationum et actuum, esse subiectum incorruptibilium, esse causam gubernationis corporis absque eo quod a corpore aliquid accipiat, esse imaginem et sigillum quoddam separatarum intelligentiarum . . .

34. In Albert's *Summa theologiae* 2, tr. 12, q. 73, m. 2 (ed. Paris, t. 33, pp. 54b–56b), Albert's presentation of the soul's incorruptibility depends entirely on its being made by God alone, in his own likeness, and on its being in no way dependent on the body for its being or operation as to pure intellection. No reference whatsoever is made to anything like St. Thomas's doctrine of form and *esse*. The Cologne editors of St. Albert, writing in 1978, have argued very forcefully for the authenticity of this work, dating it after 1268 and (for part 2, tr. 18) even after 1274: cf. D. Siedler and P. Simon, "Prolegomena" in *Summa theologiae*, Munster, 1978: Aschendorff (ed. Cologne, t. 34/1), pp. v–xvi for authenticity, xvii for date.

35. Albert, *De natura et origine animae*, tr. I, c. 6 (ed. Cologne, t. 12, p. 15.74–86):

Amplius, iam patet, qualiter inter omnes naturales formas anima intellectualis verius forma est, eo quod est magis separata et nobilior omnibus . . . Et est ista iuxta primam causam et immediata ei inter omnia quae per generationem esse accipiunt. Haec igitur vera natura est animae hominis.

36. Ibid., c. 8 (p. 17.15–21):

Et ideo compositio nulla est in anima per rationem formae et materiae. Propter quod etiam non dicit Aristoteles animam esse hoc aliquid, sed formam absolute eam dicit esse. Sed melius dicitur esse intellectualis natura composita ex eo quod est de natura sua intellectuale, et ex eo quo est perfectio intellectus. Ex intellectu enim possibili, sicut iam ostensum est, est natura intellectualis id quod est, sed ex agente est perfectio ipsius secundum esse intellectuale in actu.

Cf. also Albert, *De unitate intellectus, ad* 15 (ed. Cologne, t. 17/1, p. 26.70–77):

Thomas says. Avicenna not only presents the form, in things composed out of matter and form, as pure principle of existence, but he goes on to argue that the rational soul is simple, and thus cannot include any principle of destruction, i.e. any matter. While he depends in his argument on the soul's simplicity in a way St. Thomas does not do, nevertheless it is fairly clear that this simplicity of the soul is closely tied in with its being form, principle of existence or of the "act of enduring" [*effectus permanendi*]. Though the ontology of material beings and of man in particular in the doctrine of St. Thomas is different in crucial ways from the doctrine of Avicenna, nevertheless on this particular issue of the soul's incorruptibility, Avicenna seems to have provided Thomas with the premise he was looking for.[37]

In conclusion, in St. Thomas's writings we observe an initial shyness about the approach to the incorruptibility of spiritual substances. At the same time in his career we notice the absence of the use of the notion of form as itself constituting proximity to the first principle, or as itself constituting a reason for enduring independently of the body. With the

---

Et quod intellectus est causatum luminis causae primae, verum est, sed recipiens ipsum est substantia potentialis, quae res est in seipsa . . . et hoc nec vere materia est *nec vere forma*, sed est fundamentum lucis intellectivae . . . Et ex hoc substantia distincta est omnis intellectualis substantia et una in uno et in alio alia. [my italics]

This work dates from about 1263, according to A. Hufnagel, ibid., p. x.25–26.

37. The foundation of Avicenna's discussion is the distinction between the nature of potency and that of act. Thus, in his *Liber de anima* 5.4 (ed. Simone Van Riet, Louvain/Leiden, 1968: Editions orientalistes/Brill, p. 120.36–46), we read:

Quidquid enim solet destrui ex aliqua causa, in illo est potentia destruendi in quo est ante destructionem effectus permanendi; aptitudo autem eius ad destructionem non est ex suo effectu permanendi: intentio enim potentiae alia est ab intentione effectus, et relatio huius potentiae alia est a relatione huius effectus: relatio enim huius potentiae est ad destruendum, et relatio huius effectus ad permanendum: ergo ex duabus causis diversis sunt in re hae duae intentiones. Dicemus igitur quod in omnibus compositis et simplicibus existentibus in compositis possunt coniungi effectus permanendi et potentia destruendi; in rebus autem simplicibus separatis per se impossibile est haec duo coniungi.

Also, Avicenna focuses on the form as the principle of actual existence in the composite of matter and form (ibid., ed. Van Riet, p. 121.58–62):

. . . ut eius essentia sit composita ex aliquo quod, cum habuerit, essentia eius *sit in effectu*, quae est *forma* in unaquaque re, et ex aliquo habenti hunc effectum quod habebat in natura sua potentiam eius, quod est materia eius.

It is by presenting the soul as simple (ibid., p. 121.64) that he can go on to argue its incorruptibility (p. 122.71–77):

Manifestum est igitur quod in eo quod est simplex non compositum aut radix compositi, non conveniunt effectus permanendi et potentia destruendi comparatione suae essentiae: si enim fuerit in ea potentia destructionis, impossibile est esse in eo effectum permanendi; si autem fuerit in eo effectus permanendi et habuerit esse, tunc non est in eo potentia destruendi: ergo manifestum est quod in substantia animae non est potentia corrumpendi.

De ente et essentia, we see St. Thomas use the doctrine of form as cause of being, in order to envisage the possibility of form existing independently of matter: the nature of form becomes a reason for independence vis-à-vis the body. So also, the nature of form coalesces with the notion of proximity to the first cause. *Quodlibet* 10 shows us St. Thomas attempting to deal with radical incorruptibility with the means provided by physical arguments alone. The *Question on the Immortality of the Soul*, I suggest, presents us with a look at the mind of St. Thomas at the moment of transition. The principal argument for essential or radical incorruptibility is still physical, while the answer to the fifth objection begins as a mere defensive move, but turns, before our eyes, into the new metaphysical approach. In *SCG* 2.55 and ever after, the doctrine of *esse* as accompanying the form as such is the primary reason for incorruptibility. One might conjecture not merely that the *Question* dates from very shortly before *SCG* 2.55, but even that the significant doctrinal advance to which the two texts together bear witness led St. Thomas to decide against formal publication of the *Question*.

While it might be thought that it is the simplicity more than the nature of form as principle of being which is in play in the argument, one should note that Avicenna goes on to argue that in corruptible composites, the power to be destroyed is not in the nature *(in intentione)* which gives the composite unity, but is in the matter which is potential with respect to both contraries: (p. 122.78–81) "... *potentia vero destrui non est in intentione secundum quam compositum est unum, sed in materia quae est in potentia receptibilis utrorumque contrariarum* ..." He also says that the potential for destruction of the simple things which are in matter is in the substance which the matter has, not in their substance: (p. 123.86–88) "*Potentia vero destructionis simplicium quae sunt in materia est in substantia quam habet materia, non in substantia eorum.*" He thus seems to be pointing out the entire freedom-from-tendency-to-destruction which constitutes the nature of *form*.

Chapter 11

ST. THOMAS AND THE DISTINCTION BETWEEN FORM AND *ESSE* IN CAUSED THINGS

INTRODUCTION

The present paper concerns the oft-stated doctrine of Thomas Aquinas that the act of being attends upon form, just because of the sort of thing form is: *"Esse . . . per se consequitur ad formam"*;[1] *"esse secundum se competit formae"*;[2] *"esse . . . per se convenit formae, quae est actus."*[3]

The close relationship between form and *esse* is of great importance for the understanding of both these targets of metaphysical attention. They are so closely associated that they are most easily confused. Accordingly, my topic is how we know, with Thomas, that they are indeed *really*, and not merely notionally, distinct.[4]

St. Thomas is not as helpful as he could be. In the *Sentences*, he seems to affirm that the *esse* of a caused thing is itself the formal cause of being

---

1. *SCG* 2.55 (ed. Pera, 1299):

. . . being accompanies form through itself: for "through itself" means "inasmuch as [it is] itself"; but each thing has being according as it has form.

The idea is that it is just because of what form is, in itself, that being is its companion. Cf. chapters 9 and 10 above.

2. *ST* 1.50.5 (321a8–10):

. . . being belongs to form according to itself; for each thing is a being in act [*ens actu*] according as it has form.

3. *ST* 1.75.6 (445b2–6):

. . . being belongs to form through [form] itself, which is act. Hence, matter [precisely] through this acquires being in act [*esse in actu*], that it acquires *form;* but corruption occurs in it [precisely] through this, that *form* is separated from it.

4. In Etienne Gilson, *Elements of Christian Philosophy*, Garden City, N.Y., 1960: Doubleday, we read: ". . . no one has ever been able to demonstrate the conclusion that, in a caused substance, existence is a distinct element, other than essence, and its act." (p. 128, my italics)

of that thing. At least, to an objector who says that the *esse* of creatures must be "through itself" and thus not caused (and consequently is God himself), Thomas replies:

... created *esse* is not *through* something else, if the word "through" expresses the intrinsic formal cause; on the contrary [*immo*], through it [*ipso*], formally, the creature is . . .[5]

In this passage, it is clear enough that *esse* is being viewed as the intrinsic formal cause. However, toward the end of the *De veritate*, we read:

... God causes in us natural *esse* by creation, without the mediation of any efficient cause, but nevertheless through the mediation of a formal cause: because natural form is the principle of natural *esse* . . .[6]

And it is this doctrine which will prevail.[7]

When it comes to explaining the distinction, we still do not get as much help as we would like. Consider what Thomas says in *Quaestiones disputatae de anima:*

... In substances composed out of matter and form we find three [items], viz. matter, and form, and, [as a] third, *esse*, whose principle is form. For matter, by the fact that it receives form, participates in *esse*. Thus, therefore, *esse* follows upon form itself, nor nevertheless is form its own *esse*, since it is its principle [*cum sit eius principium*].[8] And though matter does not attain to *esse* save through form, form nevertheless, inasmuch as it is form, does not need matter for its *esse*, since *esse* follows upon form itself [*cum ipsam formam consequatur esse*]; but it needs matter since [*cum*] it is such form as does not subsist by itself . . .[9]

5. In Sent. 1.8.1.2.ad 2 (ed. P. Mandonnet, Paris, 1929: Letheilleux, p. 198).
6. St. Thomas, DV 27.1.ad 3 (Leonine ed., t. 22/3, lines 182–186). An important remark is to be found at DP 3.1.ad 17. The question is posed: can God make something out of nothing? The objector reasons that the maker gives esse to the thing made. If what receives the esse is nothing, then it is nothing which is constituted in existence [esse]: and thus nothing is made. If, on the other hand, it is something which receives the esse, then this is not making something out of nothing. Thomas replies:

... God, simultaneously giving *esse*, produces that which receives *esse*: and thus it is not necessary that he work on something already existing.

This allows us to see that, God being posited on high as agent, we analyze his product, a being, i.e. *ens*, in which are found together a multiplicity of intelligible ontological factors, such as *esse*, form, matter, etc. That is, *only* by what I would call "formal analysis" does metaphysics make sense. One should not view the *esse* of the thing as something that itself *has esse* and gives it to essence; this is to view it as an agent, i.e. a subsisting thing.
7. Cf. e.g. CM 4.2 (ed. M.-R. Cathala, Turin, 1935: Marietti, 558. the criticism of Avicenna on *esse*. See chapters 9 and 10 of this book.
8. I translate *"cum"* here as "since" rather than "though," because a few lines below it twice clearly means "since."
9. Thomas Aquinas, *Quaestiones disputatae de anima* q. 6, lines 229–240 (*Opera omnia*, t. 14/1. Roma-Paris, 1996: Commissio Leonina/Cerf. Ed. B.-C. Bazan). On the argument

Here it is merely asserted that form is the principle of *esse* and therefore cannot be identified with the *esse*. So also, in the *Summa contra gentiles*, Thomas has us depend merely on the different modes of speech about form and *esse:*

> ... neither is form *esse* itself, but they are situated relative to each other in an order: for form is related to *esse* as "light" [*lux*] to "shining" [*lucere*], or as "whiteness" [*albedo*] to "being white" [*album esse*].[10]

Accordingly, I propose to explain this real distinction, basing myself on various considerations in Thomas's works.

THAT 'ESSE' IS

There is a real composition out of the subsisting thing and its being-actually in any caused thing (i.e. caused, as by an efficient cause).[11] And since ultimately Thomas will say that there is only one being which is not caused by an efficient cause, namely God, only in God is there identity of subsisting thing and act of being.

In the subsisting thing, as we find it in sensible things, there are many distinct items of metaphysical analysis. Thus, we speak of matter, we speak of form, we speak of essence (or nature or quiddity). None of these items can be identified with the *esse* of the caused thing. And so one finds Thomas, at one time or another, discussing a variety of compositions involving *esse*. Sometimes he will speak of the *creature* being other

---

concerning form in this passage, see my paper, "St. Thomas Aquinas against Metaphysical Materialism," in *Atti del'VIII Congresso Tomistico Internazionale*, t. 5, pp. 412–434, Vatican City, 1982: Libreria Editrice Vaticana.

10. *SCG* 2.54 (ed. Pera, 1290). Just how fragile such an indication is can be suggested by *ST* 1.18.2 (127a24–37): at first, Thomas seems to be saying that *"vita"* signifies the substance; but he goes on to say that *"vivere"* signifies being [*esse*] in a nature capable of self-activation, and that *"vita"* signifies that very being [*hoc ipsum*], but abstractly, just as *"cursus"* signifies the same thing as *"currere,"* but abstractly.

On the other hand, Thomas at *ST* 1.75.5.*ad* 4, wishing to distinguish between the soul as subsisting form and its own act of being, says:

> ... But whatever created form is posited as subsisting, it is necessary that it participate in *esse;* because even life itself [*ipsa vita*], or whatever would be so said, "participates in being itself [*ipsum esse*]," as Dionysius says, in *On the Divine Names*, c. 5 [5; *PG* 3.820] ...

Cf. Thomas, *In De divinis nominibus* 5.1 (ed. Pera et al., Rome/Turin, 1950: Marietti, 635). This seems to be a direct appeal to the universality of *esse:* there are things that do not have life, and nevertheless have *esse*. I am not sure how this fits with the idea that life *is* the being of living things.

11. *ST* 1.3.7.*ad* 1:

> ... But this belongs to the intelligibility of the caused thing [*causati*], that it be in some way a composite; for at the very least, its being [*esse eius*] is other than its essence [*quod quid est*] ...

than its *esse*.[12] Sometimes he will speak of the *substance or essence* being other than the *esse*.[13] Where should one begin, and what pathway should one follow?

I take it for granted that the subsisting thing, i.e. that which is [*ens*], is not only well known, but is what we all first know intellectually, since it is best known both in itself and to us.[14] Obviously this knowledge of *ens* already includes a knowledge of *esse*,[15] but that is still a somewhat confused knowledge of *esse*, since it is only as included in a composite.[16] However, knowledge of *esse* just in itself cannot be too difficult of access. Thus, Thomas takes as his example of a *per accidens* sensible object, i.e. what jumps to the attention of intellect on the occasion of sense cognition, the life (considered universally) of a living thing.[17] Now, we know that life is the being, i.e. the *esse*, of the living thing.[18] This is obviously an in-

12. *Quaestiones de quolibet* 2.2.1 [3], in Leonine ed., t. 25/2, Rome/Paris, 1996: Commissio Leonina/Cerf, p. 214, lines 46–48:

. . . in qualibet creatura est aliud ipsa creatura que habet esse, et ipsum esse eius [. . . in any creature, the creature itself which has *esse* is one item, and its very *esse* is another].

[There is a translation by Sandra Edwards: Thomas Aquinas, *Quodlibetal Questions 1 and 2*, Toronto, 1983: Pontifical Institute of Mediaeval Studies, pp. 78–79.]

Properly speaking, by "the creature" is meant the subsisting thing, not a merely inherent item: it is the subsisting thing which *"has esse"*: *ST* 1.45.4.

13. *SCG* 2.52, e.g.

14. Thomas Aquinas, *Sententia libri Ethicorum Aristotelis* 6.5 (Leonine ed., t. 47/2, Rome, 1969: Ad Sanctae Sabinae, lines 102–106 (concerning Aristotle at 1141a12–17) (ed. Pirotta, 1181); there we read that metaphysics is most certain, i.e. more certain than any other science, inasmuch as it attains to the primary principles of beings. Though some of these principles, viz. immaterial things, are *less* known to us than other things, thus placing in doubt metaphysics' claim to being "most certain," nevertheless this claim is well founded, inasmuch as the most universal principles, pertaining to being as being, are *both best known in themselves and best known to us*. And these pertain to metaphysics.

15. *ST* 1.5.1.*ad* 1 (27a39–47):

. . . Now, since *"ens"* says something properly being in act [*aliquid proprie esse in actu*], and act properly has an order to potency, it is in function of this that something is called *"ens"* unqualifiedly, viz. in function of that whereby first of all it is distinguished from that which is merely in potency; and this is the substantial *esse* of each thing; hence, through its substantial *esse* each thing is called *"ens"* unqualifiedly.

16. See chapter 3 above, at n. 16.

17. Thomas, *Sentencia libri De anima* (in *Opera omnia*, t. 45/1, Rome/Paris, 1984: Commissio Leonina/Vrin), 2.13 (lines 182–190). Cf. Aristotle, *De anima* 2.6 (418a7–26). Thomas says that when I see someone speaking and setting himself in motion, I apprehend that person's *life* (considered *universally*), and I can say that I *"see"* that he is alive (thus speaking of the intelligible object as a "visible.")

18. Cf. *ST* 1.18.2 (127a32–37), following up on the *Sed contra* reference to Aristotle, *De anima* 2.4 (415a13). The text of Aristotle is arguing that the soul is the cause of the living body, as its form. The passage in the Latin which Thomas, in his *Sentencia libri De anima*, comments upon is:

. . . Quod quidem igitur sit sicut substancia, manifestum est. Causa enim ipsius esse omnibus substancia est, uiuere autem uiuentibus est esse, causa autem et principium horum anima.

stance of *esse*, considered universally.[19] Indeed, when we move from the first operation of the intellect to the second, i.e. from the apprehension of simple objects to composition and division, Thomas presents as the maximally first principle: "it is impossible for the same thing to *be* and not to *be*."[20]

That esse is, then, everyone knows. The problems arise when we seek to know *what* it is, i.e. to distinguish it from every other item with which it might be confused.[21]

What Esse Is (1)

The first step is to distinguish it from that which is [*ens*]. This Thomas does in his *Commentary on Boethius's De hebdomadibus*. There, he tells us that Boethius is presenting, in the chapter (II) which interests us, a series of principles known just by virtue of themselves [*principia per se nota*].[22]

In the Leonine ed., t. 45/1, Rome/Paris, 1984: Commissio Leonina/Vrin, this is at 2.7 (p. 93).

Thomas paraphrases, 2.7 (lines 176–181):

... that is the cause of something in the role of substance, i.e. in the role of *form*, which is the cause of being [*causa essendi*], for *through the form* each thing is in act [*est actu*]; but the soul is the cause of being for living things, for through the soul they live; and living itself [*ipsum uiuere*] is their being [*esse*]; therefore, the soul is the cause of living things in the role of form.

I note that W. S. Hett, in the Loeb Classics translation of the *De anima* [Cambridge, Mass./London, 1964 (1st ed., 1936; revised 1957): Harvard University Press/Heinemann, p. 87], translates Aristotle's *"einai"* here as "existence":

... substance is the cause of existence in all things, and for living creatures existence is life, and of these [Hett notes: existence and life] the soul is the cause and first principle.

19. The senses, of course, know *esse* but merely concretely, as here and now: *ST* 1.75.6 (445b31–32):

... Sensus autem non cognoscit esse nisi sub hic et nunc, sed intellectus apprehendit esse absolute, et secundum omne tempus.

20. *CM* 3.5 (392) and 4.6 (605). In the former, we read:

... ad philosophum potius pertinet consideratio dignitatum, inquantum ad ipsum pertinet consideratio *entis* in communi, *ad quod per se* pertinent huiusmodi principia prima, ut maxime apparet in eo quod est *maxime primum principium, scilicet quod impossibile est idem esse et non esse* ... [my italics]

[... to the philosopher pertains especially the consideration of the axioms, inasmuch as to him pertains the consideration of *that which is* in general, to which essentially pertain such first principles, as appears most of all in what is most of all a first principle, viz. that it is impossible for the same thing *to be and not to be*.]

21. See *ST* 1.87.1 (541a5–22). I apply what is said there of the two modes of knowing the soul, to knowledge of *esse*.

22. *Expositio libri Boetii De ebdomadibus*, in *Opera omnia* t. 50, Rome/Paris, 1992: Commissio Leonina/Cerf, (Henceforth *"DH"*) I (Leonine ed., line 125).

They are such as are immediately approved of when heard. Their structure is such that the predicate is contained in the intelligibility of the subject. Such principles are of two grades, depending on whether the terms involved are the sort which everyone whatsoever knows, or such as are known only to the learned. The principles presented by Boethius in chapter II are known by virtue of themselves only to the learned, even though they are analyses of notions which are known to all.[23] It seems as though the principles we will see involve an *exploration* of the meanings of the most common terms, an exploration requiring education.

The first principle presented is: "that which is and being are diverse." However, this is not a doctrine of the *real* diversity of these two targets of metaphysical attention, that which is and being. It is presented by Thomas as speaking of the very *notions,* not about the realities. The two are presented as the concretely expressed and the abstractly expressed. Accordingly it is taught that one cannot predicate "being" of being itself, but only of that which is, which is viewed as receiving being. Also, that which is is open to participation in other intelligibilities, but being cannot participate in anything else. Furthermore, that which is can have mixed in with it some other intelligibility, but being has nothing foreign admixed. All this flows from the abstractness and supreme universality of being.

It is when we come to the next set of principles, those based on the notion of unity, that we find Thomas dealing with our topic. Under the notion of unity come the notions of compositeness and simplicity. The principle is proposed: *in every composite,* 'THAT WHICH IS' *and* 'BEING' *are really distinct.* The point is that a composite is something that contains, in one "that which is," at the very least a duality or diversity. However, we have seen that "being" [*esse*] signifies something which cannot include composition. Thus, "being" is what a composite has, that renders it deserving of the title "that which is." To anyone who has thought about the idea of a composite, i.e. something one which includes diversity, it is evident, from the very notions, that the composite includes a principle of unity which is not identifiable with the diversity as a diversity.[24]

Thomas's actual explanation runs as follows:

23. *DH* II (lines 6–7): rules of the wise or learned; yet the terms are known to all (lines 9–18).

24. Cf. *Quodl.* 9.2.2 [3].*ad* 2:

. . . sed *esse* est id in quo fundatur unitas suppositi: unde *esse* multiplex praeiudicat unitati essendi.

[. . . but being is that on which is founded the unity of the subsisting thing: hence, multiple being precludes unity of being.]

. . . just as *esse* and *quod est* differ as to notions, so also they differ *really* in composites. Which indeed is evident from the foregoing. For it was said above that *esse* itself neither participates in anything such that its intelligibility [*ratio*] be constituted out of many, nor does it have anything extrinsic admixed such that there be in it an accidental composition; and therefore *esse* itself is not composite; therefore, the composite thing is not its own *esse* . . .[25]

One might wonder here at the procedure. If the earlier discussion was not about things but merely about notions, one might think that from its data one could not conclude to the *real* simplicity of *esse*. What one must consider is that we are here taken as knowing the composite to be really a composite. How is this known? Generally, it is change that reveals to us composition.[26] Thus, we come to appreciate the reality we are attempting to express. Its "being" pertains directly to its being a unit, to its overcoming the duality of composition. Since the words and the notions, "that which is" and "being," are designed to express the reality which confronts us, "that which is" (which has been seen to accommodate participation) can signify the composite itself, but this cannot be true of "being."

Still, thus far we have no reason to distinguish *form* from *esse*. Of both, it could be said that they pertain to the composite's being a unity.

However, we cannot ignore what Thomas says about the next principle: *in every simple thing, 'THAT WHICH IS' and 'BEING' are identical.* He carefully explains that one must understand "simple" here to mean "altogether simple" [*omnino simplex*], not merely "simple in some respect" [*secundum quid simplex*]. Supposing that there are some forms which are not in matter, each is "simple" as lacking matter and quantity (which is a disposition of matter). However, he says:

Because, nevertheless, any form is determinative of being itself, none of them is being itself, but is something having being; for example, according to the opin-

25. *DH* II (lines 204–215; Calc. 32):

. . . sicut esse et quod est differunt secundum intentiones, ita in compositis differunt realiter. Quod quidem manifestum est ex premissis. Dictum est enim supra quod ipsum esse neque participat aliud ut eius ratio constituatur ex multis, neque habet aliquid extrinsecum admixtum ut sit in eo compositio accidentalis; et ideo ipsum esse non est compositum; res ergo composita non est suum esse; et ideo dicit quod in *omni composito aliud est* esse ens et *aliud* ipsum compositum quod est participando *ipsum esse.*

The Boethius text has, at line 17:

Omni composito aliud est esse, aliud ipsum est.

The Leonine editors (Louis J. Bataillon and Carlo A. Grassi) have attempted to italicize this in Thomas's exposition. The *"ens"* is awkward. Without it, one would think one could underline:

. . . et ideo dicit quod in *omni composito aliud est esse* [ens] et *aliud ipsum* compositum quod *est* participando ipsum esse.

26. Cf. e.g. *SCG* 1.18 (ed. Pera, 141, 143, 144).

ion of Plato, suppose we posit that an immaterial form subsists which is the idea and intelligibility of material human beings, and another form which is the idea and intelligibility of horses, it will be evident that the subsisting immaterial form itself, since it is a something determined to a species, is not common being itself [*ipsum esse commune*], but participates in it. And it makes no difference in this regard if we posit other immaterial forms of a higher grade than are the intelligibilities of these sensible things, as Aristotle maintained; for each of them, inasmuch as it is distinguished from another, is some special form participating in being itself, and thus none of them is truly simple.[27]

Thomas goes on to argue that the subsistent act of being, which is God, is alone truly simple [*uere simplex*].

A text like this already helps us grasp the difference between form and *esse*. It asserts with some ease that "any form" [*quelibet forma*] is determinative of *esse*, meaning by "determinative" that it particularizes it, limiting it to a species. Now, this is not true of form inasmuch as it is form. Thus, the rest of the above text is an argument to make the point. It does so by noting the diversity of the things being discussed, one from the other. Whether they be Platonic forms or Aristotelian separate entities, "being" signifies something all have in common, and so the "*special* forms" (note well this expression) cannot be identified with it. *Esse*, in spite of the "*quelibet forma*" statement, really appears in the above as a sort of *universal* form.[28]

That is why Thomas can say, in *ST* 1.3.2, that God is "*per essentiam suam forma,*" form by his very own essence, and "*primo et per se forma,*" i.e. what has primacy in the realm of form.[29] So also, speaking of *ipsum esse*, which Dionysius had called "the substance and perpetuity" of each existent, Thomas can paraphrase: "the *form* participated in, so as to subsist and to endure."[30]

In an earlier paper,[31] I have noted that Thomas seems to have changed

27. *DH* II (Leonine ed., lines 230–249). The use of the Platonic forms is perhaps to be traced to Dionysius as we see presented in Thomas, *In De divinis nominibus* 5.1 (ed. Pera et al., Rome/Turin, 1950: Marietti, 639), commenting on Dionysius at 267.

28. For the expression "universal form" as applied to *ens* (and by implication, I would say, to *esse*), see *ST* 1.19.6 (136b1–4). We should, of course, take seriously Thomas's designation of *esse* as "most *formal* of all" [*maxime formale omnium*] in such a crucial and careful argument as *ST* 1.7.1 (37a43–44).

29. *ST* 1.3.2 (17a40–49).

30. Thomas, *In De divinis nominibus* 5.1 (ed. Pera, 635):

. . . *nihil est existens cuius ipsum per se esse non sit substantia et aevum,* idest forma participata ad subsistendum et durandum.

[. . . there is no existent of which "being through itself" itself is not the substance and the duration, i.e. the form participated in so as to subsist and endure.]

The italicized words are the Latin translation of the text of Dionysius.

31. Cf. chapter 10 above.

his approach to form somewhat, between the *Sentences* and the *SCG*. As he points out in his *Disputed Question on the Immortality of the Soul*, "form," like "act," is said analogically of diverse things.[32]

What Esse Is (2)

The above type of argument helps us, but it is somewhat dialectical or logical; I am looking for something closer to things in their real being.[33] If we take "form" in its metaphysical reality, why must it be really distinct from *esse* in caused things? Notice that the above argument made use of both God and realities intermediate between material beings and God in order to make its distinction.

The general argument I wish to stress insists on the doctrine that the cause as such is more noble than its effect, and insists on causal *hierarchy*. This is a doctrine somewhat obscured by the prominence of univocal causes in our experience. Since dogs cause dogs, it would seem that the effect is just as noble as the cause.[34] Still, it is universally true that the agent is more noble than the patient. The cause as such has being in act, and the effect, inasmuch as it is an effect, derives its actuality from its cause.[35]

Let us simply note that univocal causality is essentially *derivative* causality. It presupposes a higher sort of cause. It consists in communicating a form, existing in matter, to other matter. It cannot cause the form itself as such, for then it would be cause of itself, and so prior to itself: in act and in potency in exactly the same respect. Yet a form existing in matter requires a cause. One sees this from the order and composition it involves. This means that ultimately the forms of material things can only have as their origin some more noble sort of form.[36]

Now, causal hierarchy is not merely a hierarchy of "acts of being" one

32. Thomas Aquinas, *De immortalitate animae, ad* 17 [ed. Kennedy at p. 222]:
. . . forma et actus et huiusmodi sunt de hiis que analogice predicantur de diversis.

33. Cf. Armand Maurer, C.S.B., "Dialectic in the *De ente et essentia* of St. Thomas Aquinas," in *Roma, magistra mundi. Itineraria culturae medievalis*, Mélanges offerts au Père L. E. Boyle à l'occasion de son 75ᵉ anniversaire, ed. J. Hamesse, Louvain-la-Neuve, 1998: Fédération Internationale des Instituts d'Etudes Médiévales, pp. 573–583. Cf. also chapter 8 above, concerning "logical consideration" in metaphysics.

34. In this line, Thomas himself at *SCG* 1.28 (ed. Pera, 265, Pegis, 7), says merely that while it is impossible for the effect to be more noble than the cause, it is possible for the cause to be more perfect than the effect.

35. Aristotle, *De anima* 3.5 (430a18); Thomas, *In De anima* 3.4 (Leonine ed., t. 45/1, Rome/Paris, 1984: Commissio Leonina/Vrin, lines 75–86): the agent, inasmuch precisely as it is in act, is more noble than the patient; cf. *ST* 1.4.1 (23b44–46).

36. *SCG* 3.65 (ed. Pera, 2400). The doctrine that the forms of things are like numbers implies that the cause must have a form more noble than its effect, once one leaves univocal causality.

of which would have the "upper hand" for no good reason at all. Rather, causal hierarchy is a hierarchy of *natures,* diverse kinds of things, one kind more noble than another.[37] Of course, to such a hierarchy there corresponds a hierarchy of acts of being.[38]

In our vision of a causal hierarchy, then, it is clear that the ultimate effect has a nature of its own, distinct from and inferior to the nature of the immediately superior cause. I can speak here of "nature" or of "form," since form in material things is what has primacy in the essence, and is the source of the thing's species.[39]

Now, we make use of artificial things in our effort to imagine and understand natural things (art partly completes and partly imitates nature).[40] To begin to get an idea of the three factors in a material being: matter, form, and the act of being, let us imagine an alphabet made of metal or wood, and a person to hold up a row of letters. Let us say that the person can succeed, with two hands, to present three letters. Take the letters T, A, and C. The person can hold up the letters in this way: ACT, or else in this other way: CAT.[41] In each case, we have an English *word* presented. The letters, taken one by one, have the role of *matter,* whereas the letters' *order* has the role of *form.* Thirdly, and of crucial importance for our present topic, the letters only have that order because

37. Our own bodies provide an example of causal hierarchy: the hand is by its very nature ordered toward particular modes of operation, and it operates under the (by nature) more all-embracing or universal operation of the brain; St. Thomas himself uses the example of the particular sense powers as ordered under the *sensus communis,* the universal sense power which has a more universal proper object, the sensible in general: cf. *ST* 1.1.3.*ad* 2. One could even argue that the hierarchy has as its essential levels nature and mind, i.e. that the work of nature is, by priority, a work of intelligence: cf. *ST* 1.19.4 (134a34–44). However, I do not need that point here.

38. Let us remember the passage in the *De ente:*

. . . But because *"ens"* is said absolutely and primarily of substances, and posteriorly and in a somewhat qualified sense of accidents, thus it is that *essentia* also properly and truly is in substances, but in accidents it is in a certain measure and in a qualified sense. But of substances, some are simple and some are composite, and in both there is *essentia;* but in the simple in a truer and more noble degree, inasmuch as they also they have more noble *esse;* for they are the cause of those which are composite, at least [this is true of] the first simple substance which is God. [*De ente et essentia* c. 1 (Leonine ed., lines 53–63)].

I would say we need everything that Thomas deploys in such a text: causal hierarchy, hierarchy of *esse,* hierarchy of essence. A causal hierarchy is understood in terms of grades of natures. And a hierarchy of *esse* is an integral part of the same picture.

39. *CM* 7.11 (1531), concerning Aristotle at 1037a28–29.

40. *CP* 2.4 (170 [5]–171 [6]), on art imitating nature, and why; concerning Aristotle at 2.2 (194a22); and *CP* 2.13 (258 [4]) concerning Aristotle, 2.8 (199a15–17), on adding to nature as well as imitating.

41. Other helpful groups of letters, in the four-letter range, are S,P,O,T and I,T,E,M. We get "spot," "pots," "tops," "opts," "stop," "post"; but "otsp" and "opst" and "otps" and "ostp" and "ptso" and "ptos," etc. are all monstrosities. We get "item," "time," "mite," "emit"; but "tmei" and "eitm," etc. are monstrosities.

of the activity of the person presenting them. That person's "input"[42] is the word's "actual existence" or being. Notice that it is of the essence of the situation that the person gives form as well as actuality, and gives actuality by giving form.

If we consider these different factors, we can see something of the roles played. The letters, taken by themselves, are not "beings," are not "things which are," in the (conveniently restricted) domain which we are considering: i.e. they are not *words* (in fact, the domain is that of *three-letter English words*). It is when we make a *word* that we can say: "Now, you've really got *something!*" Indeed, we have the experience of arriving at *a goal* (i.e. at a good: the good and that which is are identical)[43] when we add the T to the CA, or when we add the T to the AC. Form has been added, or arrived at, and now something exists. When matter acquires form, matter acquires being. Thus, it is a doctrine expressed by St. Thomas that *"form gives being to matter."*[44] Matter, just in itself, *can* participate in being. It is potentially a being.[45] Thus, it has kinship with *being*, but not as strongly as *form* has. Form is the factor through which the matter comes to participate in being. Form is thus very close in nature (or ontological character) to what we call *"esse."* Indeed, form and being are *indissociable;* being follows upon or necessarily accompanies form, just because of the kind of thing form is.

We should reflect on this "almost-identity" of form and *esse*. Form is something which satisfies the mind. When we see that a thing has form, we see that it is "all there," a finished product. To see form is to see totality, completeness, something like the completeness of a circle (nothing can be added or taken away without ruining it).[46]

Our experience of form, completeness, in the realm of artifacts is

42. The word "input," like "influence," suggests that what we are talking about is really *in* the effect, as coming from the cause.

43. *ST* 1.5.1.

44. *De ente et essentia* c. 4 (Leonine ed., line 46); *On Being and Essence*, tr. Armand Maurer, C.S.B., Toronto, 1968 (2nd ed.): Pontifical Institute of Mediaeval Studies, ch. 4, para. 3, p. 53.

45. *CP* 1.15 (131 [3]). As regards "kinship with being," note *ST* 1.14.11.*ad* 3 [the objector claimed that God could not know singulars because knowledge requires some likeness and God, being pure act, is totally unlike matter, which is pure potency. The reply:

. . . matter, though it recedes from the likeness of God in accordance with its potentiality, nevertheless inasmuch as it has being even in that way [*vel sic esse habet*], it retains some likeness to the divine being [*esse*].

46. *ST* 1.76.8 (461b39–43 and 462a8–11):

. . . There is a *whole* which is divided into the parts of the intelligibility and of the essence: as the thing defined into the parts of the definition, and the composite is analysed into the matter and the form. . . . [The] *totality* which is noted as regards the perfection of the intelligibility and of the essence belongs properly and essentially [*proprie et per se*] to *forms* . . .

And *ST* 1.76.4.*ad* 4 (457a10–16):

linked to the artifact's having a function, an operation, which it is designed to perform. A bicycle is made for an operation. Our grasp of the bicycle as complete or perfectly formed is related to our seeing it as perfectly proportioned to the carrying out of that operation.

And this grasp of form is also found in our knowledge of *natural* things: cats, dogs, human beings, trees, spiders. We see the operation, e.g. feeding oneself, and we see what it is for such an animal to be *all there*. We see its form. And when kittens are born, we can judge whether they are as they should be—whether a being has come upon the scene, or whether there has been some accidental variation in the generative process, and the offspring is dead (not "a cat," not "a being").

Why distinguish, then, between form and *esse?* Let us remember that the distinction holds only for *caused* things, caused by another, i.e. things that are produced by an *efficient* cause. In the case of God, form and esse are *identical,* and in the case of things which more closely resemble God, they are *closer* to each other in intelligible character: one might say that form becomes closer to, i.e. more like, *esse* as one mounts the metaphysical hierarchy, and coincides with it "at infinity," i.e. at God.[47] Still, in such things, things other than God, the form always stands relative to the *esse* as potency to act. Let us see why this must be the case.

We must consider efficient causality. While we have a certain experience of efficient causality in any body pushing another body (David Hume's billiard balls, pushing each other around, where one body is quite homogeneous with another), eventually we have to turn our minds to the situation where one thing has a nature such as to be active vis-à-vis another thing which has a different nature which renders it passive (relative to the first).[48] While the influence of the hot on the cold is the most sensibly evident manifestation of this, we find examples of agent and patient abundant in our knowledge of nature. We speak familiarly of some-

---

... the substantial being [*esse substantiale*] of each thing whatsoever consists in [or: is found in] an indivisible [*in indivisibili consistit*]; and every addition or subtraction varies the species, as in numbers, as is said in *Metaph.* 8 [1044a9]. Hence, it is impossible that any substantial *form* admit of more and less . . .

47. Cf. *Super Librum de causis expositio,* ed. H. D. Saffrey, O.P., Fribourg/Louvain, 1954: Société Philosophique/Nauwelaerts, prop. 4, at p. 32, lines 7–17. In English translation, cf. *Commentary on the Book of Causes,* translated and annotated by Vincent A. Guagliardo, O.P., Charles R. Hess, O.P., and Richard C. Taylor, Washington, D.C., 1996: The Catholic University of America Press, pp. 34–35.

48. Cf. Thomas, *ST* 1.115.1:

. . . It is sensibly apparent that some bodies are active.

Unlike David Hume, according to whom efficient causality is not an observable object, Thomas teaches that it is one of those things that leaps to the attention of the mind through the mediation of sense perception.

Natural agent-to-patient relationships, the agent having a nature such as to be active, the patient having a correspondingly passive nature, are easy to find. Consider the human

one or something "having the upper hand" (the dominant nature or position). So, in our example taken from artificial beings, viz. the example of the letters, the agent is the human being (mind and fingers), and the things manipulated, the letters, are of a nature such as to be subject to human manipulation. So also, in the full picture of Hume's billiard balls, we must include *the player*.

The causal situation thus includes higher and lower (i.e. active and passive) natures, higher and lower grades of *form* (and higher and lower grades of *esse*, whether *esse* is seen as identical with form or merely concomitant with form). We should realize the difference between the two levels. They are two levels such that the upper level can *be* without the lower, but the lower cannot be without the higher. The being of the one is, as such, dependent, while the being of the other is, as such, independent.[49]

Indeed, for true causal *hierarchy*, i.e. a series of causes yielding one effect, the situation must be such that the higher cause can bring about the very same effect without the aid of the lower cause, whereas the lower cause cannot bring about the effect without the contribution of the higher cause. This is the sort of thing meant by St. Thomas in the example he uses sometimes: the hand or man using the stick to move the stone. The idea is of a movement one could give to the stone without bothering to use the stick.[50]

---

or any animal body. There are muscles which have an active role in turning the eyeball, e.g., the eyeball itself being designed to be passive in their regard. The wrist is active relative to the hand, etc. Thomas generally uses the most immediately sensible active feature of things, i.e. the power of hot things to affect our own bodies. We learn very early in life not to touch the stove: it is ready to *act* upon us.

49. This is, in a way, more evident in the case of an agent which gives substantial being to its effect, for example parents (the agent) relative to their children (the effect of the agent). The parents have being independently of the children, but the children depend for their being upon the causality provided by the parents. Even in this situation, one must be careful to take the cause precisely in its role of causing, and to take the effect precisely in its role of being caused. Thus, the parents are the cause of the coming into being of the child. The child is the effect precisely as being *brought into* being. Once the child is present in being, then it no longer depends for its being on the parents. It exists independently (as compared with those parents), though, of course, it is dependent on other things (e.g. the air we breathe). In the cases I have mentioned in the previous note, e.g. the wrist and the hand, we are considering agency as regards, not substantial being, but local movement. Thus, the wrist is a principle or origin of local movement of the hand. It is precisely as viewed in function of certain local movements that one sees the primacy or independence of the wrist vis-à-vis the hand, the dependence of the hand upon the wrist. (However, the wrist also needs the hand for the wrist's fulfillment.)

50. In *CP* 8.9 (1039 [3]) we read:

. . . [Aristotle] presents a comparison of first mover and second. For, though we say "brings about movement" of both the first mover and the last, we say that the first mover brings movement about moreso [*magis*] than does the last. And this is clear for two reasons. One is that the first mover moves the second mover, but not the converse. The

The form of the caused thing is an *inferior* form. Since it is a form, it is a principle of being *(esse),* but only as presupposing the contribution of a *higher* thing, the efficient cause. In the case of our letters making a word, it is the presence of order (the FORM) which makes of the letters a being, a word: thus, we can say that with the coming of the order there comes also an act of being *(esse);* being accompanies form. However, order is present in the letters only "under the influence" of the man who holds up the letters. The man (having a higher, more active form) is a being *more fully established in being* than are the words made out of wooden letters. The words have being only by receiving a share ("participating in") the wealth of being of the man.

This is why we must distinguish between the *form* of the lower thing and the *esse* of the lower thing. The *esse,* i.e. the being-actually, of the caused (or lower) thing pertains to the caused thing's participating in the perfection *proper to the nature of the higher thing,* the nature of the *efficient cause as such.* The form of the lower thing, on the other hand, pertains to the *nature proper to the lower thing.*[51] The two natures being different, so also the *esse* and the form of the caused thing must be different from each other, the *esse* being the *actuality* even of the form.

There is another point which we must bring out to complete the doctrine that form and *esse* in efficiently caused things cannot be identical. Remember that we are speaking here primarily of the analysis of the *substance* and its *substantial components.* Now, substance is the *absolute* thing. The efficient cause we wish to speak of should be cause of the substance of the inferior thing. The formal superiority and inferiority between cause and effect mean that the cause has a higher substantial nature, the effect a lower substantial nature.

Now, a thing's substantial nature is its *selfhood,*[52] so that the form of the lower thing is really what sets it off as a distinct thing vis-à-vis the higher thing, which has its own nature, its own selfhood. This makes it even clearer that we must distinguish between the *form,* whereby the effect has

---

second reason is, because the second mover cannot bring the movement about without the first, but the first mover can bring the movement about without the second; for example, the stick cannot move the stone unless it is moved by the man, but the man can move [the stone] even without the stick.

This is, of course, the example Thomas uses in *ST* 1.2.3 (the "first way").

51. Thus, if we envisage a *hierarchy* of efficient causes, each one has a composition of *form* and *esse,* precisely inasmuch as it has above it a higher cause. In demonstrating that one *cannot go to infinity* in ascending an efficient causal hierarchy, one demonstrates that there must exist a cause which is first by nature, and so a thing in which form and *esse* are identical. And this is God. This is, of course, the argument of the "second way" in *ST* 1.2.3.

52. I say this because, among the modes of unity, sameness or identity or selfhood is the mode proper to substance as substance; cf. *CM* 4.2 (561) and 10.4 (2002–2005).

its own identity as a being, and its *esse*, whereby it partakes in what is "owned" (my "own" is what relates to my "self") by higher reality. This, I would say, is the argument used by Thomas in the following passage, taken from the *Summa contra gentiles:*

> . . . The substance of each thing is present to it just by virtue of *itself* [*est ei per se*] and not through another; hence, to be actually illuminated is not [something] of the substance of air, because it is present to it through another. But for any created [read: caused] thing, its being [*suum esse*] belongs to it through another. Therefore, in the case of no created substance is its being [identical with] its own substance.[53]

Form or essence ("substance"), as such, is not limitation or finitude. Rather, it is identity (also called "whatness"). It happens to form or essence that it be finite, inasmuch as it is *such* essence, viz. distinct from infinite essence. "Essence" does not name something intrinsically involving imperfection.[54] It rather names an ineluctable metaphysical dimension, something pertaining to every being as such. Identical with *esse* in God, it can only be present in anything else as potency to *esse*.[55]

CONCLUSION

Lastly, among the many discussions provided by St. Thomas concerning the distinction between *esse* and the other items in the metaphysical analysis of caused beings, there is one which has seemed to me most helpful for the development of the line of thinking I have presented. It is to be found in *Quodlibet XII* (Easter, 1272), the fruit of Thomas's

53. *SCG* 2.52 (1278).
54. *SCG* 4.11 (ed. Pera, 3472–3473) is a passage from St. Thomas which shows something of the variety of intelligible roles of the various items in the metaphysical analysis:

> . . . it has been shown in the first book (ch. 31) that those things which in creatures are divided are unqualifiedly one in God: thus, for example, in the creature essence and being [*esse*] are other; and in some [creatures] that which subsists in its own essence is also other than its essence or nature: for this man is neither his own humanity nor his being [*esse*]; but God is his essence and his being.
>
> And though these in God are one in the truest way, nevertheless in God there is whatever pertains to the intelligible role [*ratio*] of the subsisting thing, or of the essence, or of the being [*esse*]; for it belongs to him not to be in another, inasmuch as he is subsisting; to be a what [*esse quid*], inasmuch as he is essence; and being in act [*esse in actu*], by reason of being itself [*ipsius esse*].

55. *ST* 1.3.4 (19a7–12) gives us the argument as to why, *if* the distinction is real, the essence must be potential:

> . . . being is the actuality of every form or nature; for goodness or humanity is not signified [as] in act save inasmuch as we signify that it *is*. Therefore, it is necessary that being itself be compared to the essence which is *other* that it as act to potency.

last academic activity in Paris, before returning to Naples.[56] Thomas had been asked whether the *esse* of the angel is an accident. His reply is a strong rejection of such an idea (though he does save the wider use of the word "accident" regarding *esse,* in connection with the saying of Hilary of Poitiers that *esse* is not an accident in God).

In making his point, the technique he uses involves first presenting *causal hierarchy as such.* If a thing is at first in potency and then in act, it comes to be in act only by participating in a higher nature, a higher actuality:

. . . one must know that each thing which is in potency and in act is rendered in act through precisely this, that it participates in a superior act . . .[57]

In this setting, Thomas goes on to present *esse* as what renders a thing maximally in act. In order to do so, he begins by saying, in keeping with the first point, quoted above, that a thing is rendered maximally in act through participation in the highest act, the act which involves no potency whatsoever. We read:

. . . but something is maximally rendered in act through this, that it participates, through likeness, in the first and pure act . . .[58]

And he identifies this "first and pure act" as *esse* subsisting by itself, i.e. (we may say) that to which one attains at the summit of causal consideration (as one sees in *ST* 1.2 and 1.3). And so we read:

. . . but the first act is *esse* subsisting by itself . . .[59]

And he draws the conclusion, this time in terms of "completion":

. . . hence, each thing receives completion precisely through this, that it participates in *esse.*[60]

The effect of this argument is that we now know how to consider *esse* in caused things. We read:

56. *Quaestiones de quolibet* 12.4.1 [6] [= "*Q12*"], in Leonine ed.., t. 25/2, Rome/Paris, 1996: Commissio Leonina/Cerf, pp. 403–404. For the date, see the Introduction by R.-A. Gauthier, O.P., in t. 25/1, p. 160*; Easter in 1272 was April 24, and Thomas had to be in Florence for the Chapter of his province in June. The *Twelfth Quodlibet* is a set of notes from St. Thomas himself, not themselves intended for publication, but for the eventual preparation of a publication never actually produced.

57. *Q12* (lines 16–18). The point here might be filled out by *ST* 2–2.2.3, on the activities of things as involving a movement under the influence of a higher nature.

58. *Q12* (lines 18–20).

59. *Q12* (lines 20–21).

60. *Q12* (lines 21–23).

. . . Hence, *esse* is what is completive of every form, because it is completed through this, that it has *esse*, and it has *esse* when it is in act [*est actu*]; and thus no form is, save through *esse*.

And thus I say that the substantial being of the thing [*esse substanciale rei*] is not an accident, but rather the *actuality* of any existent form whatsoever [*actualitas cuiuslibet forme existentis*], whether [it is a form] without matter or with matter. And because it is the completion of all [*completio omnium*], thus it is that the proper effect of God is *esse*, and no cause gives *esse* save inasmuch as it participates in the divine operation. And thus, properly speaking, it is not an accident.[61]

The forms here are the acts proper to the lower things. The *esse* always moves us toward the higher thing. What interests me here is the way the entire discussion is introduced through the idea of lower modes of act having to participate in higher modes of act. In the context, the existence of God and his character as subsistent act of being are presupposed. Obviously, this is the fruit of the doctrine that one cannot go to infinity in efficient causes. There must be a supreme actuality which is pure actuality subsisting. Thus, *esse* in caused things can be nothing but a participation in what is proper to the highest as highest.

My point amounts to a focus on the role of a hierarchy of causal natures for a sound understanding of the *reality* of the distinction between form and *esse* in caused things.[62]

---

61. *Q12* (lines 23–33). Of interest is Thomas's use of the word *"actualitas,"* suggesting that *"esse,"* even in lower things, names act at its purest, what is first in the order of *"actus."*

62. Later note: *ST* 2–2.23.3.*ad* 3 is a good text to confirm the view I have presented of form and *esse;* it presents light in the transparent as of a higher nature than the transparent itself. Thomas often compares the relation of form or essence to *esse* to the relation of air or the transparent to light: cf. above, ca. n. 53 and *SCG* 2.54 (para. 5):

> . . . ad ipsam etiam formam comparatur ipsum esse ut actus. Per hoc enim in compositis ex materia et forma dicitur forma esse principium essendi, quia est complementum substantiae, cuius actus est ipsum esse: sicut diaphanum est aeri principium lucendi quia facit eum proprium subiectum luminis.

> [. . . the very act of being has the status of act relative to the form itself; for it is through this that in composites of matter and form the form is said to be the principle of being, viz. because it is that which completes the substance, whose act is the very act of being: just as the transparent is for air the principle of illumination, because it constitutes it as the proper subject of light.]

Chapter 12

NATURE AS A METAPHYSICAL OBJECT

GENERAL CONSIDERATIONS

A paper on nature as a metaphysical object[1] is, as we shall see, a paper on essence.[2] Is there anything more to say about essence? Essence had a difficult time in the twentieth century, when the insistence was decidedly on existence. It might be wise to begin with a reminder of essence's right to "equal time." Since there are actually metaphysicians "out there" who think of essence as a mere limit on actual existence, or as a metaphysical item only needed to make possible the existence of creatures, beings other than the supreme being,[3] perhaps the best recommendation of es-

---

1. By "a metaphysical object" I mean what is a proper target of attention of the science of metaphysics; thus, in *ST* 1.11.3.*ad* 2, Thomas, speaking of the "one" which is interchangeable with "a being," calls it *"quoddam metaphysicum,"* in contrast to the "one" which is the principle of number; this latter, he says, is *"de genere mathematicorum."* In *CM* 5.5 (808), he carefully explains how *"natura,"* as said of all substance, pertains to first philosophy, just as does "substance," taken in all its universality.

At the outset of his *Commentary on the Nicomachean Ethics* Thomas lists among the orders with which reason has to do, the order of *natural* things. He says:

> There is a certain order which reason does not make, but only considers: such as is the order of natural things [*ordo rerum naturalium*]. [*In Eth.* 1.1 (1).]

And he goes on to list the diverse sciences which relate to the various orders mentioned. As regards the order of natural things, he says:

> . . . to natural philosophy it pertains to consider the order of things which human reason considers but does not make: we are taking "natural philosophy" as including within it also metaphysics [*ita quod sub naturali philosophia comprehendamus et metaphysicam*]. [*In Eth.* 1.1 (2).]

2. *ST* 1.60.1 (ed. Ottawa, 362b5–7):

> . . . nature is prior to intellect, for the nature of each thing is its essence.

3. In his book *Introduction à la philosophie chrétienne,* Paris, 1960: Vrin, looking for the basis for the possibility of having beings other than God himself, Étienne Gilson tells us:

> The difficulties to be surmounted are particularly serious in a theology like this one, where the first Cause *transcends the order of essence.* Indeed, it is a matter of understanding how essences can emanate from the being in which no distinctive essence is added to the *esse* to form a composition with it? This way of posing the question should,

sence we can provide is its status in the case of God. Suffice it to say, then, that while in God the subsisting thing, the essence, and the act of being are one simple identical item, nevertheless that simple item verifies what is *proper* to each: inasmuch as God is not in another, he is a subsisting thing; inasmuch as he has whatness, he is an essence; and inasmuch as he is, actually, he is the act of being.[4] Indeed, what we call "essence" in creatures exists by priority in God, and exists there in a higher way: essence is most truly essence in God.[5]

The word "nature" has many meanings. Aristotle presented a whole series of meanings of *"phusis"* in *Metaphysics* 5.[6] Boethius also had occasion to leave us a set of meanings of *"natura,"* the most relevant Latin

---

besides, suffice to allow us to see in what direction the answer must be sought. *If one located God in the order of essence, even at its summit,* it would become extremely difficult, not to say impossible, to find outside of God a place for the world of creatures . . . But we begin here with the notion of a God *entirely transcending the order of essences,* which includes the totality of creatures, whence one can infer that no problem of addition or subtraction will arise as between him and the being he creates. [170–171; my italics; the question-mark is Gilson's]

And toward the end of the meditation, he tells us:

The *property of essence* [*Le propre de l'Essence*], finite mode of participating in being, is to render possible the existence of a *natura rerum* which is neither nothing nor God [198, my italics].

Thus, it is clear that the word "essence," for Gilson, means properly a finite participation in being.

Of course, one can say that God transcends the entire order of being, as including both essence and existence; but that is obviously not what Gilson had in mind; cf. Thomas, *Expositio libri Peryermenias* 1.14 (Leonine ed., t. 1*1, Rome/Paris, 1989: Commissio Leonina/Vrin, lines 438–442):

. . . the divine will is to be understood as standing outside the order of beings [*ut extra ordinem entium existens*], as a cause pouring forth being in its entirety [*totum ens*] and all its differences. Now, the possible and the necessary are differences of being . . .

In another late text, *ST* 3.75.4 (2943a18–19), we have:

. . . his [i.e. God's] action extends to the entire *nature* of being [*ad totam naturam entis*] . . .

This is in the context of the discussion of the change involved in the sacrament of the Eucharist. In the *ad* 3, there, God is called the author of *ens,* and the nature is also termed *"entitas,"* "entity."

4. Cf. *SCG* 4.11 (ed. Pera, 3472–3473), quoted above in chapter 11, n. 55.
5. Cf. *De ente et essentia* c. 1 (Leonine ed., lines 53–63. My italics.):

. . . But because *"ens"* is said absolutely and primarily of substances, and posteriorly and in a somewhat qualified sense of accidents, thus it is that *essentia* also properly and truly is in substances, but in accidents it is in a certain measure and in a qualified sense. But of substances, some are simple and some are composite, and in both there is *essentia;* but in the simple *in a truer and more noble degree* [*ueriori et nobiliori modo*], inasmuch as they also have more noble *esse;* for they are the *cause* of those which are composite, at least [this is true of] the first simple substance which is God.

6. Aristotle, *Metaphysics* 5.4 (1014b16–1015a19).

term.[7] Thomas Aquinas recounted several times the findings of these authors, sometimes offering personal reflections on them.[8]

Aristotle begins with the generation or birth of living things as a meaning; in Thomas's Latin, *"natura"* in that meaning is equated with *"nativitas."*[9] Aristotle subsequently moves to the principles, within things, of such an event, and to the principle of a thing's other changes or movements.[10] The word is extended in use even to the *essence* of changeable things. Lastly, by what Aristotle describes as a *"metaphor,"* the word is applied to *all ousia.*[11] It is with this last "metaphorical" use of the word that I will be concerned. Lest the word "metaphor" lead one to think of this use as negligible, let us recall Thomas's treatment of the word "light" [*lux*]. Is it said properly or metaphorically[12] as applied to spiritual things? Well, if you consider the word as regards its first imposition, it is indeed metaphorically applied to spiritual things; however, if you consider its subsequent history in the mouths of speakers [*"secundum usum loquentium"*], it is said properly as applied to spiritual things.[13] I would say that the same is true of the use of "nature" as applied to the essence of all beings.

Aristotle is, of course, reporting on actual Greek usage. One has an impressive use of *"phusis"* placed by Plato on the lips of the youthful Socrates in the dialogue *Parmenides*. Socrates speaks of the Forms of things as "patterns fixed in nature" [*paradeigmata hestanai en té phusei*], where "nature" clearly means the realm of the unchangeable, i.e. true being.[14] In fact, the relation of this area of vocabulary to the expression of being is striking. Thus, the English word "be" is cognate with the Greek *"phusis,"* and

7. Boethius, *Contra Eutychen et Nestorium*, c. 1. Cf. *The Theological Tractates*, with an English translation by H. F. Stewart and E. K. Rand, London and New York, 1918 [reprint 1926]: Heinemann and Putnam [Loeb Classics].

8. E.g. *ST* 1.29.1.*ad* 4; also 3.2.1.

9. Thomas, *CM* 5.5. (808).

10. Here we have the meaning which will be given primacy in both the *Metaphysics* and the *Physics*. In *Physics* 2.1 (192b21–23), nature is a cause or principle of being moved and of being at rest, being *within* firstly and by virtue of itself and not by accompaniment. This is primarily the substantial form, secondarily the matter (193b3–8). In the *Metaphysics*, it is ultimately the form [*ousia*, which Thomas, *CM* 5.5 (826), interprets as *form* here] of things having a principle of movement within themselves as themselves (1015a13–15). The importance of the notion of substance for this conception cannot be too strongly underlined; selfhood or a primary "within" depends on the notion of substance, since among the modes of unity, identity or selfhood is the mode proper to substance as substance; cf. *CM* 4.2 (561) and 10.4 (2002–2005).

11. Aristotle, *Metaph.* 5.4 (1015a11–13); cf. Thomas, *CM* 5.5 (823).

12. For Thomas's explanation of the difference between things said metaphorically and things said properly, cf. *ST* 1.13.3.*ad* 1 and *ad* 3.

13. *ST* 1.67.1.

14. Plato, *Parmenides* 132d (tr. J. Owens).

stems from the Sanskrit *"bhu,"* meaning "to become," i.e. to arrive at the terminus of generation.[15]

Again, Plato, in the *Cratylus,* writes:

[*Socrates*] . . . [things] must be supposed to have their own proper and permanent essence [*ousian*]; they are not in relation to us, or influenced by us, fluctuating according to our fancy, but they are independent, and maintain to their own essence the relation prescribed by nature [*hêper pephuken*].[16]

And:

[*Socrates*] Are not actions a class of being [*ti eidos tôn ontôn*]? . . . Then the actions also are done according to their proper nature [*kata tén autôn phusin*], and not according to our opinion of them?[17]

Clearly, in this metaphysical discussion, what a thing is "as to nature" is contrasted with the mere "being" in human opinion.

My aim, then, in this paper, is to consider to some extent Thomas's use of this notion of nature as an object found universally, but analogically. What texts come to mind? Their great variety is already suggested by the variety of topics proposed by speakers for this week's proceedings.[18] Certainly, the texts include those on natural intellectual knowledge; on natural love in intellectual creatures; on nature and will in God; on the distinction between natural being and intentional being; on such a question as "is death natural?" etc. The point is to see what special task this notion of "nature" performs as applied universally. Why is it needed? Obviously, I can only hope to stimulate interest in so wide a topic.

But what is a "metaphysical outlook"? We might begin to answer that by recalling Aristotle's characterization of the science which seeks the first causes as the science of being as being. As Thomas reads him, Aristotle tells us that a cause must be the cause of some *nature,* and that the highest cause must be *the cause of the nature of being.*[19] Thus, to engage in metaphysics, one must grasp the beings themselves which we experi-

---

15. Cf. *Concise Oxford Dictionary,* London, 1964 [5th edition]: Oxford University Press, concerning "be."

16. Plato, *Cratylus* 386d–e [tr. Benjamin Jowett].

17. *Cratylus* 387a.

18. This paper was written for and read at the Summer Thomistic Institute, Maritain Center, University of Notre Dame (Indiana), July 13–20, 2001.

19. As Thomas, *CM* 4.1 (533), on Aristotle at 1003a26–32, paraphrases:

. . . Every principle is the essential principle and cause of some *nature.* But we seek the *first* principles and the *highest* causes . . . therefore, *they* are the essential cause of some *nature.* But of no other nature than that of *being* . . . [Italics mine]

In *ST* 1.45.5.*ad* 1 (288b35–38), Thomas qualifies his use of the term *"natura"* for the field of reality as falling under the cause of being as such:

ence as exhibiting the sort of unity we mean by "a nature."[20] It will not
be a specific nature or a generic nature. It will, nevertheless, have a unity
which can well be described as "natural."[21]

In order so to view reality, we do not start with the "biggest picture."
We start with the relevant sort of unity, but exhibited more locally. Thus,
in *CM* 4, Thomas explains the Aristotelian conception of the unity of the
field of metaphysics by means of a presentation of being in four modes or
measures. In presenting four "modes of being," Thomas begins with the
weakest, the least, and moves toward the strongest. The four are (1) negations and privations, (2) generations and corruptions and movements,
(3) inhering accidents, and (4) substances. Here is his presentation:

> . . . sicut hic homo participat humanam naturam, ita quodcumque ens creatum partici-
> pat, *ut ita dixerim, naturam essendi;* quia solus Deus est suum esse . . .

> [. . . as this [individual] man participates human nature, so also each created being
> whatsoever participates, *if I may so speak,* the nature of being, because God alone is his
> own being . . .]

20. I will cite an early text along these lines, *Commentary on the Sentences* 2.1.1.1 (ed.
Mandonnet, pp. 12–13), part of the prehistory of the Fourth Way (*ST* 1.2.3); Thomas is
aiming to show that there must be one and only one unqualifiedly first principle:

> . . . This is apparent . . . from the very nature of things [*ex ipsa rerum natura*]. For there
> is found in all things the nature of entity [*natura entitatis*], in some [as] more noble
> [*magis nobilis*], and in some less [*minus*]; in such fashion, nevertheless, that the natures
> of the very things themselves are not that very being itself [*hoc ipsum esse*] which they
> have: otherwise being [*esse*] would be [part] of the notion of every quiddity whatso-
> ever, which is false, since the quiddity of anything whatsoever can be understood even
> when one is not understanding concerning it *that it is.* Therefore, it is necessary that
> they have being [*esse*] from another, and it is necessary to come to something whose
> nature is its very being [*cujus natura est ipsum suum esse*]; otherwise one would proceed
> to infinity; and this is that which gives being [*esse*] to all; nor can it be anything else but
> one, since *the nature of entity* [*natura entitatis*] *is of one intelligibility* [*unius rationis*] *in all,*
> *according to analogy* [*secundum analogiam*]: for unity in the caused requires unity in the
> proper [*per se*] cause. This is the route taken by Avicenna in his *Metaphysics* 8.

Here, then, the unity of the first principle is concluded to from the unity of the hierarchy
of acts of being, a unity described as the "nature of entity."

21. We might recall *ST* 1–2.10.1.*ad* 3, concerning whether the human will is moved toward anything naturally. The objector argues that nature is determined to something one,
but that the will relates to opposites; thus, it has no natural movement. Thomas replies:

> It is to be said that to a nature something one always corresponds, [but] something
> proportionate to the nature. For to the generic nature [*naturae . . . in genere*] there cor-
> responds something generically one [*unum in genere*]; and to the specific nature there
> corresponds something specifically one; while to the individuated nature there corre-
> sponds one individual something. Therefore, since the will is a certain immaterial pow-
> er, just as is the intellect, there corresponds to it naturally some one common thing,
> viz. the good; just as to the intellect there corresponds some one common thing, viz.
> the true, or that-which-is [*ens*], or the what-it-is [*quod quid est*]. Still, under the good,
> taken universally [*sub bono . . . communi*], many particular goods are contained, to none
> of which is the will determined.

The point of the reply is that there is a *unity* proper to the altogether universal intelligibles.

One should know that the aforementioned [by Aristotle] modes of being [*modi essendi*] can be reduced to four. For one of them, which is the weakest, "is" only *in the mind*, namely *negation* and *privation;* we say they "are" in the mind, because the mind treats them as though they were some sort of beings, when it affirms or negates something in their regard. (The difference between negation and privation will be explained later.)

Another mode is close to the first as regards weakness, according to which *generation* and *corruption* and *movement* are called "beings." The reason [they are weak] is that they have, mixed in, something of negation and privation. Thus, it is said in [Aristotle's] *Physics,* book 3, that movement is *imperfect* actuality.

Now, in third place those items are called ["beings"] that have no admixture of not-being, and yet still have weak being, because they "are," not *by themselves,* but *in another,* the way *qualities, quantities,* and *properties* of substances "are."

But it is the fourth kind which is most perfect, namely that which has being *in nature* [*esse in natura*] [i.e. not merely in the mind], and without an admixture of privation, and has *solid* and *firm* being, as *existing by virtue of itself,* the way substances "are."

And to this, as to what is first and principal, all the others are referred back. Thus, qualities and quantities are said to "be," inasmuch as they have "being-*in*" substances; movements and generations [are said to "be"] inasmuch as they *tend* toward substance, or to one of the others [i.e. quality or quantity]; and privations and negations [are said to "be"], inasmuch as they *remove* something pertaining to the other three modes.[22]

It is this kind of "sizing up" of what we immediately experience which constitutes the metaphysical outlook.[23]

Thomas obviously considers that reality is constituted with a unity along the lines suggested by this fourfold presentation. Thus, in other texts we see that *substances themselves* are presented to us in modes or levels or intensities of being. Thus, in *ST* 1.12.4, on whether any created intellect can by its own *natural* powers see the divine essence, Thomas establishes the premise that:

. . . the knowing [performed] by any knower is in keeping with the mode of its [the knower's] *nature.*

And he continues:

Therefore, if the mode of being of any known thing exceeds *the mode of the nature* of the knower, necessarily the knowledge of that thing is beyond the *nature* of that knower.

22. *CM* 4.1 (ed. Cathala, 540–543). We note the use here of "being in *nature,*" as contrasted with being in the mind.
23. This is an approach mainly in terms of being as divided by the categories, though the inclusion of change shows that being as divided by act and potency is also in play; change is "imperfect actuality" [*actus imperfectus*]. Thomas teaches that the approach in

And we are then presented with the hierarchy:

> Now, there are many modes of being.
> Some things are, whose *nature* does not have being save in this individual mat-
> ter; and of this mode are all corporeal things.
> But some things are, whose *natures* are subsistent by themselves, not in some
> matter; which nevertheless are not their own being, but are [things] having be-
> ing: and of this mode are incorporeal substances, which we call "angels." Of God
> alone the proper mode of being is that he be his own being subsisting.[24]

Clearly, this is a vision which has to be built up, and we see many signs
of the process of building in various places. However, one thing is especially clear: that in the presentation of the hierarchy as a hierarchy of
being as being, the importance of cognition, and particularly *intellectual
cognition*, as constituting a principle of division, is most evident. The reason for this is the ineluctable role of ontology in the explanation of cognition. Aristotle's dictum that the soul, through sense and intellect, is in
a way all things suggests that there is a difference from the viewpoint of
being itself, as between the thing which has intellect and the thing which
does not. Thus, Thomas, in explaining why the rational creature is a subject of divine providence in a special way, says:

> It is evident that all parts are ordered toward the perfection of the whole: for
> the whole is not for the sake of the parts, but the parts are for the sake of the
> whole. But intellectual natures [*naturae intellectuales*] have a greater affinity with
> the whole than [do] other natures [*aliae naturae*]: for each intellectual substance
> is in a way all things, inasmuch as through its intellect it is inclusive of being in
> its entirety [*totius entis comprehensiva est*]; whereas any other substance has a mere-
> ly particular participation in being [*particularem solam entis participationem habet*].
> Thus, fittingly, the others are provided for by God for the sake of the intellectual
> substances.[25]

Both levels of substance have being, but one has it in a more complete
and so meaningful way. Accordingly, it occurs to me that a consideration

---

terms of act and potency is wider than that in terms of the categories; the latter is about
perfect being, while the form includes even the imperfect: *CM* 5.9 (889).

24. *ST* 1.12.4 (64b13–23). In this article, we seem to have the use of the word "nature"
very much in the sense of "essence as ordered toward operation." One might even say that
the act of being of the thing is being viewed as a quasi-*movement* caused by the essence. Cf.
ST 1–2.10.1.*ad* 1, where the act of being [*esse*] is called *"motus proprius naturae"* (unless
"motus" there should read *"modus"?*). Cf. also *ST* 1.42.1.*ad* 1, where the form or nature is
seen as having two effects, the act of being and the operation. Thus, the notion of magnitude of perfection is applied even to the divine nature. For a remarkable presentation
of ontological hierarchy of substances, cf. *SCG* 3.20 (especially paras. 1–4), on how things
imitate the divine goodness.

25. *SCG* 3.112 (2860).

of the presentation of this mode of nature will serve to stimulate interest in nature as a metaphysical object.

Among the various presentations by Thomas of the meanings of the word *"natura,"* the foregoing texts put me in mind of one which contains an especially illuminating specification. In the *De ente et essentia,* commenting on the use of "nature" to mean the *essence* of a thing, Thomas says:

> [Essence] by another name is also called "nature," taking "nature" according to the first way of those four which Boethius presents in the book *On the Two Natures:* according as every item which can be grasped by intellect in any way is called a "nature": for a thing is intelligible only through its definition and essence; and thus also the Philosopher says in *Metaphysics* 5 that every substance[26] is a nature. Nevertheless, the word "nature" taken in this way seems to signify the essence of the thing according as it has *an order toward the proper operation of the thing,* since no thing is bereft of a proper operation.[27]

It is this conception of essence as ordered to the thing's proper operation[28] which will be the key to my approach here today.

---

26. Here, "substance" is translating Aristotle's *"ousia,"* and clearly means essence; cf., on the variety of meanings of the Latin *"substantia,"* Thomas, *De potentia* 9.1.

27. *De ente et essentia* c. 1, lines 36–49:

> Hoc etiam alio nomine natura dicitur, accipiendo naturam secundum primum modum illorum quatuor quod Boetius in libro De duabus naturis assignat: secundum scilicet quod natura dicitur omne illud quod intellectu quoquo modo capi potest, non enim res est intelligibilis nisi per diffinitionem et essentiam suam; et sic etiam Philosophus dicit in V Methaphisice quod omnis substantia est natura. Tamen nomen *nature* hoc modo sumpte uidetur significare *essentiam rei secundum quod habet ordinem ad propriam operationem rei, cum nulla res propria operatione destituatur.*

Thus, here Thomas relates this general usage of "nature" to the first meaning proposed by Boethius:

> Natura est earum rerum quae, cum sint, quoquomodo intellectu capi possunt. [*De persona et duabus naturis* c. 1 (PL 64, 1431 B)]

(This is not the meaning from Boethius used in other presentations of "nature" as bearing upon essence, and notably not the meaning used in presenting Boethius in *CM* 5.)

The statement that no thing is without its proper operation is presented in *DV* 19.1.*sed contra* 1 as coming from St. John Damascene's *De fide orthodoxa* 2.23. Cf. Saint John Damascene, *De fide orthodoxa,* Versions of Burgundio and Cerbanus, ed. Eligius M. Buytaert, O.F.M., St. Bonaventure, N.Y., 1955: Franciscan Institute, cap. 37, pp. 142–143:

> . . . Operatio enim est naturalis uniuscuiusque substantiae virtus et motus. Et rursus, operatio est naturalis omnis substantiae innatus motus . . . Impossibile enim substantiam expertem esse naturali operatione. [lines 1–10, in part]

28. Cf. *ST* 1.42.3.*ad* 4:

> . . . "natura" quodammodo importat rationem principii, non autem "essentia" . . .
> ["Nature" in some measure conveys the notion of a principle, whereas "essence" does not.]

Thomas in this statement from the *ST* does not seem to agree with what he wrote about the term "essentia" in the *De ente:* that it is called "essentia" inasmuch as "through it and in it a being has being" [*Sed essentia dicitur secundum quod per eam et in ea ens habet esse.*] That suggests very much a principle.

We should reflect on the idea of a proper operation, and, indeed, on the conception of operation. Obviously, it pertains to the move from a consideration of "nature" as naming the proper principles of physical things, as presented in Aristotle's *Physics* 2.1, to what is meant by "nature" as said of every essence. The Aristotelian definition in *Physics* 2 speaks of a principle of *movement* or *change*. As Boethius says in this connection: "every body has its proper *movement*."[29] Thomas, I might add, relates the doctrine that "nothing is without its proper *operation*" to St. John Damascene.[30] Now, consider the following argument from an objector to the view that life pertains to God:

Some things are said to "live," inasmuch as they move themselves . . . But to be moved does not befit God. Therefore, neither does "to live."

Thomas answers:

. . . as is said in *Metaphysics* 9, action is twofold: one which goes forth into external matter, as to heat and to cut; the other, which remains within the agent, as to understand, to sense, and to will. The difference between the two is as follows: that the first [sort of] action is not the perfection of the agent which brings the movement about, but rather [is the perfection] of the very thing moved; whereas the second [sort of] action is the perfection of the agent. Hence, because movement is the act of the moveable thing, the second [sort of] act, inasmuch as it is the act of the one performing the operation, is called its "movement," on the basis of this likeness, that just as movement is the act of the moveable, so this sort of action is the act of the agent: though, admittedly, movement is the act of the imperfect, i.e. of that which exists in potency, whereas this sort of action is the act of the perfect, i.e. of that which exists in act, as is said in *De anima* 3. Therefore, in this mode in which understanding is a movement, that which understands itself

---

29. The work of Boethius to which Thomas regularly refers as *"Liber de duabus naturis"* is usually presented under the title *Contra Eutychen et Nestorium*. It can be found in Boethius, *The Theological Tractates,* with an English translation by H. F. Stewart and E. K. Rand, London and New York, 1918 [reprint 1926]: Heinemann and Putnam [Loeb Classics]. Boethius in his chapter 1 presents the meanings of the term *"natura."* He begins with the widest meaning and only comes in the end to the meaning given in Aristotle's *Physics* 2. We read:

> Quod si naturae nomen relictis incorporeis substantiis ad corporales usque contrahitur, ut corporeae tantum substantiae naturam habere uideantur, sicut Aristoteles ceterique et eiusmodi et multimodae philosophiae sectatores putant, definiemus eam, ut hi etiam qui naturam non nisi in corporibus esse posuerunt. Est autem eius definitio hoc modo: "natura est motus principium per se non per accidens." Quod "motus principium" dixi hoc est, quoniam *corpus omne habet proprium motum,* ut ignis sursum, terra deorsum. Item quod "per se principium motus" naturam esse proposui et non "per accidens," tale est, quoniam lectum quoque ligneum deorsum ferri necesse est, sed non [?] deorsum per accidens fertur. Idcirco enim quia lignum est, quod est terra, pondere et grauitate deducitur. Non enim quia lectus est, deorsum cadit, sed quia terra est, id est quia terrae contingit, ut lectus esset; unde fit ut lignum naturaliter esse dicamus, lectum uero artificialiter.

30. Cf. above, n. 27.

is said to move itself. And in this way also, Plato held that God moves himself, not in the way that movement is the act of the imperfect.[31]

This sort of extension of the vocabulary of "movement" to operation in general helps to explain the movement of thought from "nature" in the *Physics* 2 sense to "nature" in the sense of essence as ordered toward its proper operation. Thomas, commenting on the text of Aristotle's *De anima* 3 referred to above, stresses the difference between sensation and physical motion [*a motu physico*, line 32]; sensation, along with intellection and volition, is *properly* called an "operation."[32]

The term "act," also, is used for both movement and operation, as is clear from the above. Movement is the act of a thing in potency, whereas operation is the act of a thing in act.[33] Indeed, Thomas will, in a metaphysical context, use the vocabulary of "operation" and "action" for the movement or change proper to the physical thing. Thus, we read:

... the bodies of those things whose being is in [the domain of] change imitate incorruptible bodies in this respect, that they always act; thus, for example, fire, which just in virtue of itself always heats, and earth, which just in virtue of itself always performs its proper and natural operations. And this indeed is the case because they have movement and their own proper operation just in virtue of themselves, and within them, inasmuch as their forms are the principles of such movements and actions.[34]

We must also recall the doctrine of the *importance* for a thing of its proper operation. We remember the text:

... it is evident that operation is the *ultimate* act of the one performing the operation: hence, it is called "second act" by the Philosopher in *De anima* 2 [412a23]: for the thing having form can be merely potentially operating, as for example, the scientist is potentially considering. And thus it is that in other things "each thing is said to be for the sake of its operation," as is said in *De caelo* 2 [286a8].[35]

31. *ST* 1.18.3.obj. 1 and *ad* 1.

32. *In De anima* 3.6 [Leonine ed., lines 8–36], commenting on *De anima* 3.7 (431a6).

33. For the three modes of act, viz. form, operation, and imperfect act (which includes the movement of the mobile thing), cf. Aristotle, *Metaph.* 9.6 (1048b6–17) as commented upon by Thomas at *CM* 9.5 (1828–1831). For the origin of the vocabulary of "act" for the discussion of being, as coming from the vocabulary of movement, cf. Aristotle, *Metaph.* 9.3 (1047a30–b2) as commented upon in *CM* 9.3 (1805–1806).

34. *CM* 9.9 (1880), paraphrasing Aristotle, *Metaph.* 9.8 (1050b28–30). The Latin of the cited passage runs:

... corpora eorum, quorum esse est in transmutatione, imitantur corpora incorruptibilia in eo, quod semper agunt; sicut ignis, qui secundum se semper calefacit, et terra quae secundum se semper facit operationes proprias et naturales. Et hoc ideo est, quia habent motum et operationem suam propriam secundum se, et in eis, inquantum scilicet formae eorum sunt principia talium motuum et actionum.

35. *ST* 1–2.3.2 (ed. Ottawa, 727b28–36):

An especially good general picture of the nature and its order toward both being and operation is provided in the *ST* discussion of the Trinity; speaking of the *equality of magnitude* which obtains among the three Persons in God, Thomas says:

> The *magnitude* of God is nothing else but *the perfection of his very nature*.[36]

In the question's first article, an objector is introduced to argue that there can be no equality in God because there is no quantity. And to this, Thomas provides the following reply:

> . . . quantity is twofold. One is called "quantity of mass" or "dimensional quantity," which is found in corporeal things only, and so has no place in the Divine Persons. But the other is "quantity of power" [*quantitas virtutis*], which is caught sight of in connection with the *perfection* of some *nature or form*. It is this [latter] quantity which is signified when something is said to be "more" or "less" warm, inasmuch as it is more *perfect* or less *perfect* as regards such a quality.[37] Such quantity of power [*quantitas virtualis*] is seen first of all at its root, that is, in the very perfection of the *form or nature*, and thus one speaks of "spiritual greatness" [*magnitudo spiritualis*], as one speaks of heat as "great" because of its intensity and perfection. And thus Augustine says in *De trin.* 6, that "in those things which are 'great,' not by reason of their mass, that is 'greater' which is *'better'*"; for the more *perfect* is what one calls "better."
>
> Secondly, however, quantity of power [*quantitas virtualis*] is seen in the *effects* of form. And the first effect of form is *being*, for every thing has being in accordance with its form. The second effect is *operation*, for every agent acts by virtue [*per*] of

---

> Manifestum est autem quod operatio est ultimus actus operantis; unde et actus secundus a Philosopho nominatur, in II *De anima;* nam habens formam potest esse in potentia operans, sicut sciens est in potentia considerans. Et inde est quod in aliis rebus "res unaquaeque dicitur esse propter suam operationem," ut dicitur in II *De caelo.*

In his *In Aristotelis De caelo et mundo expositio* 2.4 (334 [5]), Thomas says:

> . . . [Aristotle here says] that each thing which has a proper operation is for the sake of its operation [*propter suam operationem*]: for anything whatsoever has appetite for its own perfection, as for its goal [*suum finem*]; and the operation is the ultimate perfection of the thing (or at least the product of the operation, in those things in which there is some product besides the operation, as is said in *Ethics* 1 [1094a3–7]); for it is said in *De anima* 2 [412a23] that form is first act, while operation is second act, as the perfection and the end of the one operating. And this is true both in corporeal things and in spiritual things, for example in the habits of the soul; and both in natural things and in artificial things.
>
> But [Aristotle] says "which has a work" because of those things which are against nature, as are monstrosities; they do not have any work, taken precisely as such, but rather they have a deficiency as regards the operative power, as is evident in the case of those which are born lame or blind: for lameness is not an end intended by nature, for the sake of which it brings about the birth of the lame animal; but rather this happens aside from the intention of nature, from the deficiency of the natural principles.

36. *ST* 1.42.4 (268a24–25).
37. Here, the text says: *"in tali caliditate,"* i.e. "in such warmth," but I am conjecturing *"in tali qualitate,"* i.e. "in such a quality."

its form. Thus, quantity of power is seen as regards being and as regards operation; as regards being, inasmuch as those things which are of a more perfect nature have a greater duration; and as regards operation, inasmuch as those things which are of a more perfect nature, are more powerful as regards action . . .[38]

While we see these considerations applied, in the above quotation, to any *particular* nature, thus making being [*esse*] the *effect* of the nature, ultimately Thomas regularly takes the case of what is most *formal* of all, namely *being* itself.[39] Thus, he will speak of God, presented as being itself, subsisting by itself, as possessed of the entire *perfection* of being. We see this in a text such as the following:

. . . God is being itself, subsisting by itself [*ipsum esse per se subsistens*]: hence it is necessary that the total perfection of being [*totam perfectionem essendi*] be contained in him. For it is evident that if something warm does not have the total perfection of the warm, this is because warmth is not participated in according to its perfect character [*perfectam rationem*]; but if warmth were subsisting by itself, there could not be lacking to it anything of the power of warmth. Hence, since God is being subsisting, nothing of the perfection of being can be lacking to him. But the perfections of all things pertain to the perfection of being: for it is according to this that some [particular] things are called "perfect," viz. that they have being in some measure [*aliquo modo esse habent*]. Hence, it follows that the perfection of no thing is lacking to God.[40]

This text, showing what I would call the "Fourth Way" viewpoint, is absolutely typical of Thomas's metaphysical overview, for the whole of his career. It is a vision wherein being itself is considered as a nature.[41]

MORE PARTICULARLY: THE NATURE
OF THE HUMAN SOUL

The presentation of the human soul in *ST* 1.75–89 affords us the opportunity to watch Thomas contemplate a nature precisely as a nature. In the prologue to q. 75, in the midst of the treatise on the divine work of

38. *ST* 1.42.1.*ad* 1.
39. *ST* 1.7.1 (37a43–44), and 1.4.1.*ad* 3.
40. *ST* 1.4.2.
41. Cf. above, notes 19 and 20; also *ST* 1.14.6 (97b43–51):

. . . the proper *nature* of each thing has solidity [*consistit*] inasmuch as it participates in the divine perfection in some measure. But God would not perfectly know himself if he did not know in whatever measure his perfection is participable by others; nor would he know *the very nature of being* [*ipsam naturam essendi*] if he did not know all the modes of being.

[By "the Fourth Way" viewpoint, I refer, of course, to the fourth of the Five Ways of proving the existence of a God, as given in ST 1.2.3. This Way seems to me to present the essential structure of metaphysics.]

distinction,[42] we arrive at the consideration of the human being, a composite of spiritual and corporeal substance. However, after dividing the presentation into consideration of (1) the nature of man and (2) the production of man, it is immediately noted that it belongs to the theologian to consider the nature of man as regards man's *soul*. The body enters into the discussion only as regards its relation to the soul. Thus, qq. 75–89 are on *the essence of the human soul*. Thomas finds in pseudo-Dionysius's *On the Celestial Hierarchy* the approach he requires for this study, a three-step approach suitable to the study of spiritual substances, in terms of essence, power, and operation.[43] Philosophically, this is clearly an exercise in metaphysics.[44]

Thomas has considerable confidence in the quality of his knowledge of the human soul. In discussing the limitations of our knowledge of God and angels, he raises the question whether our intellect through knowledge of material things can come to understand the immaterial substances. An objector argues in favor of such understanding:

The human soul is in the genus of immaterial substances. But it can be understood by us through its act, by which it understands material things. Therefore, also other immaterial substances can be understood by us through their effects on material things.

Thomas, however, replies:

... the human soul understands itself through its own act of understanding, which is its proper act, *perfectly demonstrating its power and its nature*. But neither through this, nor through other things which are found in material things, can *the power and nature* of the immaterial substances be perfectly known; because such [effects] do not adequately measure up to their powers.[45]

---

42. Cf. *ST* 1.44.prologue (qq. 47–102 are on the divine work of distinguishing created things, one from another); 1.48.prologue (qq. 50–102 are on the distinguishing of the spiritual and the corporeal creature).

43. *ST* 1.75.prologue; and cf. 1.77.1.*sed contra*.

44. Notice the discussion of the limits of physics relative to metaphysics, as found in *CP* 2.4 (ed. Maggiòlo, 175 [10]), concerning Aristotle at 2.2 (194b13–15). We read:

Hence, the consideration of the physicist which is concerning forms extends right up to the rational soul. But how it is with forms totally separate from matter, and what they are, or even how it is with this form, i.e. the rational soul, according as it is separable and able to exist without the body, and what it is as separable in virtue of its essence: to determine all this pertains to primary philosophy.

Cf. *ST* 1.76.1.*ad* 1. Also cf. Aristotle, *Parts of Animals*, 1.1 (641a33–b10): only the science that considers all being can adequately treat of intellect and so of the human being as a whole.

45. *ST* 1.88.2.obj. 3 and *ad* 3. The Latin of the reply reads:

... anima humana intelligit seipsam per suum intelligere, quod est actus proprius eius, perfecte demonstrans virtutem eius et naturam. Sed neque per hoc neque per alia quae in rebus materialibus inveniuntur, perfecte cognosci potest immaterialium substantiarum virtus et natura; quia huiusmodi non adaequant earum virtutes.

While qq. 75–89 are rich in materials relevant to our topic, q. 77, located between the discussion of the essence of the soul in itself and the discussion of the operation of understanding, is an ideal focal point for seeing the essence ordered toward operation, i.e. the *nature*. The first issue is the very distinction between essence and power. As Thomas himself points out, not everyone sees the need to make this distinction.[46] The single article here depends on a three-step presentation already given in treating of the angels, viz. 1.54.1–3. Thomas there begins by distinguishing between the substance of the angel (and of any creature) and its act of understanding (or any operation); he next shows the necessity to distinguish between the angel's act of being and its act of understanding (indeed, between any creaturely act of being and any operation); and lastly he argues that the essence of the angel (or of any creature) cannot be identified with its operative power.

Of these three articles, the most important and enlightening is the second, distinguishing between the act of being and the act of understanding. Thomas recalls the distinction between actions which remain in the agent, such as to sense, to understand, and to will, and actions which project forth and influence something else, such as to heat and to cut. The problem is not here with these latter, since they are not easily confused with the substance or the act of being of the agent. However, "I understand" and "I am" might be confused, and so the basis of distinction is the *object* of the operation: such operations as understanding and willing have an *infinite* object, viz. all things, whereas the creaturely act of being is finite.[47]

As I said, 1.77.1 is based on 1.54.1–3, and concludes that in no creature can there be identity between essence and operative power. The passage at 1.77.2 presents the rationale for the *multiplicity* of powers of the human soul. The point is that the multiplicity of powers pertains to the place of man and human soul in the hierarchy of reality. Man belongs in the upper echelon of reality inasmuch as he can attain to "the universal and perfect good," i.e. to beatitude. However, among things so endowed, he is at the lowest level, and so needs many kinds of operation to do so.

The passage at 1.77.3 explains how one distinguishes one operative power from another, i.e. on the basis of the objects of the operation. One notes here how important it is that the distinctions are rather evident in the realm of the external senses, thus providing a model for the discussion of the more immaterial powers.

With 1.77.4 we come to what more directly concerns us at present. Is

46. *ST* 1.77.1 (463b6).
47. *ST* 1.54.2; one should pay special attention to the remarkable reply *ad* 2.

there an *order* among the powers of the human soul? Without this vision of order, we would have little conception of the unity of the source, i.e. of the soul as a nature. That this is so is brought out in 1.77.6, where the first objection against the powers flowing from the essence of the soul is the simplicity of the soul versus the multiplicity of powers:

From one simple item diverse items do not proceed. But the essence of the soul is one and simple. Since, therefore, the powers of the soul are many and diverse, they cannot proceed from its essence.

And Thomas replies:

It is to be said that from one simple item many can *naturally* proceed in some *order*. And, again, because of the multiplicity of recipients. Thus, therefore, from the one essence of the soul many and diverse powers proceed, for one reason, because of the *order* of the powers, for another, because of the diversity of corporeal organs.[48]

This means that, in order to have a decent conception of the order of the essence toward the powers and operations, i.e. of the essence as a nature, one must consider the order of the powers, already presented in a. 4.

We might note in a. 4, first of all, the sort of thing we have in the *sed contra*, recalling that Aristotle had compared the powers of the soul to the sequence of geometrical figures. The idea that one must proceed from one to many by virtue of an order is linked to the *coherence* of the procession, its *per se* character. Obviously one can associate a merely chaotic variety of accidental entities with a substance, but they are not *per se* associates if they do not have something to do with the very *unity* of the substance.[49] Thus, Thomas begins precisely on this point:

48. *ST* 1.77.6.*ad* 1.
49. Cf. 1.76.4.*ad* 3:

. . . in matter there are considered diverse grades of perfection, viz. being, living, sensing, understanding. But always the following supervening one is more perfect than the previous one. Therefore, the form which gives merely the first grade of perfection to matter is most imperfect; but the form which gives the first and the second and the third, and so on, is most perfect; and nevertheless, it is immediately [united] to the matter.

And cf. also *ST* 1.76.5.*ad* 3:

It is to be said that the parts of the animal, as the eye, the hand, the flesh, and the bone, and such, are not in a species; but rather [it is] the whole [which is in a species]; and so it cannot be said, properly speaking, that they are of diverse species, but rather that they are of diverse dispositions. And this suits *the intellective soul, which though it is one as to its essence, nevertheless because of its own perfection is many as to power;* and therefore for the sake of the diverse operations it requires diverse dispositions in the parts of the body to which it is united. And for this reason we see that the diversity of parts is greater in the perfect animals than in the imperfect, and in these latter than in plants.

It is to be said that since the soul is one, while the powers are many, and it is by some order that there is procession from something one to a multiplicity, it is necessary that there be order among the powers of the soul.

He then specifies:

Now, a threefold order is seen among them. Two of them are considered as to the dependence of one power on another; the third is taken from the order of [their] objects.

But the dependence of one power on another can be taken in two ways: in one way, according to the order of *nature*,[50] inasmuch as the more perfect are prior to the less perfect; in the other way, according to the order of generation and time, inasmuch as from the imperfect one comes to the perfect.

Therefore, according to the first order of powers, the intellective powers are prior to the sensitive powers: hence, they direct them and dominate them. And, similarly, in this order the sensitive powers are prior to the powers of the nutritive soul.

But according to the second order, the converse is the case. For the nutritive powers of the soul are prior, on the pathway of generation, to the sensitive powers: hence, they prepare the body for the actions of the latter [powers]. And it is similar for the sensitive powers relative to the intellective powers.

But as regards the third order, some sensitive powers are ordered among themselves, viz. sight, hearing, and smell. For the visible is naturally prior, because it is common to superior and inferior bodies. And audible sound is brought about in air, which is naturally prior to the mixture of the elements, which odor follows upon.

Notice here the following objection and reply. The second objector says:

. . . The powers of the soul relate to their objects and to the soul itself. But based on the soul there is no order among them, because the soul is one. Similarly also, based on the objects, which are diverse and altogether disparate, as is clear in the case of color and sound. Therefore, there is no order among the powers of the soul.

Thomas replies:

It is to be said that this order of the powers of the soul has its base in the soul, which according to a certain order stands related to the diverse acts, even though it is one as to its essence; and also, as based on the objects; and also as based on the acts, as was said.[51]

The third reply here notes that in the case of the first two sorts of order, the *operation* of one power depends on the *operation* of another.

---

50. On the natural order in being, cf. *CM* 5.13 (950–953), concerning Aristotle, *Metaph.* 5.11 (1019a2–14).
51. *ST* 1.77.4.*ad* 2.

Obviously, here in 1.77.4 we are close to the vision of human unity itself, inasmuch as we see this order in the multiplicity.

The passage at 1.77.5 asks whether all the powers are in the soul as in a subject. Here we have the distinction between the intellect and will, on the one hand, viz. the powers which have no corporeal organ, and all the other powers which do have an organ. The latter have as their subject the composite of soul and body, the former the soul alone. However, it is noted already, all the powers have the soul as their principle.[52]

It is aa. 6 and 7 of q. 77 which most concern us here. Do the powers *flow* from the essence of the soul? Does one power *flow* from another? If we are to see the essence of the soul as a nature, i.e. as ordered toward its proper operation, this doctrine is central.

In a. 6, the *sed contra* sends us to Aristotle's *Metaphysics* 7, that the subject is introduced into the very definition of the proper accident.[53] The idea is that the powers of the soul are its natural properties, and thus are caused by the soul.

The body of the article could not be more metaphysical. It consists mainly in a distinction between the role of the substantial form and that of the accidental form (where the accidental form is a proper accident of the substance). It begins:

It is to be said that the substantial form and the accidental form partly agree and partly differ. They agree in this, that each is act, and in function of each something is in some measure in act.

But they differ in two respects. Firstly, because the substantial form brings about being, unqualifiedly, and its subject is a being in potency only. The accidental form, on the other hand, does not bring about being, unqualifiedly; but rather, being such, or so much, or in some relation; for its subject is a being in act. Hence, it is clear that actuality [*actualitas*] is found by priority in the substantial form rather than in its subject; and because what is first is cause in every order, the substantial form causes being in act in its subject. But, conversely, actuality is found by priority in the subject of the accidental form rather than in the accidental form; hence, the actuality of the accidental form is caused by the actuality of the subject. And this takes place in such a way that the subject, inasmuch as it is in potency, is receptive of the accidental form; while inasmuch as it is in act, it is productive of it.—And I say this regarding the proper and essential [*per se*] accident; for relative to the extraneous accident, the subject is merely receptive; an extrinsic agent is productive of such an accident.

---

52. This doctrine will affect the reply in the last article of q. 77, viz. a. 8, as to whether the powers remain in the soul when it is separated from the body. Only the intellect and will remain actually, though the others remain as in their source [*virtute*]. Notice *ST* 1.77.8.*ad* 2: the powers having the composite as subject are not natural properties of the soul alone, but are properties of the composite.

53. The footnote in the Ottawa ed. sends us to *Metaph.* 7.4 (1029b30), but I would add 7.5 (1030a17–1031a14); cf. *CM* 7.4.

But, secondly, the substantial and accidental forms differ, because since the less principal is for the sake of the more principal, matter is for the sake of the substantial form; but, conversely, the accidental form is for the sake of the completion of the subject.

All this is said subsequent to a. 5, in which we saw that some powers, viz. the intellect and the will, have the soul itself as their subject. Thus, Thomas now briefly makes his point:

But it is evident from things already said [1.77.5] that the subject of the powers of the soul is either the soul alone, which can be the subject of an accident inasmuch as it has something of potentiality, as was said above [1.77.1.*ad* 6; 1.75.5.*ad* 4]; or else the composite. But the composite is in act through the soul. Hence, it is manifest that all the powers of the soul, whether their subject is the soul alone or the composite, flow from the essence of the soul as from a principle; because it was just said that the accident is caused by the subject according as it is in act, and is received in it inasmuch as it is in potency.

This concludes the body of the article. The basic idea is that the substantial form as such is source of actuality for the accidental forms.

The doctrine of the powers flowing from the essence of the soul is thus based on the priority as to actuality of the subject of the accidental form over the accidental form itself; which in turn is based on the priority of substance and hence substantial form over accident. It is the fundamental doctrine of being which is in play.[54]

Let us move quickly on to a. 7, on the flow of one power from another. The body of the article begins:

It is to be said that in those things which proceed in a *natural* order from something one, just as the first is the cause of all, so also that which is closer to the first is in some measure [*quodammodo*] the cause of those which are more remote.

---

54. On the ontology of substance and accident, cf. *SCG* 4.14 (para. "*Quamvis autem in Deo . . .*"):

> . . . in us relations have dependent being [*esse*], because their being is other than the being of the substance: hence, they have a mode of being proper [to them] in function of their own proper character [*rationem*], just as is the case with the other accidents. Indeed, because all accidents are certain forms added to the substance, and caused by the principles of the substance, it is necessary that their being be added on, over the being of the substance, and depending on it [the being of the substance]; and the being of each of them is prior or posterior inasmuch as the accidental form, as regards its proper character, is closer to substance or more perfect. For which reason, a relation really added to the substance has the last and most imperfect being: last, because not only does it presuppose the being of the substance, but also the being of other accidents from which the relation is caused: as, for example, one in quantity causes equality, and one in quality likeness; but most imperfect, because the proper character of relation consists in the fact that it is toward another: hence, its proper being, which it adds to the substance, depends not only on the being of the substance, but also on the being of something external.

But it has been shown above [1.77.4] that among the powers of the soul there is manifold order. And so one power of the soul proceeds from the essence of the soul through the mediation of another. [470a19–27]

Having made this general point, Thomas now looks at the situation more closely. We read:

But because the essence of the soul compares to the powers both [1] as active and final principle and also [2] as receptive principle, either separately by itself or together with the body; and the agent and the end is more perfect, whereas the receptive principle, as such, is less perfect; the consequence is that the powers of the soul which are prior according to the order of perfection and of nature are the principles of the others in the mode of end and active principle: for we see that sense is for the sake of intellect, not the converse; moreover, sense is a lesser [*deficiens*] participation in intellect; hence, according to natural origin it is in some measure [*quodammodo*] from intellect, as the imperfect from the perfect.

But in function of the pathway [*viam*] of the receptive principle, conversely, the imperfect powers have the role of principles with respect to the others; just as the *soul*, inasmuch as it has the sensitive power, is considered as a subject and a sort of material with respect to the intellect; and for that reason, the more imperfect powers are prior on the pathway of generation: for animal is generated prior to man.[55]

The comparison with the soul, as having a conception in terms of the sequence of types of soul, is to be noted here. The nobility of the soul is seen in its being the single principle of the variety of powers.[56]

This is the entire body of the article. My point is, as always, that the order of causal flow of the powers pertains to the doctrine of the unity of source, and so to the vision of the essence of the soul as a nature, a nature with a certain proper perfection.

Before concluding, I wish to add a few points which complete the picture. Thomas takes on the complex task of presenting the essence of the soul as source of all the powers of *man*. I will focus for the moment on the soul as source and subject of the two spiritual powers, the intellect and the will. In terms of what we have seen, it is clear that one of these powers flows from the other, and in fact, the will flows from the intellect, the less perfect from the more perfect. This is the significance of the articles in which Thomas makes the comparison of the one power to the other, e.g. *ST* 1.82.3. We might note one objection and reply in that context, one which harmonizes very much with what we have seen. The objector, arguing for the greater nobility of the will, says:

55. *ST* 1.77.7.
56. Cf. *ST* 1.76.3 (454b28–56).

Natural things are found to proceed from the imperfect to the perfect. And this also is apparent among the powers of the soul: the process is from sense to intellect, which is more noble. But the natural process is from the act of the intellect to the act of the will. Therefore, the will is a more perfect and more noble power than the intellect.

To which Thomas replies:

It is to be said that that which is prior as to generation and time is more imperfect: because in one and the same thing potency temporally precedes act and imperfection perfection. But that which is prior, unqualifiedly, and as regards the order of *nature*, is more perfect: for thus act is prior to potency. And it is in this way that intellect is prior to will, as the motive principle [*motivum*] to the mobile item, and as the active to the passive: for the understood good moves the will.[57]

We note that the sequence here is not temporal, but rather one of the imperfect following upon the perfect. The act of the will which follows upon that of the intellect can very well be *simultaneous* with that of the intellect.[58]

We should note how Thomas conceives of the "flow" of powers from the essence of the soul, and of one power from another. In 1.77.6.*ad* 3, the objector argues:

. . . "Emanation" names a sort of movement. But nothing is moved by itself, as is proved in *Physics*, book 7 [241b24], save perhaps by reason of a part: as an animal is said to be moved by itself, because one of its parts is the mover and another is the moved. Nor, also, is the soul moved, as is proved in *De anima* 1 [408a34]. Therefore, it is not the case that the soul causes in itself its own powers.

That is, this whole idea of the *flow* of the powers, which have their *seat in* the essence, from the essence *itself*, doesn't make sense: one identical thing would be both mover and moved. And Thomas replies:

It is to be said that the emanation of the proper accidents from the subject is not by virtue of any change [*transmutationem*]; but rather by a natural following forth [*naturalem resultationem*]: the way in which from one item another naturally [*naturaliter*] results: as, for example, color from light.[59]

Here, the idea is that light and color are given together in one same instant, but that color is able to affect the transparent medium (e.g. the air around the colored body) only with the aid of light (color being a

57. *ST* 1.82.3.*ad* 2.
58. Cf., e.g., *DV* 29.8 [Leonine ed., lines 212ff.].
59. *ST* 1.77.6.*ad* 3; this is explicitly applied to the flow of one power from another in 1.77.7*ad* 1.

participation of light by the body limiting the transparent medium).[60]

One would have eventually to discuss the outmoded character of this example. I had at first thought that our best examples of what Thomas means are such sequences as arm and hand, or eye and socket muscles. We find in things a natural order of forms, without which a thing which is one would be incomplete. However, that is more a case of final causality than of productive causality. We might better resort to something more intellectual. When one already knows the major premise and one comes to see the minor in its role as minor, at the same moment one sees the conclusion. The conclusion is an effect of the premise, a natural sequel.[61]

We see something of the importance of the doctrine of emanation of powers from soul and power from power when, speaking later of how the intellect knows the act of the will and the will itself, Thomas first of all faces an objector who argues that the intellect, being an entirely different power than the will, the act of the will is not in the intellect and so is not known by the intellect. Thomas replies:

> . . . the argument would work if the will and the intellect, just as they are diverse powers, so also they differed as to subject: for thus what is in the will would be absent from the intellect. Now, however, since both are rooted in the one substance of the soul, and one of them is in some measure [*quodammodo*] the principle of the other, the consequence is that what is in the will is also in some measure in the intellect.[62]

So also, explaining what Augustine meant by saying that the affections of the soul are known through certain *"notiones,"* Thomas says:

> . . . the affections of the soul are not in the intellect merely through likeness, as bodies are; nor through presence as in a subject, as [in the case of] the arts; but

60. Cf. *In De anima* 2.14 (Leonine ed., lines 342–387, especially lines 373–380 as follows):
> . . . it is to be said that the power of color in acting is imperfect, as compared to the power of light: for color is nothing else but a light in some measure obscured by being mixed with the opaque body; hence it does not have the power to render the medium in that disposition by which it is rendered receptive of color; which pure light can do.

61. Cf. *De substantiis separatis,* c. 9 [Leonine ed., lines 180–234] (Lescoe tr., p. 63): what is brought into being by change must have being *after* not being, whereas in the mode of production which is by simple emanation or influence the effect or result can be understood as always having being. Thomas sees the sort of thing he has in mind best exemplified for us humans, not in corporeal causes and effects, but rather in "intellectual things which are at a greater remove from motion." Thus, he points out that the truth of the principles is the cause of the truth which is in the conclusions, which conclusions are always true; he introduces Aristotle on necessary things which have a cause of their necessity: *Metaph.* 5.6 (1015b9) and *Phys.* 8.3 (252a32–b6).

62. *ST* 1.87.4.*ad* 1. On the natural sequence: substance, intellect, will, cf. my paper, "The Real Distinction between Intellect and Will," *Angelicum* 57 (1980), pp. 557–593.

rather as the result [or: sequel] in the principle [*sicut principiatum in principio*] in which one has the notion [*notio*] of the result . . .[63]

Lastly, we should note a problem: if the power cannot be identical with the essence of the soul because, it would seem, of the very nobility of the object of the power (at least in the case of intellect and will), how can the essence itself still be seen as the source of the power? Can the greater come from the lesser? A manifestation of this problem is seen in the particular case of the agent intellect. Thomas teaches that the agent intellect is a power of the human soul. The argument for this point in the *ST* is not simple. Thomas first teaches that there must be, above the human intellect, a higher intellect on which it depends, and from which it obtains the power [*virtus*] to understand. That this is a power within the soul itself, participated from the higher mind, Thomas concludes both on general principles and in view of our own actual experience.

However, one of the objections runs:

If the agent intellect is something belonging to the soul, it must be some *power*. . . . But every power flows from the essence of the soul. Therefore, it would follow that the agent intellect would proceed from the essence of the soul. And thus it would not be in the soul by participation from some higher intellect; which is unacceptable. Therefore, . . .

Thomas answers:

. . . since the essence of the soul is immaterial, created by the supreme intellect, nothing stands in the way of the power which is participated from the supreme intellect, [the power] by which it abstracts from matter, proceeding from its essence, just as the other powers.[64]

We see that, for an adequate conception of the essence of the soul as a nature, i.e. as ordered to operation, and in particular to the intellectual operation, it must be seen as itself flowing from the divine creative cause.

This falls in with the picture we were given in 1.77.6: the property relates to the essence both as in potency relative to the essence and as act relative to the essence. As act relative to the essence's potency, it indicates the need for something above the essence of the soul. This is in accord with the need for completion which the soul (and every creature) has. It is to this situation Thomas refers when explaining later how supernatural grace can be a quality of the soul. A most important ontological remark is found in the reply to an objection. Substance, it is objected, is nobler

63. *ST* 1.87.4.*ad* 3.
64. *ST* 1.79.4.*ad* 5.

than quality, and grace is nobler than the nature of the soul. Thus, it cannot be its quality. Thomas replies:

It is to be said that every substance either is the very *nature* of the thing of which it is the substance, or else is a part of the nature (in which way the matter or the substantial form is called "substance"). And because grace is above human nature, it cannot be that it is the substance or the substantial form: rather, it is an accidental form of the soul itself. For that which is in God substantially is brought to be accidentally in the soul participating in the divine goodness: as is clear in the case of *science*. Therefore, in accord with that, because the soul imperfectly participates in the divine goodness, the very participation in the divine goodness which is grace has being in a more imperfect mode in the soul than [the mode of being by which] the soul subsists in itself. Nevertheless, it is more noble than the nature of the soul, inasmuch as it is an expression or participation of the divine goodness, though not as to the mode of being [*non autem quantum ad modum essendi*].[65]

This is true even of a natural virtue such as theoretical science, which is a participation in beatitude.[66] The mode of being is accidental, but the sort of participation in the divine goodness is so noble that it cannot be substantial in creatures.

To complete this picture of the divine agent above the human soul, let us look now at *ST* 2–2.2.3. It asks whether believing something beyond natural reason is necessary for salvation. It uses the vision of the natural cosmic hierarchy as a basis for a conception of the relation of the human mind to God. We read:

In all ordered *natures* it is found that two things concur for the perfection of the lower *nature:* one which is according to its proper movement; the other which is according to the movement of the *superior nature.*

For example, water, according to its proper movement is moved toward the center [of the universe], but according to the movement of the moon it is moved about the center as regard flowing and flowing back; similarly, also, the spheres of the planets are moved by their proper movements from west to east, but by the movement of the first sphere from east to west.

Now, only the created rational nature has *immediate* order to God. Because the other creatures do not attain to anything universal, but only to something particular, participating in the divine goodness either as to being only, as inanimate things, or also in living and knowing singulars, as plants and animals; but the rational nature, inasmuch as it knows the universal intelligibility of being and the good [*universalem boni et entis rationem*], has an *immediate* order to the universal principle of being [*ad universale essendi principium*].

65. *ST* 1–2.110.2.*ad* 2.
66. *ST* 1–2.66.3.*ad* 1.

Therefore, the perfection of the rational creature does not consist merely in that which befits it according to its own nature, but in that also which is attributed to it from some supernatural participation of divine goodness. Hence, earlier it was said that the ultimate beatitude of man consists in some supernatural vision of God.[67]

Thomas goes on to explain the role of faith in the attainment of this beatitude. My primary point in citing this text is not the general doctrine of hierarchy of natures, where the examples are in obvious need of updating; nor am I concerned for the moment with the need for faith; rather, I underline the view of the rational *nature* as such, as *immediately* under the divine influence.[68]

There should be no hesitation in seeing here a metaphysical conception of nature. Thus, Thomas speaks of the divine nature as the "higher nature":

It is to be said that because the nature of man depends on a higher nature, natural knowledge does not suffice for his perfection, but some supernatural [knowledge] is required . . .[69]

CONCLUSION

My aim today has been to recall how all-embracing and important is the conception of nature as essence ordered toward operation. After indicating the presence of this notion in the very conception of metaphysics as a science, I have focused on a particularly prominent case, the essence of the human soul as exhibiting such an order.

67. *ST* 2–2.2.3 [1415b41–1416a25].
68. This was also seen in the fact that the human soul can only come into existence by being itself created, unlike other substantial forms (*ST* 1.90.1–3); and in the fact that it is God who, as supreme in the order of immateriality, is the source of the intellective power (*ST* 1.105.3).
69. *ST* 2–2.2.3.*ad* 1.

Chapter 13

THE INDIVIDUAL AS A MODE OF BEING ACCORDING TO THOMAS AQUINAS

Recently Timothy Noone[1] and Kevin White[2] have published papers touching in different ways on individuation in Thomas Aquinas. Both express a degree of approval of the position of Joseph Owens,[3] who holds that for St. Thomas the "global"[4] explanation of individuation is to be found in the doctrine of *esse*, the act of being. In the present paper I wish to challenge that Owensian view. To do so, I will first criticize the textual claims of Fr. Owens. Secondly, I will propose a different approach to the issue, less focused on individuation as something requiring a cause or principle, and more focused on the individual as a mode of being.

I

Fr. Owens presents us with the role of the act of being, and it is one which seems to make things individual. We read:

. . . [Being] is forging all the various elements of the thing into a unit. It is thereby making them what we understand to be an individual. [174]

He is basing himself here on a text from Thomas's youthful *Commentary on the Sentences of Peter Lombard*. We read:

1. Noone, Timothy B., "Individuation in Scotus," *American Catholic Philosophical Quarterly* 69 (1995), pp. 527–542.
2. White, Kevin, "Individuation in Aquinas's *Super Boethium De Trinitate*, Q. 4," *American Catholic Philosophical Quarterly* 69 (1995), pp. 543–556. White (p. 545) sees himself as expanding on Owens's line of thinking.
3. J. Owens, "Thomas Aquinas (b. ca. 1225; d. 1274)," in *Individuation in Scholasticism: The Later Middle Ages and the Counter-Reformation, 1150–1650,* ed. Jorge J. E. Gracia, Albany, 1994: State University of New York Press, pp. 173–194. I will refer to this paper simply by page number, e.g. "[173]," in my own text.
4. This word is from Noone. He tells us:

. . . According to Fr. Owens . . . Aquinas is really a global theorist on the issue of individuation. What he actually holds, in Owens' opinion, is that *esse* is the ultimate onto-

... the being of the thing composed out of matter and form, from which [the human mind] obtains knowledge, consists in some composing of form with matter, or of an accident with a subject [*consistit in quadam compositione formae ad materiam vel accidentis ad subjectum*].[5]

Is Thomas saying that the *esse* itself is a composite? That is what the *ad* 2 referred to by Owens does indeed say. We read:

But our intellect, whose knowledge arises from things, which have *composite being* [*esse compositum*], does not apprehend that *esse* save by composing and dividing.[6]

Owens provides his own reflection on and interpretation of what is being said. Taking first the case of a multiplicity of *per accidens* accidents (tallness and musical accomplishment) and the person in whom they inhere, certainly a rather *per accidens* unity, he stresses the "existential" character of the bond uniting them. We read:

... they are brought together by real existence in the one person. [174]

And he goes on to make the same point about the concrete substance, as regards its substantial components. We read:

... there is no reason in the essence of a person why his or her form (the soul) should be actuating the particular matter of which the body is constituted at the moment. Different matter keeps coming and going with the anabolism and catabolism of nutrition, yet the soul remains the same. There is no essential reason, either in the form or the matter, why this particular form should be in this particular matter at the given instant. The reason is existential. The two are united in the existence they are actually enjoying at the time. The existence *makes* them a unit. [174]

---

logical principle of individuation, just as it is the ultimate source of actuality in all created things. If this is so, Thomas escapes immediately from the charge of failing to develop a general account of individuals as such, whether physical or non-physical, which is one of the methodic objections Scotus marshals against [William Peter] Godinus in their debate. [p. 540]

In a review of the Gracia book containing the Owens essay, Noone says:

... Owens' interpretation of Thomas' many seemingly disparate descriptions of the principle of individuation is unparalleled in its ability to render Aquinas' account of individuation self-consistent without appealing to awkward genetic hypotheses ...

He obviously approves of this account.

5. [Owens, n. 6, p. 189] *Sent.* 1.38.1.3 [ed. Mandonnet, p. 903], and in the same place the *ad* 2 [Mandonnet, p. 904]. (Owens transl.) While the Latin word *"consistit"* does not always mean "is made out of," as English "consists" would suggest, but can mean "is found with" (cf. *ST* 1–2.2.7: that in which beatitude *"consistit"* is distinguished from beatitude itself; the former expression refers to that object in which the soul finds beatitude), here it does seem to mean something like the English "consists in."

6. *Sent.* 1.38.1.3.*ad* 2 [Mandonnet, p. 904]. (Owens transl.)

Two points should be made here. One has to do with the doctrine of *esse* found in the texts cited. The other has to do with Owens's conception of the role of *esse* as related to *ens per accidens* and *ens per se*.

While Thomas in the cited text does make the *esse* of composite things a composite, we know that he will subsequently stress the simplicity of *esse*.[7] In commenting on Boethius's *De hebdomadibus* he says that *esse* is not a composite:

... just as *esse* and *quod est* differ as to notions, so also they differ really in composites. Which indeed is evident from the foregoing. For it was said above that *esse* itself neither participates in anything such that its intelligibility [*ratio*] be constituted out of many, nor does it have anything extrinsic admixed such that there be in it an accidental composition; and therefore *esse itself is not composite;* therefore, the composite thing is not its own *esse* . . .[8]

And in the *SCG* we read:

... Nothing is more formal or more simple than *esse*. . .[9]

And what about the causal role which Owens attributes to *esse* with the word "makes"? This has much to do with his view of *esse* as a "cause of individuation." In the *Sentences,* it is true, Thomas seems to affirm that the *esse* of a caused thing is itself the *formal* cause of being of that thing. Thus,

7. Noone thinks Owens does well to avoid "awkward genetic hypotheses" (see above, n. 4), but Thomas obviously changes his views on some key issues.

8. *Expositio libri Boetii De ebdomadibus* 2 (Leonine ed., t. 50, Paris/Rome, 1992: Cerf/Commissio Leonina), lines 204–215 [ed. Calcaterra, 32]):

... sicut esse et quod est differunt secundum intentiones, ita in compositis differunt realiter. Quod quidem manifestum est ex premissis. Dictum est enim supra quod ipsum esse neque participat aliud ut eius ratio constituatur ex multis, neque habet aliquid extrinsecum admixtum ut sit in eo compositio accidentalis; et ideo *ipsum esse non est compositum;* res ergo composita non est suum esse; et ideo dicit quod in omni composito aliud est esse ens et aliud ipsum compositum quod est participando ipsum esse. [my italics]

See also lines 140–145, on *esse* as abstract and thus pure as to its "essence."

9. *SCG* 1.23 (ed. Pera, 214; Pegis, 2):

... Ipsum enim esse non potest participare aliquid quod non sit de essentia sua: quamvis id quod est possit aliquid aliud participare. *Nihil enim est formalius aut simplicius quam esse.* Et sic ipsum esse nihil participare potest. Divina autem substantia est ipsum esse. Ergo nihil habet quod non sit de sua substantia. Nullum ergo accidens ei inesse potest. [my italics]

Cf. also *DP* 1.1:

... Verbi gratia "esse" significat aliquid completum [*lege:* completivum] et *simplex* sed non subsistens; "substantia" autem aliquid subsistens significat sed alii subjectum. Ponimus ergo in Deo substantiam et esse, sed substantiam ratione subsistentiae, non ratione substandi; esse vero *ratione simplicitatis* et complementi, non ratione inhaerentiae quae [*lege:* qua] alteri inhaeret. [my italics]

to an objector who says that the *esse* of creatures must be "through itself"
and thus not be caused (and consequently is God himself), Thomas has
occasion to say, in replying:

> . . . created *esse* is not *through* something else, if the word "through" expresses the
> intrinsic formal cause; on the contrary [*immo*], through it [*ipso*], formally, the
> creature is . . .[10]

In this passage, it is clear that *esse* is being regarded as the intrinsic formal
cause. However, toward the end of the *De veritate*, we read:

> . . . God causes in us natural *esse* by creation, without the mediation of any effi-
> cient cause, but nevertheless through the mediation of a formal cause: because
> natural form is the principle of natural *esse* . . .[11]

And it is this doctrine which will prevail.[12]

A first point, then, is that Owens is starting us out with a conception of
esse, as to its nature and as to its causal role, which Thomas does not seem
to have retained.

Secondly, Owens seems to be using the *per accidens* itself as a sort of
"scope" in which to see actual existence as work. This is surprising for
many reasons.[13] The one reason I will mention here is that Thomas himself takes quite a different line in a particularly prominent text in the
SCG. We read:

> . . . even in those things whose *esse* is not subsistent, that which is present within
> the existent besides its *esse* is indeed united to the existent, but it is not one with
> its *esse*, save by attachment [*per accidens*], inasmuch as there is one subject which
> has *esse* and that which is besides *esse:* as is clear [in this case, viz.] that in Socrates,
> besides his own substantial *esse*, there is present the white, which is diverse from
> his substantial *esse;* for being Socrates and being white are not the same thing,

10. *In Sent.* 1.8.1.2.*ad* 2 (ed. P. Mandonnet, Paris, 1929: Letheilleux, p. 198). For a text
which goes very much along the lines of Owens's idea, cf. another early text, *Quodl.* 9.2.2
[3].*ad* 2:
> . . . sed *esse* est id in quo fundatur unitas suppositi: unde *esse* multiplex praeiudicat uni-
> tati essendi. [. . . but being is that on which is founded the unity of the subsisting thing:
> hence, multiple being precludes unity of being.]

11. St. Thomas, *De veritate* 27.1.*ad* 3 (Leonine ed., t. 22/3, lines 182–186).

12. Cf. e.g. *CM* 4.2 (ed. M.-R. Cathala, Turin, 1935: Marietti, 558, the criticism of Avicenna on *esse*). See above, chapters 9 and 10.

13. This is far from a late development in Owens's metaphysics. He already has it in his
Doctrine of Being in the Aristotelian Metaphysics, Toronto, 1963 (2nd ed.): Pontifical Institute
of Mediaeval Studies, p. 209. See my paper, "Being *per se,* Being *per accidens,* and St. Thomas' Metaphysics," *Science et Esprit* 30 (1978), pp. 169–184, for a criticism of this view.

The *per accidens* certainly relates in a special way to the individual, as distinct from the
universal: cf. *CM* 5.7 (845) and 5.11 (910), but that does not mean that *esse* is the "tie that
binds."

save by attachment. If, therefore, *esse* is not in some subject [the autograph has "substance"], there will not remain any way in which that which is besides *esse* can be united to it [viz. to *esse*] . . .[14]

Obviously, in such a doctrine, *esse* is no bond uniting or "forging . . . into a unit" all the items. This role rather belongs to the subject, i.e. the subsisting substance as such. And this is the doctrine which one finds in the *ST tertia pars,* written in Thomas's later years.[15]

It might be noted, furthermore, that Fr. Owens, in his presentation of the unity of the concrete substance, composed of this matter and this form, complicates matters slightly by taking the case of the human person, whose soul of course subsists in its own being. In fact, even in the case of nutrition in general, as applying to all living things, there is need for a special doctrine of individuation. How does Thomas handle the case of nutrition in general? In the *In De gen. et corr.,* Thomas, taking the case of any substance which changes its matter, and raising the question of its enduring identity, sees the need to provide a special mode of substantial form, somewhat immaterial, and thus somewhat akin to the subsisting form which is the human soul. It is the *form,* in such a case, which guarantees the substantial unity.[16] Thomas does not appeal to *esse* as Fr.

14. *SCG* 2.52 (ed. Pera, 1274, i.e. para. 2). Pera notes the reading of Thomas's autograph.

15. *ST* 3.17.2.*ad* 1. This article asks whether there is only one *esse* in Christ. The first objector makes his case on the basis of form as that upon which *esse* follows. We read:

. . . Damascene says in book 3 that those things which follow upon the nature in Christ are duplicated. But *esse* follows upon the nature; for *esse* is from form [*esse consequitur naturam; esse enim est a forma*]. Therefore, in Christ there are two *esse*'s.

And Thomas replies:

. . . *esse* follows upon the nature not as [something] *having esse* [*habentem esse*], but as that *by which* something is [qua *aliquid est*]; but it [*esse*] *follows* upon the person or hypostasis as [something] *having esse.* And so it rather retains unity in accordance with the unity of the hypostasis, than that it have duality according to the duality of nature. [my italics]

The idea is obviously that when one has to do with something which has all that it takes to be a complete thing, then *esse* is on the scene in its proper setting. Rather than simply saying that *esse* is what gives unity or individuation to the thing, Thomas sees the unity of *esse* as *resulting* ("follows") from the unity of subject or hypostasis.

16. *In Aristotelis De generatione et corruptione* 1.17 (ed. Spiazzi, Rome-Turin, 1952: Marietti, 118). This work of Thomas is incomplete, ending at *De gen.* 1.5 (322a33). Aristotle is discussing growth and diminution, and the nutrition involved with it. The general picture is of a being which maintains its identity through its form, while its matter changes. The translation of Aristotle which Thomas is using seems to speak of the form as "immaterial" though in matter. Thomas thus provides the following explanation:

. . . the power of the form, in living things, does not determine for itself any designated matter [*aliquam materiam designatam*], since one part flows forth and another arrives, as was said above. Nevertheless the power of the form cannot be without all matter, but [is] indeterminately in this or that: because, as is proved in *Metaphysics* 7, the power of

Owens does. I submit that the reason is that he has a different conception of the being of things than does Fr. Owens.

What we should insist on is that Fr. Owens uses this conception of the
role of *esse* in order to introduce his reader to the whole issue. *Esse* is presented as "forging . . . a unit," i.e. bringing unity about. While such words
can signify formal causality[17] (and even that, as I have said, is not Thomas's mature conception of the role of *esse*), Fr. Owens's conception of the
"accidentality"[18] of *esse* seems to make the causality verge on the efficient,
a sort of intrinsic efficient cause binding things together.[19]

Fr. Owens immediately introduces us to the case of God, in whom
esse is itself subsisting. He speaks of the "unifying" feature of existence as
even more striking in the case of God.[20] We read:

> It [existence regarded as a nature] necessarily individualizes itself. Subsistent ex-
> istence is its own individuation. [175]

We notice that he maintains the causal conception here. Obviously this
is not truly causality, nor does Fr. Owens mean it to be taken causally.
Nevertheless it is important to specify just which intelligibility is assigned
which role, even in the case of the divine simplicity. Thus, for example,

---

the generator is the form which is in this flesh and these bones . . . Therefore, in this
way, the power of the form of flesh or other such things, inasmuch as it does not determine for itself any designated matter, but at one moment is preserved in this, at another moment in that, is like an immaterial form [*est sicut species immaterialis*].

He also speaks of the form of the living thing as *"quodammodo immaterialis."*

17. Cf. *ST* 1.48.1.*ad* 4.

18. See above, chapter 9, where I criticize this view of his.

19. Étienne Gilson, in *Being and Some Philosophers*, Toronto, 1952 (2nd ed.; 1st ed.,
1949): Pontifical Institute of Mediaeval Studies, p. 172, explicitly makes *esse* an intrinsic
efficient cause. We read:

. . . Actual existence, then, is the *efficient cause* by which essence in its turn is the formal
cause which makes an actual existence to be "such an existence." [my italics]

This hardly corresponds to Thomas's conception. If one insists on making the *esse* of
the creature a cause, Thomas rather regards *esse* more as a *final* cause, and the effect of
all the other sorts of causality: cf. *DP* 7.2.*ad* 10.

In affirming what he does, Gilson refers (p. 172, n. 23; and cf. p. 169) to the doctrine
that causes are causes of each other, but in diverse genera of causality: *CM* 5.2 (755).
However, in that text, Thomas carefully explains that doctrine in terms of (1) the relation
between efficient and final causality, and (2) the relation between form and matter. Nowhere does he say anything about efficient and formal causality as reciprocal.

20. Thomas Aquinas, on the other hand, sees *substance* (in the sense of essence) as play-
ing the unifying role. Thus, at *ST* 1.11.4, on whether God is maximally one, an objector
holds that since each thing is one through its own essence, and what is by its own essence
such is maximally such, every being is maximally one. Thomas replies [*ST* 1.11.4.*ad* 3]:

. . . though admittedly every being is one through its own substance, nevertheless it is
not the case that the substance of each thing relates equally to causing unity; because
the substance of some is composed out of many, but the substance of others [is] not
[thus composite].

Thomas specifies that beatitude belongs to God precisely in function of his intellect, not in function of his essence or his will.[21] Here, as Fr. Owens sees it, it is of the very nature of existence that it have the task of individuation attributed to it.

The texts he cites to support his doctrine here merely say that God has the characteristics that constitute the individual. True, the first, taken from the *Sentences,* does say that the divine *esse* is determinate in itself and divided from all others; but it does not attribute that to *esse* precisely as *esse.* It is rather because God is subsistent *esse,* thus perfect, and so cannot receive any addition, which pertains to its being an individual.[22]

There is nothing, as far as I can see, to justify giving the role of "individuation" to the divine *esse* as such. I think rather of a text from the *SCG* which shows something of the variety of intelligible roles of the various items in the metaphysical analysis:

. . . it has been shown in the First Book (ch. 31) that those things which in creatures are divided are unqualifiedly one in God: thus, for example, in the creature essence and being [*esse*] are other; and in some [creatures] that which subsists in its own essence is also other than its essence or nature: for this man is neither his own humanity nor his being [*esse*]; but God is his essence and his being.

And though these in God are one in the truest way, nevertheless in God there is whatever pertains to the intelligible role [*ratio*] of the subsisting thing, or of the essence, or of the being [*esse*]; *for it belongs to him not to be in another, inasmuch as he is subsisting;* to be a what [*esse quid*], inasmuch as he is essence; and being in act [*esse in actu*], by reason of being itself [*ratione ipsius esse*].[23]

"Not to be in another," as we shall see, pertains precisely to the individual. Accordingly, I am not at all ready to say that, for Thomas, God is an individual precisely because of his *esse* as *esse.*

However, that is Fr. Owens's definite meaning, in pointing to the divine *esse* as self-individualizing. He says:

. . . This unifying and individuating feature follows upon existence wherever it is shared. [175][24]

And again we read:

21. *ST* 1.26.2.

22. *Sent.* 1.8.4.1.*ad* 1 [Mandonnet, p. 219]. The second text he refers to says that God, through his *essence,* is something undivided in himself and distinct from all those things which are not God (*DP* 8.3). This is "essence" used in a sense which does not necessarily distinguish between "essence" and "substance"; Thomas is merely contrasting the essence with the Trinity of Persons, about which he is speaking in the context.

23. *SCG* 4.11 (ed. Pera, 3472–3473). My italics.

24. Notice that Owens has practically identified the issues of individuation and unity. This in itself is highly questionable, since "one" is said in as many ways as "being" is. Owens himself wants to see the *esse* of a thing as the cause of its unity. He points to a problem text (*DV* 21.5.*ad* 8: whether the created good is good through essence) which seems to allow

. . . This individuating function of existence may be expressed tersely: "For everything in accordance with the way it has existence has unity and individuation."
[175]

All that the phrase Owens cites from Thomas[25] need (or does) mean is that *esse*, unity, and individuation all have the same causes or principles. But Owens continues:

. . . Whether as subsistent in God or as accidental in creatures, existence is, in the order of being, the basic "cause of individuation." [175]

This sentence from Owens includes the item in quotation marks, "cause of individuation." This is because in the footnote to the previous citation (note 11, p. 190), he said concerning the statement that existence, unity, and individuation go together:

. . . The context is the *"causa individuationis animarum."* The point is that bodies are only in a way *(aliqualiter)* the cause of individuation of souls.[26]

The implication he is leaving with the reader is that Thomas is referring to *esse* as the "cause of individuation."

Actually, in the text Owens is using, viz. the response to Johannes de Vercellis,[27] the real argument is that "cause of individuation" and "cause of being" go together. Is matter cause of being? To the extent that it is, it has some claim to be cause of individuation. Since the former claim is quite limited, so is the latter. There is no suggestion that the *esse* is the

---

essence, just in itself, a unity, and in this respect contrasts calling a thing "one" and calling it "a good" or "a being," the latter two names being said of created essence only by participation. In the context, Thomas rules out an argument which rejects participation in being and goodness, an argument claiming that this gets one into an infinite regress, an argument originally used by Averroes to reject unity by participation. Owens explains the unity involved as something along the lines of the negative unity attributed to primary matter. This is odd, to say the least. In fact, Thomas later in his career changes his approach in this matter, himself using the argument of Averroes even to apply to the case of being; i.e. Thomas eventually (*CM* 4.2 [555]) treats of both "one" and "a being" as signifying the essence as such, though he continues to reject the argument as regards the case of "a good" (*ST* 1.6.3.obj. 3 and *ad* 3). Notice that, in obj. 2 and *ad* 2, he allows that "anything whatsoever is a being [*ens*] through its essence." The thing is good through its *esse*, not merely through the essence). Moreover, in the *ST* 1.11.1.*ad* 1, he uses the argument of Averroes for "one," and that in a way which can hardly be reduced to the sort of unity of matter Owens tried to exploit. In fact, it is a "one" which is explicitly identified with "a being."

25. *Responsio ad magistrum Ioannem de Vercellis de 108 articulis* [in the Leonine *Opera omnia*, t. 42] article 108 [lines 1185–1187]:
. . . unumquodque enim secundum quod habet esse, habet unitatem et individuationem.

26. Owens here throws in another text, from *CT* 1.71, but it shows neither more nor less than the other text.

27. The passage is as follows:
. . . The 118th item proposed: "Souls are individuated by the matters of bodies, though [when] separated from them they retain individuation, like wax [retaining] the im-

cause of individuation of the soul. That would require, as per the argument, that it be a cause of *esse* of the soul. God, not *esse*, is the cause of the *esse* of the soul (and the soul itself, by virtue of its own nature, is formal cause of its having *esse*).[28]

Owens continues by claiming that Thomas says that existence is what "makes one thing differ from another." And he quotes in proof the example:

> . . . As existents, however, they differ, for a horse's existence is not a man's, and this man's existence is not that man's. [175]

This is from *ST* 1.3.5. Once more, all it shows is that existence and individuation stand and fall together. It does not show that existence is a cause of individuation. The text occurs in an article showing that God is not in a genus. It says that things in a genus have their generic essence in common, but differ *"secundum esse,"* i.e. taken in function of their existence. This is shown by stating the fact that the being of man and the being of horse are not the same. And it is added that the being of this man and that man are not the same. What this shows is that when a thing has *esse*, it must have in it something other than the quiddity itself (and particularly the quiddity of the genus). That is, there must be a *subject* which has *esse* and the essential nature. The idea is certainly not that *esse* as such is intrinsically individual and the cause of individuation. But that is what Fr. Owens's position involves.[29]

Hence, as regards this first section of Fr. Owens's paper, so crucial for his entire outlook, I do not agree that *esse* is a "synthesis," or that "it *makes*

pression of the seal," can be understood in a good way or a bad way. For if it is understood that souls are individuated by bodies, in such a way that the bodies are the total cause of the individuation of souls, it is false. But if it is understood that bodies are in some way the cause of the individuation of souls, it is true; for each thing according as it has being, has unity and individuation. Therefore, just as the body is not the total cause of the soul, but the soul as to its own nature [*rationem*] has some order to the body, since it belongs to the nature of the soul that it be unitable to a body: so also, the body is not the total cause of the individuation of *this* soul, but it is of the nature of *this* soul that it be unitable to *this* body, and this remains in the soul even after the body has been destroyed. [lines 1177–1194]

28. On the subsisting form as formal cause of its being, see chapter 9 above.

29. I am reminded of *ST* 1.12.4, where it is said of material things that their natures do not have *esse* save in "this individual matter." There can hardly be any doubt that in this part of the *ST esse* is presented as what is most common of all, and as having the nature of the received and formal: cf. 1.4.3: all things are like God in function of *esse*, which is analogically common to all; and 1.4.1.*ad* 3:

> . . . when I say "the *esse* of a man, or of a horse, or of anything else," *esse* itself is considered as formal and received; not as that item to which *esse* belongs.

It is true that the text used by Owens (viz. 1.3.5, main argument 3) is one of the more Avicennian texts in the *ST* 1, and requires very careful handling. Notice that it is the third of three arguments given.

each a unit in itself and renders it distinct from all others" (my italics). He has not shown (nor is it true) that existence is the basic "cause of individuality" in Thomas's philosophical thinking. [175] However, it is certainly true that individuation and *esse* stand and fall together. They have the same causes.

Owens concludes the first part of his paper, the part that concerns us, with a reference to a text wherein Thomas cites the *Liber de causis* on God's individuation. This we will reserve for the second part of our paper.[30]

II

I propose to present Thomas's doctrine of "the individual," calling attention to a few rather all-encompassing ("global") texts. But first I wish to introduce the idea that "the individual" names a mode of being. We will even say that there are modes of being an individual, i.e. that "individual" is said of many things which are so called only by analogy.[31]

First, there are texts which present the contrast between the universal and the individual (or singular) as pertaining to beings as beings. Thus, in the *SCG* we are told:

... The nature of a genus cannot be perfectly known unless its primary differences and essential accidents [*differentiae primae et per se passiones*] are known: for one cannot perfectly know *the nature of number if the even and the odd* remain unknown. *But the universal and the singular are differences or essential accidents of being* [*entis*]. If, therefore, God knowing his own essence knows perfectly the common nature of being [*naturam communem entis*], it is necessary that he perfectly know the universal and the singular. [my italics][32]

30. Continuing to prove his point, Owens says:
> ... In the language of the *Liber de causis,* God's individuation is his own pure goodness. [175]

Here we are referred to two texts, *Sent.* 2.3.1.2 [Mandonnet, pp. 90–91] and *De ente* 5.23–24. However, I would urge the reader to see how Thomas handles God's being an individual in his *In De causis.* For this, see below.

31. *Sent.,* I, d. 22, q. 1, a. 3, *ad* 2 (Mandonnet, pp. 538–539):
> ... an analogue is divided in virtue of diverse modes. Hence, since "a being" is predicated analogically of the ten genera, it is divided among them in virtue of diverse modes. Hence, to each genus there is owing a proper mode of predicating.

Thomas is here contrasting the analogical, divided by diverse modes, with the univocal, divided by differences, and the equivocal, divided by signified things.

32. *SCG* 1.65 (ed. Pera, 532; Pegis, para. 4). Avicenna, *Liber de philosophia prima sive scientia divina,* (ed. S. Van Riet, Louvain/Leiden, 1997: Peeters/Brill, I–IV), 1.2 (p. 13, lines 42–44), speaking of the subject of the science, *"ens inquantum est ens,"* and the items which follow upon it (line 37), says:
> ... Et ex his quaedam sunt ei quasi accidentalia propria, sicut unum et multa, potentia et effectus, *universale et particulare,* possibile et necesse. [my italics]

Thus, in discussing the individual, we may expect to be in a deeply ontological discussion.[33]

If we pursue this view of the individual as related to the nature of *ens* or "that which is," we find the *ST* discussion of Boethius's definition of the person, viz. an individual substance of a rational nature, most helpful. Thomas's main reply, explaining with thoroughgoing approval this definition, takes the form of a lesson on the individual [*individuum*]. We begin:

> . . . though admittedly the universal and the particular [*particulare*] are to be found in all the genera, nevertheless the individual is to be found in a special mode [*speciali quodam modo*] in the genus of substance. For substance is individuated through itself [*per seipsam*], whereas accidents are individuated through the subject, which is substance; for one speaks of "this" whiteness inasmuch as it is in "this subject." And so also, suitably, the individuals of substance have a special name, apart from the others: for they are called "hypostases" or "primary substances."[34]

This is certainly a controlling text. Notice that "universal" and "particular" (interchangeable with "individual") are found in all the Aristotelian categories of being. This is to say again that this is a difference which pertains to beings as beings.[35]

Moreover, we will be primarily considering what takes place within the genus of substance. Any accidents are already excluded from the issue. As is well known, the accident which is quantity regularly has attributed to it some sort of individuality and some role as "principle of individuation."[36] It should be clear from the above text that such a role must be secondary, at best.

Thomas continues his lesson on the individual, as follows:

> . . . But in a still more special and more perfect mode [*quodam specialiori et perfectiori modo*], the particular and the individual [*particulare et individuum*] is to be found in *rational* substances, which have mastery over their own action, and are not merely acted upon, but rather act by virtue of themselves [*per se agunt*]. Now, actions are in *singulars*. [my italics].[37]

---

33. Cf. Jorge J. E. Gracia, *Individuality: An Essay on the Foundations of Metaphysics*, Albany, 1988: State University of New York Press. Gracia says:

> . . . My suggestion, then, is that individuality may be interpreted as one of the two fundamental ontological modes, the other being universality. [136]

Whether they are "the two" fundamental modes, they are surely fundamental ontological targets of attention.

34. *ST* 1.29.1 (192a16–27).

35. The fact that "the individual" is found in all the categories itself entails that it is an analogous term: no predicate is predicated univocally of substance and accident, as St. Thomas says in *DP* 7.7.

36. See especially *ST* 3.77.2 (2961a35–b24).

37. From the point of view of the building up of human metaphysical experience, the

And therefore, also, in contrast to other substances, the singulars [*singularia*] of rational nature have a special name. And this name is "person."

And therefore in the aforementioned definition of the person is placed "individual substance," inasmuch as it ["the person"] signifies the singular in the genus of substance; but "of rational nature" is added, inasmuch as it signifies the singular among rational substances.[38]

We see from the key consideration in the above, viz. the citation of the dictum: "actions are in singulars," that we are on the trail of what essentially constitutes singularity or individuality. It is something which is seen in modes or levels, but which is realized most fully in the extent to which a substance is an agent, a source of events.

To an objector who claims that the individual cannot be defined, and thus Boethius cannot be correct, Thomas responds that "the general character of singularity" [*communem rationem singularitatis*] can be defined, and points to the definition of primary substance given by Aristotle.[39]

However, the most important objection and reply for our present interest come in third place. The objector, criticizing the Boethian definition, points out that "individual" is not the name of a thing outside the mind, but is rather a logician's consideration; not the name of a "*res*," but merely of an "*intentio*"; and yet the person is a real thing. Boethius's definitional procedure is thus, he claims, unsuitable.

---

association of individuals (or subsisting things) and operations should be related to the experience of *composite* things as the proper subjects (the "vehicles," one might say) of both (1) *actual existence* and (2) *motion* or *change*. Thus, in *Metaph.* 9.3 (1047a31–b2), Aristotle points out that while we attribute "being thought about" to things which do not exist, nevertheless we attribute *motion* only to the *existent*. Cf. Thomas's *CM* 9.3 (1805–1806). Cf. also Aristotle, *Metaph.* 1.1 (981a12–24). Aristotle's doctrine that the question of the separability of soul turns on its having an operation of its own derives from the foregoing considerations: cf. *De anima* 1.1 (403a10–12).

38. *ST* 1.29.1 (192a28–42). The same points are made in *DP* 9.1.*ad* 3 and *ad* 8. However, in the *ad* 3, Thomas is more complete on the relation of the individual to action. We read:

> . . . just as individual substance has it as proper that it exist through itself [*per se existat*], so also it has it as proper that it act through itself [*per se agat*]: for nothing acts save a being in act [*ens actu*]; and because of this, heat, just as it is not through itself, so also neither does it act through itself; but rather the hot heats through heat. But that which is *to act through itself* [*per se agere*] belongs in a more excellent degree to substances of rational nature than to others. For only rational substances have mastery over their own act, such that there is in them to act and not to act; but other substances are more acted upon than acting. And therefore it was suitable that the individual substance of a rational nature have a special name.

39. *ST* 1.29.1.*ad* 1–the reference is to Aristotle, *Categories* 3 (2a11):

> Substance, in the truest and primary and most definite sense of the word, is that which is neither predicable of a subject nor present in a subject; for instance, the individual man or horse. [tr. E. M. Edghill]

Thomas replies, explaining carefully the meaning of "individual" in the definition. We read:

... because substantial differences are not known to us, or else are not named, it is necessary sometimes to use accidental differences in place of substantial [differences], for example, if someone were to say: "fire is a simple, hot, and dry body"; for proper accidents are the effects of substantial forms, and reveal them. And similarly the names of *logical notions* [*intentiones*] can be accepted in order to define *real things* [*res*], inasmuch as they are accepted in the role of some names of real things which [names] have not been invented. And thus this name "individual" [*individuum*] is inserted in the definition of the person in order to signify the mode of subsisting, which belongs to particular substances [*modum subsistendi qui competit substantiis particularibus*].[40]

In another objection in the same article, the meaning of the term "substance," as used in the definition of person, is questioned. The preferred reply of Thomas is as follows:

... "substance" is taken universally [*communiter*], inasmuch as it is divided into primary and secondary; and by the addition of "individual," it is narrowed down to stand for primary substance.[41]

Thomas's only slightly earlier *DP* 9.2 discussion explains more fully:

... when "substance" is divided into primary and secondary, this is not a division of a genus into species—since nothing is contained under "secondary substance" that is not contained under "primary [substance]"—but rather it is a division of the genus in function of diverse modes of being [*secundum diversos modos essendi*]. For "secondary substance" signifies the absolute nature of the genus, just by itself; but "primary substance" signifies it [the nature] as individually subsisting [*ut individualiter subsistentem*]. Hence, it is more of a division of an analogue than of a genus [*magis est divisio analogi quam generis*]. Thus, therefore, "the person" is indeed contained in the genus of substance, though admittedly not as a species, but as determining a special mode of existing [*ut specialem modum existendi determinans*].[42]

Thus, we see the extent to which the entire discussion is one of dividing being into modes, relative to what subsists, as having its own *esse*.

---

40. *ST* 1.29.1.*ad* 3. In *DP* 9.2.*ad* 5, on the same point, we have:

... "individual" is inserted into the definition of the person in order to signify the individual mode of being [*ad designandum individualem modum essendi*].

At *Sent.* 1.25.1.1 [Mandonnet, p. 601], the discussion of Boethius's definition of "person," note how different is Thomas's handling of "individua" than in *ST* 1.29.1 and *DP* 9.2; in the *Sent.* it is still merely the name of an intention.

41. *ST* 1.29.1.*ad* 2 (192b11–15).

42. *DP* 9.2.*ad* 6.

It is not easy to see just what is meant by this division of "that which is" into the universal and the individual. Can we say that universals are beings? Certainly, an *SCG* argument maintains that they have less right to this title than does the individual. Arguing that God's providence extends to contingent singulars, Thomas says:

. . . Since God is the cause of that-which-is inasmuch as it is that-which-is [*entis inquantum est ens*], as was shown above, it is necessary that he be the provider [*provisor*] for that-which-is inasmuch as it is that-which-is: for he provides for things inasmuch as he is their cause. Therefore, whatever *is* in any degree [*quocumque modo est*] falls under his providence. But singulars are beings [*entia*], and more so [*magis*] than universals; because universals do not subsist by themselves, but *are* [viz.: have being, *sunt*] only in singulars. Therefore, there is divine providence even as to singulars.[43]

Thus, we see that the universal is viewed as the inherent, in contrast to the individual which precisely subsists, i.e. properly *has its own esse.* Inherents are found even in the genus of substance, as in the case of the substantial forms lower than the human soul.[44]

Having located our topic as the mode of being proper to the subsisting thing,[45] let us note how Thomas provides a tableau or panorama of

43. *SCG* 3.75 (ed. Pera, 2513; Pegis, 13). Cf. also *Expositio libri Posteriorum* 1.37 (Leonine ed., lines 173–187, commenting on Aristotle, 85b15; Spiazzi, 330):

And he [Aristotle] says that if the universal is said of many in function of one intelligibility [*rationem*] and not equivocally, the universal as regards what pertains to reason [*quantum ad id quod rationis est*], that is, as regards science and demonstration, will not be less of a being than the particulars, but rather more, because the incorruptible is more of a being [*magis ens*] than the corruptible, and the universal intelligibility [*ratio universalis*] is incorruptible whereas the particulars are corruptible, corruptibility happening to them in function of the individual principles, not in function of the intelligibility of the species, which is common to all and preserved by generation; thus, therefore, as regards what pertains to reason, the universals *are* more than the particulars, but as regards natural subsistence [*quantum vero ad naturalem subsistenciam*], the particulars are more [*magis sunt*], [and thus] are called "primary and principle substances."

44. See *ST* 1.45.4. In referring to the substantial forms lower than the human soul (which subsists), I am trying to be as "realistic" as possible regarding the universal. The substantial form is not the universal, but is its principle. The essence or quiddity of the material thing is distinct from the material thing itself, and has the role of "formal part": cf. *ST* 1.3.3 (18a16–21). For an indication of the problems in discussing quiddity, substantial form, and thing, cf. above, chapter 8.

45. "Mode of being" itself deserves prolonged study. The general notion of "mode" here is one of *measure* of a formal feature: cf. *ST* 1.5.5:

Praeexigitur autem ad formam determinatio sive commensuratio principiorum, seu materialium, seu efficientium ipsam, et hoc significatur per modum: unde dicitur quod mensura modum praefigit.

[The prerequisite for form is determination or commensuration of its principles, whether material or efficient: and this is signified by "mode": hence, it is said that measure pre-establishes the mode.]

being, viewed as to the different modes of the subsistent or individual. In terms of subsistence or "*having* being," we get this:

Now, there are many modes of being of things [*modus essendi rerum*].

For some things are, whose nature does not *have* being [*habet esse*] save in this individual matter; and of this mode [*huiusmodi*] are all corporeal [things].

But some things are, whose natures are subsistent by themselves, not in any matter, which nevertheless are not their own being [*esse*], but rather they are [things] *having* being [*esse habentes*]; and of this mode are incorporeal substances, which we call "angels."

Of God alone the proper mode of being [*proprius modus essendi*] is that he be his own subsistent being [*suum esse subsistens*].[46]

We should note the use of the word "have," as in "have being," which St. Thomas sometimes stresses in order to present the subsisting thing as such. Thus, for example, in presenting the sort of thing which is truly "made," he tells us that "being made" is ordered to "being," and so that is properly made which properly *is*. And what is that? We read:

. . . that is properly said to "be" which itself *has* being [*quod ipsum* 'HABET' *esse*], as subsisting in its *own* being [*quasi in* 'SUO' *esse subsistens*]: hence, only substances are properly and truly called "beings" [*entia*]. (ST 1.90.2)

However, we can find the above tableau set out expressly as regards the individual. Let us consider a text from *In De causis* prop. 9. We are in one of the most important lessons in the work, since it concerns the causality of the highest cause and how it stands as to being, relative to all the rest. Thomas is presenting the author's conception of God as pure *esse*, and the created separate substance as a composite of form and *esse*. At the very end of the discussion, there comes a possible objection. If God is pure *esse*, he will not be an *individual* being; he will rather be that "*esse commune*" predicated of all; and since only individuals act or are acted upon, he will not be a cause. The contention is that the divine *esse*, in order to be individuated, must be *received in something*. The obvious point is that it does not suffice to posit *esse* as such, in order to have something individuated.[47]

Thus, we are regularly considering a "receiver" which *has* some perfection. In the case of God, the simplicity of the divine essence requires that God *be* whatever he *has*; cf. *SCG* 1.23 (218).

46. *ST* 1.12.4, in part.

47. *Super Librum de causis expositio*, prop. 9 [ed. H. D. Saffrey, O.P., Fribourg/Louvain, 1954: Société philosophique/Nauwelaerts, pp. 64, lines 28–65, line 7; italics in the edition, indicating words from the commented text]:

. . . Posset enim aliquis dicere quod, si causa prima est esse tantum, videtur quod sit esse commune quod de omnibus praedicatur et quod non sit aliquid individualiter ens ab aliis distinctum; id enim quod est commune non individuatur nisi per hoc quod in

Does Thomas answer that *esse* as such everywhere provides individuation? Not at all. He rather relates individuation in the first cause to its *not being received in anything*. We read:

But to this [the author of the *De causis*] responds that the very infinity of the divine *esse*, inasmuch as it is not limited to some receiver, has in the first cause the role of the *yliatim* which is in other things. And this because, as in other things the individuation of a received common thing is brought about by the receiver, so the divine goodness and being [*esse*] is individuated from its very own purity, i.e. through the fact that it is not received in anything; and from the fact that it is thus individuated by its own purity, it has it that it can issue forth in goodnesses [bestowed] upon the intelligence and the other things.[48]

One sees that it is very much the receiver which accounts for individuation in all the common things; one should remember that *esse*, in everything other than God, is as something received in a receiver.[49] It could

---

aliquo recipitur. Causa autem prima est aliquid individualiter distinctum ab omnibus aliis, alioquin non haberet operationem aliquam; universalium enim non est neque agere neque pati. Ergo videtur quod *necesse* sit dicere causam primam habere *yliatim*, id est aliquid recipiens esse.

Cf. St. Thomas Aquinas, *Commentary on the Book of Causes*, translated by Vincent A. Guagliardo, O.P., Charles R. Hess, O.P., and Richard C. Taylor, Washington, D.C., 1996: The Catholic University of America Press, p. 72.

Cf. M.-D. Roland-Gosselin, O.P., *Le "De ente et essentia" de s. Thomas d'Aquin*, Le Saulchoir, Kain (Belgique), 1926: Revue des sciences philosophiques et théologiques, containing "Études," the first of which is "Le principe de l'individualité" (pp. 49–134). The very first theologian he presents, William of Auvergne, in his *De universo* (ca 1231–1236), refers to the *Liber de causis* without mentioning that name, in connection with divine individuality. Roland-Gosselin (p. 73, n. 3) cites Guillaume d'Auvergne, *Opera omnia* (Orléans, 1674), t. I. *De universo* I 2 c. 9, p. 852 a D:

. . . et posuerunt ei individuum dicentes quia individuum ejus est bonitas pura.

48. *In De causis*, ed. Saffrey, p. 65, lines 7–15:

Sed ad hoc respondet quod ipsa *infinitas* divini *esse*, inquantum scilicet non est terminatum ad aliquod recipiens, habet in causa prima vicem *yliatim* quod est in aliis rebus. Et hoc ideo quia, sicut in aliis rebus fit individuatio rei communis receptae per id quod est recipiens, ita divina *bonitas* et esse individuatur ex ipsa sui puritate per hoc scilicet quod ipsa non est recepta in aliquo; et ex hoc quod est sic individuata sui puritate, habet quod possit *influere bonitates super intelligentiam et alias res*.

Cf. Guagliardo, p. 72. The translation is my own, but this is no reflection on the fine translation of Guagliardo, Hess, and Taylor. I might note, however, that for ". . . per id quod est recipiens . . . ," they have ". . . through what the recipient is . . . ." I think it would better be rendered: ". . . by the receiving that-which-is," i.e. the receiver has always the role of "*quod est,*" or the subsisting thing.

49. *ST* 1.4.1.*ad* 3. I am reminded of the way Johannes Capreolus expresses the doctrine of St. Thomas concerning *esse*, as that item in the metaphysical analysis of the creature most remote from the nature of that which subsists as such. He says [Johannis Capreoli, *Defensiones theologiae divi Thomae Aquinatis*, ed. C. Paban et T. Pègues, Turonibus, 1900: Alfred Cattier, t. 1, p. 327a]:

. . . since the *esse* of the creature least of all subsists, it is not properly created or annihilated, nor is, nor is not, nor begins [to be], nor ceases [to be]; but all those things are

hardly serve, in the doctrine of St. Thomas, as something giving individuation to all else.

Since Thomas has been obliged to work with the text of someone else, which as he reads it seems to require something material (or quasi-material) for individuation, he goes on to provide his own proper account of individuation. We read:

> So that this may be evident, it is to be considered that something is called an "individual" from this fact, that it is not of its nature to be in many: for the universal is that whose nature it is to be in many.
>
> But that something is not of a nature to be in many can occur in two ways. In one way, by the fact that it is limited to something one in which it is [present], for example whiteness by the character of its species is of a nature to be in many, but this whiteness which is received in this subject cannot be save in this.
>
> But this way [of not being of a nature to be in many] cannot proceed to infinity, because in formal and material causes one cannot proceed to infinity, as is proved in *Metaphysics* 2; hence it is necessary to arrive at something which is not of a nature to be received in something, and from this it has individuation, as for example primary matter in corporeal things, which is the principle of singularity.
>
> Hence, it is necessary that everything which is not of a nature to be in something, by that very fact is individual; and this is the second way in which something is not of a nature to be in many, i.e. because it is not of its nature to be in something, as for example if whiteness were existing separately without a subject, it would be an individual in that way.[50]
>
> And in this way there is individuation in separate substances, which are forms having *esse*, and in the first cause itself, which is *esse* subsisting.[51]

said of that which is through that *esse*, and not of *esse* itself. [*Cum ergo esse creaturae minime subsistat, non proprie creatur, aut annihilatur, aut est, aut non est, aut incipit, aut desinit; sed omnia talia dicuntur de illo quod est per illud esse, et non de ipso esse.*]

See my paper, "Capreolus, saint Thomas et l'Être," in *Jean Capreolus et son temps 1380–1444, Colloque de Rodez* [special number, no. 1 of *Mémoire dominicaine*], ed. Guy Bedouelle, Romanus Cessario, and Kevin White, Paris, 1997: Cerf, pp. 77–86.

50. There is a most interesting text in *Quaestiones de quolibet*, 7.4.3 [10] (Leonine ed., Rome/Paris, 1996: Commissio Leonina/Cerf, t. 25–1, pp. 22–24). Thomas is asked whether God can bring it about that whiteness or any other corporeal quality exist without quantity. He answers that God could do it. One must distinguish, in any quality, between the nature through which it obtains a specific character and the individuation by which it is this *sensible* whiteness distinct from that other sensible whiteness. God could, by a miracle, bring it about that the nature subsist without any quantity, but that whiteness would not be this *sensible* whiteness; it would be an intelligible form, something like the separate forms which Plato posited. However, that this individuated *sensible* whiteness be without quantity is something that cannot be brought about. In the *ad* 1, he describes the hypothetical miraculously separate whiteness as "a spiritual, not a corporeal, quality."

In this relatively early text, Thomas reserves the word "individuation" for the sensible whiteness, as found in dimensive quantity, whereas our present text presents as individual the hypothetical whiteness itself subsisting, and speaks of "individuation" regarding subsistent form.

51. *In De causis*, ed. Saffrey, p. 65, line 16–p. 66, line 7:

What could be clearer? Thomas has ample opportunity to bring in "*esse* as such"; he does not do so at all.[52]

There is, then, a "global" theory of the individual in St. Thomas's doctrine, viz. that something does not have a nature such as to be received in something. In corporeal things, this derives from the matter. In subsisting forms, the form itself (not the *esse*) has the requisite nature. In God, the *esse* itself is of such a nature as to subsist. "The individual" is *analogically* common, or is divided into modes.

Thus far I have said nothing about the role of quantity in individuation. I have focused rather on the mode of being of the subsisting thing, which obviously cannot stem from quantity or any accident. In earlier texts Thomas treats individuation as a kind of package, focusing on the multiplication of beings in the same species.[53] How are the instances of human nature distinct one from the other? The answer lies neither in form just in itself nor in matter just in itself, but in matter as subject to dimensive quantity. Dimensive quantity is presented as following upon the substantial form, corporeity, a substantial form which is present in all matter. This general doctrine is never abandoned by Thomas, but in later presentations it is more carefully distinguished from the primary metaphysical issue, the mode of being of the subsisting thing.[54] Dimen-

---

Ad cuius evidentiam considerandum est quod aliquid dicitur esse individuum ex hoc quod non est natum esse in multis; nam universale est quod est natum esse in multis. Quod universale aliquid non sit natum esse in multis hoc potest contingere dupliciter. Uno modo per hoc quod est determinatum ad aliquid unum in quo est, sicut albedo per rationem suae speciei nata est esse in multis, sed haec albedo quae est recepta in hoc subiecto, non potest esse nisi in hoc. Iste autem modus non potest procedere in infinitum, quia non est procedere in causis formalibus et materialibus in infinitum, ut probatur in II *Metaphysicae;* unde oportet devenire ad aliquid quod non est natum recipi in aliquo et ex hoc habet individuationem, sicut materia prima in rebus corporalibus quae est principium singularitatis. Unde oportet quod omne illud quod [p. 66] non est natum esse in aliquo, ex hoc ipso sit individuum; et hic est secundus modus quo aliquid non est natum esse in multis, quia scilicet non est natum esse in aliquo, sicut, si albedo esset separata sine subiecto existens, esset per hunc modum individua. Et hoc modo est individuatio in substantiis separatis quae sunt formae habentes esse, et in ipsa causa prima quae est ipsum esse subsistens.

Cf. Guagliardo, pp. 72–73.

52. Cf. *DP* 7.2.*ad* 5; the first argument in the body of *DP* 7.3 should be read in the light of this text.

53. The fundamental work here is that of Roland-Gosselin mentioned earlier. Roland-Gosselin (p. 105, n. 2), hunting for discussions of individuation in *Sentences* 1, tells us that we have the doctrine of the multiplication of individuals in a species by "division of matter" in 1.9.1.2 [Mandonnet, pp. 248–249]. Notice that we are talking here about the problem of multiplication, and not merely of "not being in something."

54. I notice that *DP* 9.5.*ad* 13 gives us the two aspects I think Thomas eventually sees have to be carefully distinguished. Notice that in that text the individuating principles are called the *"principium subsistendi."* This seems right to me, and not the somewhat Boethian doctrine in the *ST* 1.29.2.*ad* 5. But I cannot deal with that here.

sion serves to limit a form which can be in many, so that it still has "being in," but has being in one only. Primary matter serves to remove altogether the aspect of "being in." This distinction of the two issues is clearest in *ST* 3.77.2, on whether the dimensive quantity of the bread or the wine is the subject of the other accidents in the sacrament of the Eucharist.[55] We have seen it above, also, in the text from the *In De causis*. I believe that this distinction of issues is crucial for understanding Thomas on the individual and individuation.

In the present paper my main objectives have been (1) to criticize the association of individuation with the act of being, taken precisely as such; and (2) to show a truly global approach, on Thomas's part, to the individual as such, the individual conceived as a mode of being. Enough has been said to alert the reader of Thomas to the fact that in diverse levels of being there are diverse "principles" of individuation.

I notice that in *Quodl.* 2.2.2 [4], on the distinction between nature and supposit in angels, supposedly a later text, Thomas holds that the angel's nature is not individuated by matter, but by itself: because such a form is not of a nature to be received in some matter. However, there is a distinction between nature and supposit, since things are predicated of the supposit which cannot be predicated of the nature as such. This line of thinking strikes me as more akin to the earlier approach to individuation, tending to distinguish between individuation and subsistence. The later view makes subsistence the primary individuation.

55. The doctrine in *ST* 3.77.2 is the same as in the *De causis*. I have used the latter only because I have actually encountered readers who object to the "theological" character of the former.

Bibliography

Albert the Great, *De anima*, ed. Clemens Stroick, Monasterii Westfalorum, 1968: Aschendorff [hereafter "ed. Cologne"], t. 7/1.

——, *De homine* (i.e., *Summa de creaturis* 2), ed. Steph. C. A. Borgnet, Paris, 1896: Vivès [hereafter "ed. Paris"], t. 35.

——, *De natura et origine animae*, ed. Cologne, t. 12, with Introduction by B. Geyer.

——, *De unitate intellectus*, ed. Cologne, t. 17/1, with Introduction by A. Hufnagel.

——, *Metaphysica*, ed. Cologne, t. 16/1 and 2, with Introduction by B. Geyer.

——, *Sentences* 2, ed. Paris, t. 27 (1894).

——, *Summa theologiae* 2, ed. Paris, t. 33 (1895).

Allard, Jean-Louis, ed., *Etre et savoir*, Ottawa, 1989: Les Presses de l'Université d'Ottawa.

Aristotle, *Categories*, tr. E. M. Edghill, in *The Basic Works of Aristotle*, ed. Richard McKeon, New York, 1941: Random House.

——, *De anima*, tr. W. S. Hett, Loeb Classics, Cambridge, Mass./London, 1964 (1st ed., 1936; rev. 1957): Harvard University Press/Heinemann [also tr. J. A. Smith, in McKeon].

——, *De generatione et corruptione*, tr. Harold H. Joachim, in McKeon.

——, *Parts of Animals*, tr. William Ogle, in McKeon (in part).

——, *Physics*, tr. P. Wicksteed, Loeb Classics, Cambridge, Mass., 1929: Harvard University Press [also tr. R. P. Hardie and R. K. Gaye, in McKeon].

Ashley, Benedict M., O.P., "The River Forest School and the Philosophy of Nature Today," in *Philosophy and the God of Abraham*, ed. R. James Long, Toronto, 1991: Pontifical Institute of Mediaeval Studies, pp. 1–16.

Aubenque, Pierre, "Sens et structure de la *Métaphysique* aristotélicienne" (Séance du 23 mars 1963), *Bulletin de la Société française de Philosophie* 58 (1964).

Avencebrolis (Ibn Gebirol), *Fons Vitae*, ed. Clemens Baeumker, Münster, 1895: Aschendorff (Beiträge zur Geschichte der Philosophie des Mittelalters. Band I, Heft 2–4).

Avicenna, *Avicenna Latinus. Liber de philosophia prima sive scientia divina* I–IV, ed. S. Van Riet, Louvain/Leiden, 1977: Peeters/Brill.

——, *Liber de anima*, ed. Simone Van Riet, Louvain/Leiden, 1968: Editions orientalistes/Brill.

Behe, Michael J., "Darwin Under the Microscope," *New York Times*, Oct. 29, 1996.

——, *Darwin's Black Box: The Biochemical Challenge to Evolution*, New York, 1996: The Free Press.

——, "The Sterility of Darwinism," *Boston Review*, February/March 1997.

Boethius, *Contra Eutychen et Nestorium* [*De persona et duabus naturis*], in *The Theological Tractates*, tr. H. F. Stewart and E. K. Rand, Loeb Classics, London/New York, 1918 (reprint 1926): Heinemann/Putnam.

————, *De trinitate*, in *The Theological Tractates*.

Bower, T. G. R., "The Object in the World of the Infant," *Scientific American* 225, no. 4 (October 1971), pp. 30–38.

Browne, Malcolm W., "Despite New Data, Mysteries of Creation Persist," *New York Times*, May 12, 1992, pp. C1 and C10.

Cajetan, Thomas de Vio (Cardinal), *De nominum analogia*, in Hyacinthe-Marie Robillard, O.P., *De l'analogie et Du concept d'être*, Montréal, 1963: Les presses de l'Université de Montréal.

Capreolus, Johannes, O.P., *Defensiones theologiae divi Thomae Aquinatis*, ed. C. Paban and T. Pègues, Turonibus, 1900: Alfred Cattier.

Concise Oxford Dictionary, London, 1964 (5th ed.): Oxford University Press.

De Koninck, Charles, "*Le cosmos* (1936)—Extrait," *Laval théologique et philosophique* 50 (1994), pp. 111–143.

————, *The Hollow Universe*, London, 1960: Oxford University Press.

————, "Metaphysics and the Interpretation of Words," *Laval théologique et philosophique* 17 (1961), pp. 22–34.

————, "Le problème de l'indéterminisme," in *L'Académie Canadienne Saint-Thomas d'Aquin* (Sixième session, 9 et 10 octobre 1935), Québec, 1937: Typ."L'Action Catholique," pp. 65–159.

————, "Random Reflections on Science and Calculation," *Laval theologique et philosophique* 12 (1956), pp. 96–100.

————, "Réflexions sur le problème de l'indéterminisme," *Revue thomiste* 43 (1937), pp. 227–252 and 393–409.

————, "Thomism and Scientific Indeterminism," in *Proceedings of the American Catholic Philosophical Association 1936*, Washington, D.C., 1937: The Catholic University of America Press, pp. 58–76.

Delsol, Michel, "Où mène la biologie moderne? Questions aux théologiens et aux philosophes," *Laval théologique et philosophique* 52 (1996), pp. 339–353.

Delsol, Michel, Philippe Sentis, Roger Payot, Régis Ladous, and Janine Flatin, "Le hasard et la sélection expliquent-ils l'évolution? Biologie ou métaphysique," *Laval théologique et philosophique* 50 (1994), pp. 7–41.

Dewan, Lawrence, O.P., "Capreolus, saint Thomas et l'Être," in *Jean Capreolus et son temps 1380–1444*, *Colloque de Rodez* [special number, no. 1, of *Mémoire dominicaine*], ed. Guy Bedouelle, Romanus Cessario, and Kevin White, Paris, 1997: Cerf, pp. 77–86.

————, "Charles De Koninck," in *Oxford Companion to Canadian Literature*, ed. William Toye, Toronto/New York, 1983: Oxford University Press.

————, "The Distinctiveness of St. Thomas' Third Way," *Dialogue* 19 (1980), pp. 201–218.

————, "Does Being Have a Nature? (Or: Metaphysics as a Science of the Real)," in *Approaches to Metaphysics*, ed. William Sweet, Dordrecht, Holland, 2004: Kluwer Academic Publishers, pp. 23–59.

————, "The Interpretation of St. Thomas's Third Way," in *Littera, sensus, sententia*, Studi in onore del Prof. Clemente J. Vansteenkiste, O.P., ed. A. Lobato, O.P., Milan, 1991: Massimo.

————, "Is Truth a Transcendental for St. Thomas Aquinas?," *Nova et Vetera* [English edition] 2 (2004), pp. 1–20.

————, "Jacques Maritain, St. Thomas, and the Birth of Metaphysics," *Études Maritainiennes/Maritain Studies* 13 (1997), pp. 3–18.

————, "Laurence Foss and the Existence of Substances," *Laval théologique et philosophique* 44 (1988), pp. 77–84.

————, "The Number and Order of St. Thomas's Five Ways," *Downside Review* 92 (1974), pp. 1–18.

————, "Something Rather than Nothing, and St. Thomas' Third Way," *Science et Esprit* 39 (1987), pp. 71–80.

————, "St. Thomas and the Divine Names," *Science et Esprit* 32 (1980), pp. 19–33.

————, "St. Thomas Aquinas against Metaphysical Materialism," in *Atti del'VIII Congresso Tomistico Internazionale*, t. 5, ed. A. Piolanti, Vatican City, 1982: Libreria Editrice Vaticana, pp. 412–434.

————, "St. Thomas, Aristotle, and Creation," *Dionysius* 15 (1991), pp. 81–90.

————, "St. Thomas, Capreolus, and Entitative Composition," *Divus Thomas* 80 (1977), pp. 355–375.

————, "St. Thomas, the Fourth Way, and Creation," *The Thomist* 59 (1995), pp. 371–378.

————, "St. Thomas, Joseph Owens and Existence," *New Scholasticism* 56 (1982), pp. 399–441.

————, "Thomas Aquinas and Being as a Nature," *Acta Philosophica* 12 (2003).

Doig, James C., *Aquinas on Metaphysics*, The Hague, 1972: Martinus Nijhoff.

Dondaine, Antoine, O.P., "Les 'Opuscula fratris Thomae' chez Ptolémée de Lucques," *Archivum Fratrum Praedicatorum* 31 (1961), pp. 142–203.

————, "Saint Thomas et la dispute des attributs divins (I *Sent.*, d. 2, a. 3): authenticité et origine," *Archivum Fratrum Praedicatorum* 8 (1938), pp. 253–262.

Fabro, C., "The Transcendentality of *Ens-Esse* and the Ground of Metaphysics," *International Philosophical Quarterly* 6 (1966), pp. 389–427.

Garrigou-Lagrange, Réginald, O.P., *Le sens commun, la philosophie de l'être et les formules dogmatiques*, Paris, 1909: Desclée de Brouwer.

Gauthier, R.-A., O.P., "Preface" to *Sentencia libri de anima*, in St. Thomas, *Opera omnia*, t. 45/1, Rome/Paris, 1984: Commissio Leonina/Vrin, at pp. 256*–257*.

————, "Quelques questions à propos du commentaire de St. Thomas sur le De anima," *Angelicum* 51 (1974).

Gilson, Étienne, *Being and Some Philosophers*, Toronto, 1952 (2nd ed.; 1st ed. 1949): Pontifical Institute of Mediaeval Studies.

————, *D'Aristote à Darwin et retour*, Paris, 1971: Vrin [*From Aristotle to Darwin and Back Again: A Journey in Final Causality, Species, and Evolution*, tr. John Lyon, Notre Dame, Ind., 1984: University of Notre Dame Press].

————, "Doctrinal History and its Interpretation," *Speculum* 24 (1949), pp. 483–492.

————, *Elements of Christian Philosophy*, Garden City, N.Y., 1960: Doubleday.

————, *Étienne Gilson, Jacques Maritain, Correspondance, 1923–1971*, ed. Géry Prouvost, Paris, 1991: Vrin.

————, *History of Philosophy and Philosophical Education*, Milwaukee, 1948: Marquette University Press.

————, "L'innéisme cartésien et la théologie," in *Etudes sur le rôle de la pensée médiévale dans la formation du système cartésien*, Paris, 1975 (4th ed.): Vrin, pp. 9–50.

————, *Introduction à la philosophie chrétienne*, tr. A. Maurer, Paris, 1960: Vrin.

————, "Les principes et les causes," *Revue thomiste* 52 (1952), pp. 39–63.

————, *The Unity of Philosophical Experience*, New York, 1937: Scribners.

————, "Wisdom and Time," tr. Anton C. Pegis, in *A Gilson Reader*, ed. Anton C. Pegis, Garden City, N.Y., 1957: Doubleday Image Books, pp. 328–341 [published in French in Lumière et Vie 1 (1951), pp. 77–92].

Gracia, Jorge J. E., *Individuality: An Essay on the Foundations of Metaphysics*, Albany, 1988: State University of New York Press.

Hull, David L., "The Effect of Essentialism on Taxonomy—Two Thousand Years of Stasis," British Journal for the Philosophy of Science 16 (1965), no. 60, pp. 314–327, and no. 61, pp. 1–18.

Hume, David, *An Enquiry concerning Human Understanding*, ed. L. A. Selby-Bigge, Oxford, 1902 (2nd ed.): Clarendon Press.

————, *The Letters of David Hume*, ed. J. Y. T. Greig, Oxford, 1932: Clarendon Press.

————, *A Treatise of Human Nature*, ed. L. A. Selby-Bigge, Oxford, 1888: Clarendon Press.

John Damascene, *De fide orthodoxa, Versions of Burgundio and Cerbanus*, ed. Eligius M. Buytaert, O.F.M., St. Bonaventure, N.Y., 1955: Franciscan Institute.

Kennedy, Leonard A., C.S.B., "A New Disputed Question of St. Thomas Aquinas on the Immortality of the Soul," *Archives d'histoire doctrinale et littéraire du moyen âge* 45 (1978), pp. 205–208 (introduction) and 209–223 (text).

Laverdière, Raymond, *Le principe de causalité*, Bibliothèque thomiste 39, Paris, 1969: Vrin.

Maritain, Jacques, *Le paysan de la Garonne*, Paris, 1966: Desclée de Brouwer.

————, *La philosophie bergsonienne*, Paris, 1948 (4th ed.): Téqui.

————, *Sept leçons sur l'être et les premiers principes de la raison spéculative*, Paris, 1932–1933: Téqui.

————, "La vie propre de l'intelligence et l'erreur idéaliste" (dated 1924), in *Réflexions sur l'intelligence et sur sa vie propre*, Paris, 1926 (2nd ed.): Nouvelle librairie nationale.

Maurer, Armand, C.S.B., "The Analogy of Genus," *The New Scholasticism* 29 (1955), pp. 127–144.

————, "Dialectic in the *De ente et essentia* of St. Thomas Aquinas," in *Roma, magistra mundi. Itineraria culturae medievalis*, Mélanges offerts au Père L. E. Boyle à l'occasion de son 75ᵉ anniversaire, ed. J. Hamesse, Louvain-la-Neuve, 1998: Fédération Internationale des Instituts Médiévales, pp. 573–583.

McInerny, Ralph, *Aquinas and Analogy*, Washington, D.C., 1996: The Catholic University of America Press.

Nicolas, Jean-Hervé, O.P., "Chronique de philosophie," *Revue thomiste* 48 (1948), pp. 546–547.

Noone, Timothy B., "Individuation in Scotus," *American Catholic Philosophical Quarterly* 69 (1995), pp. 527–542.

————, Review of Jorge J. E. Gracia, ed., *Individuation in Scholasticism, Review of Metaphysics* 49 (December 1995), p. 411.

Orr, H. Allen, "Darwin v. Intelligent Design (Again)," *Boston Review*, December 1996/January 1997, pp. 28–31.

Owens, Joseph, C.Ss.R., "The 'Analytics' and Thomistic Metaphysical Procedure," *Mediaeval Studies* 20 (1964), pp. 83–108.

————, "The Causal Proposition—Principle or Conclusion?" *The Modern Schoolman* 32 (1955), pp. 159–171, 257–270, 323–339.

———, "The Causal Proposition Revisited," *The Modern Schoolman* 44 (1966–1967), pp. 143–151.

———, *The Doctrine of Being in the Aristotelian Metaphysics*, Toronto, 1963 (2nd ed.): Pontifical Institute of Mediaeval Studies.

———, *Elementary Christian Metaphysics*, Houston, Tex., 1985: Center for Thomistic Studies [reprint of the volume published by Bruce, Milwaukee, 1963].

———, *History of Ancient Western Philosophy*, New York, 1959: Appleton-Century-Crofts.

———, "Thomas Aquinas (b. ca. 1225; d. 1274)," in *Individuation in Scholasticism: The Later Middle Ages and the Counter-Reformation, 1150–1650*, ed. Jorge J. E. Gracia, Albany, 1994: State University of New York Press, pp. 173–194.

Plato, *Cratylus*, tr. Benjamin Jowett, in *Plato, The Collected Dialogues*, ed. Edith Hamilton and Huntington Cairns, New York, 1961 (with corrections, 1963): Pantheon Books.

———, *Phaedo*, tr. H. N. Fowler, Cambridge, Mass., 1960 (original 1914): Harvard University Press.

———, *Republic*, tr. Allan Bloom, New York, 1968: Basic Books.

———, *Sophist*, tr. F. M. Cornford, in Hamilton and Cairns.

———, *Theaetetus*, tr. F. M. Cornford, in Hamilton and Cairns.

———, *Timaeus*, tr. Benjamin Jowett, in Hamilton and Cairns.

Robillard, Hyacinthe-Marie, O.P., *De l'analogie et Du concept d'être*, Montréal, 1963: Les presses de l'Université de Montréal.

Roland-Gosselin, M.-D., O.P., *Le "De ente et essentia" de s. Thomas d'Aquin* (containing "Études"), Le Saulchoir, Kain (Belgique), 1926: Revue des sciences philosophiques et théologiques.

Thomas Aquinas, *Compendium theologiae*, with Introduction by H.-F. Dondaine, O.P., in *Opera omnia*, t. 42, Rome, 1979: Editori di San Tommaso.

———, *De ente et essentia*, in *Opera omnia*, t. 43, Rome, 1976: Editori de San Tommaso.

———, *De substantiis separatis*, in *Opera omnia*, t. 40, Rome, 1969: Ad Sanctae Sabinae.

———, *Expositio libri Boetii De ebdomadibus*, in *Opera omnia*, t. 50, Rome/Paris, 1992: Commissio Leonina/Cerf.

———, *Expositio libri Peryermenias* [Editio altera retractata], in *Opera omnia*, t. 1*1, Rome/Paris, 1989: Commissio Leonina/Vrin.

———, *Expositio libri Posteriorum*, Leonine ed., t. 1*2 [Editio altera retractata], Rome/Paris, 1989: Commissio Leonina/Vrin [also ed. Spiazzi, Rome/Turin, 1955: Marietti].

———, *Expositio super librum Boethii De trinitate*, ed. Bruno Decker, Leiden, 1959: Brill.

———, *In Aristotelis libros De caelo et mundo, De generatione et corruptione, Meteorologicorum expositio*, ed. R. Spiazzi, Rome/Turin, 1951: Marietti.

———, *In librum beati Dionysii De divinis nominibus expositio*, ed. C. Pera, O.P., Rome/Turin, 1950: Marietti.

———, *In librum Boetii De hebdomadibus expositio, lect. 1*, in *Opuscula theologica*, vol. 2, ed. M. Calcaterra, O.P., Turin/Rome, 1954: Marietti, nos. 14–18.

———, *In octo libros Physicorum Aristotelis expositio*, ed. M. Maggiòlo, Rome/Turin, 1954: Marietti.

———, *In XII libros Metaphysicorum Aristotelis Commentarium*, ed. M.-R. Cathala, Turin, 1935: Marietti.

————, *Liber de Veritate Catholicae Fidei contra errores Infidelium seu "Summa contra gentiles,"* ed. C. Pera et al., Rome/Turin, 1961: Marietti.

————, *On Being and Essence*, tr. Armand Maurer, C.S.B., Toronto, 1968 (2nd ed.): Pontifical Institute of Mediaeval Studies.

————, *Quaestio de immortalitate animae* (see Kennedy above).

————, *Quaestiones de quolibet*, in Leonine ed., t. 25/2, Rome/Paris, 1996: Commissio Leonina/Cerf, with Introduction by R.-A. Gauthier, O.P., in t. 25/1.

————, *Quaestiones disputatae de anima*, ed. B.-C. Bazan, in *Opera omnia*, t. 24/1, Rome/Paris, 1996: Commissio Leonina/Cerf [also ed. James H. Robb, Toronto, 1968: Pontifical Institute of Mediaeval Studies].

————, *Quaestiones disputatae de malo*, in *Opera omnia*, t. 23, Rome/Paris, 1982: Commissio Leonina/Vrin.

————, *Quaestiones disputatae de potentia*, ed. P. Bazzi et al., Rome/Turin, 1953 (9th ed. rev.): Marietti.

————, *Quaestiones disputatae de veritate*, qq. 21–29, in *Opera omnia*, t. 22/3, Rome, 1976: Editori de San Tommaso.

————, *Quodlibetal Questions 1 and 2*, tr. Sandra B. Edwards, Toronto, 1983: Pontifical Institute of Mediaeval Studies.

————, *Responsio ad magistrum Ioannem de Vercellis de 108 articulis*, in *Opera omnia*, t. 42, Rome, 1979: Editori di San Tommaso.

————, *Scriptum super libros Sententiarum Magistri Petri Lombardi*, tt. 1 and 2, ed. Pierre Mandonnet, O.P., Paris, 1929: Lethielleux.

————, *Sentencia libri De anima*, in *Opera omnia*, t. 45/1, Rome/Paris, 1984: Commissio Leonina/Vrin.

————, *Sententia libri Ethicorum*, Leonine ed., t. 47/2, Rome, 1969: Ad Sanctae Sabinae [also ed. Pirotta, Rome/Turin, 1934: Marietti].

————, *Summa theologiae*, Ottawa, 1953 (Editio altera emendata): Commissio Piana.

————, *Super Librum de causis expositio*, ed. H. D. Saffrey, O.P., Fribourg/Louvain, 1954: Société Philosophique/Nauwelaerts [*Commentary on the Book of Causes*, translated and annotated by Vincent A. Guagliardo, O.P., Charles R. Hess, O.P., and Richard C. Taylor, Washington, D.C., 1996: The Catholic University of America Press].

Wallace, William A., O.P., "Are Elementary Particles Real?," in *From a Realist Point of View: Essays on the Philosophy of Science*, Washington, D.C., 1979: University Press of America, pp. 187–200.

Weinberg, Stephen, *Dreams of a Final Theory*, New York, 1993: Pantheon.

Weisheipl, James, O.P., *Friar Thomas D'Aquino, His Life, Thought, and Work*, Garden City, N.Y., 1974: Doubleday.

————, "The Life and Works of St. Albert the Great," in *Albertus Magnus and the Sciences*, ed. J. Weisheipl, Toronto, 1980: Pontifical Institute of Mediaeval Studies, pp. 13–51.

————, "Medieval Natural Philosophy and Modern Science," in *Nature and Motion in the Middle Ages*, ed. William E. Carroll, Washington, D.C., 1985: The Catholic University of America Press, pp. 261–276 [originally published in *Manuscripta* 20 (1976), pp. 181–196, under the title: "The Relationship of Medieval Natural Philosophy to Modern Science: The Contribution of Thomas Aquinas to its Understanding"].

White, Kevin, "Individuation in Aquinas's *Super Boethium De Trinitate*, Q. 4," *American Catholic Philosophical Quarterly* 69 (1995), pp. 543–556.

INDEX OF NAMES

INDEX OF TOPICS

Act: has more of the nature of being
than potency, 30; nobler than, better
than, more intelligible than, truer than
potency, 30

Act and potency: abstracted from
all matter, 49n.7; and Avicenna's
doctrine of incorruptibility of the soul,
186n.37; not considered by particular
sciences, 51n.9; and emergence, 102;
more evident as found, respectively,
in incorruptible and corruptible
substances, 30n.71; intelligibly prior
to motion, 53; among the primary
differences of being, 53; priority of act
over potency, 3–4, 8–9, 30n.71, 79n.64,
224; role of proportion in the grasping
of act and potency, 79n.64; and the
viewpoint of being, 109

Act of being [*esse*]: act of the essence, 71,
170n.14, 174; actuality even of the
form, 201, 204n.62; actuality of every
form or nature, 202n.55; not a bond
forging a thing into a unity, 233–34
(against Owens, 229); caused by God
through mediation of formal cause,
189; completive of every form, 204; as
composite once in *Sent.*, 230; conceived
once by Gilson as intrinsic efficient
cause, 234n.19; confused knowledge
of *esse* in our knowledge of a being
[*ens*], 44–46, 191; considered through
form, 43; not difficult of access, as
regards knowing *that* it is, 191; distinct
from operative acts in creatures, 218;
esse of creature least of all subsists, is
not properly created or annihilated,
neither is nor is not, neither comes
to be nor ceases to be (Capreolus),
244n.49; in everything other than

God is as received item in receiver,
244; is the form participated in order
to subsist and endure, 195n.30; most
formal,195n.28; cannot be identified
with form or essence or substance in
caused things, 190–91; cannot include
composition, 193; too intimate to the
essence to be a mere property, 174;
knowledge of *esse* and knowledge of the
maximally first principle, 192; knowing
what esse is requires careful investigation,
192; knowledge of the mode of *esse* as
found in the natural thing, 76; life, as
particular case of *esse*, prime example of
per accidens sensible, 191–92; name of an
act or actuality, 18; does not participate
in anything else, 193–94; not a *per
accidens* predicable, 174 (against Owens,
169); *per se* result of form as form, 176;
proper effect of the first agent, thus
having role of ultimate end, i.e. final
cause, 170–71, 204; reflection back on
the phantasms and our knowledge of
the nature of *esse*, 45; in *Sent.* appears
once as formal cause, but in subsequent
works as following formal cause, 189;
in what sense called an "accident," 174;
most simple, 231; too simple to be first
known just in itself, 44; substantial *esse*
that whereby a thing is called "a being,"
unqualifiedly, 191n.15; nothing suffices
to be cause of its own *esse*, 169; universal
form, 195; as a verb, 19

Action: remaining within the agent, is the
act of the perfect, i.e. of a thing in act,
and properly called "operation," 213–
14; as ultimate act in a thing is called
"second act," and is the perfection and
end of the thing, 214–15; vocabulary of

metaphysician or physicist, 92–93; as
preliminary approach in metaphysics,
140; its use in metaphysics requires
completion by the properly scientific
treatment, 152. *See also* metaphysical
method.

Magnitude: defined by metaphysician
for the geometer, 83; magnitude
of perfection pertains even to the
divine nature, 211n.24, 215; spiritual
magnitude, 215
Man: by nature "onto-centric," 119;
reason, more than anything else, is man
(Aristotle), 3
Matter (primary): and common matter,
41, 78n.63, 84, 156, 158; difficulty of
the conception, 24; importance of the
doctrine, *see* hylomorphism; individual
matter, 39–40, 46, 78n.63, 150, 155–59,
211, 237n.29, 243; intelligible matter
a diminished materiality, 42; has
kinship with *esse*, but less than form has,
198; known to us through succession
of forms, 120; material cause, no
metaphysical demonstration by means
of, 136–37; matter in mathematical
objects, 42, 49n.7, 156; metaphysical
matter in Albert the Great, 135–36; its
mode of reception of form, 28n.64;
ontological indetermination of matter,
and the conception of form as cause of
being, 126n.96, 149, 165; in potency to
an infinity of forms, 126n.96; potentially
a being, 24, 114, 128, 198; a real
potency for not-being (De Koninck),
122; retains a likeness to the divine *esse*,
198n.45; is for the sake of substantial
form, 126n.96; sensible matter,
42, 49n.7, 155–56; what matter is,
sufficiently known only through motion,
generation and corruption, 147n.62,
149–50. *See also* form; individuation.
Metaphysical method: and modes
of consideration, 140–52; logical
consideration (using predication),
145–48; philosophical consideration
(using the proper principles of things),
148–51. *See also* logical consideration.
Metaphysics: achieved only very gradually,

53n.15; most ambitious of human
studies, 15; and certainty, 3–5; as
considering being [*ens*], demonstrates
by formal cause, 21, 139–40, 152;
considers things as regards the
conditions of their actual existence,
25–26, 85, 150–51; knowledge of cause
of nature of being, 31–32, 208–09;
knowledge of the highest causes, 15,
52, 98n.7, 131, 208n.19; maximally
intellectual, 51n.9, 83n.12; metaphysical
objects, 49, 205n.1; need for, p. 51n.9;
objectivity and difficulty of, ix, 1n.6,
2–4; only science that treats anything
from viewpoint of being, 53–54. *See also*
wisdom.
Mind: as a cause (Anaxagoras), 7, 8, 99,
106n.28, 108; contemplating the good
(Plato), 8; and design theory (Behe),
7n.34, 105–09, 119n.70; first and
second operations of, 5, 46n.25, 192;
self-formation of the educated mind, x,
36–38, 57–60. *See also* intellect.
Mode of being, 242n.45; being as
presented in four modes, 49, 209; and
the existence of logic, 82; of form as
form, 41; of God alone the proper mode
is to be the subsistent act of being, 211,
243; imperishable substance a higher
mode, ix; the individual as mode proper
to substance, xi; of the intellective
soul, 25; there are many mode of
being of things, 78, 211; of our mind's
connatural object, 56n.20; in Plato,
1n.3, 15n.8. *See also* individual.

Nature: Aristotle and the meanings of
"nature," 207; art partly completes and
partly imitates, 197n.40; Boethius and
the meanings of "nature," 212–13; the
created rational nature in immediate
relation to the universal cause of being
and goodness, 38, 227–28; is essence
as principle of operation, xi, 211n.24,
212–14; hierarchy of natures and
participation in higher operation, 197,
227–28; of the human soul, 216–28;
metaphorical use and proper use, 207;
as metaphysical object same as essence,
xi, 205; nature or form has as effects

Physics: Aristotle sees early physicists as
metaphysicians, 15n.10, 51–52, 53n.15;
as second philosophy, 110; Socrates
and the school of the physicists, 7, 9,
16n.10; can be a source of forgetfulness
of being, 114; should be studied before
metaphysics, 49n.4, 60.

Plato: Aristotle's criticism of, 6–7n.30, 21,
156; on awakening the mind to being,
6–8, 15; on God as self-mover, 214; on
immortality of soul in the *Phaedo*, 29,
175; on modes or intensities of being,
15; on the need for intelligence and
life in the highest being (*Sophist*), 8–9;
on ontology, 1, 16, 23, 100; on the
permanent war about being (*Sophist*), 1,
15, 100; Thomas's criticism of, x, 82n.6,
112; his use of word "nature" [*phusis*],
207–8

Potency: active and passive (and Plato's
Sophist), 6n.30; as a division of being,
1, 24, diverse modes of, in corruptibles
and incorruptibles, 93n.32; prior, in a
qualified sense, to act, 10; its posteriority
to act, 3–4, 8, 9, 10; potency to several
the subject of habits, 58; not all potency
is towards opposites: some is entirely
to *esse* and not to non-*esse*, 173. *See also*
being [*ens*]; act of being; form; matter.

Powers of human soul: how distinguished,
218; flow from the essence of the soul,
and from one another, 221–26; never
identical with essence in creatures,
218; order of powers and human unity,
221; the subject in which they inhere,
222; three sorts of order, 220. *See also*
substantial form.

Predication, denominative or concretive vs.
univocal, essential, 149

Presocratism, a perennial intellectual
stance, 97–109

Principles of knowledge: best known in
themselves and to all of us, 56; interest
in principles of identity, sufficient
reason, finality, and causality (Maritain
and Garrigou-Lagrange), 61; knowledge
of their terms most noble, 60; known
by virtue of themselves, 56n.21, 65,
193; metaphysician's interest in, 63–66;
metaphysics treats of the terms out of

which they are formed, 5, 65; the most
certain principle regarding the being
of things, 5; the principle "an effect
depends on its cause", 66–80; principles
of metaphysical knowledge, 2; a realistic
principle of identity, 71–72; result from
divine providence, 109n.34

Principles of things: philosophical
consideration and the proper principles
of things, 140, 151–52, 155n.89, 165;
use of the term "principle" in Thomas's
CM 8, 161–65. *See also* essence; form;
matter; nature.

Property: and the Aristotelian schema of
scientific demonstration, 167; as both
in act and in potency relative to the
essence, 226; essence and properties
(essential accidents) depend on the
same cause, 31. *See also* act of being.

Providence: compatible with the existence
of the contingent, 31–33; extends to
contingent singulars, 242; pertains to
it that all grades of being which are
possible be fulfilled, 23n.39; provides for
all else for sake of the rational creature,
211; results in the determinate being
of things and the necessity of the first
principles, 109n.34; transcends the
necessary and the contingent, 32, 173

Quantity. *See* magnitude.

Quiddity [*quod quid erat esse*]: for Albert
the Great, 155n.89; for Averroes, 155;
for Avicenna and Aristotle, the true
view, 155–56; not in categories other
than substance, or only in a secondary
sense, 148; according to logical
consideration, a thing and its quiddity
are identical, but not in material things,
considered according to their natural
principles, 144; predicated of a thing
according to itself and not according
to accompaniment, 147; as cause or
principle of being, 161; and refutation
of Plato's doctrine of Ideas, 156; in
subsisting forms identical with the thing,
150; study of quiddity as approach to
substantial form, 147; and substantial
form, difference between, 154–59. *See
also* essence; form; unity.